BUSH LEAGUE, BIG CITY

BUSH LEAGUE, BIG CITY

THE BROOKLYN CYCLONES, STATEN ISLAND YANKEES, AND THE NEW YORK–PENN LEAGUE

MICHAEL SOKOLOW

EXCELSIOR
EDITIONS

Published by State University of New York Press, Albany

Excelsior Editions is an imprint of State University of New York Press

For information, contact State University of New York Press, Albany, NY
www.sunypress.edu

Library of Congress Cataloging-in-Publication Data

Name: Sokolow, Michael, author.
Title: Bush league, big city : the Brooklyn Cyclones, Staten Island
    Yankees, and the New York-Penn League / Michael Sokolow.
Description: Albany : State University of New York Press, 2023. | Series:
    Excelsior editions
Identifiers: LCCN 2022046509 | ISBN 9781438492636 (pbk. : alk. paper) | ISBN
    9781438493053 (ebook)
Subjects: LCSH: Brooklyn Cyclones (Baseball team)—History. | Staten Island
    Yankees (Baseball team)—History. | New York-Penn League (Baseball
    league)—History. | Baseball fields—New York (State)—New York—History. |
    Baseball—New York (State)—New York—History.
Classification: LCC GV875.B69 S65 2023 | DDC 796.35709747/1—dc23/eng/20221219
LC record available at https://lccn.loc.gov/2022046509

10 9 8 7 6 5 4 3 2 1

To the late Sam Nader, who opened a window into the past

and

To my grandson Nadav Shahar,
who is opening a window into the future.

A regular professional ball field at Coney Island would pay in July and August for exhibition games; but it would cost a good round sum to construct such a ground properly.

—*Brooklyn Eagle*, September 14, 1884

So his dream is to go to Brooklyn. You know, the usual—sane businesspeople become misty-eyed over this whole thing.

—Robert F. Julian, former president
of the New York-Penn League

There's going to be a new terminal, there will be a museum, and there will be a baseball field where these young ballplayers will be trying to hit home runs in between the World Trade Center towers because the outfield faces the World Trade Center. It would be great for Staten Island.

—New York City Mayor Rudolph W. Giuliani,
January 14, 1999

Mostly in the old days we were concerned with our little own communities, we were from the community, and had some loyalties to the community. Now there is very little loyalty to the communities. What the hell does the league care? I get a better offer from Joe Blow, I'm gonna leave. That's true not only with the young ones, it's true with the old ones. That loyalty isn't in existence with players, with everything else. It's all money.

—Sam Nader, team owner of the Oneonta Yankees

Contents

Illustrations

Acknowledgments

Many individuals and institutions helped me along my journey of writing this book, and I owe thanks to a very large number of people. First I would like to express my gratitude to all of the archivists and librarians who keep and maintain the records that I drew from. These include the fine staff members at the Brooklyn Public Library, the research librarians at the New York Public Library (the other NYPL in this book about the NY-PL), my friends and colleagues at the Kibbee Library at Kingsborough Community College, library staff at several CUNY campuses and the Berkshire Athenaeum in Pittsfield, Massachusetts, and the helpful folks at the A. Bartlett Giamatti Research Center at the National Baseball Hall of Fame in Cooperstown, New York. I also thank the many internet users who create and maintain the many labor-of-love sites devoted to minor league baseball and its ballparks, some of which appear in the notes. Finally in terms of information access, my deep thanks to David Shelley of the New York City Economic Development Corporation, who responded to my Freedom of Information Act requests in 2006 with efficiency and warmth. He provided me with a treasure trove of materials that took more than three months to explore at my leisure, and a cubicle and copy facilities to boot.

I thank my friends and colleagues at Kingsborough and CUNY for their interest and support over the years that I worked on this project. I am especially grateful to my mentor, advisor, and friend Dr. Michael Barnhart for his guidance, patience, and friendship throughout the long writing and publication process, along with my previous department chair Fran Kraljic. Particular thanks to Joe Felser and Michael Miranda for their friendship and support, along with KCC Donuteers Jacek Czarnecki, Rich Legum, and Rick Repetti. "Cre-deet" also goes to retirees Rick Fox, Fred

Melamet, Stu Suss, Ollie Klapper, Peter Cohen, Barbara Ladman, Loretta DiLorenzo, and the late Dr. Bernard Klein and a host of other mentors who brought me along over the years at KCC. While I never took any sabbaticals or time off—which might explain why the book took me twenty years to write—I did receive a PSC-CUNY Research Grant at a crucial juncture that enabled me to move forward. I also thank the faculty organizers of the KCC Dreamlands Pavilion: Brooklyn and Development conference for giving me a forum to present some of my work on Coney Island in 2009. Two KCC History Department travel awards allowed me to present my research at meetings of the Cooperstown Symposium on Baseball and American Culture in 2011 and 2014. I also thank Bill Simons and his panel at the Cooperstown Symposium for choosing my paper "The Rise and Demise of Minor League Baseball in Oneonta, 1966–2010" to appear in the collected proceedings titled *The Cooperstown Symposium on Baseball and American Culture, 2011–2012*, William M. Simons, ed. (McFarland, 2013) where earlier versions of parts of chapters 3, 5, and 7 previously appeared.

I am especially grateful to the many minor league baseball personnel, front office staff, team owners, and commissioners who were welcoming, honest, and forthcoming with me when I interviewed them. Heartfelt thank-yous to Steve Cohen (longtime executive with the Brooklyn Cyclones), Gary Perrone, Bill Potrecz, Pittsfield Mayor James Ruberto, and Ontario's Finance Minister Greg Sorbara for finding precious time to speak with me. It is bittersweet to thank two individuals who have passed on since I interviewed them in 2006, team executive R. C. Reuteman and NY-PL historian Charlie Wride. British expatriates Nick and Pam Cannon took me out to a pub in St. Catharines where they regaled me with tales of Canadian team ownership and presented me with a purple Stompers cap that I still wear. Rick Murphy talked with me at great length about Wahconah Park and the perils of small-town team ownership, providing me with eye-opening details of life behind the scenes. The Honorable Robert F. Julian gave me two hours in his judge's chambers in Utica, offering tremendous insight into a crucial period of league growth and change and into how team owners think. The late Sam Nader inspired me with his perspective on the game, the league, community loyalty, and life in general, and so this book is partly dedicated to him and his memory. Finally, Josh Getzler joined me for four hours of Zoom conversations in 2020–2021 during the pandemic. He shared stories of Watertown and Staten Island, the intricacies of breaking in a new stadium, being part of the Yankees organization, and the highs and lows of NY-PL team ownership. He is a consummate mensch, and I cannot thank him enough for his generosity of spirit.

I owe a great debt to my friends and community for helping me survive and thrive during and since the pandemic. Steven Z., Steven G., Judah, Dov, Shlomo, Joe, and pedant Jacob Z. provided an intellectual outlet and hours of laughter and learning. The hospitality of the Ackerman family provided me with the workspace where I restarted the book and completed multiple chapters. Siyata D. Schmier gave me the lift I always needed. Everyone at Kingsway Jewish Center offered me a new home and full audiences for my lectures over the past three years. Longtime family friend Henry Sapoznik matched me a match with stellar editor Richard Carlin at SUNY Excelsior Press, and both made it possible for this book to see the light of day. *A sheynem dank.* My brother Dan took amazing photos thanks to the generosity of the folks at Maimonides Park (Coney Island) and Community Park (Staten Island) who let us on the field—Bryan Wynn, Kaitlin Hertz, and Ricky Viola in Brooklyn, and Gary Perrone and Ray Irizarry in Staten Island.

Without the love and support of my family and extended family I could never have begun, procrastinated, and finally completed this book. From the bottom of my heart, thank you to my mom and dad, Vera and Peter Sokolow, my brother Dan and his family, and to Faye and Dennis Wilbur and their sons Benjo and Yosef and their families. My wife and life partner, Arden, was the original inspiration for this entire project, and she and our children Zahava, Nat, Aviva, and Doron have kept me going ever since. Finally my grandson Nadav Shahar has been a joy to all of us since he was born on July 9, 2021. The dedication of this book is a partial birthday present. Good job!

INTRODUCTION

This is a story that was eighty years in the making and took me twenty years to tell.

In the fall of 2002, I was a young community college professor coming up for tenure review. While getting my file in order, I taught a full course load of five classes, prepared my PhD thesis for publication, and helped manage a busy household with three rambunctious children under the age of nine. In the meantime, my wife was finishing up her master's degree in urban planning at Hunter College, where she was running a perfect 4.0 GPA. One of her classes that semester was called "Cases in NYC Planning," taught by a Staten Island architect and planner named Pablo Vengoechea. Professor Pablo lived in a neighborhood called St. George, where he had previously headed the Staten Island Office of the NYC Department of City Planning. Although he'd left that position several years earlier, he maintained an active interest in the biggest construction project to hit St. George in decades: the construction of a fabulously expensive minor league baseball stadium along the waterfront. In his class at Hunter College Graduate School he provided his students with access to a wealth of municipal paperwork and local sources about the ballpark. My wife wrote a term paper using the St. George stadium as her case study and eventually received a grade of A– for the class, the only imperfect grade she ever got at Hunter. She was furious. I was fascinated.

When she brought home newsletters, documents, and reports with exotic initials like FEIS or ULURP, I hauled them to my workplace to make surreptitious copies for myself. They raised all sorts of questions that I could not answer. Was the soil beneath the stadium really filled with toxins from its days as an abandoned railyard? How had the site been chosen for the ballpark? Why would the mighty New York Yankees situate a minor league team in their home city, a huge market already crowded with over a half-dozen professional sports franchises? And the most baffling question of all to me was, why in the world did this stadium cost $80 million to build? Several months later I belatedly realized that Staten Island's Richmond County Bank Ballpark was just one of a matched set of brand-new stadiums in the five boroughs. The other was Keyspan Park in Coney Island, located less than three miles from Kingsborough Community College where I was about to be granted tenure. In fact, my college's radio station broadcast Brooklyn Cyclones games, and our logo was emblazoned on an outfield sign at the stadium. Together the two facilities had cost New York City taxpayers like me approximately $120 million, at that time the most expensive minor league stadiums ever built. Yet I could not remember ever voting to allocate that money, and I had been unaware of any public discussion of plans to construct them.

I sensed that I might be on to something and decided that my next project would focus on minor league baseball. I spent the next several years assembling background information about many disparate subjects. I pored over books and articles and microfiches about the structure and history of minor league baseball, the economics of sports stadiums, and the political era of the 1990s and early 2000s. After filing a slew of FOIA requests I spent several months cloistered in a cubicle at the offices of the New York City Economic Development Corporation, combing through files marked "classified" that I extracted from boxes labeled "Weekly Baseball Meetings." In the year 2006, I spent the most glorious summer of my life immersed in New York-Penn League baseball. I traveled to stadiums and libraries all over New York, Massachusetts, Maryland, Pennsylvania, and Canada, printing up detailed Google maps because I didn't yet own a GPS or a smartphone. I interviewed team owners, league commissioners, general managers, baseball lifers, and the finance minister of Ontario, and then stayed afterward to enjoy live baseball games in their company. I was treated with warmth and courtesy by every member of the minor league baseball community, which I came to see as an extended family of individuals who truly loved their sport. Over the next four years I constructed a plan for a book and completed three and a half chapters. Then I put the manuscript down in 2010 and did not pick it up again for the next ten years.

I spent much of the next decade alternating between being too busy to think about my baseball project and berating myself for my lack of progress on my baseball project. I served on college committees, wrote memos and task force reports, got deeply involved in departmental and college governance, and taught history classes to thousands of students. Every so often I would take the time to wonder why I could not simply finish writing a story that I found so engaging even when I was deep into procrastination mode. And then in March 2020 the Covid-19 pandemic hit, lockdowns began, and all external activities outside my basement ceased for the foreseeable future. Seven long months later my phone pinged with a news alert that Major League Baseball had made the unilateral decision to dissolve the New York-Penn League as part of a massive minor league consolidation plan. And in that instant I finally realized that what my baseball project had lacked all along was an ending. Now that it had been provided to me, it was time to get back to work.

Most of this book has been written or reedited over the past eighteen months since the axe fell on the Staten Island Yankees along with most of the New York-Penn League (but not the Brooklyn Cyclones, as we shall see presently). It has been bittersweet to review and revisit the research and interviews I conducted during the golden summer of 2006. Several of the people I spoke with have passed away and some moved on from baseball, but the majority have remained active in the sport in some capacity. As I navigated my way through warm memories while focusing on the task of assembling an objective historical narrative, I identified the core theme of this book. Professional baseball exists at the intersection of cultural nostalgia and the business of sports. The inherent tensions between these two qualities suffuse the history of the sport, local and national marketing campaigns, and the loyalty that fans and communities feel toward their teams. This has been especially true in the borough of Brooklyn and at Steeplechase Park in Coney Island where the Cyclones team makes its home. It proved to be less impactful in Staten Island, where the lack of a nostalgic past combined with many challenging real-world limitations ultimately doomed a once-promising franchise.

The story's starting point is the tiny hamlet of Batavia, New York, where the original iteration of the New York-Penn League was created back in 1939. The league always portrayed that historic moment through a haze of nostalgia, fondly looking back at an era of community-minded small-town baseball that emphasized the homespun appeal of America's pastime. Nobody dwelled on the fact that the entire enterprise was originated by a bottom-line businessman seeking to build a competitive advantage for his employers in Major League Baseball. They also preferred to overlook the financial instability and near bankruptcy of the league's early years, when teams winked in and out of existence on an almost annual basis.

This book tells a multifaceted story of the relationship between nostalgia and business, from Batavia to Brooklyn and many places in between. It examines the slow transformation of a hardscrabble, low-level, short-season league into a profitable commercial enterprise replete with millionaire team owners and expensive stadium deals. It shows how the confluence of that growth with the development plans of New York City Mayor Rudolph Giuliani would expand the league into the biggest sports market in the nation and unprecedented popularity. It offers insight into the memorable individuals who helped their league flourish and thrive, as well as the avaricious outsiders who euthanized it. And it tells the story of two franchises that went in opposite directions, one achieving astronomical success while the other sank under the weight of debts, failure, and recriminations.

One of the truisms of baseball is that it is a sport with no game clock, and the players play out nine innings for however long that may take. The New York-Penn League's nine innings took eighty years to play out before their game was called, and although the ending was fairly abrupt there were quite a number of memorable highlights along the way.

CHAPTER ONE

OUR OWN LITTLE COMMUNITIES

On November 28, 1938, a group of twenty-three entrepreneurs, local investors, community boosters, and baseball organization men gathered at the Olean House Hotel in Olean, New York, the biggest city in tiny Cattaraugus County in southwestern New York state. The members of this select group hailed from twenty-one different cities, including nearly every major enclave in a region that encompassed western New York state, northwestern Pennsylvania, and a southeastern slice of Ontario, Canada. They had come to Olean at the behest of Oliver French who was then the president of the Rochester Red Wings, a minor league baseball team affiliated with and owned by the St. Louis Cardinals of the National League. When the meeting finally began French got right to the point, proposing that the attendees and their communities work together to create a new minor league. The circuit would be comprised of all-new teams, located in small to mid-size communities that had no current affiliation to professional baseball. Using the full authority of his employer, French committed the renowned Cardinals organization to the success of the incipient league. With St. Louis on board, several other big-league ball clubs also indicated that they would participate as well. The new and as-yet unnamed league was already off to a good start.[1]

Over the next five months, French continued to build on the momentum he had begun in Olean, spending the winter off-season traversing the frozen roads that led to each of the cities that had expressed interest. In January 1939, unfazed by a month that dumped more than three feet of snow on western New York, the principals gathered once again in the city of Batavia, halfway between Rochester and Buffalo. Hosted by Joseph Ryan, a local meat merchant and the Democratic chairman of the New

York State Liquor Authority, that successful meeting led to a third and final organizational session at a Buffalo hotel in March. There the representatives from Batavia and Olean were joined by men from Bradford, Pennsylvania; Hamilton, Ontario; and the western New York communities of Jamestown and Niagara Falls. After depositing a fee of $630 apiece to close the deal, they wrapped up the meeting by electing Buffalo sportswriter and editor Bob Stedler as inaugural league president. The name suggested by Ryan for the fledgling organization was at once practical and whimsical, and in short order their six teams became the first members of the Pennsylvania-Ontario New York League, better known as the PONY League.[2]

As conceived by Oliver French and his major league cronies, the PONY League would be a Class D minor league. This designation referred to baseball's classification system, which dated back to a historic truce declared in 1903 between the established National League (NL) and its junior competitor at the time, the American League (AL). The agreement, which ended two years of so-called baseball wars between the two organizations, imposed order on both major leagues and established their shared professional legitimacy. Together the longtime rivals set up a governance structure for the sport that handled arguments over player contracts, laid out rules for the drafting of players, and created the World Series as an interleague championship. At the same time, this represented both a renewal and a modification of the National Agreement that had previously defined professional baseball. Originally crafted in the 1880s, the agreement had formalized relationships between all of the various professional leagues, not just the NL and AL. Among its provisions were rules regarding clubs' territorial rights and the infamous reserve clause that bound players to their teams even after their playing contracts expired, inhibiting free agency. To the detriment of thousands of baseball players over the next seven decades, the leagues and team owners were quick to carry over all of these conditions before signing the truce of 1903.

Many lesser leagues were also party to this deal, particularly those who would soon become known as baseball's minor leagues. Two years earlier in 1901, fourteen smaller independent leagues had merged into a single entity called the National Association of Professional Baseball Leagues (NAPBL) to protect themselves from the baseball wars between the NL and AL. As the wars now came to a peaceful conclusion, the association joined in to negotiate the restoration of baseball's earlier National Agreement. For their part, the leagues of the NAPBL accepted a permanent, hierarchical division of professional baseball into major leagues and minor leagues, with the majors to be restricted solely to the National League and the American League. The minor circuits would then be divided into a hierarchy of their own. Each minor league would now be slotted into one of four levels or classes, which were designated A, B, C, and D.[3]

By the time the PONY League was created in 1939, Class D was the largest in all of professional baseball. Its circuits were comprised of regional clusters of four, six, or eight teams each, playing against their local rivals for full six-month seasons lasting from April through September. The nationwide popularity of live baseball was reflected by the numerous Class D teams supported by small and medium-sized towns across the country, with fans turning out for games in the Arizona-Texas League, the Alabama-Florida League, rural North Carolina's Tar Heel League, the Northeast Arkansas League, and more than a dozen others. Even at the end of a decade of economic depression, hard times, and sinking profits among even major league teams, baseball was flourishing in the Class D hinterlands. The twenty-two Class D leagues outnumbered all of the rest of the minor leagues, as a combined total of only nineteen leagues played in the classes then known as C, B, A-1, A, and AA. And while 144 teams played D ball that year, only 46 teams were in C leagues, 38 in B leagues, 16 at the A-1 level, 8 in the one Class A league, and 24 teams in the three top Class AA leagues.[4]

Yet the size of Class D belied its importance in the overall scheme of organized baseball. These leagues were at the bottom of the sport's food chain in almost every way. Because they represented the lowest level of professional ball, their players were nearly all young and underdeveloped in terms of their baseball skills and acumen. Teams in towns as small as Paducah, Kentucky, and New Bern, North Carolina struggled to find the revenues to pay even the piddling wages due to their players or to maintain their rapidly deteriorating facilities. Cash-strapped owners often resorted to selling their best players to higher-class minor leagues, a standard strategy that was encouraged by the sport's governance and its legendary commissioner Judge Kenesaw Mountain Landis. This practice only diluted the on-field Class D product even more, which often led to resentment or disinterest on the part of local fans. One PONY League general manager later recalled that "when the Yankees had the farm team here in the 1940s, there was one year when we had 75 players go through. It seemed like every train that came in would have two guys with suitcases getting on and two getting off. Finally some of the fans hung a sign on the gate of [the] field where we played that said, 'New York Yankees Experimental Station.'"[5]

The lowly status of the D leagues was exacerbated by the machinations of the St. Louis Cardinals, who employed baseball men like Oliver French to transform the minor leagues into a pure feeder system for the majors. Beginning in the 1920s under the visionary leadership of team business manager Branch Rickey, the Cardinals had begun purchasing ownership stakes in minor league franchises around the country. By the end of that decade the team owned all or part of seven clubs, with their top players moving up through the minors and into the majors at little or no cost to the parent organization. Now rich in developed talent, some homegrown and some obtained through trades made possible by their overstocked farm system, the St. Louis Cardinals went on to spectacular success, winning multiple National League pennants and three World Series titles between 1926 and 1942. This in turn fueled even greater minor league expansion. By 1940 the Cardinals had working agreements with eight farm teams and owned another thirty-two teams outright, including every single team in the Class D Nebraska State League. The organization established tryout camps all across the country, enticing young players everywhere to sign contracts binding themselves to its many Class D franchises. Branch Rickey insisted that his ubiquitous farm system represented the salvation of professional baseball. His critics, commissioner Landis chief among them, derided the Cardinals' farm teams as "chain gangs."[6]

The newly created PONY League would provide yet another source of inexpensive talent for the Cardinals, which is why Oliver French was willing to go to such lengths to get it underway. The club's main interest was its Ontario team the Hamilton Red Wings, which was wholly owned by the organization. As its name suggested, the Hamilton group was officially designated a farm club of the AA International League's Rochester Red Wings. Originally known as the Syracuse Stars, that team had been purchased by Rickey in 1921 at the outset of his minor league expansion plan. After a successful seven-year run in Syracuse the Cardinals summarily relocated the team to Rochester in 1929, seduced there by the promise of a brand-new ballpark built at no cost to the club. Rickey promptly renamed the team the Red Wings to emphasize its connection to the redbird logo of its major league parent and installed his loyal underling Oliver French as team president. Much to the chagrin of the abandoned fans in Syracuse, the reconstituted Rochester team went on to win four consecutive International League pennants. Bolstered by recruits moved up from the lower minors, the AA Red Wings were now the crown jewel of the Cardinals' developmental system. The team's new PONY League subsidiary would add even more depth to one of the deepest talent pools in all of professional baseball.[7]

Following the successful model established by the Cardinals, all fifteen of the team's major league competitors had minor league affiliates by 1939, though few had even half as many farm clubs as the St. Louis outfit. When the PONY League commenced operating that year, several big-league clubs seized the opportunity to invest in its first season. Pennsylvania's Bradford Bees arranged an affiliation with the National League Boston Bees (a name briefly adopted by the Boston Braves during the late 1930s). The Niagara Falls Rainbows played under the banner of the Cleveland Indians, the PONY League's sole American League member. The Olean Oilers became part of the Brooklyn Dodgers organization under the management of their newly hired farm director, Branch Rickey Jr., possibly at the recommendation of his father. The last remaining teams in the PONY League, the Batavia Clippers and the Jamestown Jaguars, did not manage to secure an agreement with any major league team and instead operated as independents, owned and administered by local community investors.[8]

PONY League original teams, 1939

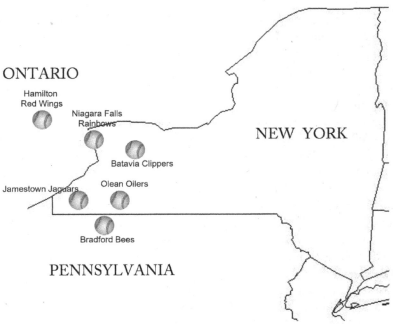

Figure 1.1. NY-PL Map, 1939. Photo by author.

From the outset, the league's independent teams faced significant problems as they tried to establish themselves. This was especially true in Batavia, which had no previous experience in professional baseball. In the 1920s and 1930s the city had been home to a pair of amateur teams, whose games against African American barnstormers like the Canadian Clowns and the New York Colored Giants attracted a few hundred curious fans. But as of the March 1939 inception of the PONY League, Batavia's newly proposed team had no front office or ownership structure, no roster of prospective players, no stadium to hold the games, not even an official name. With only two months to go until the beginning of the season, the local businessmen who had put up Batavia's franchise fee redoubled their efforts.

With assistance from the city's Chamber of Commerce, the Batavia Baseball Club was formed to operate the team, and Joseph Ryan was formally announced as its president. On the stadium front, Mayor James J. Mahaney had spent the better part of two years agitating for federal funds to build a baseball facility. Two weeks before the commencement of the first PONY League season, the regional director of the Works Progress Administration finally approved plans to spend $33,000 to construct a permanent grandstand. A hastily arranged newspaper contest resulted in the name Batavia Clippers for the club, and local Clippers prospects began trying out and practicing at a nearby public park while they awaited the completion of the team's ballfield. Undaunted by the obstacles that still remained, the mayor blithely declared Opening Day a civic holiday and arranged for a citywide parade featuring three drum corps, the American Legion Band, and a brand-new Blue Bus Lines coach to carry team and city officials.

When the Clippers finally took the field the following afternoon on May 10, 1939, only the concrete foundations for the stadium were completed. The stadium lights would not be erected for another three weeks, the outfield fences would not be constructed for another month, and President Roosevelt still had not formally signed off on the WPA funding to pay for everything. Nevertheless, Batavia's first professional baseball game began before a packed crowd of 3,000 spectators. The fans swelled sections of bleachers temporarily relocated from municipal parks, with the overflow seated on folding chairs borrowed from the local funeral parlors. Amid raucous cheers and excitement in the stands, the Clippers went on to lose by a score of 9–4.[9]

The team that beat the Clippers in their first game was the Jamestown Jaguars, who were in dire straits themselves. Like the Batavia club, the

Jaguars were independently owned and lacked any major league backing. Although the team had an existing baseball field inside Jamestown's Celoron Park, its facilities were antiquated and had no concessions or even restrooms for patrons. Drinking water for the players had to be hauled in pails from private homes outside the park, usually by unpaid batboys. The edges of the outfield were thick with trees, which interfered with play. In addition to all of the ballpark issues, the locals who ran the team were frankly incompetent, and it became apparent almost immediately that they would soon fold without even finishing the season. Total failure was averted only through the intervention of Oliver French, who reorganized the Jamestown club a mere ten days after Opening Day. Using his big-league connections, French convinced the Pittsburgh Pirates to take over the management of the team and add it to their meager seven-team farm system. With heavy subsidization provided by their new major league parent, the renamed Jamestown Pirates eked out an existence for the remainder of 1939.[10]

Although they survived their first season, both Jamestown and Batavia entered the 1940s in a state of disarray. The Pirates were so dissatisfied with their experiences in Jamestown that they hauled the franchise out of town after its single season and moved it to London, Ontario. After a second year of limited success the Batavia Baseball Club management team was no happier with its own bottom line, and Batavia's 1941 season was marked by steep financial deficits, bitter turmoil in its front office, and a desperation plan to raise funds through the sale of public stock. The team hoped for salvation in the form of an affiliation agreement with the powerful New York Yankees, which would hopefully boost local interest and fan loyalty. But the deal fell through when the Yankees instead picked Wellsville, New York for their new franchise.

Against all odds the PONY League maintained a presence in Batavia and Jamestown, not only throughout the 1940s but for many decades to come. Jamestown's initial rescuer was the owner of the Niagara Falls Rainbows, who was looking for an escape route for his team after an equally disappointing inaugural season. Despite their own record of baseball failure, the leading citizens of Jamestown were so committed to fielding a team that they managed to scrape together the resources to build a facility to replace Celoron Park. By 1941 the erstwhile Rainbows, now the Jamestown Falcons, were playing out a full schedule at brand-new Municipal Stadium as members of the Detroit Tigers organization. The Batavia Clippers needed a little longer to secure their own future, but shortly after the collapse of their negotiations with the Yankees in April 1942 the team signed on with the Cleveland Indians, jilted patrons of the Niagara Falls ball club.[11]

It was already clear that while Oliver French's brainchild league had the potential for success, it would not be characterized by any long-term stability among its member franchises. Over the next several years, teams winked in and out of existence in towns like Bradford and Hornell in New York, and London in Ontario. Some clubs exchanged major league dance partners nearly every year, luring affiliates with the promise of improved facilities or better attendance. Most if not all of them flirted with financial disaster each season. This forced teams to pinch pennies wherever they could, often at the expense of their employees. Adam Warshal, a player on the 1942 Wellsville Yankees, later recalled that "we traveled in a dilapidated bus to places like Lockport, Batavia, Jamestown, Olean, Hornell, and Hamilton, Ontario. We played night games and immediately after the games we would shower and return to Wellsville to save the management money. Because our pay was so skimpy, we didn't eat too well or have any money left over. I got $75 a month then."

Conditions were even worse for club managers, who were forced to take on many responsibilities in addition to coaching their players on the field. One long-time follower of the teams in Wellsville was local resident and baseball fan Paul Ryan: "The managers had a really miserable job back then . . . They weren't just managers. They were also the trainer, the clubhouse boy and on top of everything else, they had to drive the team bus. Most of them were on the way down. Maybe they'd had a cup of coffee with a major league team and had gotten to know someone in the front office. They'd get a job with a team like Wellsville and get their retirement time in." Life in the PONY League meant life on the margins of professional baseball for everyone involved.[12]

Despite the very real challenges threatening its continued existence, the PONY League not only survived but even flourished throughout the 1940s. After its six teams recorded a combined attendance level of 267,212 in the inaugural 1939 season, league attendance rose slightly in 1940 and then broke 350,000 in 1941. Although the advent of World War II doomed nearly every Class D minor league in the country, the PONY League became one of only two low-level minors to maintain continuous operation right through the war. Undeterred by the paucity of young ballplayers due to the military draft and the difficulties of budgeting in a wartime economy, the league expanded from six to eight teams and kept attendance above

370,000 each year. After topping 400,000 fans in 1944 the PONY League celebrated the end of the conflict by breaking the half-million mark in 1946 and 1948, and then tallied more than 600,000 in attendance in 1949. Most teams like the Batavia Clippers continued to operate on a shoestring, their administrators fretting publicly about the possibility of folding each off-season. But the majority of the league's clubs survived (although the Erie Sailors lasted a mere two seasons before failing in 1945), even if they were not exactly thriving. The league's affiliation agreements generally remained consistent as well, though some teams like the Hornell Maple Leafs, Wellsville Nitros, and Lockport White Socks were forced to operate independently for a season or two between major league contracts. As the PONY League entered its second decade it seemed to have good cause for at least a cautious sense of optimism.[13]

This sudden burst of popularity in the immediate postwar era coincided with a baseball boom throughout the country. During the period between 1946 and 1948 major league teams recorded a startling surge in attendance, attracting nearly 20 million fans each year. This represented a significant increase from the 1945 season, which drew fewer than 11 million. Major league ballparks now attracted crowds of more than 16,000 to an average game, dwarfing not only the low Depression-era average of approximately 6,500 but even the legendary 1920s heyday of the sport, when games usually filled only 7,500 seats. In 1946 alone, eleven out of the sixteen major league baseball teams broke their previous attendance records. Most notable was the New York Yankees, who drew 1.3 million more fans than the year before despite fielding a third-place team that finished seventeen games behind the league-leading Boston Red Sox. This big-league success was replicated throughout the minors, which drew a record 40 million fans in 1949 to the delight of small-town owners and front office personnel throughout circuits like the PONY League.[14]

The sport's resurgence reflected its growing significance to the national psyche throughout the war years. President Franklin D. Roosevelt had made this clear just after war was first declared. In his famous January 1942 "green light letter" to commissioner Landis, the president gave his blessing for major league baseball to continue playing for the duration. "It would be best for the country to keep baseball going," he wrote, recommending not only that games should be held but even that more night games be scheduled to accommodate larger audiences of war workers. As a wholesome and inexpensive leisure activity, baseball would provide a welcome recreation for those on the home front. At the same time, the game's emphasis on teamwork, sportsmanship, and victory reaffirmed the values the government sought to instill throughout American society. The new practice of playing the national anthem before games further infused the sport with a deeper spirit of patriotism, as did the presence of several prominent baseball stars within the ranks of the military forces.[15]

In the aftermath of World War II baseball took on even greater meaning. The war ended with a resounding military success that established America as a true world superpower and set off a period of prosperity nearly unmatched in the nation's history. Richard Ben Cramer's observations about the popularity of 1920s baseball are just as cogent in describing its significance following World War II: "America had made the world safe for democracy. We were rich. We were strong . . . we were ready to play, with truly American force. While the market soared, we knew God loved America." The return of the country's baseball heroes from the battlefield to the ballfield underscored the completeness of victory. It also reassured the citizenry that traditional values and pastimes would now be resumed after the long periods of upheaval during depression and war.[16]

During this period of consensus, American values and patriotism triumphantly suffused the culture of the United States, and the baseball world in particular. In rousing orations and interviews, league executives hailed the sport's purported contributions to the nation at large. In a 1948 speech to a large audience of minor league front-office personnel, Branch Rickey proudly opined that "the sport is making a worthwhile contribution to the welfare of the community and country and give [sic] an unconquerable devotion to it." Three years later, National League president and future baseball commissioner Ford Frick went far beyond that modest statement in a hyperbolic address to the Columbus, Ohio, Rotary Club. "If Germany had had baseball," Frick expostulated, "World War II would have been prevented, and if Russia had a sports program like the Americans, with a chance to let off steam, there would be no danger of Communism." In the Cold War rhetoric of the day, baseball was hailed as a uniquely democratic institution, even more so after major league integration commenced with the Brooklyn Dodgers' signing of Jackie Robinson in October 1945. In its own self-congratulatory narrative, postwar baseball was a color-blind meritocracy. Its entertainment value was secondary to its main function of teaching American youth core virtues such as competitiveness, a drive toward individual achievement, and loyalty to one's teammates. Furthermore, as interest in the sport spread to Japan, Latin

America, and other third-world regions, baseball also became a vehicle for extending America's cultural hegemony throughout the world.[17]

Unfortunately, this period of unprecedented success did not last long into the 1950s. The decade began on a sour note when teams noticed an abrupt decline in attendance. After three years of hovering at the 20-million mark, major league teams experienced a 30 percent drop at the gate before bottoming out at 14.3 million tickets sold in 1953. Minor league attendance plummeted in similar fashion and declined by more than two-thirds by 1959, when combined ticket sales barely topped 12 million after peaking at 42 million ten years earlier. The financial pressures caused by empty ballparks wrought major transformations at all levels of professional baseball over the ensuing decade. Several major league teams relocated westward in search of wider audiences and more profitable markets in Kansas City, Milwaukee, Los Angeles, and San Francisco. At the farm team level more than half of all leagues folded, as only twenty-one out of fifty-nine minor leagues were still in business by 1960. The PONY League was one of the fortunate survivors, but it would have to make some key adjustments in its struggle to continue.[18]

Baseball's attendance problems were only one symptom of a series of challenges facing the sport. Many major league stadiums were aging hulks, located in declining inner-city neighborhoods with inadequate parking facilities. As white middle-class Americans rose in affluence and moved out to the suburbs, they came to view a trip to the ballpark as inconvenient or even racially undesirable. The growing popularity of men's outdoor sports such as tennis, golf, hunting, and fishing, may have further whittled away at the time they once spent attending ballgames. This period also marked the golden era of New York baseball, when the Dodgers, Giants, and Yankees dominated the sport to such an extent that one or more of these teams appeared in the World Series for eighteen straight years. The lack of competitive balance likely hurt nationwide interest, even as all three New York teams struggled to sell out their games and watched their own attendance tail off.[19]

The biggest culprit behind baseball's attendance crisis was the television set. During the early 1950s millions of American families purchased televisions, creating massive audiences and revenue streams for broadcasters. Baseball men like Branch Rickey were initially skeptical of the new medium, fearing that televised play would fulfill fans' desire to see baseball games without actually buying tickets at the ballpark. While this proved to be true, major league teams quickly realized that their gameday losses would be offset by the huge profits they reaped from selling their lucrative broadcasting rights. The first indication of the popularity of televised baseball was the 1947 World Series between the Brooklyn Dodgers and the New York Yankees, which drew an estimated 3.9 million viewers. Within a year the three New York teams were being paid a combined $700,000 for television rights to their games, and by 1955 the Brooklyn Dodgers alone collected $800,000 from local radio and television contracts. Any hesitancy on the part of major league baseball dissolved as teams experienced an explosion of revenues and nationwide interest despite the growing number of empty seats in their stadiums. The sport's huge viewership also attracted large national sponsors such as beer companies, further inflating profits. Baseball was transformed by television, and a slump in ticket sales seemed a small price to pay in exchange.[20]

While the major leagues could trade off sagging attendance for the benefits of televised games, the minor leagues were devastated. As part of the bargain between the networks and the majors, home games were generally not shown on local television so that at least some ticket sales would still be guaranteed. However, there was no such mechanism to protect minor league games played within the broadcast areas of major league parents. Instead of traveling to the nearest ballpark, paying the nominal cost of a ticket, and watching a local farm team struggle with their fundamentals, fans could now spend their evenings or weekends in the comfort of home and pay nothing to watch the big leaguers play. The relocation of major league franchises to historic minor league communities such as Baltimore and cities on the West Coast further extended the hegemony of televised baseball. Throughout the 1950s and into the 1960s, the expansion of baseball's national television audience steadily sapped fans away from local ballparks and hastened the demise of more than half of the nation's minor leagues.[21]

The PONY League suffered significantly during this fallow period. After attendance peaked at a high of 602,273 in 1949, the league lost more than a quarter of its fans when it dropped to 448,012 the following year. Gate receipts dipped slightly in 1951 and then more seriously in 1952, when attendance fell below 400,000 for the first time since World War II. Only 291,325 tickets were sold in 1953, the lowest number since the league's second season in 1940. Yet while other minor leagues across the nation accelerated into a similar downward spiral, the PONY League staged a mini-comeback. In 1954 its teams attracted nearly 376,000 fans, and in 1955 attendance reached a respectable 339,030.[22]

Unlike many of its contemporaries, the league had some unique advantages that allowed it to persevere and hope for the best. The majority of its teams were located in remote areas in western New York state, at a relative distance from any big-league home territory (defined by major league baseball rules as "the circumference of a circle having a radius of fifty (50) miles, with its center at the baseball park of such baseball club").[23] This limited their direct competition for fan attention, with the notable exception of the national broadcast of the Game of the Week. Furthermore, the region was well known for its historic and ongoing support of the minor leagues. Its largest cities, Buffalo and Rochester, were International League stalwarts and had hosted high-level farm teams without interruption since the 1890s. Most of the PONY League's eight teams played in small towns and cities with stable or growing populations, expanding their potential fan base. They also continued to maintain their long-standing affiliations with popular East Coast major league parents including the Dodgers, Yankees, and Philadelphia Phillies.[24]

In the end, the league's temporary reprieve was short-lived. The 1956 season was an unmitigated disaster from the outset. Only twelve games into the year, the New York Yankees abruptly cut off their brand-new affiliation with the team from Bradford, Pennsylvania. This effectively ended professional baseball in Bradford, one of the six founding members of the PONY League. Even more shocking was the dissolution of the Hamilton Red Wings after a mere fourteen games. The only team to retain a single parent organization for the seventeen-year duration of the league, St. Louis's Class D affiliate had once been a model example of a successful farm system. But with the days of Branch Rickey and Oliver French long since passed, the Cardinals' front office made the dispassionate decision to pull the plug on the Hamilton franchise, which disappeared without a trace. The shrunken PONY League limped through the rest of the season, its paltry attendance figure of 161,973 representing less than half that of a year earlier.[25]

It was left to Vince McNamara to save the league. Described by one team president as a "dapper leprechaun," McNamara was a Buffalo native with a strong will and an abundance of Irish charm. As a young shortstop on the Class AA Buffalo Bisons, he had gained minor league experience fielding "ground balls off infields with chunks of coal where there was supposed to be grass." When his major league aspirations failed to materialize, McNamara made a successful switch from player to PONY League umpire in the early 1940s before leaving baseball for a five-year stint in the military during World War II. Upon his return home in 1948 he was elected to succeed Robert Stedler as the second president of the PONY League. He was fortunate enough to take office during the postwar baseball boom that would be the league's high-water mark for the remainder of his thirty-seven-year term. However, the 1957 season represented the crucial test of his leadership capabilities.[26]

Like minor league executives throughout the country, McNamara knew that he could not expect any support from the upper echelons of organized baseball. The major leagues' preoccupation with expansion, relocation, and broadcasting dominance demonstrated their lack of regard for the survival of the minors. The National Association that governed the minor leagues also offered little help to lowly Class D leagues on the brink of dissolution. The association's president, George Trautman, was a major league apparatchik who had most recently served as executive vice president of the Detroit Tigers. It was under his watch that the position of the minors eroded to the point of complete subservience and near-extinction for the majority of his member leagues.[27]

In fact, there was little Vince McNamara could do for his league besides advocate belt-tightening and a strong commitment to weathering the crisis. Under his stewardship the league took an aggressive approach, expanding from six to eight teams even after the worst season in its history. Clubs continued to pursue affiliation agreements that would secure their short-term future, extending the pool of candidates to include the Boston Red Sox, Washington Senators, and even the relocated Milwaukee Braves. His efforts helped reenergize the league, and in both 1957 and 1958 attendance once again topped 250,000. In recognition of this spirit of renewal, President McNamara and the leaders of the league decided that the time had come to change its name. The 1956 demise of the Hamilton Red Wings had marked the end of the PONY League era, not least because Ontario would no longer field a team. Beginning with the 1957 season, the circuit would be known as the New York–Penn League.[28]

As the 1950s gave way to the 1960s, the outlook remained grim. The brief surge in attendance dissipated in 1960, rebounded to nearly 300,000 by 1962, and then relapsed to below 200,000 the following year. Once again the league dwindled from eight teams to six. Host cities Batavia, Corning, Jamestown, Olean, and Wellsville were periodically joined or replaced by communities of similar size and demographics, such as Auburn, Elmira, Geneva, and Erie, Pennsylvania (the sole "Penn" member left in the New York-Penn League, or NY-PL as it became known). Franchises found it harder and harder to retain long-term affiliations with major league teams; perhaps the most hapless victim of this process was the 1962 Auburn team, which was forced into an unlikely flip-flop from the world champion New York Yankees to the expansion New York Mets. The league did receive a reclassification from Class D to a rebranded lowest-level Class A in 1963, when the minor leagues were reorganized in a belated response to a decade of contraction. Fans responded with a shrug and attendance drooped further to 167,639.[29]

The turmoil of the late 1960s provided the impetus for the unexpected salvation of the league. As the nation committed to the escalation of the Vietnam War and the institution of the military draft, young ballplayers suddenly were in short supply. This not only threatened the minor leagues, which had been languishing in the doldrums for more than a decade, but also endangered major league rosters. Major league teams began to urge their top prospects to enroll in colleges to avoid the draft, taking liberal advantage of the military's policy of granting student deferments. These so-called students would then spend their summer breaks developing their baseball skills in the minor leagues.

Vince McNamara, now president of the declining and near-defunct NY-PL, saw this as a unique opportunity. With the assent of the league's team owners, he proposed that the schedule be reduced from a full season of 126 games to a short season of only 78 games. This would make the league an attractive playing option for the student population on limited break, since the schedule would only extend from late June through early September. The plan had additional benefits as well. Because of their northerly location and proximity to the Great Lakes, the league's member cities were frequently forced to cancel games due to inclement weather in the months of April and May. Eliminating those months would remove the inconvenience of rescheduling these postponed games. It would also serve as a welcome cost-cutting measure, particularly since poor weather led to sparse attendance at that time of year anyway. Following the examples set by the Appalachian League, Pioneer League, and Northwest League in the mid-1960s, the NY-PL officially became a short-season A circuit in 1967. Displaying their usual lack of enthusiasm, the fans responded with the worst attendance record in league history as only 115,175 people showed up for the games.[30]

Although it was off to a rocky start, the revamped short-season league soon turned a corner. After hitting rock bottom in 1967 attendance rose for three consecutive years. The league once again surpassed 200,000 fans in 1970, and it would never again fall below that benchmark. By the late 1970s attendance reached the 300,000 plateau for the first time since 1950, a remarkable feat considering that the number of games played had been reduced by 39 percent. The roster of teams expanded back to eight and even to ten in 1977, the most in league history. Despite or because of reducing its schedule, the NY-PL had emerged from near-collapse into a period of stability and incremental growth. Vince McNamara's key role in achieving this success was acknowledged at professional baseball's winter meetings in 1972. By the balmy beaches of Honolulu, far from the frigid conditions of western New York, McNamara was awarded the minor leagues' "King of Baseball" award for his "long-time dedication and service" to his league and his sport.[31]

The reincarnated NY-PL was not only larger but also more geographically diverse than before. Besides the western cluster of teams in Erie, Jamestown, Batavia, Newark, and most recently a new Niagara Falls club, the league now extended further to the east. In addition to central New York communities such as Elmira, Geneva, and Auburn, which had come and gone since the mid-1950s, the league's newest entries from Utica, Little Falls, and Oneonta were its first members to the east of Syracuse. The league also reached affiliation deals with new parent organizations in the 1970s, including the Milwaukee Brewers, Toronto Blue Jays, Boston Red Sox, and Montreal Expos. In this way the circuit managed to benefit from major league expansion instead of suffering from it, as other minor leagues did.

Inside the ballpark, the game remained essentially unchanged. Life in the lowest echelons of baseball still consisted of underpaid personnel trying to perform amid squalid conditions. Most NY-PL teams played in aging if not antiquated stadiums, their small to mid-size communities unable or unwilling to upgrade them just for the sake of thirty-nine home games per season. Undermanned front offices pressed staff members into performing multiple jobs for little or even no pay. Some clubs took advantage of unpaid summer interns, and the community-owned team in Batavia relied on local volunteers to run concessions.[32] Teams took any and all measures to fill the stands, turning to every promotion and gimmick they could think of to sell tickets. Even the league office was not immune to such tactics, as it demonstrated in 1969 when it became the first professional baseball league in the country to sign a woman, Bernice Gera, to an umpiring contract.[33]

Through all of the challenges, teams and their host cities persevered. "We felt that having a minor league franchise was good for our community," Oneonta team owner Sam Nader later recalled. As mayor of the Otsego County town where he had been born and raised, the fierce local booster helped spearhead the group that brought baseball back to Oneonta after its Class C league had failed in the mid-1950s. In 1966 Nader reached out to his remaining baseball contacts and convinced them to bring an NY-PL club back to his town of 13,500 residents. "I thought that professional baseball, as in the old days, when they used to be proud of their local baseball teams, their fire departments, their bands, . . . it would give us a flag to fly," he said. At the same time, Nader knew better than to expect that anyone would get rich off Oneonta's new Class A team. "Owning a minor league franchise was almost a license to lose money. You could hardly give away franchises. The original franchise was given to [us] for one dollar." Undeterred by the defection of his first affiliate after only one year, the determined small-town mayor aggressively courted and won an affiliation with the New York Yankees in 1967. Oneonta responded by winning three out of the next five league championships and went on to win seven championships in its first fifteen seasons. Sam Nader's combination of community spirit and baseball success was rewarded by the Yankees in the form of an unbroken thirty-two-year affiliation with the town, a relationship unmatched in the history of the league.[34]

As the NY-PL reached its milestone fortieth anniversary in 1979, it could rightfully claim to be a model minor league success story. It was the unlikely survivor of a period that had destroyed many larger and higher-level circuits, and at one point nearly the entire minor league system. Under the leadership of only two very capable presidents, a marginal collection of undersized remote communities had achieved economic and competitive stability in a sports business not known for either one. Looking toward the future, it is doubtful that the masters of the NY-PL realized that they were on the cusp of a time of momentous change. Over the next fifteen years minor league baseball would be transformed into a huge potential moneymaker, often at the expense of the individuals and communities that had nurtured it through good times and bad. A new breed of baseball owners and executives would redirect the sport's priorities based on the bottom line. In this environment, a small-time short-season league could expand into markets much larger and more profitable than it had ever thought possible. Even the largest market imaginable, a city so vast that it was already host to two major league baseball teams, was no longer out of bounds.

The New York–Penn League was coming to New York City. But that move would be two decades in the making.

CHAPTER TWO

DICTATING THINGS FROM A DISTANCE

The summer of 1988 was one of the best in minor league history. Attendance was way up, fan enthusiasm was high, and the outlook for the future was brighter than it had been since the early 1950s. Minor league baseball was so hot that it ruled not only the ballpark but even the cineplex, thanks to a tremendously popular movie called *Bull Durham*.

Set in the rough-and-tumble world of Class A minor league baseball, the film was based on the personal experiences of its writer and director, Ron Shelton. As a young farm prospect Shelton had spent five years as a utility player on several minor league squads, most notably the AAA Rochester Red Wings. Building on his authentic knowledge and feel for the game, *Bull Durham* was widely lauded for capturing the atmosphere and rhythms of minor league baseball. Although it never rose higher than fourth on the box-office charts that summer, the film still took in a respectable $50 million in domestic grosses.[1] The movie succeeded thanks to its witty script and its talented lead actors, Kevin Costner, Susan Sarandon, and Tim Robbins. At the same time, it also touched something deeper in the public psyche. The movie, later chosen by *Sports Illustrated* as the greatest sports movie of all time, had heart and soul, and at its center was the special meaning of baseball within American culture.[2]

Unlike more worshipful baseball movies like *Pride of the Yankees* or *The Natural*, *Bull Durham* purported to present a warts-and-all inside look at the wildly idiosyncratic characters who populated the minor leagues. The film's protagonists include a washed-up catcher, a bonus-baby rookie with "a million-dollar arm and a five-cent head," and a sexually voracious woman named Annie, a nod to the ever-present baseball groupies called

23

Annies by the players. The hardships of minor league life appear onscreen as well, such as the meager salaries and rock-bottom facilities, and the numbing effects of the endlessly repetitive cycle of travel, practice, and playing games day after day.

At the same time, *Bull Durham* asserted both implicitly and explicitly that baseball, particularly in its purest minor league incarnation, had great cultural significance. In an interview conducted twenty years after the film's release, Ron Shelton identified its core message as "the American dream [of] hope and promise," achieved both despite and because of the challenges faced at the minor league level. The movie itself ended on this note, as now-retired groupie Annie Savoy intoned the closing lines: "Walt Whitman once said, 'I see great things in baseball. It's our game. The American game. It will repair our losses and be a blessing to us.' You could look it up!"[3]

The release of *Bull Durham* coincided with a tremendous upswing in baseball's popularity. After more than a decade of relatively flat growth, baseball teams experienced a distinct rise in attendance figures beginning in the late 1970s. The biggest beneficiaries were the major leagues, which drew an unprecedented 30 million fans in 1976 and more than 55 million by 1989. At the same time, soaring profits were accompanied by a corresponding rise in expenses. Abetted by a federal ruling mandating free agency for players with expiring contracts, team payrolls and marketing budgets exploded. The resulting media attention fed even more public interest in the sport and its newly bloated economic structure, and the fervor grew unabated even through a pair of work stoppages in 1981 and again in 1985. Meanwhile, fans were finding new and novel ways to interact with the game through rotisserie leagues and fantasy baseball camps, which gave them the chance to share a vicarious experience of the game as if they were general managers or players themselves.

The popular fascination with the statistical and economic aspects of the sport was accompanied by a tendency among writers and filmmakers to romanticize its legacy. In an era dominated by conservative rhetoric of American exceptionalism and traditional values, the game seemed to epitomize the ideals of a past golden era. Like Annie Savoy, many Americans saw great things in baseball, its history, and the lessons it could teach. Baseball's audience ran the gamut, from intellectual readers of Roger Angell's poetic essays in *New Yorker* magazine to the mass millions of filmgoers who embraced the naked sentimentality of Kevin Costner's 1989 hit movie *Field of Dreams*. Baseball fever had America in its grip throughout the 1980s, and the nation's appetite for the sport was insatiable.[4]

The minor leagues also benefited enormously from the rejuvenation of the game. Attendance had dipped to an all-time low during the 1970s but rallied to 12.3 million in 1980 and over 23 million when *Bull Durham* came out in 1988, the highest level since the early 1950s. The popularity of the film spurred fan interest even further, although league personnel downplayed the film's influence. Sal Artiaga, president of the umbrella National Association that governed the minors, put it this way: "Did *Bull Durham* help us? No, I think it was the reverse; they made the picture because of the success the minor leagues have been enjoying."[5]

Artiaga did his best to make the most of that success. Under his leadership and that of his predecessor Johnny Johnson, the minors were urged to think big league rather than bush league. Some aggressive teams established marketing deals with national firms to maximize media exposure and profitability. Clubs were encouraged to renovate or even replace their facilities whenever possible, hoping that these improvements would influence more people to spend their leisure dollars at the ballpark. More creative and (sometimes) sophisticated promotions helped the minors market themselves and their image of "good, wholesome entertainment at a reasonable price in a nice setting," tapping into the romanticized popular vision of the national pastime. As these efforts translated into higher and higher revenues, the financial worth of minor league teams skyrocketed. In some leagues franchise values rose by ten times between 1980 and 1989. The president of the AA Eastern League bragged that his franchises had increased in value from $50,000 apiece to "between $2 million and $3 million." This in turn attracted a new type of big-time owner with deeper pockets, marketing savvy, and high expectations of a return on their increasingly large investments in minor league teams.[6]

The baseball boom of the 1980s even trickled down to the Class A teams inhabiting the lowly New York-Penn League (NY-PL). In 1981 league attendance broke the 300,000 mark for the first time since 1955, and then topped 500,000 two years later. By the end of the decade the league was averaging more than 600,000 fans each season, despite its abbreviated three-month regular season schedule of only seventy-eight games. Spurred by this unprecedented local interest, the league expanded back to ten teams in 1982, to twelve the following year, and finally to a permanent membership of fourteen teams in 1989, the same year attendance hit an all-time high of 714,561 tickets distributed. After suffering through decades of shrinkage and dwindling revenues, the league's fortunes were finally on the rise.[7]

The expansion plan centered on New York State, as it had throughout the league's existence. Of the original members, three were still based in the western New York communities where the league was born in 1939: Jamestown, Batavia, and a reconstituted Niagara Falls organization. They had since been joined by several teams situated further east in central New York communities like Newark, Elmira, and the Finger Lakes towns of Geneva and Auburn. New single A clubs in Binghamton and Oneonta soon extended the league's boundaries even further into central New York, and by the mid-1980s its ongoing march eastward led into Utica, Watertown, and the Adirondack community of Little Falls.

By now the league's appeal to potential club owners extended beyond the borders of New York and even the United States. In 1981, after spending nearly fifteen years outside organized baseball, the Erie Cardinals reestablished the league in Pennsylvania for the first time since Erie's former teams went under during the 1960s. Several Ontario communities also joined up, starting with the city of St. Catharines in the greater Niagara region. St. Catharines was soon followed by a second club from Hamilton, once home to the Red Wings team that had been a cornerstone of the original PONY League. Welland, Ontario, completed the Canadian triumvirate in

Figure 2.1. NY-PL Map, 1987. Photo by author.

1989, marking the strongest international presence in the league's history. With its teams so numerous and widely dispersed, the league introduced an East-West divisional structure to enhance local rivalries and build interest in the end-of-summer playoff series.

The NY-PL's newfound popularity ushered in a welcome period of relative stability for many of its teams. About half the clubs now maintained long-term affiliations with a single major league partner. Although franchise agreements were generally short term, teams like the Auburn Astros, Jamestown Expos, and Geneva Cubs had little difficulty arranging multiple extensions that eventually lasted for more than a decade. Even the Little Falls Mets and St. Catharines Blue Jays maintained a similar equilibrium, though both were expansion franchises in communities that had never before supported a minor league team. The league's sole nonaffiliated club was the Utica Blue Sox, abandoned in 1981 by the Blue Jays organization to ignominy and debt. Kept alive by an outside investment group, sheer stubbornness and an unlikely league championship victory in 1983, the Blue Sox persevered on their own for several years until they were finally adopted by the Philadelphia Phillies organization. And when Philadelphia dropped them for Batavia after a single two-year contract, the Blue Sox acted quickly to secure a replacement affiliation with the Chicago White Sox.[8]

The tribulations of the Blue Sox reflected the fundamental vulnerabilities faced by all of the clubs. Minor league owners paid the lion's share of costs and assumed all of the financial risk involved in running their franchises. Cash-strapped front offices had to cover virtually all expenses including local housing, some travel, and stadium-related payments for leases, utilities, and groundskeeping. Many were forced to operate on shoestring budgets that were threatened by even an incremental rise in the price of baseballs at Wilson Sporting Goods, the league's preferred supplier. At the same time, outlays were rarely matched let alone exceeded by profits. Despite the league's rising profile, teams often struggled to fill seats and hawk enough concession items to break even by the end of the season. As owners faced financial disaster on an almost daily basis they could take some solace in the fact that their largest potential expense, the payroll for their on-field staff, was underwritten by their major league affiliates.

The relationship between minor league clubs and their major league parents was governed by player development contracts (PDCs), the legal heart of the farm system. The PDC structure was laid out in the sport's Professional Baseball Agreement between the major leagues and the minors'

National Association of Professional Baseball Leagues, a compendium of on-field and business operational guidelines which was rubber-stamped and renewed by both sides every four years. The rules mandated that major league clubs were responsible for subsidizing salaries for minor league players and coaches and providing their minor league affiliates with additional money for travel and meal expenses. In return, major league front office personnel expected to exert tremendous authority over their farm teams. Major league farm directors appointed the coaching staff and provided the players to fill team rosters. They decreed how those players were to be used in games, deciding when they should play and which positions they should play, and for how many innings on a given day. This caused complications for minor league personnel and often the players themselves, as described by Oneonta Yankees and Jamestown Expos manager Q. V. Lowe:

> One of the big frustrations in managing in the minor leagues is not having control, not being able to make the moves and play the kids that you need to win, and not being able to do the things that you know are best for the kids. We had a kid out there on the mound last night, a kid to whom we had given lots of money. He gave up six runs in the first inning and was really struggling. I took him out in the fourth and put in a kid I thought could give us a chance to win. We did win. But then the front office gets on me for not giving the bonus kid one hundred pitches . . . It doesn't do the kid any good psychologically to leave him on the mound when he is getting shelled.
>
> But the front office isn't here. They can't see the whole situation. They only see the damn numbers. So many times I have seen organizations make decisions with no regard to the kid, almost as if his welfare didn't even cross their minds. There is too much of the [front office] dictating things from a distance.[9]

At any time, either a player or a coach could be shuffled between affiliates at the behest of the parent club, regardless of the effect this might have on his former team's record or performance. The mantra of the farm system was not winning but player development—that is, to develop the skills of players until they were ready to leave the minors behind and become major leaguers. Since the vast majority of minor league players would never reach that level, the entire farm system existed to identify and train only a handful of individuals for eventual promotion to "the show." More than one contemporary observer likened minor league baseball to corporate R&D at firms like IBM, a far cry from the freewheeling world of *Bull Durham*.[10]

The player development contracts between major and minor league clubs only lasted for a period of either two or four years before renewal, and that decision inevitably rested in the hands of the major league partner. This kept the pressure on the minor league affiliates to provide the best environment judged suitable for developing prospects, or else risk abandonment and the uphill battle to secure a replacement. In addition, all player drafts, signings, and other roster moves were conducted under the auspices of the major leagues. The chief function of the minors was the breeding and feeding of talent to the majors, just as it had been since Branch Rickey's Cardinals pioneered the farm system six decades earlier.

Under these rules, it was virtually impossible for an independent minor league operation like the Utica Blue Sox to survive for long. Without a parent club to contribute to its payroll and excluded from the talent pool that fed the competition, it was a miracle that the Blue Sox lasted even a single season on their own. When the team unexpectedly won the NY-PL championship it did so as the sole independent club in all of the minor leagues, the only team out of approximately 170 franchises that necessarily valued winning over player development. Within a short time Utica was back in the fold as a minor league affiliate, its aberrant years as an independent all but forgotten. The price for security was victory, as Utica would never again play in a league championship series, let alone win another title.

Meanwhile on the major league level, baseball's meteoric success was breeding tensions. Despite or because of the massive profits generated by their lucrative franchises, team owners were focusing obsessively on the bottom line. They squabbled with players over the higher salaries of the free agency era, even as they initially rushed to outbid one another to obtain the best talent available. Several owners ratcheted up pressure on local governments to fund expensive stadium upgrades, threatening to relocate unless their demands were met. And as the sports pages became increasingly financial in tone, fans began to express contempt for the greed they perceived in both camps, players and owners.

The nadir of this trend was the revelation that team owners had engaged in an organized and illegal collusion effort. Major League Baseball's collective bargaining agreement with the Players' Association forbade teams from conspiring with each other to artificially hold down player salaries or block free agents from switching teams. In 1987, after three seasons with virtually no free agent movement at all, the players brought a formal grievance alleging that collusion was clearly taking place. Three separate arbitration hearings all found in favor of the players. Abetted by the league presidents and baseball commissioner Peter Ueberroth, the owners had illicitly shared information about their free agent plans and tacitly agreed not to poach each other's players even once they became available. These findings were a black eye for baseball, which endured a public relations nightmare and threats of losing its invaluable antitrust exemption. The teams were also forced into paying a whopping $280 million settlement to the players, with each major league team contributing more than $10 million.[11]

At the epicenter of the collusion conspiracy and the increasing owner conflict were Jerry Reinsdorf and Eddie Einhorn of the Chicago White Sox, two partners with much in common. Both were born in 1936 in the New York City metropolitan area, Reinsdorf in Brooklyn and Einhorn in Paterson, New Jersey. In the late 1950s they were classmates at Northwestern University Law School in Chicago before each found his route to success and fortune. Reinsdorf used his innate savvy with numbers to make a killing in real estate before going on to amass even more millions in partnerships and investment firms. Along the way he developed a reputation as a fierce negotiator and a master at manipulating his opponents into giving him what he wanted. He first demonstrated this ability when he convinced Northwestern to grant him a major scholarship by pitting the school against an alleged but unconfirmed offer from the University of Chicago. This innate cunning and guile would make Reinsdorf an ideal major league owner.[12]

The more gregarious Einhorn was a pioneer in televised sports media, earning the nickname "Fast Eddie" for his limitless energy and deal-making abilities. After creating one of the first nationally syndicated college basketball networks in the late 1960s, the mop-topped dynamo tried promoting pro wrestling and college bowling before moving on to CBS Sports. As executive producer of *CBS Sports Spectacular* Einhorn crafted a ratings blockbuster by featuring anything and everything that would attract an audience—"I'm as big a whore as anybody else," he admitted at the time—such as Mr. Universe contests, tractor-pulling championships, and *Battle of the NFL Cheerleaders*. While raising his profile as a media executive, Einhorn was also keeping his eyes open for sports ownership opportunities. When the White Sox went on the market in 1981, Reinsdorf reached out to Einhorn and the two multimillionaires teamed up to purchase the franchise from renowned baseball man Bill Veeck for $19 million. According to the terms of their partnership, Reinsdorf took over as team chairman and Einhorn as vice chairman and team president.[13]

Brash, blunt-spoken, and spoiling to make their mark on a moribund franchise, the new owners immediately began ruffling feathers inside and outside the organization. In one of his first public comments Reinsdorf derided the team's Comiskey Park as a "park full of drunks." Einhorn then chimed in by calling Comiskey "the world's largest outdoor saloon." South Side fan response was predictably resentful, and many agreed with Chicago sportswriter Richard Lindberg's assessment of the two as a pair of rich fat cats who "flew around in Lear jets and operated under the protection of a tax shelter." Within a few months the new owners were further quoted disparaging the fans as classless and popular former owner Veeck as inept. They also ran off legendary White Sox broadcaster Harry Caray, who hissed "snake oil" at the new management team on his way across town to call games for the rival Chicago Cubs.[14]

Their next target was a massive facilities upgrade for their antiquated stadium. After securing $5 million in Chicago city funding to add field-level luxury seating and a bank of skyboxes to the existing facility, Reinsdorf and Einhorn kicked off an ultimately successful campaign to squeeze the state of Illinois for a fully subsidized state-of-the-art ballpark. Their tactics combined a highly public flirtation with moving the team to St. Petersburg, Florida, along with some old-fashioned arm-twisting local politics. After several years of wrangling, a last-minute deal was struck, and in 1991 old Comiskey Park fell to the wrecking ball, new skyboxes and all. It was quickly replaced with a new stadium featuring unobstructed views, improved amenities, and more than eighty skyboxes that were even more lucrative than their predecessors. New Comiskey was hailed as a model of a modern facility by team executives. The team's working-class fans, sitting in bleacher seats now moved further back from the field to accommodate the expensive luxury boxes, were less complimentary. Dan Bickley of the *Chicago Sun-Times* summed up the prevailing popular opinion when he called the stadium "a monolithic mall."[15]

The scorched-earth approach taken by the White Sox front office extended into baseball politics as well. Exhibiting the same force of will that propelled him to success in Chicago, Reinsdorf quickly established

major clout within the owners' circle. He took positions on several of the
sport's most significant committees, including Player Relations, Labor Policy,
and the powerful Executive Council of Major League Baseball. Reinsdorf's
hard-nosed style and hardline fiscal positions won him influential allies like
Milwaukee Brewers owner Bud Selig, his co-ringleader in both collusion and
the owners' subsequent eviction of Fay Vincent from the commissioner's
seat. Some owners were nettled by the pushiness of the White Sox pair.
George Steinbrenner, no milquetoast himself, was overheard more than
once referring to Reinsdorf and Einhorn as "the Katzenjammer Kids" and
"Abbott and Costello" (Reinsdorf famously retorted, "How do you know
when George is lying? When you see his lips move."). But their unerring
nose for profit and strong-arm strategies delighted most of their peers,
and even Steinbrenner later praised Reinsdorf as "the one guy I'd have
in the trenches with me."[16]

While Reinsdorf exerted his influence over political power brokers
and fellow owners, Eddie Einhorn took the lead in reshaping the White
Sox baseball operations, particularly in the minor leagues. When he first
stepped in as team president in 1981 the Sox farm system was in sham-
bles. The club had a long history of abysmal player development and
draft busts, which helped explain why the White Sox had appeared in
the playoffs only once since the infamous "Black Sox" team of 1919 had
thrown the World Series. By the end of the Veeck years the franchise had
fewer resources than ever to develop young talent. That was expected to
change with the infusion of cash provided by new ownership. But the front
office chose to spend their money on a slew of high-priced free agents
instead, refusing to direct any additional funds to rebuilding the team's
minor league infrastructure. From the outset it was clear that the White
Sox had become "the franchise that doesn't believe in the minor leagues."[17]

Einhorn's penurious approach to minor league budgeting was the
result of intentional planning, not merely inexperience. After years as a
cost-conscious media executive Einhorn was appalled at the high expenses
associated with signing and developing young players, most of whom
never even made it to the majors. In an era when the most successful
organizations had seven minor league farm teams, the White Sox refused
to authorize more than five. Instead of investing in an effective scouting
program, the front office cut the club's full-time scouting personnel from
thirteen to five employees. Young prospects were viewed as bargaining
chips to be traded away in exchange for proven big-leaguers, rather than
talent to be nurtured. Among players and other organizations the team got

a reputation for being hard on minor leaguers, an image they seemed to welcome (one White Sox VP was quoted on the record saying "the days of babying players are gone"). While lifelong baseball men scoffed, Einhorn saw it as his mission to proselytize among major league owners until they understood how wasteful and inefficient the farm system had become.[18]

Convinced that it was high time for "baseball people [to] get together and build a better mousetrap," Einhorn commissioned a series of statistical studies on the minor leagues. Then he presented the results before a succession of committees comprised of major league owners and administrators. The core of his argument was that "baseball has a low level of return of investment for the numbers of players who make it." Einhorn's numbers were damning indeed: in the previous decade clubs had spent $1 billion developing more than 8,500 minor league players, but only 425 of them—5 percent—ever reached the major league level. In full-out Fast Eddie mode, Einhorn claimed to worry not only for cash-strapped teams but for the young hopefuls who traded away their futures in pursuit of their unlikely big-league dreams. "It's a morally reprehensible system to me. We pay a first-round draft choice $150,000 bonus just so he won't go to college. That's reprehensible. Children should be encouraged to go to college. The odds are that he won't make the major leagues anyhow. If he doesn't make it in three or four years, does he go back to college?"[19]

Minor league executives were scornful of the questionable conclusions reached by Chicago's "television guys." They pointed at the recent success of organizations like the California Angels, renowned for their emphasis on drafting and developing their own players. Some baseball people argued that Einhorn's studies were far less accurate than the research of Allan Simpson, editor of the highly regarded magazine *Baseball America*. In a completely opposite set of conclusions, Simpson had found that more than 10 percent of players who signed pro contracts reached the majors, double Einhorn's figure. Furthermore, players who advanced to higher levels of the minors had a significantly better chance of success, as 73 percent of players on Class AAA teams would go on to appear in a big-league uniform. Then again, critics could point out that *Baseball America* was owned by Miles Wolff, whose Durham Bulls were among the most successful minor league franchises in the country. As an employee of a prominent minor league owner, Simpson may not have been entirely unbiased either.[20]

Eddie Einhorn was unfazed by his rough reception and continued to advocate sweeping changes. The current system was financially unsustainable, he insisted. Major league teams had no choice but to cut their runaway spending on minor league operations. After visiting Japan three separate times to examine the Japanese approach to player development, Einhorn was convinced that their example was worth emulating. Based on his observations he suggested that developmental rosters should be trimmed by half and the number of teams fielded by each organization should be slashed as well. He also urged a cap on investment to relieve the onerous burden of player development costs, limiting each team's annual contribution to $3–4 million. Instead of fielding five clubs with rosters of 120 players each, teams would now fund only two minor league clubs with 60 players apiece. At one point he even advocated that the minor league hierarchy be scrapped in favor of a single developmental program under the centralized auspices of Major League baseball. "It's hard to believe we'd miss anybody," Einhorn concluded.[21]

Most career baseball executives were skeptical of Eddie Einhorn and his recommendations. But many team owners were swayed by his notion of a streamlined sport. Einhorn was hugely popular at the moment, as he was lauded for laying the groundwork for baseball's new billion-dollar television deal with CBS and ESPN. His partner Jerry Reinsdorf was already entrenched as one of baseball's most powerful owners in committee meetings and behind the scenes. To their fellow owners, the White Sox leaders were both a source of bountiful profits and a model to emulate. Their organization was a big-market cash cow, yet they remained dedicated to cost-cutting. Although they were always active in the free agent market, the White Sox were sharp negotiators who routinely managed to avoid ruinous salary arbitration cases. Their new stadium deal was a masterstroke of profitability in every way.

By the end of 1990 the lords of baseball were facing record salary levels, a new labor deal that seemed to favor the players, and collusion payments that they were loath to fund out of their own pockets. For the past several years the White Sox had been proposing that teams seek fiscal relief by slashing minor league costs. With the Professional Baseball Agreement (PBA) between the major and minor leagues set to expire in January 1991, many clubs had reached the point where they were inclined to agree. As the PBA deadline approached, a determined coalition of team owners and the commissioner's office decided it was time to take a hardline approach to their negotiations with the minor leagues.

Major league front offices began their public relations assault on the minors in 1989, more than a year before the PBA expired. Following Eddie Einhorn's lead, team officials bemoaned the millions they invested in a system that would only yield one or two players each year. Minor league salaries had reached "ridiculous" levels, they charged. As savvy prospects began to hire agents and demand high signing bonuses up front, developmental costs multiplied even faster. "Everything we have is going out," complained Ed Kenney, director of player development for the Boston Red Sox. "We get nothing back."[22]

Minor league personnel were bewildered by the suddenness and ferocity of the attacks. Despite their recent surge in popularity many farm teams were still barely breaking even. The inflated franchise valuations reported by the press mostly reflected potential sale prices for teams whose local owners had no intent to sell. It made no sense to them when a big-market operator like the Mets' Joe McIlvaine accused minor league clubs of "crying wolf" as their profits allegedly outstripped some major league teams. Everyone knew that Major League Baseball had made more than $200 million in profits in 1989 alone, with more to come from the $95 million in fees demanded from two new expansion teams. The $14 million each team was to receive in television money alone would be more than enough to offset the collusion settlement, with plenty left over to lavish on free agents. If anyone was crying wolf, it was the major leagues and not the minors.[23]

For most of 1990 the PBA negotiations remained at a standstill. In the early part of the year major league owners had suffered twin defeats. First a monthlong lockout of the players failed to wring any significant economic concessions and resulted instead in higher salaries and less leverage for ownership. Then the full collusion settlement figures were announced shortly afterward, frustrating many owners even further. Unable to punish the real culprits—the players, arbitrators, and themselves—owners directed the brunt of their anger against minor league executives. They chose Bill Murray, Commissioner Fay Vincent's executive director of baseball operations, as chief negotiator in the PBA talks. With the full authority of the commissioner's office and the owners behind him, Murray brought a list of demands to the table. Major league baseball wanted concessions from the minors and would walk away if they were not met.

The stalemate came to a head in November as the agreement deadline loomed. Completely overmatched at every stage of the negotiations, minor league representatives had already agreed to capitulate on most of the terms dictated to them. They would surrender a significant percentage of their annual revenues to the major leagues, including ticket sales, television, and merchandising. They would continue to pay the majors for the privilege of using the organizations' names and logos in marketing their own farm teams, a deal forced upon them by then-commissioner Peter Ueberroth in the previous PBA. All minor league clubs would have to open up their financial records and submit annual profit-loss statements to the major leagues, who were under no reciprocal obligation to do likewise. For their part, the major league teams would reduce their subsidies of the minors even further, forcing farm teams to pay a higher share of the expenses for travel, hotels, meals, and equipment for their players. They also wanted to draft a new set of minimum standards for minor league stadium facilities and enforce compliance on teams whose ballparks failed to pass muster. Prostrated in total and abject defeat, the minors agreed to these conditions too.[24]

Despite all of these concessions, Murray and his masters were not yet satisfied. Major League Baseball now demanded an even higher percentage of minor league revenues than the $3 million combined figure they were being promised. The commissioner's office also insisted on total centralized authority over the minor leagues, as opposed to the semi-independent control that had been wielded by minor league presidents and the president of their National Association for nearly a century. Minor league owners were outraged, to put it mildly. Durham Bulls owner Miles Wolff fumed about the "firing squad" poised to execute the minors. Fellow owner Joe Buzas excoriated the hypocrisy of the major leagues and their commissioner. "We're under a gag rule, but I don't give a damn . . . My first twenty-one years as a minor league owner were hell. Now that we've built it up, they want to take over and get rid of us."[25]

In response, Bill Murray threatened to establish a new developmental system completely owned and operated by Major League Baseball along the lines proposed by Eddie Einhorn. As the standoff stretched into December, major league owners went a step further and refused to attend the annual Baseball Winter Meetings in Los Angeles. Instead of gathering together with minor league executives as they had for decades, the lords of baseball met separately in Jerry Reinsdorf's Chicago for their own grim council of war. Their mood was matched by the weather outside the Chicago Hyatt, as subzero temperatures were punctuated by harsh winds and snow squalls.[26]

Less than two weeks later the major leagues got nearly everything they wanted. Their slice of minor league revenues was increased to $5 million over the next four years, and their annual subsidy reduced by more than $300,000. The commissioner's office was given most if not all of the authority it sought over minor league operations. From now on it would be the commissioner who granted final approval over franchise relocations, sales or transfers, and minimum facilities standards, although the leagues retained a modicum of control over approving ownership changes. The minors would benefit from a new joint licensing agreement with Major League Baseball's marketing arm, although the profits were minimal once they were divided among the 170 clubs. They also persuaded the majors to raise their minimum number of affiliates from 78 to 119, guaranteeing security for a much larger number of teams. But in exchange they lost all rights to define and divide up their own territorial rights. As the Utica Blue Sox discovered years earlier, the price for minor league survival was giving up self-determination.[27]

In one of his first acts as overlord of all of organized baseball, commissioner Vincent appointed a new director of minor league operations, Jimmie Lee Solomon. The son of a cattle rancher and a onetime Dartmouth football player, the dignified black attorney was ostensibly charged with healing the rift with the humiliated and disgruntled minor leagues. In reality he ensured that the transfer of power was smooth and that full compliance took place, particularly in the area of facilities standards. Although his boss was ousted by the owners within the year, Solomon remained in place communicating the mandates of Major League Baseball to its minor league vassals.[28]

In the short term the minor leagues' deal with the devil had little appreciable effect. Overall attendance continued to rise, with more than 27 million fans coming to minor league ballparks during the 1992 season. Franchise valuations continued to surge to record levels. Minor league baseball continued to grow in popularity among families attracted by its affordability, entertainment value, and generally wholesome reputation. While Major League Baseball tore itself apart over labor strife and economic issues in the mid-1990s, the minors retained their appeal for a fan base weary of the spectacle of feuding multimillionaires.

But behind the scenes the new PBA rules were placing enormous pressure on franchise owners and front offices. Few clubs made even a 10 percent profit each season, and that margin was razor-thin. Now that teams were forced to pay for travel and hotel arrangements, every precious penny had to be stretched further than ever. "[We're] like kids on the playground having our lunch money taken from us by the bullies," said Miles Wolff, who had purchased the Durham Bulls when they were bankrupt and now watched his hard-earned revenues trickle into bottomless major league coffers. While minor league teams were thrilled by rising attendance figures, they also knew that the more tickets they sold, the higher their payments to the majors. Instead of paying $5 million over four years, minor league executives estimated that they paid that $5 million to the major leagues in the first year alone. And still Bill Murray insisted that the minors had gotten the better part of the deal.[29]

The stadium issue loomed largest of all. Major League Baseball wasted no time in drawing up a set of standards for all new minor league facilities. To ensure that player development took place in the best possible environment, they compiled rules for the appropriate size of the field, composition of the playing surface, lighting requirements, drainage, and any other factors that might affect the quality of play or the safety of the players. While they were at it, they added a laundry list of amenities that had nothing to do with the players, ranging from concessions to construction details to the minimum number of toilets in fan restrooms. Although the PBA specifically excluded existing ballparks from the new stadium standards, the commissioner's office demanded that every minor league facility either conform to the rules or make at least some progress in that direction. The deadline for compliance was 1994.[30]

This edict sent a palpable shudder throughout the minor leagues. Many teams—perhaps the majority of them—played in aging if not downright elderly ballparks. In the New York-Penn League alone the average stadium was fifty-seven years old. Rotting wooden facades and metal bench bleachers were the rule rather than the exception, and the less said about the restroom conditions the better. Few franchises owned their own facilities. Most belonged to the small to mid-sized municipalities that leased them to the teams, often at discounted rates that were all the cash-strapped tenants could afford.

To comply with the new standards teams would have to ask their municipal landlords to spend hundreds of thousands if not millions of dollars on improvements. The alternative was to demand even more millions to build entirely new stadiums designed to fulfill all of the requirements imposed by Major League Baseball. Once the stadium improvements were funded, teams could offer no guarantees that they would stick around long enough to validate the huge expense of construction. Since the Player Development Contracts that governed affiliation agreements lasted only two years, a club might conceivably move out or even cease to exist shortly after the new or improved facility opened its gates.

The new PBA set the stage for chaos and greed to engulf the minor leagues. An industry that had never been about profitability was now obsessed with it. Owners were pitted against their local communities in a stadium struggle pressed upon them by the major league owners who now controlled all of professional baseball. Mom-and-pop teams who were unwilling or unable to engage in these conflicts were pressured to sell their franchises to carpetbaggers without such compunctions. Instability and uncertainty were to be the hallmarks of a new era in the minor leagues.

In short, they were turning into the majors.

CHAPTER THREE

WHAT THE HELL DO THEY CARE?

Part One: The Oneonta Yankees

If anyone understood and feared the implications of the new Professional Baseball Agreement, it was Sam Nader.

Born and raised in Oneonta, New York, Nader was almost singlehandedly responsible for his hometown's longtime relationship with professional baseball. Sam was born in 1920, one of six children of a Lebanese railroad laborer who lived on the wrong side of the tracks that separated their poor neighborhood from the better sections of town. There the Naders rode out the Great Depression, living among immigrant neighbors who didn't know they were poor at a time when nearly everyone was. As a teenager Sam played baseball at Oneonta High and had dreams of making the big leagues, but he quickly realized that he lacked the skills to be a professional ballplayer. After graduation he found a new aspiration in the study of law, but after two unsuccessful years at two different colleges it became clear that higher education wasn't in the cards either.

Ever practical, Sam found work at the age of twenty-one in nearby Sidney, New York. There he joined thousands of Otsego County residents at the Scintilla division of the Bendix Aviation Corporation, makers of airplane magnetos and one of the region's largest employers. After starting at 40 cents per hour he moved over to sales, but his career was put on hold when he was drafted into the army for the duration of World War II. Disregarding his poor eyesight, he served as a machine gunner at the Battle of the Bulge and subsequently was awarded the Bronze Star. When the war ended Sam's job was waiting for him, along with a promotion to director of purchasing.[1]

Sam was well on his way to becoming a lifelong magneto man when baseball came knocking in the early 1950s. One of his longtime Oneonta buddies was Sonny House, a local fellow whose uncle owned the town's Class C Canadian-American League baseball team. Sam had a passing interest in baseball too, and a more than passing interest in Sonny's sister Alice. His years in sales had taught Sam a thing or two about persuasion, and soon he was married to Alice and a member of the Oneonta Red Sox Board of Directors to boot. Although the marriage would be a long and happy one, his involvement with the Oneonta Red Sox was short-lived. Less than a year into his tenure the Canadian-American League folded, one of many victims of that decade's minor league contraction.

Sam went on to a forty-year career at Scintilla to support Alice and their growing family. Along the way he also got involved in Oneonta politics, first as a town alderman and then as mayor in the 1960s. Yet throughout his many town meetings about river dredging, highway construction, and antiwar unrest at local campuses, Sam Nader dreamed of bringing organized baseball back to Oneonta. As he said at the time and for decades afterward, Nader was convinced that baseball bore genuine civic benefits for the people of his town. A professional Oneonta team would hearken back to "the old days, when they used to be proud of their local baseball teams, their fire departments, their bands. It would give us a flag to fly."[2]

Determined to reestablish a team in town, Nader kept up with his baseball contacts from the old days and kept a close eye on local minor league franchise activity. "If there were two baseball people meeting somewhere," he said, "I would be the third." Finally in 1966 he got word that the Red Sox, his old affiliate, were dissatisfied with their New York-Penn League (NY-PL) team accommodations in Wellsville. Backed by a coalition of Oneonta businessmen and boosters, Nader swooped in and bought the franchise. For the first time in fifteen years, minor league baseball returned to the confines of WPA-built Damaschke Field.

But the town's relationship with the Red Sox was doomed to disappointment. After only a year the Red Sox jilted Oneonta again, this time switching their Class A affiliation from the NY-PL to the Western Carolinas League. Undeterred by their defection, Nader convinced ten prominent Oneontans to pony up $1,000 each to purchase a replacement. This got the attention of the New York Yankees, whose plans to move their Binghamton club to the AA Eastern League had left them without a team in lower Class A. They struck a deal with Nader's community-owned Oneonta

Athletic Corporation for $7,500, and in 1967 the Oneonta Yankees were born. From the outset the team was a splendid success in baseball terms. Oneonta won three championships in its first five seasons, and four more over the next decade. Sam Nader's combination of community spirit and baseball success was rewarded by the Yankees in the form of an unbroken thirty-two-year affiliation with the town, a relationship unmatched in the history of the league.[3]

The community owners of the Oneonta franchise never expected to get rich off their new Class A team. "Owning a minor league franchise was almost a license to lose money," Nader later recalled. "You could hardly give away franchises." In fact, with Mayor Nader at the helm profits were almost beside the point. Ticket prices remained abysmally low for decades, even during the salad days of minor league baseball in the 1980s. The team accepted almost no public money to upgrade its field or offices or lighting equipment, preferring to raise the funds through private contri- butions. Most damning of all, the Oneonta Yankees were the only team

Figure 3.1. Sam Nader at Damaschke Field, Oneonta. Photo credit: John S. Nader.

in all of organized baseball that refused to serve alcoholic beverages to its fans. Beer, the mainstay of concession profits throughout the nation's stadiums, was unavailable for purchase at Damaschke Field for the entire game. This continued for every game over a thirty-year period. In 2006 Nader explained his team's reasoning behind the beer ban:

> Is that by choice? Absolutely. Are we teetotalers? Absolutely not. We just feel and have felt throughout the years that [our players] are young guys. They don't need a fan that's got a couple of beers in him sitting behind a pole. He knows that he can see the balls and strikes better than the umpires, he can bat, he can throw, he can everything else better than the players. He becomes obnoxious not only to the people sitting next to him, but to the fans. We try to sell a family environment, so that's why we haven't sold beer. Does it affect us financially? Damn right!
>
> We've stood by our principles, good or bad, through the years. I think the type of fan, the type of community we are contributes to the development of a first-year player. He can focus on playing ball.[4]

The Oneonta Athletic Corporation stood by its principles when it came to league business too. Nader served as a very active league director on behalf of his team and served as the league's vice president under four presidents beginning with Vince McNamara in the late 1960s. When McNamara finally retired in 1985 the league asked Sam to take over, but he demurred in favor of longtime Auburn team president Leo Pinckney. The octogenarian Pinckney announced his own retirement in 1992, and once again Nader refused to be elevated to the president's chair. As he watched Utica lawyer Robert Julian take the reins, he knew he had made the right decision. "If I became president of the league I would have to dissociate myself from operating the Oneonta club," he observed. And that was the one thing he would never do, primarily because he knew that there would be no one to take his place. "The Oneonta club," he pointed out, "is not in a position to go out and hire a hell of a lot of people or personnel." Sam Nader dedicated much of his professional life to the survival and success of the NY-PL. But for Sam, Oneonta always came first.[5]

Under his stewardship Oneonta frequently came first in the standings as well, winning more division titles (thirteen) and league championships (eleven) than any other team in its first quarter century from 1966 to 1991. The team's success was due in large part to the experienced talent evaluators who ran the New York Yankees' scouting and farm operations. Years of good drafts brought quite a few future major leaguers to Damaschke Field, including Rex "Wonder Dog" Hudler, Don Mattingly, and Yankee world champions Jim Leyritz and Bernie Williams. One promising youngster named John Elway spent the summer of 1982 patrolling Oneonta's right field before leaving baseball to become a Hall-of-Famer NFL quarterback. Several managers and baseball personnel also made their professional debuts at Oneonta before moving on to bigger and better things. Buck Showalter coached there before being promoted to the big leagues, as did Toronto General Manager J. P. Ricciardi and Pittsburgh GM Dave Littlefield. Even Casey Close, a powerful mega-agent who later represented Ryan Howard and Derek Jeter, put in some time at Oneonta as a minor leaguer in the mid-1980s.[6]

With Nader at the helm the Oneonta Yankees were valued and recognized by the larger organization. Each season, members of the New York front office made the four-hour pilgrimage to Oneonta to examine the talent firsthand. The majority owner himself, known as "The Boss" to the media but always "Mister Steinbrenner" to Sam Nader, visited on a regular basis. By developing players as well as they did, the Oneonta club helped stock the Yankees with their best homegrown stars. As these famed big leaguers forged a winning Yankee tradition and nationwide reputation, Oneonta's owners hoped that the big-league team's name and logo would attract thousands of local fans to come to see the Yankee stars of tomorrow.[7]

Despite the popularity of the Yankee brand and Nader's promotional efforts, the franchise was simply not positioned to make much money. The club's major handicap was its tiny market share. Oneonta had fewer than 14,000 residents in 1990, making it the smallest city with a NY-PL team and the fourth smallest in all of organized baseball. The rest of the surrounding area was just as sparsely populated, with only 62,000 people living in all of Otsego County. With such a limited fan base it was unsurprising that Oneonta's annual attendance figures routinely lagged behind most of the minor leagues. In their best years in the 1980s the Oneonta Yankees might draw 53,000 fans over the course of a full season, even fewer than the capacity crowd of 57,000 that might attend a single game at New York City's Yankee Stadium. At its height Oneonta averaged only 1,400 fans per game, leaving more than two-thirds of its 4,500 seats empty each night.[8]

As the minor league doldrums of the 1970s gave way to the boom years of the 1980s, Sam Nader and his co-owners watched with growing concern as the game changed all around them. National marketing deals and sophisticated promotional strategies meant nothing to Oneonta, where the team's presence was already as high-profile as it would get. The aging shareholders of the Oneonta Athletic Corp. had little in common with the new breed of younger, wealthier investors who were coming to dominate minor league team ownership. The league's expansion into Canada and Massachusetts—which Nader had strongly opposed in directors' meetings despite being outvoted by the new guys—taxed the club's meager resources and eroded fan interest as local rivalries became long distance. The Oneonta Yankees, once the epitome of the small but successful minor league baseball franchise, had become an anachronism.

Once the 1990 PBA negotiations threatened to endanger all of the minor leagues, the level of alarm reached a peak in Oneonta. Like his friend Joe Buzas, Sam Nader had put decades of sweat equity into building up his team to this point. The previous season had been the best in the history of the Oneonta Yankees. The team had won its second championship in three years, and its incoming roster for 1991 would feature a promising pitcher-catcher battery of rookies Andy Pettitte and Jorge Posada. Attendance had reached an all-time high of 58,742, the third straight year that it surpassed the once unattainable level of 50,000. Now the growing acrimony over the PBA threatened to derail success that had been years in the making.

Although total disaster was averted once the PBA was finally renewed, the deal struck between the majors and the minors represented terrible news for Oneonta. The new revenue sharing agreement allotted a significant percentage of ticket income to the parent organization, so the Oneonta franchise would not reap the full benefits of its increased attendance. While George Steinbrenner's Yankees had always been fairly generous in the past, this would not offset the higher travel and accommodation costs that the PBA now passed on to minor league affiliates. With the NY-PL now spread out over three states and a Canadian province to boot, these expenses suddenly loomed large for an Oneonta club on the financial margins.

Nader and his partners were most worried by the new facilities standards rolled out shortly after the PBA was finalized. Oneonta's Damaschke Field was among the oldest in the country. Originally constructed in 1905, the current stadium was a product of the same Depression-era WPA funding that had built Batavia's Dwyer Park. Equipped with backless steel benches and field lights that dated back to 1940, Damaschke Field was now an aging dowager of a ballpark. The majestic views of the Catskill Mountains beyond the outfield fences provided a stunning backdrop for games, but at the bottom line the facility did not conform to the requirements now imposed by Major League Baseball.

Devoid of the financial resources to pay for refurbishing the stadium, the club found itself in a serious bind. There was no way Sam Nader was going to hold Oneonta hostage for a new multimillion dollar facility, not after twenty years of principled ownership and municipal loyalty. The community could not afford such a monstrous expense, and it was obviously wasteful to build a brand-new stadium for the sake of thirty-nine annual home games that never sold out anyway. Working with league president Robert Julian, Nader joined a statewide effort to secure more than $10 million in New York State legislative funding for minor league stadium projects. Although very little went to improve Damaschke Field, the efforts were sufficient to stave off the commissioner's office.

The easiest way for the Oneonta Yankees to raise cash would have been to sell the team. Despite its lack of profitability the franchise had many suitors over the years. The prospect of owning a minor league club, and an established Yankee franchise in particular, was a huge selling point. Nader had already turned down several offers of millions of dollars, even when they were accompanied by promises to keep the team in Oneonta. But he didn't trust the fast talkers or their promises.

> Anybody's going to buy the ball club, they aren't going to be satisfied—and I work for no salary—to keep the ball club going. What the hell do they care about the city of Oneonta? My concern is Cooperstown, my county seat, being the birthplace of baseball . . . Christ, I think it would be a mortal sin if they let professional baseball get out of here! But you know what? I don't think they really give a damn. That's my philosophy.[9]

Unlike virtually any of his minor league peers, Sam Nader did not have his price. He was committed to keeping the Yankees in Oneonta no matter what and would remain loyal to his team to the end.

Part Two: The Pittsfield Mets

As opposed to Sam Nader's Oneonta Yankees, the Little Falls Mets had their price. It was $230,000, and in 1989 a slick Massachusetts operator named Michael T. Casey paid it. Then he drove the team bus straight out of town, heading east.

The Mets first brought professional baseball to Little Falls, New York, in 1977. The franchise was the team's third NY-PL venture in its short fifteen-year history, after two brief and uninspired affiliations with local teams from Auburn and Batavia. Like those two previous franchises, the Little Falls front office ran a typical 1970s minor league operation with field personnel provided by the Mets and a handful of local community investors pitching in the capital to form an ownership group. While the town was further to the east than any of the league's other members, it was only twenty miles away from its closest rival in Utica. It was also close enough to Oneonta, Auburn, and Elmira to start up a handful of natural rivalries, which allowed the league to pursue realignment into Eastern and Western divisions once Little Falls came aboard.[10]

In an era when the larger Mets organization was characterized by inept ownership and mismanagement, the Little Falls club was a modest success. The team's chief asset was its playing facility, Veterans Memorial Park. Built in 1949, the tiny stadium boasted only basic amenities in terms of its clubhouses, one miniscule concession stand, and a press box fashioned to look like a log cabin. The two foul line bleacher sections consisted of ten rows of wooden and metal benches that seated a mere 2,000 fans, by far the fewest of any club in the league. Yet the playing surfaces and surrounding grounds were immaculate, tended with loving care by townspeople. Unlike the ruinous Murnane Field in nearby Utica, the Little Falls infield was packed smoothly with red New Jersey clay and its lush outfield was entirely free of bare patches, divots or foreign objects. The knolls between paved walkways were thick with sculpted hedges and rosebushes. The Mets did their part by installing one of the league's best lighting systems and a full-size electronic scoreboard. "If I ever saw a jewel," declared league president Vince McNamara on more than one occasion, "it's Little Falls."[11]

Unfortunately for the team, even the cozy confines of "the Little Vet" were too expansive for its few fans. With fewer than 6,000 residents, Little Falls was not even half the size of small-market Oneonta. Like the Oneonta Yankees, their top rival, the Mets franchise achieved great on-field success during the 1980s. Blessed with talented players like future major leaguers Dwight Gooden and Wally Backman, the Little Falls Mets won several division championships and even a league championship. But the club was fatally handicapped by its tiny market and lacked an indomitable leader like Sam Nader who could keep it alive by sheer force of will. By 1988 the local owners were running out of both money and options, and so they put the team up for sale.[12]

Their first offer came from Stuart Revo, a well-connected oil tycoon eager to make a big splash in baseball. Based in New York City, Revo was an impetuous and impatient minor league owner who once bought and sold a partnership interest in an AAA team within the span of less than six months. By the late 1980s he was part-owner of two AA teams, one in the Texas League and the other being the Pittsfield Cubs, an Eastern League team based in Massachusetts. As part of his plan for an incipient minor league empire, Revo now sought to bring the Little Falls Mets into the fold. As described later by local news sources, his plan was to shuffle his teams around in his own best interests. With the blessing of his entrepreneurial partner Marvin Goldklang, Revo planned to move the underachieving Cubs to the larger and more profitable market of Binghamton, New York. He would then relocate the short-season Class A Little Falls Mets to Pittsfield, where the Cubs' low annual attendance figures of 60,000 would seem quite respectable in the context of the NY-PL.

The grandiosity of Revo's plans proved to be his undoing. The Binghamton move hinged on the construction of a new $6 million facility at public expense. The requisite approvals lagged beyond ownership's desire or ability to wait, and so Goldklang and Revo moved the Pittsfield Cubs to Williamsport, Pennsylvania, instead. Dissatisfied with the lateral move to yet another small market, the Cubs yanked their affiliation agreement and left the new Williamsport Bills scrambling to join the lackluster Seattle Mariners organization as their AA Eastern League team. Meanwhile, the demise of his Binghamton strategy so disenchanted Revo that he gave up and sold out his Pittsfield interests to Goldklang. There must not have been many hard feelings over the Williamsport debacle, as the two would-be baseball impresarios immediately joined forces to purchase yet another struggling club, the Miami Marlins of the Class A Florida State League. Along with actor Bill Murray, singer Jimmy Buffett, and a handful of other wealthy investors, they purchased not only the ballclub (now rechristened the Miami Miracle) but also the major league territorial rights to Miami and its environs. With major league expansion on the immediate horizon, Revo and his group were on the fast track to baseball prominence. Meanwhile, Pittsfield and Little Falls faded to nothingness in Revo's rearview mirror.[13]

With Revo and Goldklang out of the picture, Pittsfield had no ball team and the Little Falls Mets had no buyer. But the pieces were in place for the franchise to relocate, and a new investment group with local ties quickly stepped in to consummate the deal. The front man for the partnership was Michael Casey, a moderately successful nursing home operator, businessman, and amateur baseball coach. Casey was from Dalton, Massachusetts, a town of fewer than 7,000 residents just east of Pittsfield, up the long Route 9 hill that led deeper into the heart of the Berkshires. He had first learned of the Mets opportunity from fellow Dalton native Dan Duquette, an old friend who happened to be the farm director of the Montreal Expos. In early 1988, as the Revo plan faltered and ultimately fizzled, Casey pitched the idea of minor league ownership to two acquaintances in Pittsfield. His first partner was funeral director Francis Devanny, whose reluctant involvement in the project would last less than a year before he cashed out. The junior member of the triumvirate, Rick Murphy, was a recent Boston College graduate with a small residential cleaning business. Together the budding Massachusetts entrepreneurs scraped together $230,000 and bought the Mets franchise just in time to play the 1988 season in Little Falls. Less than six months later, Michael Casey charmed the Mets organization and the NY-PL into letting him move the team to Pittsfield.[14]

Initially it appeared that the move would pay off. In their first season in Pittsfield the Mets attracted nearly 97,000 fans, doubling the 1988 attendance figures for the Pittsfield Cubs and more than tripling the Mets' previous season in Little Falls. Then in 1990 they broke the 100,000 mark despite placing only third in their division. The team reached the NY-PL championship series in two out of its first three seasons, and successfully developed eleven future major leaguers including home-run slugger Jeromy Burnitz. The local owners made friends in town by maintaining a hands-on approach to running the team, with Rick Murphy in charge of the club's day-to-day operations. After a single year, the club even reported a profit of $70,000. In every way, the Pittsfield Mets appeared to be a prosperous, model franchise.

But for Mike Casey, hometown success was breeding a growing restlessness. After pulling off the first stage of Stuart Revo's plan by bringing the Mets to Pittsfield, Casey figured that he could go even further by following the rest of his blueprint as well. In early 1990 he took steps to secure a prospective Class AA Binghamton franchise. First, with some financial contribution from Pittsfield co-owner Murphy, Casey plunked down $350,000 to buy the foundering last-place Williamsport Bills from a very willing Marvin Goldklang. Casey's next step was to sign a formal agreement to relocate the Bills to Binghamton, pending public approval of the $6 million stadium that was still languishing in bureaucratic limbo. From all indications the new franchise would easily secure an affiliation deal with the New York Mets, who were unhappy with their current AA partner in Jackson, Mississippi. Embraced by Binghamton politicians and fast-tracked for approval by the Eastern League, Casey was sure he'd succeed where Revo had failed.[15]

But the experienced Revo had been far savvier than the novices from Massachusetts. The red tape strangling the Binghamton stadium proposal never loosened. Seven months after signing his purchase agreement with Williamsport, Casey still had no stadium and consequently could not line up the necessary financing for his new team. His personal finances were now in ruins. In addition to the estimated $150,000 he spent on administrative preparations for the Binghamton move, he had paid in advance a nonrefundable $350,000 franchise fee to Goldklang for the currently homeless Williamsport club. Casey had taken on even more losses dating back to 1988, when a separate sale of a nursing home (presumably to raise cash to buy the Little Falls Mets) had gone sour. In all, Michael Casey was in the hole for more than $2 million by the end of 1990. His last remaining significant asset was his half-ownership share in the Pittsfield Mets, but Casey's fiscal troubles were endangering the future of that team as well.[16]

More than a year of litigation followed between Casey and his partner Rick Murphy. For Murphy, this would be a painful period of great personal and professional stress. He had known Mike Casey for most of his adult life and had played under him in amateur summer league baseball during Casey's coaching days. But now his years of mentoring were subsumed by the rancor of their catastrophic financial losses. As Casey mounted a desperate effort to retain his hold on the Pittsfield franchise, the relationship fractured beyond repair. After filing for chapter 11 bankruptcy, Casey claimed that he could raise $900,000 to purchase the team himself. Several months later he said he'd come up with $3 million to buy out Murphy and also pay off all his creditors. But no amount of fast talking could save Michael Casey this time. In the end he lost his team, his businesses, his homes, and his friends. A few years afterward he even lost his freedom after he was apprehended as a fugitive in a mobile home park, charged with bank fraud and larceny after passing bad checks in Kentucky.[17]

In December 1990, just two years after purchasing the team, Casey bowed to the inevitable. He transferred his entire ownership stake in the Pittsfield Mets to Rick Murphy to clear his accumulated debts to both the team and Murphy (who had just returned home from Binghamton after trying and failing to salvage the AA Binghamton Mets plan), with the understanding that no additional cash would be exchanged in the buyout. Murphy spent the next several months trying to straighten out the unsettled ownership situation in Pittsfield but was continually tied up in litigation by Casey over the half-stake he now refused to relinquish. Throughout all of 1991 the lawyers for the two sides wrangled, even as Murphy struggled to keep the team afloat all on his own amid sinking attendance and revenues. Finally, under pressure from the Mets and his own mounting financial difficulties, Murphy found a buyer for the team: Bill Gladstone.[18]

William L. "Bill" Gladstone had a professional resume that far surpassed any owner in the history of the NY-PL, which he would help transform over the next two decades. Born in Brooklyn in the early 1930s, Gladstone graduated Lehigh University in 1951 and immediately found work at Arthur Young, one of the nation's major corporate accounting firms. After earning a law degree and rising through the ranks for more than three decades, he was named managing partner and CEO of the company in 1985. He continued on as co-CEO after a huge 1989 merger created Ernst & Young, the world's largest accounting firm with revenues over $4 billion. After overseeing the merger—and spending some very uncomfortable hours testifying before Congress about his company's role in the deepening national Savings and Loan Scandal—Gladstone gracefully stepped down in 1991 and entered a well-deserved and lucrative retirement.[19]

The sudden surplus of free time allowed the former executive to pursue his lifelong love for baseball. Over the years, Gladstone and his wife Millie had accumulated one of the world's foremost collections of baseball-related art and artifacts. Their contacts within the worlds of collecting and baseball led to his election to the board of directors of the Baseball Hall of Fame shortly after his retirement, and he soon became a very active member and committee chair at the Hall. Yet these activities were not enough to satisfy his passion for the sport. Unused to sitting on the sidelines, Gladstone was already seeking a more hands-on role in the baseball world. He gathered several investors from among his wealthy acquaintances and incorporated the National Pastime Corporation, with himself as president. Then he went looking for a team to buy.

One of Gladstone's baseball contacts was Fred Wilpon, a real estate magnate who also happened to be half-owner and team president of the

New York Mets organization. When they were approached by Gladstone about acquiring a team, the Mets saw a golden opportunity to resolve the unstable ownership situation of their Pittsfield affiliate. According to Rick Murphy, at Wilpon's urging Gladstone soon called him with an offer to buy the P-Mets outright. After selling his ownership share, pending the resolution of his messy legal battles with Mike Casey, Murphy was welcome to stay on as general manager and operate the team as an employee of the National Pastime Corporation. After some delaying tactics by the Casey side the deal was consummated in April 1992, and the team was sold for $850,000, a development that a relieved Rick Murphy termed "refreshing."[20]

In both public press statements and private discussions, Gladstone asserted that he had no intention of disrupting his team's ongoing operations in Pittsfield. As his first season as owner wound down in September 1992, he expressed satisfaction with the club's performance and its positive relationship with the parent Mets organization, which confidently renewed its affiliation with Pittsfield for the next four years. He also signed a new one-year lease on the city-owned ballpark, although he did insist on a new indoor batting tunnel for players to use in inclement weather. In a classic statement reminiscent of every new team owner in minor league history, Gladstone told reporters, "We look forward to staying in Pittsfield."[21]

By 1995 the New York-Penn League was flourishing. League attendance was at an all-time high, and new team owners like Bill Gladstone were pouring funds and energy into making their clubs successful. But despite these additional efforts and investments, in Pittsfield both attendance and revenues were shrinking daily. As their league rivals moved into larger markets and secured team-friendly deals, Gladstone's Pittsfield Mets front office could only watch in helpless envy. The team was in an especially frustrating situation because its surrounding fan base should have been sizable enough to put it among the NY-PL's profit leaders. But the limitations of its current facility were extreme, the demands of the PBA could not be ignored for much longer, and the local municipality seemed unwilling to spend the amount of money needed for upgrades to keep the team in the black. Over the next three years Bill Gladstone would show more patience than nearly any other new NY-PL owner as he conducted deliberate negotiations with his recalcitrant host city. Yet as the discussions dragged on without much discernible progress, the chances that the P-Mets would remain in Pittsfield were dwindling.

The situation was especially dire mainly due to the huge challenges and awful conditions at Wahconah Park, where the P-Mets played their home games. The subject of numerous profiles in the national sports media, the current stadium had hosted many professional baseball teams since its construction in 1919. Even as it was hailed by sportswriters as a quirky and quaint reminder of the purity of baseball's bucolic origins, the ballpark was reviled by players, front office staff, and team owners for decades. The gap between the public's nostalgic perceptions of the ballpark and the practical limitations of playing there eventually led to the crisis that forced out professional baseball entirely.[22]

Baseball was first played in Wahconah Park in 1892, many years before an actual stadium was constructed on the site. Conveniently located not far from the center of town, the privately owned greenscape was a sizable grassy area that was naturally irrigated by the Housatonic River that bisected it. Almost two decades later, after a number of semi-pro and minor league teams like the Eastern Association Electrics came and went, the field became home to the Eastern League's Pittsfield Hillies upon their relocation there from Saugerties, New York, in 1919. As part of the attempt to attract professional baseball to town, Wahconah's owners donated the fifty-acre site to the municipality, which promptly used public funds to erect a wooden ballpark for the Hillies to lease at a nominal cost. Although there would be several renovations over the ensuing decades, the same original Wahconah Park facility would remain substantially unchanged through the 1990s and even today.[23]

After playing in Pittsfield for eleven years and winning two early league championships, the Hillies went belly-up after the 1930 season. The Wahconah Park grandstands remained vacant for the remainder of the Great Depression, until the Class C Canadian-American League came to town in 1941. In only its sixth year of operation, this new minor league was comprised of eight teams located in upstate New York and Quebec. The league's sole Massachusetts entry would be the Pittsfield Electrics, a new incarnation of an old name from three decades earlier. After a brief affiliation with the Detroit Tigers organization, the Pittsfield club shifted its allegiance and eventually its name to the Indians, before playing out its final season in 1951 as the Pittsfield Phillies. By that time the league and minor league baseball as a whole had sunk into a period of postwar doldrums, and the Canadian-American League was one of many regional minor leagues to fold. Once again the stadium lacked a professional tenant, but playing conditions at the park had been untenable for so long that not many baseball people mourned its loss.[24]

The fundamental problems of Wahconah Park were structural, beginning with the orientation of the playing field. When the stadium was first constructed in 1919, the left field line was laid out to run due west. Some writers have surmised that this was fairly common practice at the time, as ballpark planners sought to minimize afternoon sun glare for outfielders attempting to track fly balls. Before the advent of electric stadium lighting all baseball games were played during the day, and so fielders benefited from having the sun shine over their shoulders rather than from directly in front of them. At the same time, the sun's position high overhead would not trouble hitters or umpires facing west during a midday or early afternoon contest.

However, by the mid-twentieth century professional baseball had evolved into a late afternoon and evening sport, and this caused serious problems for players at Wahconah Park. When the city of Pittsfield finally approved major renovations of the facility in 1946 and 1977, many physical improvements were made including the eventual erection of stadium lights. But the direction of the field's layout remained unaltered, and so home plate continued to face west. This meant that the individuals who were looking out at the pitcher—namely, the catcher, hitters, and the home plate umpire—were blinded by the setting sun at dusk. Over the years many Pittsfield general managers would experiment with a variety of solutions to the sun dilemma, erecting screens and overhangs and even planting tall trees in a fruitless attempt to shut out the glare. In the end they all succumbed to the simplest solution: a forty-five-minute "sun delay" during which the game was halted until the sun went down and it grew dark enough to resume night play under the lights. The players loathed the enforced inactivity of the delays, and many came to hate the Pittsfield facility with a passion.[25]

While the sun disrupted play from above, groundwater beneath the playing surface often caused problems from below. The ballpark was situated on the Housatonic flood plain, courtesy of the river that ran through the middle of the Wahconah parkland. During and just after periods of heavy rain the Housatonic River tended to flood the immediate area, soaking the field to such an extent that games would often have to be cancelled or rescheduled. A dyke constructed in 1927 proved to be ineffective at stemming the tide, and two extensive renovations in the 1940s and 1970s that raised the entire field level higher did little to improve the wet field conditions that frequently prevailed. By the 1970s and 1980s the park's newest tenants played in the Class A NY-PL, whose short season lasted from June through September and avoided the worst rainy months of April and May. Nevertheless, summer rains forced Pittsfield's players to conduct many games on a soggy home field. As onetime Pittsfield Cubs minor leaguer Rafael Palmiero later recalled, "The outfield was so damp your feet got wet immediately. And since you only wore one pair of spikes all year, you stayed wet all summer."[26]

The unusual dimensions of the field presented further challenges to the young Class A players who spent their early seasons in Pittsfield. At first glance the distance to the outfield fences seemed manageable, with a left field of 334 feet, center field of 374 feet, and the right field fence measured at 333 feet. But one section of the outfield jutted outward, the result of a decision by the city to adapt the field to accommodate high school football games during the baseball offseason. This created an enormous power alley of nearly 430 feet in right-center field where the fences were pushed back, "one of the deepest outfield areas in all of baseball" as one

Figure 3.2. Wahconah Park parking lot flooded after severe storms. Photo credit: *Berkshire Eagle.*

sportswriter noted. For hitters already struggling with the wet Housatonic humidity that reduced the distance their fly balls would carry, the expansive outfield could adversely affect their power numbers and career prospects. For fielders, chasing down long fly balls on damp, slippery grass could be a nightmare. Pittsfield outfielder Ty Quillin, looking out at the field a week before the 1992 season started, observed that "it's humongous—right-center field looks like a driving range, almost." The close proximity and sparsity of foul territory between the large outfield and the nearby stands only compounded the tribulations of inexperienced fielders.[27]

The run-down condition of the stadium's structures presented further difficulties. After the original 1919 wood grandstands rotted away (or were filched for firewood during the Great Depression, when no team was playing regularly in the park), new ones were set in place atop an all-new foundation in 1949. These stands and their wooden bench seats were still in service in the 1990s, receiving only rudimentary repairs and a few paint jobs during the interim. Two sections of uncovered no-frills metal bleachers expanded the seating capacity to 4,500, but the stadium was rarely full once each new team settled into Pittsfield every few years. Perhaps the quirkiest aspect of the seating areas were the ceramic and plastic owls hanging from the grandstand rafters to discourage pigeons from nesting in the roof—or, as Bob Ryan of the *Boston Globe* indelicately put it, "from roosting and pooping on the first couple of rows of box seats." The rusticity of the stadium was complemented by inadequate bathroom facilities and concession space, a bare minimum of access for handicapped patrons, and a cramped dirt parking area that was often underwater due to the lack of any drainage. Electric lights were not even installed until 1977, when the town reluctantly laid out the funds in order to attract a minor league team to come back after a quarter-century spent mostly without tenants.[28] Players routinely referred to Pittsfield's stadium as "the Pit," and many agreed with Boston Red Sox star Ellis Burks in his unequivocal judgement that "the worst ballpark that I played in during the Minor Leagues was Wahconah Park."[29]

Now in the 1990s, the Pittsfield Mets were occupying Wahconah Park under the ownership auspices of Bill Gladstone and his band of millionaire New York investors. In both public press statements and private discussions, Gladstone asserted that he had no intention of disrupting his team's ongoing operations in Pittsfield. As his first season as owner wound down in September 1992, he expressed satisfaction with the club's performance and its positive relationship with the parent Mets

Figure 3.3. Wahconah Park grandstands with hanging plastic owl in the upper left. Photo credit: Scott Stafford/*Berkshire Eagle*.

organization, which confidently renewed its affiliation with Pittsfield for the next four years. In late 1993 Gladstone signed a new three-year lease with the city of Pittsfield to keep his team in Wahconah Park. In press interviews Gladstone reiterated his satisfaction and his plans to keep the team where it was.[30]

Behind the scenes, however, the new owner of the P-Mets had serious concerns regarding his team's decaying, antiquated facility. On the one hand, Gladstone's acquisition of the team came at the height of public sentimentality regarding Pittsfield and Wahconah Park's quaint old-fashioned charm. For the first time in league history, the NY-PL received a prominent profile in the *New York Times*, and Pittsfield was singled out for special attention. *Sports Illustrated* ran a glowing piece by Daniel Okrent which enthused about "cozy" and "pure" Wahconah Park, which he called "baseball heaven."[31] While this burst of publicity was welcome, it ignored the reality that the stadium as it was could never hope to meet the new PBA standards for minor league clubhouses, rest room facilities, and foul territory dimensions, among many other areas of concern. Team GM Rick Murphy knew very well that a cosmetic facelift would simply not be enough, and that old-fashioned charm was no substitute for the modern amenities that fans had come to expect. As he later explained,

"They call it 'historic.' We coined it, 'historic.' What are you going to say, 'come to dumpy old Wahconah Park'? You're not going to say that. So you call it 'historic.' If people saw me in the Pump Room, manually hitting the injectors to flush the toilets, they wouldn't call that 'historic.' They'd call that 'old and decrepit.' "[32]

The club was well aware that it had to meet or at least begin meeting the PBA requirements within two years, a condition that Bill Gladstone understood when he came into full control of the team in 1992. Even as he signed his new three-year lease, Gladstone and Murphy warned the public that "the new baseball agreement has put us in the middle. We hate to ask anybody for any money, especially in these economic times, but the last thing we want is for our franchise to get pulled." And so they did in fact ask for public funding to upgrade the ballpark, with some modest success. Between 1992 and 1994 the City of Pittsfield did pay for a few improvements to Wahconah Park, but only the bare minimum that was needed for the P-Mets to retain their minor league facility standing. For example, as a sweetener to get the lease signed, the city allocated $25,000 to expand the square footage of the visitors' clubhouse. While this did help the team meet a single PBA standard, it did almost nothing to fully modernize a seventy-year-old ballpark that was desperately in need of a complete overhaul.[33]

Frustrated with the lack of movement on the stadium issue, Gladstone and Murphy soon began a calculated press campaign aimed at securing a brand-new stadium in Pittsfield. Contrasting their product to national media stories about the bitter major league players' strike of 1994, the Pittsfield Mets' front office stressed the popularity of local baseball and the team's commitment to staying put. But over the next several years they continued to push for the money they would need to improve or replace Wahconah Park. When a state emergency bond bill for $2.5 million in stadium improvements failed to pass, they enlisted Pittsfield's Mayor Edward M. Reilly to call for an entirely new facility instead of sinking more money into "an old stadium on a flood plain." When the city legislature responded with a mere $330,000 allocation for a variety of minor repairs and an annual maintenance budget increase of only $5,000, the team made it clear that stopgap measures would no longer be sufficient.[34]

Like Wahconah Park itself, the Pittsfield Mets' situation in Pittsfield was deteriorating in the mid-1990s. This took on a new urgency as several of the team's league rivals acted decisively to secure their own futures in new and imaginative ways.

CHAPTER FOUR

NEW STADIUMS DO NOT PRODUCE ECONOMIC GROWTH

In the 1990s the New York-Penn League was completely transformed by a pair of interrelated seismic shifts: an influx of new moneyed out-of-town owners and a stadium-building boom. Both of these phenomena were influenced by a combination of parochial and national baseball concerns. The rapidly increasing interest in and valuation of minor league franchises was attracting the attention of wealthy investors like Bill Gladstone, who would marry their business savvy and network connections to their passion for the game of baseball. And, like Gladstone, these new owners quickly came to realize that their team's most immediate and pressing need was compliance with the new Professional Baseball Agreement (PBA) facilities requirements. This was the primary motivator they cited in interviews and press coverage to justify their public ultimatums, as they bluntly demanded that their current host cities either provide them with completely new or refurbished ballparks or else their teams would move somewhere else that would do so. At the same time, that exact scenario was also playing out with regularity on a nationwide basis throughout the highest levels of professional sports. Particularly in Major League Baseball and the National Football League, established teams and new expansion clubs leveraged their bargaining power to negotiate sweetheart construction and lease deals on enormously expensive, publicly funded stadiums throughout this period. Although their short-season Class A New York-Penn League (NY-PL) would never compete for the hundreds of millions being spent on stadiums for the big boys, the league's new owners could and did use their positions to achieve similar ends in their smaller markets.

Strictly in terms of the numbers, the 1995 season was the most successful in the fifty-six-year-history of the NY-PL. Game attendance totaled nearly 1,182,000 over the span of the short season, the highest attendance ever recorded by the league and well more than double the figure of 490,993 recorded a decade earlier in 1985. The league's popularity, nationwide interest, and lucrative potential had experienced a steady rise since the *Bull Durham* summer of 1988, when the number of ticket buyers had topped a half-million fans for just the second time ever. The league's deliberate climb would continue for several more years to come, as ticket sales rose by at least 25,000 each year through 1999, when they crested at 1,371,054 before receding slightly the following year.[1]

Fourteen teams now played in the NY-PL, also the highest number in the league's existence. In contrast to its earlier incarnations, the league now encompassed territories in five northeastern states as well as Canada, where the St. Catharines Stompers played. The rapid growth of the league necessitated an expansion from two divisions (Eastern and Western) to three divisions (McNamara, Pinckney, and Stedler) in the 1990 season. Scheduling and travel arrangements were now much more complex and were accompanied by a major rise in per-team expenses. This trend accelerated under the conditions the new onerous PBA imposed on the minor leagues at the end of 1990, which made them responsible for a much higher portion of operational costs. As the league barreled ahead into a big-time future, its smallest-market operators would have a very hard time keeping up with the demands upon their clubs and their finances. Quite a few of them decided not to even try.[2]

As in the case of the Pittsfield Mets, the renewed energy and profitability suffusing the league attracted a number of investors eager to buy their way into professional baseball, even as some strapped franchise owners welcomed the opportunity to cash out and make a quick sale. In addition to Pittsfield's acquisition by former Ernst Young CEO Bill Gladstone, several wealthy buyers began to fill the NY-PL's ownership ranks in the late 1980s and early 1990s. Wharton-educated lawyer, banker, and New York Yankees minority partner Marvin Goldklang became a team owner when he and his investment group purchased the Erie Sailors in 1991. Alan Levin had risen through the executive ranks to become president of CBS Productions prior to buying the Welland Pirates in 1990. A few years earlier, IBM and Sperry executive Clyde Smoll purchased the Elmira Pioneers, then an affiliate of the Boston Red Sox. Barry Gordon, a Long Island–based "investment advisor that manages money for high-net-worth individuals," spearheaded a group that bought the Hamilton

(Ontario) Redbirds in 1991, rounding off a spectacular year that also brought in fellow New Yorkers Gladstone and Goldklang. Never before had the league boasted so many owners with such distinguished corporate pedigrees and deep pockets.[3]

While these new big-money carpetbaggers were committed to the financial success and viability of their new teams, they lacked any personal or sentimental attachment to their communities. Throughout the decade of the 1990s, every one of these newly acquired clubs picked up roots and relocated elsewhere. Some were data-driven, hoping to reverse downward local attendance trends by starting over in a new, larger market where they hoped to attract a greater number of new and enthusiastic fans. Several teams left in search of literally greener pastures in new or at least more modern ballparks, which would satisfy the terms of the PBA and generate wider interest and higher profits. Some of these NY-PL proprietary groups also owned more than one minor league team, and so at times they leveraged their negotiations with different municipalities by offering first one team and then another at a different minor league level, striking whichever deal benefited them the most without regard to the impact this had on each team and each league. And at least one set of new owners sought to move their franchises closer to their own homes in the New York City area, rather than to leave them isolated in the boondocks of upper and western New York State.

It took several years before any major moves took place, but after biding their time to lay some groundwork the new guys set off a raft of relocations in 1994 and 1995. After buying the Welland (Ontario) Pirates in 1990, Alan Levin's Palisades Baseball Group kept the team there for just four years before moving to Erie, Pennsylvania. To drum up local interest and enthusiasm the team was rechristened the Erie SeaWolves, keeping intact the team's front office and Pittsburgh Pirates affiliation arrangement. Previously Erie had been the home of the NY-PL's Erie Sailors, the team bought by Marvin Goldklang in 1991 (a year after Levin entered the league). Goldklang's tenure in Erie had been a mere two years primarily because of the deterioration of Ainsworth Field, a decrepit 3,000-seat stadium originally built in 1923. After Goldklang's abrupt departure, Levin was enticed to relocate the Pirates there only after the state of Pennsylvania allocated $8 million to finance most of the costs of a brand-new PBA-compliant Erie baseball stadium in 1994, with the remainder of the funds contributed by the City of Erie, Erie County, and a consortium of local private citizens. On June 20, 1995, when they held their first Erie Opening Day, Levin's SeaWolves played and won their first game at Jerry Uht Park before a sellout crowd of 6,300 fans without having to pay a nickel of the costs of their brand-new facility. The team's relocation followed a decades-old pattern of minor league franchises abandoning sagging markets for new locales with a past track record of hosting minor league baseball teams. Many a minor league club frequently changed dance partners to squeeze out every possible advantage and municipal concession, only to be replaced by another team from the same league.[4]

The Goldklang Group's departure from Erie in 1993 had been motivated by similar reasons. Although the plan for Jerry Uht Park had already been in the works, negotiations between the team and the municipality broke down over the terms of the proposed lease. Goldklang and his partners, who co-owned four minor league teams across the country, did not feel limited by geographical restrictions or league precedents in their search for a new home. They cast a wide net which soon caught the attention of the Dutchess County, New York, town of Fishkill. Although the town's population of approximately 18,000 people was just as small as that of many of the NY-PL's tinier historic locations, the surrounding Poughkeepsie-Newburgh-Middletown Metropolitan Statistical Area was home to nearly 600,000 potential baseball fans. More importantly, Dutchess County was willing and able to fork over $4.95 million for a new stadium with favorable lease terms. Roger Akeley, Dutchess County commissioner of planning and development, enthusiastically helped sell the plan to the county legislators and enthusiastic voters, saying "nothing is more solid and optimistic than, what do they call it, the boys of summer." Although dissenters considered the stadium financing plan to be far less solid and way more optimistic than it deserved, the plan sailed through the Legislature by a vote of 27–8 and Dutchess Stadium was erected in less than a year. The former Erie Sailors became the Hudson Valley Renegades, season ticket sales were brisk, and the NY-PL expanded further southeast to a town less than seventy miles from New York City.[5]

Meanwhile, investment manager Barry Gordon moved his team even closer to Manhattan, or "the City" as it was known among the locals. As early as 1991, immediately after purchasing the Ontario-based St. Louis Cardinals affiliate Hamilton Redbirds, Gordon's Minor League Heroes partnership announced they would be moving the team to a brand-new, as yet unbuilt stadium in Sussex County, New Jersey, to be called Skylands Park. The stadium project was headed up by one of Gordon business partners and was soon plagued by cost overruns, natural disasters, and Chapter 11 bankruptcy. Undeterred, the Redbirds waited out a lame-duck 1992 in Hamilton, then temporarily moved the team to Glens Falls, New

York, for a stopgap year in 1993, and finally made the final move to New Jersey in 1994. In a *New York Times* interview, team officials explained the relocation strategy that made them choose suburban New Jersey for their single-A ballclub. What they were looking for, they said, was "an area that was reasonably affluent and one that was on the fringe of a major league market." As another local general manager explained, "We've had a lot of people buying season-ticket plans who say they canceled their Mets and Yankees tickets. They say they're tired of the greed, the expense and everything else." This minor league trend was building in the years surrounding the 1994 Major League Baseball work stoppage, but it was entirely new to the New York-Penn League.[6]

Figure 4.1. NY-PL Map, 1998. Photo by author.

For Bill Gladstone and the Pittsfield Mets front office, these developments were providing a blueprint to follow. They too were determined to acquire a new facility, preferably in Pittsfield but possibly elsewhere. For personal reasons, Gladstone was especially interested in the expansion of the league into territory that was edging closer and closer to New York City, that baseball mecca of the East Coast and his own hometown. He had been born and raised in the borough of Brooklyn, once home to the fabled Brooklyn Dodgers. Gladstone was a young lawyer at the Manhattan accounting firm of Arthur Young & Company when the Dodgers left town for the West Coast in the 1950s, and he had been devastated by the defection of his favorite boyhood team. Now a baseball team owner himself, Gladstone was already thinking about the logistics of bringing baseball back to his native city, albeit in minor league form. Even as they negotiated with Pittsfield for a new stadium, Gladstone's National Pastime Inc. engaged in simultaneous talks about the future of his franchise with the Mets organization and also New York's local and state politicians. This information leaked as early as 1995, when Gladstone was named in a newspaper report that New York State Governor George Pataki and Suffolk County officials were proposing the construction of a stadium on Long Island to house his Mets affiliate. There were also strong indications that New York City Mayor Rudolph Giuliani was embracing the notion of building a new facility in Gladstone's preferred location of Brooklyn, perhaps in moribund Coney Island.[7]

Once whispers of these dealings reached the local press, Gladstone used them to his advantage as he allowed for the possibility that his team could still have a future in Pittsfield. Over a period of eighteen months in 1996–1997 he applied pressure on the city to abandon Wahconah Park altogether and instead build an entirely new modern facility in downtown Pittsfield. The Pittsfield Mets even signed an unprecedented ten-year lease arrangement with the city that freed the team from all rent payments as long as they had to play at their current ballpark, but the deal was contingent on the construction of a new stadium during that period. A study was commissioned paying $30,000 to the HOK Sports Facilities Group, one of the nation's foremost sports designers of sports venues; unsurprisingly the study concluded that Wahconah Park did not meet professional baseball standards and suggested up to fourteen possible sites for a new stadium elsewhere in Pittsfield. Less than four months after the City Council and the team approved the ten-year lease, the study was complete and the city had appointed committees to settle on any one of the potential sites and move ahead on plans for stadium financing. The project appeared to be on the fast track, and Pittsfield might keep its professional baseball team.[8]

But neither the P-Mets nor the city's top elected officials had counted on a groundswell of public opposition against the stadium project. In letters to the editor and other public forums, Pittsfield residents spoke out against the high costs of constructing a municipally funded stadium that would have little direct benefit for the community. Some opined that "bush-league" baseball would hardly enhance the reputation of the Berkshires, a region best known as a center for culture and the arts. It was pointed out that as a member of the NY-PL, the P-Mets would only utilize their expensive new facility for fewer than forty home games played over three months each year, a very low rate of return on the millions that would be spent to build it. There was also a small but vocal contingent adamantly opposed to abandoning Wahconah Park. They argued that the facility was an integral part of the city's baseball history and heritage, tapping into the nostalgic sentiment that had been celebrated by journalists and local fans in the past. When a majority of Pittsfield voters supported an anti-stadium referendum on Election Day 1997, it became clear that the town was stuck with Wahconah Park for the foreseeable future. Whether it could keep the team that leased it was another matter entirely.[9]

Even as the Pittsfield negotiations deteriorated, Gladstone continued to doggedly pursue his cherished dream to bring baseball back to Brooklyn. Of course, doing so would multiply his club's potential profitability and fan base many times over as well. This would be a bold, unprecedented move to relocate a "bush-league" product not to a similar regional area but to New York City, the largest, most crowded professional sports market in the entire country. Further complicating matters was the fact that the territory in question was officially shared between the major league Mets and Yankees under a favored-nation clause in the PBA. This meant that not just one but two NY-PL teams would have to be brought to the five boroughs, doubling the level of difficulty facing an essentially small-market product in the biggest baseball city of them all.

Gladstone's efforts would trigger a confluence of complications that would encompass both NY-PL and New York City economics, politics, and personalities. Early in the planning stages, many crucial questions needed answers: Which franchises would be moving to the Big Apple? Who would own and control them? Which boroughs would house the teams, and precisely where and how would their new stadiums be constructed and financed? Was it even realistic to expect widespread public buy-in to support and maintain a pair of developmental short-season Class A clubs in one of America's preeminent professional sports cities? The unwavering support of NY-PL League Commissioner Robert Julian, the Mets and Yankees organizations, and New York City's Mayor Rudy Giuliani went a long way toward ensuring that all of these uncertainties would be handled smoothly, if not exactly seamlessly. But it remained to be seen if even these savvy political operators could overcome all the obstacles in their way.

Even as the HOK Group was completing its $30,000 study of a new stadium for Pittsfield, another team of HOK employees was busily assembling a much more lucrative stadium proposal for a municipality around 150 miles to the south. Their client was the New York City Economic Development Corporation (EDC), a nonprofit institution whose putative mission was to promote and implement the city's economic development. In actuality, EDC was often used as a powerful tool to achieve the ends of the mayor of New York City. And in the mid-1990s, the mayor was extremely interested in building several expensive baseball stadiums within the boundaries of New York City. Aside from the potential economic or political benefits of doing so, a major motivation was the simple fact that the Honorable Mayor Rudolph W. Giuliani loved baseball.[10]

When he was on the campaign trail running for mayor of New York City, one of Giuliani's favorite personal stories focused on his lifelong love of the sport and its teams, the New York Yankees in particular. He would tell of his childhood in Brooklyn in the late 1940s as he grew up a Yankee fan, a choice more or less forced upon him by his father. When he was two years old, or so he said, his proud papa would dress Rudy in a miniature Yankees uniform and send him outdoors to play with the neighborhood children. At that time virtually every kid in the borough was a staunch Brooklyn Dodgers fan, so as soon as they caught sight of Rudy wearing the colors of the enemy they would jump on him, beat him up, and toss him in the mud.[11]

During his failed mayoral campaign of 1989 and then his successful second attempt four years later, Giuliani would repeat this anecdote again and again. It was extremely useful because it contained many of the elements he used to define himself and his subsequent career as a US district attorney and politician. Giuliani had purposefully cultivated a reputation as a tough public servant who refused to be bullied, a man who stubbornly maintained his convictions even when he faced overwhelming opposition. His lifelong loyalty to the Yankees also emphasized his deep roots in the city and attachment to its institutions. At the same time, certain aspects of his story were very telling in other ways. As he often did in his public persona, Giuliani glossed over some less plausible or pertinent details. He never explained why a pair of doting parents would repeatedly send a two-year-old outside alone to be assaulted. He also neglected to mention that his family subsequently left Brooklyn before his seventh birthday for suburban Nassau County, a more congenial environment for a nascent Yankee fan than the Dodgers' home borough. Giuliani's allegiance to the Yankee pinstripes also hinted at his preference for choosing winners over losers, even lovable ones. His own timely switch from the Democratic to the Republican party during the Reagan years, his relentless pursuit of prosecutorial victories, and many of his ruthless tactics as a mayoral campaigner and administrator reflected this quality.[12]

In November 1993 Giuliani captured the mayoralty by a very slim margin, prevailing by approximately 50,000 votes out of nearly 2 million cast. Three days after Election Day, months before he would even be inaugurated as New York City's mayor, the lifelong "Yankee nut" was forced to deal with baseball as his first major public policy matter. For the previous five months, New York State Governor Mario Cuomo had been under increasing pressure from the New York Yankees to upgrade or replace Yankee Stadium. The team's lease on its Bronx ballpark would be up in 2002, and owner George Steinbrenner was threatening to move to New Jersey if that state committed to constructing a newer and more profitable facility. Although it had been less than twenty years since the city and state spent $160 million to renovate the stadium at no cost to the Yankees, Steinbrenner insisted that the current facility did not meet the growing need for better fan access, more stadium amenities, and especially expensive luxury boxes. Even as the governor proposed plans for hundreds of millions of dollars in improvements or even a new half-billion-dollar stadium to be built on the West Side of Manhattan, the Yankees remained unsatisfied. Now that the city's mayoral contest was decided, the governor gladly passed the stadium dilemma over to the mayor-elect and stepped away from the negotiations.[13]

Giuliani's response to the Yankees' demands was conciliatory and accommodating. He went on the record immediately to say that "Yankee Stadium is a magnet New York City needs to keep," placating his good friend George Steinbrenner (with whom he had been "going to games . . . for years," though he claimed he was always scrupulous about paying for his own seat in the owner's box).[14] For his part, Steinbrenner took care to stress to the press the drawbacks his team faced in the Bronx, grabbing headlines with his unsubstantiated assertions that "there are crack houses within three blocks of the Stadium and buildings where mattresses, stoves and refrigerators are thrown out in the middle of the night."[15]

The new mayor got the message loud and clear and continued to up the ante on the city's offers to the Yankees. EDC paid a hefty $630,000 to stadium design firm HOK for a master plan that would be appealing enough to keep the Yankees in the South Bronx. Then, even as he slashed $2 billion from city agencies and the Board of Education, insisted on more than 15,000 municipal employee layoffs, and imposed heavy cuts to a wide array of social services, the mayor proposed a budget earmarking $600 million for the HOK team's plan for a new Yankee Stadium with 100 luxury boxes and a "Yankeeland" theme park. In all, the mayor floated thirteen stadium plans to the Yankees in his first two years in office, and every single one was rejected. Undeterred by the time, effort, and money this was costing the city, the administration continued the negotiations. To Mayor Giuliani, professional baseball was more than just a high political priority. It had become a centerpiece of his legacy, almost an obsession.[16]

As the city's offers to the Yankees grew more lucrative and grandiose, the other team in town began a power play of its own. While Mets co-owner Fred Wilpon insisted that the team was "perfectly happy" at Shea Stadium in Queens, several club officials began dropping unsubtle hints that the team would be even more perfectly happy with a new ballpark. In a conversation with reporters about stadium issues, Mets Vice President Dave Howard commented "we do a pretty good job with an outdated facility." In June 1995 Wilpon met with New York State officials to propose a new stadium and entertainment complex at the Shea site. Simultaneously, his co-owner Nelson Doubleday was opening discussions with Long Island legislators about relocating to the underutilized 475-acre horse racing track at Belmont Park. "I'm a big believer in Nassau County," he said, and then went on to suggest that the team could share its new facility with the New York Jets football team, which he was interested in buying. The divergent plans may have reflected the uneasy partnership between Wilpon and Doubleday, or they may have been part of a calculated attempt to convince Mayor Giuliani that they were being wooed by suitors outside the city. Either way, while the Mets brass were working multiple angles they were united in their intention to negotiate a new ballpark.[17]

The first serious Mets proposal came from Fred Wilpon. Drawing on his decades of experience as a successful New York real estate developer,

Wilpon took less than two months to assemble a comprehensive plan for a new facility. Described as "Ebbets Field with a dome," the new stadium would have a quirky, historic feel akin to Baltimore's recently erected Camden Yards. It would be built alongside the existing Shea Stadium, which would be torn down and turned into a parking lot. The projected cost for the entire project was $457 million, with the bulk coming from private financing. New York City would be asked to contribute only a quarter of the funds to pay for local infrastructure components such as new roads and highway access, a parking garage, and the demolition of the old structure, with the remainder to come from some combination of private sources and bond offerings. The highlight of the plan was the facility's retractable roof, which would enable it to serve as a year-round venue for concerts, conventions, and even professional basketball or hockey. The Queens Borough President's Office immediately expressed its enthusiastic support, calling the plan a "home run." The mayor was more circumspect, cautioning patience in the early stages of the negotiating process.[18]

In his desire to establish his baseball legacy, Mayor Giuliani now faced not one but two major league stadium projects with a combined price tag well over $1 billion. It hardly mattered that the current Yankee Stadium lease arrangement would not expire until 2002, with the Shea Stadium deal lasting two years longer until 2004. As the mayor tried in vain to placate both teams with offers that grew larger and more elaborate, the pressure continued to mount. In September 1995 the city's tabloids reported that New Jersey officials were working on a proposal for a Yankees facility in the Meadowlands. The new stadium would seat 50,000 and promised to net the team $80 million in its first year alone, far outstripping the $20 million the Yankees had earned in their best year in the Bronx. Meanwhile the Mets' friends on the Nassau County Sports Commission claimed that developers were lining up to build their Belmont facility, with $500 million in potential funding already at their disposal.[19]

As the tug of war over New York's baseball teams escalated, the press gleefully waded into the fray. Bronx political officials tumbled over one another in their rush to condemn any proposal that took the team away from the borough. At the same time, they were also sharply critical of the mayor's willingness to allocate huge sums of public moneys toward a stadium for the Yankees while the social and economic needs of their constituencies were underfunded. The team's presumptive new neighbors had complaints of their own. Letters to the editor decried the notion of a new stadium on Manhattan's West Side, citing the logistical nightmares that would ensue in terms of financing and local transportation. In addition to local coverage of the stadium standoffs, *New York Newsday* columnist Mike Lupica expanded the story to a national audience in an article published in the *Sporting News* shortly after the 1995 All-Star Game. In his piece "Destroying a Tradition," Lupica blamed the entire spectacle on Yankees owner George Steinbrenner, a "greedy windbag" who was blackmailing New York into bribing him with millions even as he murdered the great Yankee heritage in the city. All of this attention only helped the teams ratchet up the public pressure on a mayor who would do almost anything to keep professional baseball in his city.[20]

By late 1995 negotiations had stalled. It was clear that the Yankees, the Mets, and the mayor were all on the same page when it came to new stadium construction, but the practical details of location, financing, and amassing public and political support still remained to be determined. With many years remaining on their leases, the teams could afford to be patient.[21] But Mayor Giuliani was less sanguine. Already halfway through his first term, Giuliani was chafing under the constant criticism and sniping over his stadium plans. His 1997 reelection campaign would soon begin, and the delays and expenses associated with the stadium issue could adversely affect his chances of winning. The mayor knew that it would likely take a long time before two major league ballpark deals could be completed in a city with rules and politics as complex as New York's. Unfortunately, time was the one resource that he could not guarantee.

Impatient to cement his baseball legacy, Rudy Giuliani began searching for a backup plan. He firmly believed that professional baseball was a boon to New York City and to his own image as its leader. In public and private statements he continued to insist that baseball and its facilities construction would create jobs, raise revenue, and instill civic pride. He was committed to attaining these goals by building new stadiums for the Yankees and Mets and would continue the laborious planning process for these massive projects throughout his term as mayor. At the same time, he remained alert to any opportunity to achieve the same goals on a smaller scale within a much shorter timetable. The mayor's determination to impact New York City baseball was about to take him in a completely unexpected direction as he began to woo small-town baseball to the biggest metropolis in the country.

The first major problem facing the proponents of New York City minor league baseball was the growing national criticism of and opposition to public subsidies for sports stadiums. According to one estimate, during the decade of the 1990s at least twenty-eight entirely new stadiums were built to house American baseball and football teams, with three or more approved for construction in the immediate future and another twelve older facilities undergoing extensive publicly funded renovations. Another study asserted that "between 1987 and 1999, 55 stadiums and arenas were refurbished or built in the United States at a cost of more than $8.7 billion." This "unprecedented stadium construction boom" came at a high public cost, as MLB and NFL lease information revealed that taxpayer spending alone on these facilities totaled more than $7.5 billion, not including the (much smaller) contribution made by the teams themselves. As economics professors Roger G. Noll and Andrew Zimbalist observed in the summer of 1997, "new facilities costing at least $200 million [each] have been completed or are under way in Baltimore, Charlotte, Chicago, Cincinnati, Cleveland, Milwaukee, Nashville, San Francisco, St. Louis, Seattle, Tampa, and Washington, D.C. and are in the planning stages in Boston, Dallas, Minneapolis, New York, and Pittsburgh. Major stadium renovations have been undertaken in Jacksonville and Oakland." Moreover, an additional fifteen franchises were in the process of negotiating taxpayer-subsidized stadium projects by the year 2000.[22]

One reason professional team owners sought new stadiums was the enormous profit they offered. It was Joe Robbie of the Miami Dolphins who was the first to realize and then actualize this potential during this era, as Jacksonville Jaguars President and COO David M. Seldin explained shortly after the Jaguars' own stadium went up in 1993.

In 1984 Joe Robbie (founder and then owner of the Miami Dolphins) unveiled a revolutionary concept in stadium design— club seats. Wider seats on an exclusive level, offering access to an upscale concourse, partially shielded from the rain, some other added amenities—priced 300%–600% over other tickets. "Unheard of, crazy, it'll never work." Worked just fine . . . Nearly every professional sports facility built since Joe Robbie Stadium includes club seats. They are a widely accepted product, bridging the enormous gulf between regular seats and luxurious suites.

Let the fans decide where they want to sit; they'll sort themselves out . . . The same simple things that mark a successful building, development or business. Customers like choices. Customers want to be in control. Customers want value for money.

In Jacksonville, our new stadium is still a honeymoon cottage. Every one of our 200 people, from our owner to our mascot, strives to work each day to leave a fresh mint on the pillow. We'd better.

Under the guise of enhancing consumer choices and democratizing stadium luxury and amenities, sports teams characterized their new stadiums as a form of public service. The fact that they would reap huge personal revenues by increasing costs by many price points was secondary to the benefits that would accrue to millions of ticket buyers each season, they said.[23]

Proponents also argued that new stadiums would also provide more concrete benefits to the cities that built them. In addition to the amorphous concept of raising civic pride and awareness, privately commissioned economic impact studies asserted that many new jobs would be created and that their sales and salaries would generate tax revenues for local municipalities. Because these studies were invariably produced on behalf of the sports teams themselves, they were often biased and based on extremely questionable methodology to calculate positive outcomes. As the decade wore on and the number of stadium projects grew exponentially, a growing number of economists, nonprofit watchdog groups, and governmental bodies began to express doubts about these blithe assertions.[24]

A third justification for building new stadiums, voiced by major league baseball owners in particular, was the effect of design aesthetics on the gameday experience. During the previous stadium boom of the 1960s and 1970s, stadium design favored multipurpose facilities that would be used for both baseball and football games during their respective seasons, as well as any other mass public events including concerts or conventions. But their cavernous size, cookie cutter uniformity, dearth of unique identity, and—most importantly to owners—lack of expensive luxury suites left fans cold and unenthused. The exemplar of this trend was the Houston Astrodome, originally built in 1965 to provide a comfortable air-conditioned environment that protected patrons from the oppressive heat and humidity of the summer baseball season. But its monolithic institutional design turned off fans, and the artificial Astroturf playing surface disgusted players who suffered a higher rate of injury than on natural grass surfaces.[25]

The new generation of 1990s baseball parks would embrace a spirit of retro nostalgia even as they made sure to prioritize the features that appealed most to team owners, namely luxury seats, skyboxes, and club seating. The first of this new breed of ballpark was Baltimore's Oriole Park at Camden Yards which was completed in 1992 as a replacement for the city's multipurpose Memorial Stadium, then less than forty years old and utterly lacking in charm. That was quickly followed by the Texas Rangers' Ballpark at Arlington and Cleveland's Jacobs Field in 1994, the Colorado Rockies' Coors Field in Denver in 1995, Atlanta's Turner Field in 1996, and a host of additional baseball stadiums over the next decade. Design elements varied: retro-classic parks featured brick exteriors and old-timey railings which hearkened back to early twentieth-century baseball's "jewel box" stadiums, while retro-modern style construction might embrace steel and concrete facades, retractable domes, and liberal use of glass and cantilevers for a more contemporary feel. But all the new facilities boasted better views from all seats for all fans, a more natural ballpark atmosphere as a consequence of their being designed specifically for baseball and no other sport, and unique quirks that set each ballpark apart from all others, such as different outfield dimensions and color schemes. These were important points of emphasis for team owners as they bullied and cajoled cities into building these bespoke confections, all too often "pretentious by name, adorable in each obscure detail," at a cost of hundreds of millions of their taxpayers' dollars.[26]

For New York's major league teams, the fad for retro ballparks was less important than simply achieving the funding for two new stadiums at the same time. Speaking to the press on behalf of team owner George Steinbrenner in 1994, Yankees Vice President John Lawn said "the look wasn't Mr. Steinbrenner's focus. He didn't say I don't care, but he asked questions about the luxury boxes and parking and other things that get people more easily into the ball park and out." This came in response to an early proposal from Mayor Giuliani's office to spend $270 million on refurbishing the existing Yankee Stadium, with $90 million of those funds to be spent on nostalgic touches meant to evoke the history and grandeur of the original ballpark and its "elegant Gothic roof façade." But a renovation of the existing stadium was clearly insufficient to satisfy Steinbrenner, who would agree to nothing less than a completely new structure. Of course this would drive up the costs considerably, particularly in terms of the vast majority of the funding which would come from public subsidies and tax breaks.[27]

Meanwhile New York Mets co-owners Nelson Doubleday and Fred Wilpon were making it clear that if the Yankees got a new stadium, the Mets would demand the same. The Professional Baseball Agreement that governed the sport specifically granted shared territorial rights to both teams over New York City as well as Nassau, Suffolk, Rockland and Westchester Counties, most of New Jersey, and southern Connecticut. Although the municipal government was not bound by the rules propagated by the PBA, it was certain that either team would likely try to block any major action that did not benefit both equally in a most-favored-nation arrangement. It did not have to be this way, since there was ample precedent to negotiate with each team separately. Shea Stadium had been built in 1962 without a corresponding new stadium for the Yankees, and the massive Yankee Stadium renovations of the 1970s were carried out without a peep from the Mets organization. In 1991 the city of Chicago built a new $137 million stadium for Jerry Reinsdorf and his Chicago White Sox without funding any concurrent changes or upgrades for the Chicago Cubs' historic Wrigley Field. Although the two Chicago teams shared one territory in the same manner as the Yankees and Mets shared New York, their dealings with their city remained separate and independent. Nevertheless, Mayor Giuliani had no wish to alienate either fan base in advance of his 1997 reelection campaign, and his baseball mania was so advanced that he was willing to commit to two enormously expensive simultaneous stadium projects. The Mets were savvy enough to grasp this, and so even as Steinbrenner agitated for a new facility and threatened to move the team to New Jersey, Wilpon and Doubleday publicly flirted with Long Island.

But the negative press coverage of the stadium issue in 1994–1995 was an indication of a growing resistance to public funding of expensive sports facilities, at least in New York. Even as stadium after stadium was erected across the country, economists, journalists, politicians, and other public figures were fighting back against what they considered imprudent and unwarranted corporate welfare in the form of stadium subsidies. An array of studies argued that new stadiums were simply not worth the municipal investment that it took to get them built. Using statistical analysis, economic theory, and case studies, they countered each justification invoked by team owners and their lackeys in the press. These critics held a widely divergent view of the economic impacts of new stadiums from the hired stadium proponents, and they tried to cast doubt on what they regarded as unrealistic positive assumptions and predictions. Although they did generate some public attention and debate, those who cautioned against new stadium construction rarely succeeded in derailing public funding for new sports facilities. Generally they were ignored by local municipalities and politicians, or else their warnings were lost amid a torrent of positive publicity and messaging generated by the teams and their league offices. But over the course of the decade the number of detractors and outright opponents was growing, and they would influence the progress of the stadium issue in New York in the coming years.[28]

The core argument against municipal stadium financing and public subsidies was simple: the direct costs far outweighed any revenues that would be generated. Many subsidies took the form of tax-exempt bonds issued by state and local governments to provide financing, with the tax exemptions lowering the interest on debts incurred during the process. Unfortunately, these tax exemptions then resulted in large losses in federal, state, and local tax revenues for the life of the bonds. Congress noted this in the Tax Reform Act of 1986, which attempted to address "the irrationality of granting tax exemptions for interest on municipal bonds that financed projects primarily benefiting private interests." However, after Congress and industry lobbyists made a slew of edits and changes, the final version of the bill actually ended up increasing local subsidies and thus ushered in the 1990s stadium construction boom. In virtually all cases, teams took advantage of the tax exemptions and increased their own profits enormously even as the loss of tax revenues meant that localities never recouped their investments.[29]

Stadium boosters countered that the indirect economic benefits of having a new stadium would far outweigh the costs. New stadiums would generate jobs for local citizens, both in terms of immediate construction job opportunities and later long-term employment opportunities at the stadiums and in the new economic development spurred by their ongoing presence. This would lead to per-capita personal income growth for a broad swath of citizens. In the words of Thomas Chema, a Cleveland attorney and executive director of that city's Gateway Sports and Entertainment Complex:

> It is the spin-off development generated by two million or more people visiting a specific area of a city during a concentrated time frame which is critical. The return on the public investment in a ballpark or arena, in dollars and cents terms as opposed to the intangible entertainment value comes not from the facility itself, but from the jobs created in new restaurants, taverns, retail, hotels, etc., that spring up on the periphery of the sports venue . . . Development is materializing because 5,000,000 visitors are coming to games and entertainment and

they are spending their money outside the walls of the sports venues before and after the events. They are coming even when there are no sporting events.[30]

Chema and the sports teams that worked with him were relying on what they called economic multipliers, which were usually crafted for them by highly paid consultants to facilitate their projects and persuade local governments to approve them. The use of multipliers was explained in a sports context by experts Roger G. Noll and Andrew Zimbalist: "All this new spending has a 'multiplier effect' as increased local income causes still more new spending and job creation. Advocates argue that new stadiums spur so much economic growth that they are self-financing: subsidies are offset by revenues from ticket taxes, sales taxes on concessions and other spending outside the stadium, and property tax increases arising from the stadium's economic impact."[31] It is important to note that none of the projected property tax revenues would be generated by the stadiums themselves, since they were owned by the municipality and only leased to the teams, usually on very generous terms.

Skeptics of the multiplier effect dismissed these rosy predictions as exaggerated or even outright falsehoods and backed up their assertions with actual data. In city after city, economic findings showed that new stadiums had almost no effect on local manufacturing activity and did not lead to any significant increase in sales taxes, entertainment taxes, or per-capita personal income. Before-and-after profiles and economic regression analyses found no demonstrable development boom or major economic gains from dollars spent by outsiders drawn into the city by the new stadiums. Instead, job creation was often limited to low-income and labor-intensive unskilled seasonal work that did little to expand opportunities for the locals. In fact, studies argued that stadium construction often depressed local economic development by diverting funds and job opportunities that might otherwise have led to stimulation of the surrounding neighborhoods in the direction of higher-skilled and higher-wage jobs. As for increased spending on sports at the new stadiums, evidence indicated that this usually represented a redistribution of leisure and entertainment spending by existing consumers rather than new income from additional outside visitors. As economist Robert A. Baade summarized the situation fairly early in the stadium boom, "The data suggest that stadium subsidies and other sports subsidies benefit not the community as a whole, but rather team owners and professional athletes."[32]

As the Giuliani administration continued its negotiations with the Yankees and Mets between 1994 and 1997, many of these arguments both for and against new stadiums appeared in the local press. After Mayor Giuliani won reelection in November 1997 by a commanding margin, defeating Democrat Ruth Messinger by 234,000 votes and 17 percentage points, he took that as a mandate to aggressively push forward his policy agendas including stadium construction. In his Second Inaugural Address on New Year's Day 1998 the mayor referenced several issues including reducing crime and increasing support for the police, encouraging the New York City school system to adopt School Choice and support charter schools, and cutting taxes to aid businesses. He also included a fleeting mention of his baseball-related plans. "We will advance key new economic development plans . . . We will commit ourselves to keeping major city institutions like the New York Stock Exchange—the Yankees and the Mets—the institutions that help keep us the capital of the financial world and the capital of the business world." With that brief statement, Giuliani signaled his commitment to the construction of new baseball stadiums that would cost in excess of $2 billion by the time they were completed. The Yankees and Mets already had his personal assurances that their projects would come to fruition, continued to hold regular meetings with the brass at EDC, and were banking on the expensive HOK master plan that had first attracted press attention back in 1995. Now the mayor was issuing a public statement that those plans would be moving forward in the immediate future.[33]

Although the press coverage of his inaugural address generally overlooked its offhand mention of New York City baseball, the one entity that did notice was New York City's Independent Budget Office (IBO). Created in 1989 (but not actually funded by the city until 1996), the IBO was intended to provide public access and guidance regarding New York City's budget and upcoming revenue and spending forecasts. Although its own operating budget came from the administration, the IBO was an independent entity authorized to produce objective analyses and briefs on the mayor's financial plans and actions. Mayor Giuliani had opposed its creation in the first place, and after several years of delaying its funding he continued to sabotage its operations by withholding budgetary data. In 1998, shortly after his reelection, Giuliani tried no fewer than three times to abolish the agency, first through budgetary means and later through the New York State Legislature and then the New York City Charter Revision Commission, a group he controlled. The IBO survived, filing

several lawsuits and garnering widespread support from the city's Democratic politicians and other watchdog groups. With obvious reluctance,
the mayor backed off. [34]

Mayor Giuliani's misgivings about the IBO were borne out early in
1998, when the office released a detailed assessment of his baseball plans
called *Double Play: The Economics and Financing of Stadiums for the Yankees and Mets*. Widely cited by the local press and a host of anti-stadium
treatises, the twenty-page report included hard numbers, a wide-ranging
literature review, comparative data from other cities and across Major
League Baseball, and a detailed analysis of specific factors regarding New
York City and its two major league baseball teams. It included no details
provided by the Office of the Mayor, who was then withholding his budget
data in the midst of the lawsuits being filed by the IBO to gain access
to that information. But the report deftly incorporated publicly available
documentation as well as figures released by Bronx Borough President
Fernando Ferrer, an enthusiastic proponent of the Yankees' new stadium
and the rash of additional projects slated to accompany its construction.
Using these resources and some well-informed conjecture, *Double Play*
presented a much less optimistic prediction of how New York City might
benefit from new stadiums for the Yankees and Mets.[35]

The report began with the flat statement that "research consistently
finds that new stadiums do not produce economic growth in metropolitan
areas." Using studies and data on the recent surge of stadium construction
across the country, *Double Play* posited that the new facilities did produce
large identifiable revenue increases within a short time. However, nearly
all of that new revenue accrued to the major league teams leasing the
stadiums and not to the municipalities that owned them. Furthermore,
in some cases the revenue spike was only short term and stemmed from
a "novelty effect" that soon wore off. But that factor could be mitigated
by increased stadium amenities like luxury boxes, club seating with wait-
staff, and other expensive add-ons that could keep fans coming back to
the ballpark. This was a primary reason that the Yankees in particular
were insisting on an extremely expensive stadium that would include all
of these features.

But the payoff for New York City's economy, while by no means
negligible, would not necessarily justify the enormous outlay that two
new stadiums would cost. The report estimated that the Yankees and
Mets currently contributed $300 million each year to the city's overall
economic output through the nearly 2,000 jobs they created, ancillary hotel

and tourism benefits, and increased spending by fans. But many of those jobs were low-paying and seasonal. Because a majority of the fans of both teams regularly commuted to the games from nearby suburbs, most of them made no measurable contribution to the larger tourism industry or to the economies of surrounding neighborhoods. In fact, the teams' actual direct contribution to the city's treasury through tax, parking, and additional revenues was a measly $14 million. The inflated economic multiplier figures presented by the teams did not mention that the combined sales tax and payroll tax revenues accruing to the city were more than offset by the lack of property tax revenues from municipally owned stadiums, the tax rebates enjoyed by the teams—which would only rise further with the construction of the new stadiums—and the other capital costs absorbed by the city on an ongoing basis. The two new proposed stadiums would indeed provide huge new profit streams. But if past experience and the IBO's predictions held, then the lion's share would go to the teams and very little would actually go to New York City.

This conclusion was even likelier based on Mayor Giuliani's newly released annual budget, which included a proposal for funding the city's contribution to construction of the stadiums. Because of constitutional debt limit regulations and the negative optics of pushing off other infrastructure improvements, the mayor planned to forego the most common method of stadium financing through issuing general obligation debt bonds. Instead, the city's share would be provided as an ongoing stream of pay-as-you-go funding. The initial source of those moneys would be New York City's commercial rent tax (CRT), which had been scheduled for elimination as part of the mayor's pledge to reduce taxes during his reelection campaign a year earlier. As the report stated, "The resulting stream of CRT revenues would be earmarked to fund the New York City Sports Facilities Corporation, a new agency created to build the stadiums." Although the mayor's budget made it seem that this was a direct one-for-one swap to cover all stadium construction costs, that the reality would be more complicated. As construction dragged on and costs multiplied, additional funding would be needed for the expenses not covered by the CRT revenues. This would cause budgetary shortfalls and conflict with other planned tax cuts, and because the pay-as-you-go arrangement was ongoing it would necessitate spending cuts to other areas and even tax increases over time.[36]

Double Play also pointed out other drawbacks to the mayor's proposed arrangement. "Pay-as-you-go financing requires an up-front contribution many times the amount of annual debt service, and that contribution may bear little relation to the benefit current taxpayers eventually receive." The system also allowed teams to circumvent cumbersome rent regulations imposed by federal agencies on stadiums funded through traditional tax-exempt debt mechanisms. This meant that the mayor's pay-as-you-go financing plan could wind up being more expensive to taxpayers both immediately and in the long run, while the teams could potentially pay even less as they benefited from more flexible rent arrangements with a very team-friendly administration. Much of this could have been avoided with a larger privately financed contribution from the team, as in the cases of the Detroit Tigers, Milwaukee Brewers, Arizona Diamondbacks, and Texas Rangers in the early 1990s. In all of those cases, the teams increased their own share of stadium costs when larger public subsidies were not forthcoming. But Mayor Giuliani made no mention of this possibility for New York's teams, and the Yankees and Mets certainly did not bring it up either.

Determined to move forward and build the stadiums he craved, the mayor remained undaunted by the IBO's report, its damning numbers, and the unflattering picture it depicted of his plans. Unbeknownst to the public, Rudy Giuliani's ambitions were even grander than to construct just two new facilities. In fact, he was actually planning to fund and build at least twice that many.

CHAPTER FIVE
SANE BUSINESSPEOPLE BECOME MISTY-EYED

Unbeknownst to New York City's Independent Budget Office or its tax-payers, the mayor's baseball plans encompassed not just two but four brand-new stadiums. While the parent clubs were grabbing the headlines with their plans for new major league stadiums in the Bronx and Queens, behind the scenes they were simultaneously negotiating for a second pair of new minor league stadiums to be built in the city for two New York-Penn League (NY-PL) teams. With seating capacities well under 10,000 these facilities would be only a fraction of the size of the big-league ball-parks. That factor, along with their less expensive locations in the outer boroughs, would allow them to be built at a fraction of the cost as well. The Mayor's Office planned to utilize the same financial blueprint for all of the ballparks, including similar lease terms, pay-as-you-go financing, and reliance on the new NYC Sports Facilities Corporation. Since the minor league projects were smaller and cheaper in scale, it would likely be easier and quicker to set all of these arrangements in place, secure the necessary approvals, and erect the facilities. This would serve as a useful dry run for both the mayor and the teams as they deliberately set about bringing their major league vision to fruition.

The mayor's point man for stadium planning was attorney Randy Levine, deputy mayor for economic development, planning, and admin-istration. One of the mayor's closest aides, Levine had left his role as Giuliani's labor commissioner in 1995 to work for Major League Baseball as their chief labor negotiator. Two years later he returned as deputy mayor, cementing the ties between his boss, organized baseball, and particularly George Steinbrenner of the Yankees, who had recommended him for the

MLB job after using Levine for legal work of his own. Although his role took place almost completely behind the scenes, Levine's fingerprints would be all over the major league and minor league stadium deals negotiated during his tenure. Staten Island Borough President Guy Molinari would later credit Levine for doing much to convince the Yankees to bring minor league baseball to New York City. The Yankees would show their own appreciation by providing Levine with a soft landing spot once Giuliani reached the end of his final term as mayor. The Yankees hired the erstwhile deputy mayor to be their team president in the year 2000, a position he has held ever since.[1]

For NY-PL President Bob Julian, entry into the huge New York market represented the culmination of his master plan to save the league and ensure its future survival. Julian was relatively new to his position and had been brought in specifically to address the new challenges faced by the league. Over the past decade, most major league owners and officials had come around to share Jerry Reinsdorf and Eddie Einhorn's view that the existing minor league developmental model was too expensive, too cumbersome, and yielded too few benefits for the parent clubs. The passage of the 1990 Professional Baseball Agreement (PBA) codified many changes that transferred most financial control and profits to them, even as they imposed harsher obligations and facilities requirements on their minor league franchisees. These developments were extremely daunting to many shoestring operations throughout minor league baseball, but none more so than the low-level Class A short-season NY-PL. At the time the league's president was Leo Pinckney, a lifelong newspaperman who had been involved with the NY-PL since the 1950s. A native of the small Finger Lakes community of Auburn, Pinckney was characteristic of the old-fashioned breed of league owners. When his town faced the loss of its farm team during the period of baseball contraction following World War II, he had formed a consortium of local businessmen to persuade the Yankees to grant them a local franchise. Four decades later Pinckney was revered within his town and his league, but he was not prepared to engineer a complete transformation of the league's identity and vision in response to the existential crisis that threatened it. In his stead the NY-PL turned to its president-elect, only the fourth in its long history, Bob Julian.[2]

Prior to his involvement in the league, Robert F. Julian was a trial lawyer from Utica. He was also the Republican majority leader of the Oneida County Legislature and, according to the *New York Times*, a "formidable power broker" in central New York State.[3] In addition Julian was a baseball fan, and in 1985 he was brought on as local counsel to the Utica Blue Sox of the NY-PL, then under new ownership. When Leo Pinckney announced in 1992 that he was retiring from the league presidency, the owners of the Blue Sox nominated Julian as his replacement, and after a short screening process the rest of the league agreed to vote him in. Right away, the new president-elect understood the serious situation that the league faced:

> At that time, there was great concern that the league would be reduced in terms of the number of teams. I think potentially that even short-A would get eliminated as an entity. In other words, the major league teams were looking to cut costs, and the particular boogeyman, as I recollect, was Eddie Einhorn, who was one of the owners of the White Sox. Whether fairly or not fairly, I just remember him as being an advocate of cost-cutting, and minimizing or reducing the number of minor leagues, and reducing short-season was an attractive option.[4]

Working with Pinckney and other league leaders, Julian attended meetings in Albany with third-term New York State Governor Mario Cuomo, who had himself once played professionally as a minor league prospect. With Cuomo's support the State Legislature passed a budget package authorizing $60 million for the state's Urban Development Corporation to provide matching funds for minor league stadium projects that included a half-dozen NY-PL communities. In this way the league and the governor helped refurbish several antiquated facilities in Batavia, Watertown, Utica, and Jamestown to meet minimal PBA standards, even as they aided and abetted Marvin Goldklang's removal of the Erie Sailors to brand-new Dutchess Stadium in Fishkill as the Hudson Valley Renegades. Leo Pinckney's Auburn Doubledays were awarded a shiny new $2.7 million stadium named Falcon Park, which opened for business in 1995. Working together with Class AAA clubs in Syracuse and Rochester among others, the NY-PL played a major role in what Julian later recalled as "a fairly sophisticated effort."[5]

While Governor Cuomo's millions of stadium dollars staved off immediate disaster for the NY-PL, they did not necessarily ensure long-term stability for either the league or its teams. Julian gathered his constituents and told them that the only way to do so was to think bigger in ways that were both creative and, for many league owners, unprecedented.

> We had a strategic plan, [but] also we wanted to protect the
> league from franchise attrition. And I advised the Board of
> Directors and they agreed, not without some debate, that it
> would be desirable to have a minority of the teams either
> owned or strategically interconnected with major-league
> teams . . . With some rather active dissent, we pursued a
> strategy trying to marry, or cohabit at least, with as many
> major-league teams as we reasonably could.
>
> We concluded that one of several strategies would be to
> look for larger markets and rather than rejecting major-league
> baseball territory—because it was their territory—that we
> would initiate contact with major-league baseball to try to see
> if specific teams would be interested in having a minor league
> team within their territory. We reasoned it would be good for
> the major-league team in that it would potentially enhance fan
> base in the outer limits of their territory, and we reasoned that
> it would be good for our league because once major-league
> baseball begins a cohabiting arrangement, that team would
> be more likely to weigh in on the preservation of the league.[6]

Facing possible extinction due to the financial and facilities exigencies imposed by the PBA and hemmed in by MLB's hostility toward franchise independence, Julian asked his owners to consider collaboration as a survival tactic.

Many of the new breed of NY-PL owners embraced this strategy as a way to immediately increase the value and viability of their teams. The first to follow Julian's blueprint was former IBM executive Clyde Smoll, who shifted the small-town Elmira Pioneers to Lowell, Massachusetts, as part of a co-branding deal with the parent Boston Red Sox organization. Although the Spinners franchise would change hands over time, its Red Sox affiliation would remain intact for nearly a quarter-century, exactly as the league had hoped and planned from the outset. Smoll's fellow league owners like Yankees minority partner Marvin Goldklang and CBS executive Alan Levin saw no reason to spurn closer relationships with major league partners or, for that matter, Governor Cuomo's offer of matching funds toward new stadiums. When financier Barry Gordon's ownership group moved their NY-PL Cardinals affiliate from Canada to suburban New Jersey, they openly admitted that they were seeking out larger markets, following the money, and doing their best to attract the attention and patronage of fans of Major League Baseball, just as Bob Julian anticipated. So the ownership revitalization and franchise movement within the NY-PL was not the merely the result of larger shifts within baseball but actually the fulfillment of a meticulous plan by the league to save itself. By all appearances, in the mid-1990s that plan was working like a charm.[7]

One enthusiastic proponent of this approach was Bill Gladstone. In 1996 and 1997, even as he pressured the city of Pittsfield to build him a new stadium, Gladstone and his parent Mets organization engaged in serious conversations with New York State Governor George Pataki to build a stadium for the team on Long Island. Nor was this the region's first foray into trying to secure a minor league affiliate of a local New York franchise. A few years earlier, the Class AA Albany-Colonie Yankees—a second team co-owned by Barry Gordon, who was in the process of moving the NY-PL's Hamilton Redbirds to New Jersey—announced their intention to relocate to Suffolk County, Long Island. The notion had widespread support among Long Islanders, and the County Legislature was making concrete plans to finance a new $7.5 million stadium on the grounds of a local community college. But the move was successfully blocked by the Mets in early 1993 at a session of Major League Baseball's Professional Baseball Executive Council, where they made the case that "a team on Long Island, particularly one owned by the Yankees, would affect the value of their team." Now the Yankees got their chance to return the favor. At an Executive Council meeting in October 1997, committee chairman and Acting Baseball Commissioner Bud Selig held a vote where the Yankees engineered a rejection of the Pittsfield Mets' bid to move to Long Island. Less than two weeks later on Election Day, the city of Pittsfield voted down a public referendum to fund a new stadium for the team. After two strikeouts Bill Gladstone's team was down to one last at-bat, but this just happened to represent his best attempt yet.[8]

Even as he pursued both his Pittsfield and Long Island options, Gladstone had also been expending serious efforts behind the scenes to move his team to Brooklyn instead. This possibility was of special significance to Gladstone, whose most cherished dream as a minor league team owner was to bring baseball back to his hometown borough of Brooklyn in New York City. Bob Julian later described his impressions of Gladstone's approach: "Bill Gladstone had a long-standing relationship with the Mets, and he said to me 'I'd like to approach the Mets about moving Pittsfield (where the Pittsfield Mets were located) to Brooklyn.' So his dream is to go to Brooklyn. You know, the usual—sane businesspeople become misty-eyed over this whole thing. Bill had a number of conversations with the Mets, which I was only collaterally involved with. Bill [is] very capable of taking care of himself."[9] For their part, the Mets were immediately on board with the idea. Perhaps a bit misty-eyed himself, Fred Wilpon remarked, "There's no question that there's an emotional factor with Brooklyn."[10]

Although the Mets and Yankees had recently been at odds over any planned expansion into Long Island, the two organizations shared a common interest in successfully negotiating with New York City to build new major league stadiums for both clubs. The timing of Gladstone's proposal meant that his desire to establish a minor league presence in Brooklyn would now become part of the much larger conversation between the Mets, Yankees, and the mayor about the future of New York baseball. Because the major league stadium plans were interconnected, this meant that any minor league propositions would also have to include both teams. And unlike Long Island, which at that time fell outside baseball's official territorial divisions, any plans to situate new franchises within the city itself would absolutely require the explicit approval of both the Mets and the Yankees. To prevent any recurrence of the recent Suffolk County debacles, all parties recognized the need for total equity.

This meant that both teams as well as the Mayor's Office would now be considering relocation plans and new stadiums within the five boroughs of the city for not one but two NY-PL clubs. Fortunately for all parties, New York City Mayor Rudolph Giuliani was the ideal partner for the two-team minor league/major league multistadium scheme that they were concocting. "Once there was an ever-so-slight tentative expression of interest," Bob Julian later recalled, "Mayor Giuliani and his people were just all over it and drove it with vigor."[11]

Over the last several months of 1997, the Giuliani administration worked intensively with the Yankees and Mets to hammer out the fundamentals of a minor league deal. It was presumed that Bill Gladstone's Pittsfield Mets would relocate to a new stadium in Brooklyn, and if the Yankees were privately unhappy with this arrangement they gave no indication that they would again actively block it. In the meantime, following Mayor Giuliani's reelection in November his office broached the possibility that the Yankees would bring one of their affiliates to the borough of Staten Island, where they too would be the beneficiaries of a new facility. At a celebration for the mayor on New Year's Day 1998, Staten Island Borough President and fellow Republican Guy Molinari boasted to reporters that a deal was imminent. His account was cautiously corroborated by one of the mayor's spokespeople, and two weeks later in his State of the City Address the mayor proclaimed, "For the future we look forward to assisting in modernized and new Yankee and Shea Stadiums . . . a Brooklyn Sportsplex . . . and a Staten Island minor league baseball field." Molinari basked in the renewed publicity for his borough and its 400,000 residents—"I dare say a majority of them are Yankees fans," he crowed—and bragged about his multiple meetings with "a squad of mayoral aides" as well as George Steinbrenner himself. Steinbrenner was a bit more circumspect but expressed enthusiasm for the idea. "We would love to put a team in Staten Island," Steinbrenner said. "I know Guy Molinari is in the fast lane of the track on this one, and as long as he's in office over there, I'm with him."[12]

The press attention on Staten Island took a backseat to the news that baseball was finally coming back to Brooklyn. Even the few local reporters who were familiar with the interteam rivalry over Long Island did not expect to hear that the Mets were considering Brooklyn instead. The majority of the immediate stories focused on Mets co-owner and team president Fred Wilpon, who was famously Brooklyn-born and bred. Like Bill Gladstone he was a lifelong Brooklyn Dodgers fan who had been devastated when the team moved to the West Coast in the late 1950s. But without any reference to Gladstone's efforts at laying the groundwork over the previous year, Wilpon pitched a narrative where he took full credit for the idea himself. As he told the *New York Daily News*,

> I happened to be with the mayor after his (State of the City) speech and we were discussing the Yankees' interest in going into Staten Island and the quid pro quo involving our inter-est in also having a minor league team in the area . . . And then as I was taking a shower the next morning it came to me: "Why not Brooklyn?" To be honest, it would be a dream of mine to be able to bring baseball back to Brooklyn. What better thing could there be than for our fans in Brooklyn to see future Mets growing up?

Figure 5.1. Mayor Giuliani with Fred Wilpon, 1997. Photo credit: New York City Municipal Archives.

For his part Gladstone seemed content to leave all of the public credit to Wilpon and the Mets. In his own statements he feigned a sense of bewildered surprise at his farm team's good fortune. "This whole (Coney Island) thing just happened. Obviously I need to look into the business details of it, but the fact that both my wife and I were born in Brooklyn makes it a very interesting proposition. I could get very excited about this."[13]

Throughout the rest of 1998, public press accounts made it seem that the P-Mets' move to a new Brooklyn stadium was a certainty. Even as stadium negotiations encountered rough patches and local opposition over the ensuing months, reporters and observers assumed that Wilpon and Gladstone remained on the same page when it came to reviving Brooklyn baseball at long last. But behind the scenes tensions were brewing between the pair of strong-minded business tycoons, each of whom was accustomed to an organizational role as sole decision-maker with final authority. Things came to a head in late November, when Mayor Giuliani maneuvered a city commission into a vote to allocate authority over the Brooklyn stadium design to the Mets organization. With that much control over the new ballpark, the negotiations, and the minor league players who would be designated to play there, it was intolerable to Wilpon that he should not also have an ownership stake in the team itself. The establishment of a new minor league franchise in New York City also represented an opportunity for him to install his son and heir apparent Jeff Wilpon, then in his mid-thirties, to oversee all of its baseball operations. This hands-on experience would prove invaluable once the family gained full control of the Mets organization, as they eventually did when they bought out partner Nelson Doubleday less than a decade later.[14]

As the financial, political, and personal stakes rose higher, the Mets organization told Gladstone that they wanted at least part ownership and a controlling interest in running the franchise. Gladstone flatly refused, and no amount of back-and-forth would change his mind. As he remarked shortly afterward, "They wanted control and it's my team. I'd have been delighted to have them as partners, but not running the team." Dave Howard, the Mets' vice president for business and legal affairs and Fred Wilpon's top lieutenant, explained the organization's naked demand for dominance as follows: "We're bringing a minor league team into the heart of our market. We want to be sure there is no conflict with operation of the major league team." By the end of the year the deal was dead, and shortly after New Year's Day 1999 Gladstone informed the local Massachusetts press that the Pittsfield Mets would not be moving to Brooklyn after all. "Just looking over the entire move, and what it would mean in terms of how we operate the team and our relationship with the Mets, we decided it wasn't the right move for us to make," he said. For his part, Dave Howard admitted, "The fundamental issue was control. There were philosophical differences, and we decided mutually to seek alternative arrangements." Bob Julian later summarized the situation by concluding, "When they got right down to it, the Mets were only willing to have a team in their territory if they owned it. That was very disappointing for Bill."[15]

Bill Gladstone's disappointment would be short-lived. With the clock ticking on his Player Development Agreement with the Mets, he began immediate efforts to secure a new major league affiliation to take effect after his longtime Mets arrangement expired in the year 2000. Using his many baseball connections, he quickly formalized a deal with the Houston Astros. He then put his sterling business pedigree and experience to good use and opened up negotiations for a new stadium in exchange for moving the team to New York state instead. Sixteen months after he regretfully announced the collapse of his Brooklyn deal with the Mets, Gladstone held a Pittsfield press conference to announce that his team was moving to Troy, New York, just outside the state capital of Albany. New York State Senate Majority Leader Joseph Bruno had arranged a $12 million budget appropriation to build a brand-new ballpark on the campus of Hudson Valley Community College, which was also getting a new multimillion-dollar interstate highway spur to boot. As Pittsfield native and team general manager Rick Murphy wiped away tears at leaving his hometown, Gladstone was matter-of-fact about the business decision that had become inevitable. "We've had a good run in Pittsfield," he said. "We love it here. We'll miss Pittsfield. I hope Pittsfield will miss us." After expressing those sincere regrets, Bill Gladstone and his newly renamed Tri-City ValleyCats prepared to set up shop in the aptly named Joseph L. Bruno Stadium ("the Joe") for the team's next phase. With the aging and decrepit Wahconah Park deteriorating further in the absence of a major cash infusion, Pittsfield resigned itself to life without professional baseball.[16]

Meanwhile, the Yankees were facing a melancholier organizational conflict regarding their plans for a minor league team in the five boroughs. All parties agreed that the new Staten Island Yankees team would come from the NY-PL, just like the yet undecided Mets franchise. For the previous thirty-two years, the Yankees slot in the league had been occupied by Oneonta in one of the longest consecutive minor league affiliation agreements in professional baseball. Yankees owner George Steinbrenner and Oneonta Yankees managing partner Sam Nader had a relationship built on baseball success, as well as personal trust and mutual respect. So it came as a shock when the Staten Island plan came together without much advance warning. As Bob Julian recalled the sequence of events, the team first approached the league office before initiating any discussions with Oneonta.

> Once the Yankees become interested, it becomes very problematic in terms of the Professional Baseball Agreement because Oneonta then had a long-standing relationship with the Yankees. It was sentimental and emotional as well as a number of other things. So I said to [Yankees official] Lonn Trost, "All right, so now you're interested and you've got to have a discussion with Sam Nader before you go any further, because now you are in baseball. Giuliani can do whatever he wants in terms of making contact. But the notion of a disengagement of an existing Player Development Contract is governed by the rules

of baseball, and I understand you're the Yankees, but we can't dick around here."

Once they did finally get in touch with the Oneonta owner, his reaction was predictably explosive. Julian continued,

> Mark Newman, the farm director for the Yankees, had the initial discussion with Nader, and Nader's very upset about it all, quite outraged that there would even be discussions . . . We ultimately concluded that there needs to be a meeting. [In early 1998] we had a meeting in Tampa that included Trost, Cashman, Gene Michael, Newman, myself, Nader, and some of his people. Essentially Trost said to Nader "We want to do this on Staten Island, and if you want to move to Staten Island, we'd love to have you. We want to do this, and if you're not going to come with us, we're going to have to find someone else who is." And that's ultimately what they did.[17]

Sam Nader had spent much of his adult life serving as a living representation of the original community spirit of the New York-Penn League. With the support of a local ownership coalition which he organized, the onetime mayor of Oneonta had first brought minor league baseball to his hometown in 1966. Over the decades since, he had come to embody the identity of his team and his league. His peers had attempted several times to elect him league president, but he had always demurred on the grounds that he would have to dissociate himself from operating the Oneonta club, which he would never do. But the league had changed a great deal during his tenure, particularly in terms of the recent influx of the new owners that Nader called "the entrepreneurs." In a 2006 interview, he explained his perspective on the differences in modern minor league baseball:

> The philosophy of the minor league owners has changed. It's no longer the local people who want it for their community, the community-minded. It's the entrepreneurs who, in my opinion, are acquiring the minor league teams and they're going into larger markets . . . They're younger and they have a different philosophy. Mostly in the old days we were concerned with our little own communities, we were from the community, and

had some loyalties to the community. Now there is very little loyalty to the communities. What the hell does the league care? I get a better offer from Joe Blow, I'm gonna leave. That's true not only with the young ones, it's true with the old ones. That loyalty isn't in existence with players, with everything else. It's all money. The ownership in our league changed . . .

What I say is not critical of these individuals. I don't mean to say I'm right and they're wrong. But Marv Goldklang is a minority owner of the New York Yankees. Marv Goldklang has about five different clubs. He has a club in the Florida State League. He has the Minneapolis club or St. Paul club in the Independent League. He owns two or three Independent League clubs. I think he owns the Fort Myers club in the Florida State League. So he's an entrepreneur. Is he wrong and I'm right? No. I just have a different philosophy. I just think that minor league baseball, in baseball itself, there's just too damn much money already in it.[18]

Nader was approached a number of times in the 1980s and 1990s by prospective buyers brandishing offers to the tune of two or three million dollars. But he had always turned them down, knowing very well that they intended to move the team out of small-market Oneonta as soon as possible. Now it was the Yankees and "Mister Steinbrenner" who were presenting him with an ultimatum to move the team he had built from scratch. In what Bob Julian called "an honorable and very loyal act to his hometown," Nader again refused to abandon Oneonta in exchange for greater profitability elsewhere. As he explained it, "They asked me if I wanted to go to Staten Island, would I want to move my club to Staten Island. At that time I'm 81 or 82 years old. Why the hell would I want to go to Staten Island? I've lived in Oneonta all of my life, all of my roots are here. And so, no, I don't want to move to Staten Island."[19]

The story broke publicly in May 1998, four months after Mayor Giuliani's minor league bombshell announcement in his January State of the City speech. After a Staten Island newspaper cited an unnamed City Hall source in a report that the Oneonta Yankees were relocating to Staten Island, Nader issued a firm denial and promised "the O-Yanks are not going to move." Further discussions with the Yankees organization resulted in "verbal assurances" of a new plan: the Oneonta team would maintain its Yankees affiliation while another team would move to Staten Island as the organization's second NY-PL affiliate.[20] Those turned out to be empty promises, however. In September, just after the Oneonta Yankees were crowned league champions for the twelfth time in Nader's tenure, the club received official notification that the Yankees were severing their connection. "We are too small an area," Nader explained to a local Binghamton newspaper. "They are going to go where they have corporate dollars and tax dollars to help the team. There was nothing any of us could do."[21]

Because the change was mandated by the parent organization and not the minor league team owners themselves, the NY-PL was bound by the terms of baseball's PBA to find a new major league partner for Oneonta. Several other teams made offers, and Nader soon chose to hook up with the Detroit Tigers organization out of familiarity with their operations and respect for their integrity. He even had a final conciliatory phone call with George Steinbrenner, who told him he would enjoy working with the Tigers and offered to make personal phone calls to the Tigers organization on Nader's behalf to smooth things over during the transition. Over the next few years the O-Tigers developed a good relationship with their new parent club, who renewed their affiliation several times on generous terms. Although Nader did not bear a grudge against his former team, which he had once called "a relationship made in heaven," he did notice the difference.

> Has it affected us? Well, obviously we're New York State, and the Yankees are the Yankees. The Yankee name is a premium name, let's face it, you know? But from a personnel standpoint, a personality standpoint, [the Tigers are] people of integrity. They're good. They've provided me with a good, competitive team. Am I unhappy with the Tigers? No. Would I rather be with the Yankees? Hell, yes! I'm a Yankee fan, number one. But being New York State, I get some residual benefits being with the Yankees.[22]

Despite their initial hesitation, the Yankees quickly moved on from Sam Nader and Oneonta just as the Mets had from Bill Gladstone and Pittsfield. But as the minor league plans neared fruition in late 1998, both teams still faced several dilemmas. Which NY-PL teams would they be relocating to New York City, and how would their organizations ensure that they retained maximum control? Where would their new stadiums be constructed? With the mayor's help, could they overcome political hurdles and opposition without encountering years of delay? Once they did bring in the teams and complete the facilities, would anyone actually come to the games? Always the more efficient of the two baseball organizations, the Yankees would be the first to begin addressing these questions.

CHAPTER SIX

WE ARE COMMITTED TO
NOBODY EXCEPT WATERTOWN

In April 1998, Mayor Giuliani formally presented his proposed annual budget for fiscal year 1998–1999 to the New York City Council. Ordinarily a Republican mayor could expect a very hostile reception from a body dominated by entrenched Democrats. This year was no exception, despite the fact that the mayor was in an enviable position with an unprecedented $2 billion budget surplus and high popularity ratings off his landslide reelection victory the previous November. And so his $34 billion Executive Budget touched off a firestorm of criticism and months of public wrangling with the City Council, which soon passed a rival budget of its own that was promptly vetoed by the mayor. Besides the issues of tax and spending cuts that regularly caused party conflict, Giuliani's proposal sparked even more heated debate over its allocation of nearly $600 million for publicly funded baseball stadiums for the Yankees and Mets. As a citywide furor erupted over what *New York Daily News* columnist Bob Liff called "Giuliani's edifice complex," the main point of contention was the administration's plan to move the Yankees out of the Bronx. For several years the mayor and his administration had been fixated on building a new stadium for the team on Manhattan's West Side, above the underutilized Hudson Yards tract where Long Island Railroad train cars were stored. Throughout the spring and summer of 1998, the mayor and City Council Speaker Peter Vallone argued and grandstanded before the local press over the Yankee Stadium issue, with other politicians joining in the fray. Eventually their battle culminated in a lengthy council effort to put the matter to a public voter referendum, with Mayor Giuliani counterpunching with the appointment of a Charter Revision Commission for the singular purpose of preventing that from coming to pass.[1]

Almost unnoticed was the $40 million piece of the stadium budget which was earmarked for a pair of minor league stadiums in the outer boroughs. Half of that money was dedicated to the Mets' planned facility in Coney Island, which had received mostly positive media attention several months earlier. The other half was intended to build a new minor league ballpark for the Yankees in Staten Island, a project that went generally overlooked in the brouhaha over the team's major league plans. That $20 million expenditure would continue to slip beneath the radar for the next several years, even as it eventually more than tripled to over $70 million and far surpassed the costs of its counterpart in Brooklyn. With little public scrutiny or attention, the Yankees had free rein to pursue their Staten Island plans with impunity.

At the time, most of the issues relating to the construction of the facility itself were beyond the control or concern of the team. Down the road the Yankees would have significant input into the Staten Island stadium's design and amenities. But the early planning stages were required to follow the established processes for publicly funded projects of this scale, which meant that the preliminary steps would be shepherded by the Offices of the Mayor and Borough President Guy Molinari. They would be the ones to frame the numbers and the public narrative that would justify the budget allocations, legislative actions, and contractual arrangements involved in the stadium's construction. They would control the process of officially choosing and reviewing a final list of sites for consideration and presenting them to the appropriate committees and municipal bodies. It would be their administrative staff who would solicit corporate interest in purchasing naming rights for the finished ballpark, another important source of revenue. All the Yankees had to do publicly was maintain a guarded enthusiasm for housing one of their minor league affiliates in a brand-new stadium that was not costing them a penny of their own money.

The immediate question that did face the organization regarded which minor league team would play in the new stadium. It was only a few short weeks following the mayor's budget announcement that Oneonta Yankees owner Sam Nader went public with the news that his team would not move to Staten Island, contrary to the rumors previously leaked by Mayor Giuliani's staff. The Oneonta club had been a perfect candidate for the move, given the limitations of its tiny market and antiquated facilities and its lengthy history within the Yankees organization. Its relocation would also have fit right into the NY-PL's survival plan crafted by Bob Julian and embraced by several of the newer team owners. But Nader's loyalty to his community had trumped both his own economic self-interest and even his lifelong allegiance to "Mister Steinbrenner" and his team, and so the O-Yanks would not become the Staten Island Yankees.

Fortunately and by design, the Yankees already had a different NY-PL team in mind for the five boroughs: the club then known as the Watertown Indians. The city of Watertown, New York, was a relatively recent entry into the league. Situated far to the north in the Thousand Islands region on the shores of Lake Ontario, Watertown was a small-market community with fewer than 30,000 residents. After losing its first professional baseball franchise back in 1951, the city had reentered the minor leagues thirty-plus years later in 1983 when the Pittsburgh Pirates situated a NY-PL team there. After a few moderately successful but declining years in terms of attendance, the Watertown Pirates were bought in 1987 for $125,000 by a pair of New York City investors, sports psychologist Dr. Eric Margenau and literary agent Jay Acton. Almost immediately the new absentee owners engaged in a vicious war of words with the city and the local press over what they considered substandard stadium facilities at Watertown's Duffy Fairgrounds. Margenau in particular made several cutting public statements excoriating Watertown and its elected officials, displaying none of the tact or sensitivity that he espoused in his self-help book *Sports Without Pressure*. Eventually Margenau ferried his team across the lake to Welland, Ontario, and a new $3 million sports complex, spitting "I'll do everything I can to keep baseball from being successful in Watertown" on his way out of town. Less than a year later in 1990, Margenau and Acton showed their true carpetbagger colors when they cashed out their Welland Pirates franchise along with their stake in the South Bend (Indiana) White Sox as part of a two-team $4 million sale to CBS entertainment executive Alan Levin. The two New Yorkers seemed quite satisfied with the excellent rate of return on their original $570,000 investment three years before. In the meantime, Watertown's mayor and City Council voted to spend $400,000 to renovate their decrepit ballpark, and with the help of League President Leo Pinckney they convinced the Cleveland Indians to situate a replacement NY-PL affiliate in their city. The new team would have local ownership, hopefully ensuring a longer and more successful tenure than that of the Pirates franchise.[2]

It was not long before the honeymoon period ended for the new Watertown Indians. After an initial burst of local support, attendance dwindled once again to one of the lowest levels in the NY-PL. Although the Duffy Fairgrounds did receive the makeover that had been promised, the city was now dunning the team for more than $100,000 in cost over-runs that exceeded the city's official allocation of $400,000. Furthermore, despite the renovations the facility was widely considered one of the worst in all of the minor leagues. By 1992 the situation was reaching a crisis level. The new Professional Baseball Agreement (PBA) standards for minor league facilities demanded an estimated investment of up to $4 million in a new stadium, money that the city simply did not have. Meanwhile, team owners told the city and the *Watertown Daily Times* that they were already operating at a loss of $32,000 per year. After limping through another season, in 1993 the besieged owners began seeking buyers for the club. They scheduled their decision carefully to coincide with the expiration of their lease on the Duffy Fairgrounds, since that agreement included a codicil that the owners would have to split any sale proceeds during the lease term with the city. Their timing was especially serendipitous when the New York State Legislature authorized a generous matching funds plan for minor league stadiums that same year. The injection of hundreds of thousands of dollars in state funding meant a dramatic improvement in Watertown's field conditions and amenities, and so the local owners reversed course and kept the team operating under the status quo for another two years.[3]

In 1995 the Indians were crowned champions of the NY-PL. This would be the only championship in Watertown's decades-long history in professional baseball and came at the end of their third straight year atop the league's Pinckney Division. But before the season was even half over, the owners were again soliciting offers from prospective buyers. Local support had not noticeably improved despite the expensive ballpark overhaul and on-field success, NY-PL franchise valuations had never been higher, and the team's excellent performance would only enhance its worth to potential suitors. So the owners were looking to get out, and by season's end they had five candidates that they soon narrowed down to three finalists. Aside from a local fan group calling themselves the Team for Retaining Indians Baseball for Evermore (TRIBE, based on the Indians' well-known fan nickname), the other buyers were from out of state and not seeking the same local discount that TRIBE was requesting. After paying only $150,000 for the team six years earlier, the sixteen ownership group members of Jefferson County Community Baseball Inc. were now looking at a much higher payday if they accepted one of the offers from the out-of-towners. Within two months that is exactly what they did. In November 1995 they sold the team for approximately $1.1 million to a pair of New Yorkers, father and son Stan and Josh Getzler.[4]

Stanley Getzler was born in 1929 in the Bronx not far from Yankee Stadium, the fabled "House That Ruth Built." As he later recalled, "Growing up in the Bronx, walking around Kingsbridge Road, I don't know of anybody who thought about being an owner of a baseball team. You thought about being a dentist, a lawyer." After graduating from the Bronx High School of Science and New York University, followed by a stint in the Army Counterintelligence Corps in the Far East, Stan was working as a junior financial executive when he married Phyllis Resnick from Bradley Beach, New Jersey, in 1961. Phyllis was a computer programmer and mathematician, who would later serve as a tenured math professor at City College of New York for decades before keeping the books for the minor league baseball team he had never dreamed of owning. Instead of dentistry or law he launched a successful career in finance, and by the late 1960s Stan Getzler owned his own lucrative securities firm and a seat on the New York Stock Exchange. As an active member of the Orthodox Jewish community on Manhattan's Upper West Side, he also helped create the Lincoln Square Synagogue and engineered its growth and eventual purchase of a permanent building for more than $1.2 million.[5]

By the early 1990s Stan was ready to retire from running his financial services firm. The natural candidate to replace him was his son Josh Getzler. Josh had grown up in his parents' Upper West Side home, celebrating every major life event at Lincoln Square Synagogue from his bris (circumcision) to his Bar Mitzvah to his premarital bachelor send-off known as an *aufruf*. Armed with a bachelor's degree from the University of Pennsylvania (his mother's alma mater) and soon to receive an MBA from Columbia University Business School, he seemed like a perfect fit to take over the family business. But Josh had already told his father that he did not wish to follow in his footsteps at the stock exchange, and so Stan put the firm on the block, leased out his seat on the exchange—his wife had suggested holding off on selling it outright, just in case his retirement turned out to be temporary—and began to look for a new business venture to capture his interest. As Stan later told the *New York Post*, "I decided to sell the business and start looking for something to do, eventually making a list. My next career, I decided, would have nothing to do with Wall Street, had to be connected with something I understood, had to have a decent ROI [return on investment] and had to aid the public good in some way."[6]

In 1993 Stan Getzler decided that his postretirement future lay in becoming a minor league baseball team owner. The rising values and sale prices of franchises provided exactly the sort of profitable ROI that he was seeking, and many of his peers in the New York finance world were getting in on the action. Stan later said he became hooked by the possibility after reading numerous newspaper and magazine articles about baseball owners in his quest for new opportunities. His relentlessly creative businessman's mind would not allow him to ignore the siren call of team ownership, and so he began exploring the possibilities. His original plan was to secure a stadium deal in Asbury Park along the Jersey Shore, where his family owned a summer home, and then find a team to relocate there. He was disabused of that notion by several months of further research as well as networking efforts among other minor league owners. Through mutual acquaintances in financial and Jewish philanthropic circles, he met with Marvin Goldklang of the Yankees and Hudson Valley Renegades. Then he arranged a meeting with Barry Gordon, who was in the process of bringing the NY-PL Cardinals franchise to New Jersey. These more experienced multiteam owners showed him the error of his ways. As Josh Getzler later recalled, "We spent about two years working on that angle in the absolute wrong direction, the opposite way from how we should have gone. Because we didn't understand that it was not about the location initially, it was about securing a team."[7]

In December 1994 Stan Getzler attended the annual Baseball Winter Meetings in Dallas. Accompanying him was his son Josh, a twenty-seven-year-old baseball nut with a newly earned master's degree in business administration. For four days father and son sat on a couch in the hotel lobby, rubbing elbows with owners and league personnel and indicating their interest in purchasing a team. Their efforts paid off several months later, when they heard from one of their NY-PL contacts that the Watertown Indians were entering the open market. Soon the Getzlers were formally contacted by Sports Franchises Inc., a prosaically named consulting firm run by former Major League Baseball commissioner Bowie Kuhn. Kuhn and company had been hired by the current Watertown owners to solicit offers from prospective buyers, and they had heard that the Getzler family might be interested. Stan responded in the affirmative. A few months and

$1.1 million later, the Getzlers were the sole owners of the Watertown Indians.[8]

As the deal went through laborious delays throughout the winter months between December 1995 and February 1996, the nascent team owners attempted to build the foundations of a good relationship with their neighbors and patrons in Watertown. Josh Getzler immediately found and moved into a new apartment in the city as he prepared to take the reins as the club's team president and chief operating officer. In one of his first interviews with the local press the younger Getzler won approval when he promised "close partnerships with every element of the city" and promised "to do some real good for the city," a far cry from the hostile attitude displayed by previous owner Eric Margenau seven years earlier. Josh also committed right away to keeping on General Manager Jack Tracz and his front office staff, maintaining continuity for the immediate future. He even found some words of praise for the Duffy Fairgrounds, which he called "a nice little stadium," and reached out to his former rivals among the would-be local investors of TRIBE who vowed to continue supporting the team. Although the sale dragged on due to the complexities of dealing with sixteen different ownership stakeholders and their attorneys—"we're just hearing from lawyers, lawyers, lawyers," groused Stan Getzler—it was clear to all parties that it would eventually go through. In the meantime father and son trusted their attorney Lonn Trost, soon to be chief operating officer of the New York Yankees organization. During the interim they cemented their place and status in their new league, attending minor league ownership meetings at the December 1995 Winter Meetings in Los Angeles and being formally introduced to the rest of the NY-PL owners at a February 1996 meeting in Washington, DC. As Stan Getzler moved toward purchasing a home in Watertown for the upcoming summer baseball season, there was no doubt that the Getzlers were settling in and taking charge.[9]

From the outset the new out-of-town owners put the city of Watertown on notice. At his very first press conference, Josh Getzler would only guarantee that the team would remain in the city through 1998 when its lease on the Duffy Fairgrounds would expire. This had in fact been a deciding factor in the prior group's decision to sell them their team. In a prepared statement, Josh now emphasized that he and his father would not make any promises to stay in Watertown for the long run. "Our commitment to stay in Watertown is through 1998, with a penalty if we leave before 2000. We will continuously evaluate our situation as we go along. [This] proviso . . . is not an extension of the lease, nor is it a commitment of any kind to remain in Watertown after 1998. It is simply a statement of good faith and economic incentive for us to make the team succeed in Watertown." He was also very open about his family's original intent to relocate the team without playing even a single season in Watertown. "When we first thought about becoming involved with minor league baseball, it was with the intent of bringing baseball to New Jersey, where we have a home. But we have been rebuffed at every turn in New Jersey, and we have no deal with anyone in New Jersey for a stadium to be built for us. Nobody is committed to us in New Jersey or anywhere, and we are committed to nobody except for the City of Watertown." He went on to warn that the team would remain only as long as the city lived up to its responsibilities to maintain the playing facilities up to minor league standards and as long as the fans improved turnout for the games. The average ticket sales of 1,369 per game had been good enough for only tenth place out of fourteen teams in 1995, despite the team's winning the League Championship that year. "We understand coming in that it's a reticent market," he said, adding "we realize very well that a partnership is a two-way street." He promised to begin that partnership in good faith but made it very clear that the next few years would be crucial to the team's future in Watertown. For his part, Stan Getzler called the acquisition of the team "a dream."[10]

The dream did not last long before reality began to intrude. As their first season approached, the Getzlers expended a great deal of enthusiasm, energy, and money on their new investment. A new sound system and 26' x 28' electronic scoreboard were installed, paid for in part by a sponsorship from the Pepsi company. Giveaway nights were scheduled where fans could win game-worn jerseys and a real diamond worth $2,000. The team focused on reaching young fans, sponsoring more than twenty local youth baseball teams and offering a kids' group called the Indians Knothole Gang that offered discounted tickets and merchandise. They even created a new polar bear mascot named Blizzard, all part of the Getzlers' commitment "to put 110 percent of ourselves into the venture." On Opening Day on Sunday, June 16, 1996, they filled up the ballpark. On the following evening, Monday, June 17, they drew only 282 fans, basically just their small number of season-ticket holders. Despite all of their efforts attendance fell by 18 percent in 1996 to only 1,123 per game, placing the League Champion Watertown Indians second-to-last in the NY-PL. Their biggest promotional nights did not draw even 1,000 fans, with "Shirt Off Our Back Night" bringing in only 852 customers. And many were not even paying customers, as the previous owners had established a practice of distributing coupons for free game tickets all over town. Since dismal attendance numbers had been the main factor that prompted the recent sale of the team to the Getzlers, it was small wonder that the *Watertown Daily Times* commented in August that "few things are certain about the Indians' long-term future." Josh Getzler's only response was to say, "I think we will do even better next year."[11]

Before the next season was even underway, reports began to surface that the Getzlers might relocate the team. In April 1997 the Associated Press reported that they were investigating a possible move to New Jersey, a story that the Getzlers did not immediately refute because it broke on a Friday evening when their Orthodox Jewish family did not answer the phone. Once the Sabbath ended that Saturday night, Stan Getzler clarified that he often fielded calls from other communities but that "there is nothing even remotely resembling a deal." That lukewarm denial was less than reassuring in light of several stories that had appeared in New Jersey newspapers two months prior. In a February interview with the *Asbury Park Press*, Josh Getzler openly acknowledged that the team was exploring the possibility of a move to a proposed $12–$14 million stadium in the town of Lakewood, New Jersey. "What's attractive is [the Lakewood] location, the idea of having a state-of-the-art stadium, being in an area where we all have lived, and the way we have been treated by the government in Lakewood," he explained. The articles emphasized his childhood roots in nearby Long Branch at the family's summer home and even included detailed plans for kosher concession stands at the new stadium "in a nod to the township's sizable Orthodox Jewish population." As he had been since his arrival in Watertown less than eighteen months earlier, the young team president was very frank about the challenges of keeping his team there, as the article observed:

> Getzler described the Watertown metropolitan area as a "small but enthusiastic" market of about 50,000 residents. The Indians average around 1,200 fans a game paying as little as a dollar to get in to the 3,000-seat park. Contrast that with a 7,500-seat stadium in Lakewood, where fans would pay between $4 and $8 for tickets, and it quickly becomes apparent why the Getzlers are looking to New Jersey as their club's future home

base. "It's difficult for [a Watertown team] to survive in an era where a single-A franchise can look to areas like Lakewood, where you have 1 million people living within a half-hour, [Getzler] said. "They're talking about a 7,500-seat stadium, and we would expect to fill it. It's what got us excited about baseball in the first place."[12]

Despite the Getzlers' hopes, the Watertown Indians did not in fact "do even better" in the 1997 season. With a per-game average of 1,073 fans the team was dead last in the NY-PL, behind even perennial also-rans like Utica and Oneonta. This lack of enthusiasm persisted despite an increased number of giveaway events and $1 ticket coupons, a public relations blitz that included numerous news articles and editorials, a sports exhibit at the local Historical Society, school visits by Josh Getzler to drum up membership in the Knothole Gang, and community outreach by members of TRIBE (who called themselves the "sleeping giant" of Watertown baseball). The team's front office frequently alluded to how much money the team was losing, particularly in light of the baseball expenses transferred to local franchises by the terms of the PBA. As the Getzlers proceeded into their second off-season, the last before their lease with Watertown was due to expire in 1998, rumors intensified that they would soon move the team. In addition to offers from multiple communities in New Jersey, they were also contacted by interested parties from the Albany Capital region and an investment group from Concord, New Hampshire. Although Stan Getzler had ended the season by reiterating that he did not intend to leave Watertown, the events of subsequent months suggested otherwise.[13]

The onset of the following season in June 1998 brought more of the same, with relocation rumors swirling even as the team increased the number and magnitude of its promotional nights. After two straight years of losing money, the Getzlers' public statements had become bleaker and less reassuring. In an interview conducted at the first 1998 game he attended (after missing Friday's season opener due to Sabbath restrictions), Stan Getzler expressed a fairly fatalistic outlook to *Watertown Daily Times* writer Rob Oatman:

> I did say from the beginning that if there is something to talk about, we will, and I hold to that. If there comes a time, be it during the season, before the season, after the season, that

we need to make an announcement concerning the future of the team—if we are intending to move—we will make that. Whenever it happens . . .

We're in a situation, economically, where the smaller-market clubs, such as Watertown, definitely are behind the 8-ball in minor league baseball. I'm not near alone [in the problem]. You can call the ownership in Auburn and Batavia and Jamestown and Oneonta and Utica, and many places down south and in the Midwest.

Nevertheless, the team had already opened up negotiations with the city on terms for a new lease as it kept its options open. In a tepid attempt at reassurance Stan added, "It is not hopeless for Watertown," adding "we are not necessarily lame-duck."[14]

But as the 1998 season wound down in September, reports began to surface that the Getzlers were already in talks to switch their team affiliation to from the Indians to the New York Yankees and move to Staten Island. Since Sam Nader's public refusal to relocate his team in May, the Yankees had been looking for a new affiliate to settle in Mayor Giuliani's proposed $20+ million stadium in New York City's "forgotten borough." It was an open secret that the NY-PL had the inside track on both the Staten Island and Brooklyn franchise rights, as the mayor and his people had been saying so since his second inauguration in January. NY-PL president Bob Julian and several of the league's owners were very much in favor of seizing this once-in-a-lifetime opportunity to enter such a major market, which would greatly increase the profile of their entire league. And the mayor and Guy Molinari were pressing the Yankees to secure an affiliate to play in the new stadium that was already in its active planning stages. According to Josh Getzler it was around this time that Yankees executive Lonn Trost, who had represented the family as their lawyer when they bought the Watertown team several years earlier, approached them.

Lonn called and said, "you guys are dying up there," and he knew us well and he knew where we had come from, and that we would love to be back in the City. He said "we're trying to make a deal that will be complicated, between the Yankees, the Mets, the Mayor, and the Borough Presidents of Staten Island and Brooklyn. They all want to bring a Yankee and Met affiliate to [New York City], where the Mets affiliate would be in Brooklyn and the Yankees affiliate would be in Staten Island. There are a lot of moving parts and there are many ways that might not work, but if it did work, it could be really interesting. It would be good for the city, good for the politicians, a good-for-everybody project."

They said having two teams in New York City would obviously be a significant improvement over Pittsfield and Oneonta in terms of the size of the facilities and the potential attendance. That would raise the value of all the teams, and it would raise the level of the New York-Penn League considerably. [The teams] would also be under the watchful eyes of the Major League franchises, who would have more players do rehab assignments there. And then the thing that was the most tantalizing for us was to be able to do cross-promotions and be able to have add-ons to merchandise orders, to have pocket schedules in Yankee Stadium and to have ads on the jumbo vision.[15]

The Getzlers negotiated their Yankees deal for several months before the media got wind of their intentions that September. Sam Nader later remarked, "When the move was made to get Staten Island, the Watertown club eagerly grabbed the bait. I think it was kind of prearranged." Even as the Getzlers had flirted away the 1997–1998 off-season with Lakewood, Cape May, and Albany, they may have had the Staten Island deal in their back pocket.[16] But the move was just one part of a package deal that sold 49 percent of the team's ownership to George Steinbrenner and the New York Yankees. Like Fred Wilpon, Steinbrenner was unwilling to allow a minor league offshoot of his beloved Yankees play within his home territory without some significant measure of team control. Unlike Bill Gladstone of Pittsfield, the Getzlers were totally amenable to such an arrangement. As they soon found out, however, negotiating with the Yankees was very different from any negotiations they had ever conducted before.

It was 1998. We were sitting in our office in the Duffy Dome, which was a double wide. It was me, my General Manager, my parents and my wife, all sitting in this small room. My General Manager smoked and so it was very smoky, just not a great place during the summer. We'd gotten to the point with the Steinbrenners where they had asked us what we wanted for 49% of the team.

My father and I spent two weeks working out numbers and thinking "OK, what's the actual amount?" They said, you tell us an offer and essentially "remember who you're talking to." So we crunch these numbers and we [calculate] the discount, and the value of moving, and what we've lost in Watertown, and think about what we need. So we're having a phone call with Hal, who was our liaison with the Steinbrenners and who I liked a lot, and I said the number.

Before it was out of my mouth, he said "you don't want me to take that to George," which is the best line in the world! You can't argue with that, right? And I say, "excuse me," and I put my hand over the phone and say, "he says I don't want him to take that to George." And everyone in the room is looking at me, so I get back on and I say "OK, what were you thinking?" And he gave me 20% of that number.

I put my hand back over the phone again, and our general manager Jeff Dumas says, "get season tickets and make them good." So I negotiated a little bit and asked for a little bit more, and he agreed to a little bit more, but not much more. Then I said "I want eight season tickets, good ones, to the Yankees. Including playoffs."

He said, "we'll give you two." I said "four" and he agreed, so we got four seats, two rows behind the Yankee dugout. They turned out to be great seats and were worth more than we got for the team.

From that moment on, whenever somebody says something that I don't want to hear, I say "you don't want me to take that to George, right?"[17]

The NY-PL season was scheduled to end with a Championship Series between the Auburn Doubledays and the Oneonta Yankees on September 8–10, 1998. Those games never took place, as they were cancelled in the wake of a massive Labor Day storm that ripped through central New York State with wind gusts of 115 miles per hour on September 7. Precluded from postponing the series by the terms of the PBA—yet another reason for resentment among NY-PL clubs whose towns were currently facing an officially declared state of emergency—the Doubledays and O-Yanks were crowned league co-champions without ever playing an inning of their deciding contest. One week later on September 17, 1998, the New York Yankees unceremoniously declined to renew their affiliation with Oneonta and Sam Nader after thirty-two years. That announcement had barely been made when the news broke that the Indians organization would no longer be affiliated with Watertown and that the Getzlers had instead signed on with the Yankees as their new NY-PL affiliate. Counting every penny as their tenure upstate wound down, the club sold its leftover Watertown Indians game uniforms to a local semipro team at a cut-rate price. Then, as their three-year stadium lease neared its official end on October 31, the Getzlers negotiated a temporary agreement to rent the Duffy Fairgrounds on a month-by-month basis while they worked out their plans for the future. The city was desperate to retain any revenue at all from the facility, since Watertown was still $900,000 in debt on the many facility upgrades performed just a few years earlier. So they signed the monthly deal proposed by the Getzlers, but almost no one in town thought it would last long.[18]

As it turned out, the stopgap lease arrangement only lasted a few short months. In early January 1999 Stan Getzler called Watertown City Manager Jerry Hiller to inform him that the team would be playing its upcoming season in Staten Island. Although many of the details had yet to be determined, Hiller told the local press, "I think the mood was that the inevitable is finalized." After seventeen years hosting professional baseball, the city was forced to face the fact that this time it was likely gone for good. "You just have to arrive at the conclusion that we're just not a baseball community," one city councilman sighed in defeat. Stan Getzler agreed, saying, "The fans in Watertown were sensational, there just weren't enough of them." It was hard to argue, given the years of dwindling fan interest and attendance at the Duffy Fairgrounds. Saddled with nearly a million dollars in facility debt and bereft of a team, Watertown watched the Getzlers leave first, followed within the next several weeks by the contents of their stadium front office. Baseball's departure was mourned by only a handful of die-hard fans and perhaps the 515 young members of the Knothole Gang. In the absence of a team to call their own, local residents of Jefferson and St. Lawrence counties easily lapsed back into what *Newsweek* magazine had recently identified as their "high apathy" toward baseball. As Watertown's mayor Jeffrey Graham explained the following summer, "I like baseball and it was a nice atmosphere, but just the prospect of going out and sitting there for three hours didn't interest me. I didn't go."[19]

Figure 6.1. From left: Guy Molinari, Mayor Rudolph Giuliani, Josh Getzler, and Stan Getzler, January 1999. Photo credit: New York City Municipal Archives.

In contrast, the reception awaiting the Getzlers in Staten Island was rapturous. Interest in the team was high, as the New York Yankees were coming off a historic 114-win regular season and their twenty-fourth World Championship, their second in the past three years. Yankee fan-in-chief Rudy Giuliani was also spreading the word about the incoming minor league franchise and drumming up local attention.

Once they reached the point of selling tickets, they were delighted to discover that sales were brisk and far outpaced the disinterest they had encountered in Watertown. In an interview with the *New York Times*, Stan Getzler marveled, "To say that this is a dream for me, who could dream this? It is a wonderful thing for us." To the *Staten Island Advance*, his team's new hometown paper, he said, "Whoever dreamed of owning a minor league ballclub on Staten Island? You can't dream that. It's beyond dreams. It's just super to be here." Just four years earlier Stan had told a *Watertown Daily Times* reporter that it had been his family's dream to keep baseball alive in that city, 325 miles to the north of Staten Island.

The Getzlers' dreams had changed and grown since 1995, and now they were tantalizingly close to fruition. The Staten Island Yankees had built-in fan support, powerful political allies, and access to the resources available to the most successful and influential franchise in professional baseball. Now all they needed was a stadium where they could play their games.[20]

CHAPTER SEVEN

IT WILL BE GREAT FOR STATEN ISLAND

The idea of situating a minor league baseball team in a new stadium in Staten Island likely originated with the borough's president, Guy Molinari. Born in Manhattan but raised in Staten Island after his family moved there in 1929, Gaetano "Guy" Molinari was the son of "Fighting Bob" Molinari, who dubiously claimed to be the first Italian immigrant to serve in the New York State Assembly. The young Staten Islander graduated from college and law school before serving in a combat unit during the Korean War, and in the late 1950s he returned to his home borough and settled down as a husband and father with a thriving real estate practice. Over the next two decades he parlayed his father's political connections and his own growing local influence into a powerful role within Staten Island's Republican party, a conservative bastion within overwhelmingly liberal New York City. In the mid-1970s Molinari took a major political step forward by winning election to the New York State Assembly as a representative of Staten Island's South Shore, where his pugnacious and confrontational style won him many admirers among the area's working-class Irish- and Italian-American voters. After winning three straight elections to the Assembly, he ran for a seat in the United States House of Representatives and was elected to five consecutive terms in Congress. He stepped down in 1989, designating his daughter Susan Molinari (then representing Staten Island on New York's City Council) as his successor in a special election whose outcome was never in doubt. Molinari may have reached his peak when he became Staten Island's borough president from 1990 through 2001, serving as a confidante and mentor to Rudy Giuliani whose election he helped engineer. For more than a quarter-century Guy

Molinari was known as the political paterfamilias of a family referred to as the Staten Island Kennedys, with his power in the borough near absolute and rarely challenged.[1]

Although the position of borough president had been neutered and rendered mostly ceremonial by a 1989 New York City Charter revision, Molinari used his office to dispense patronage and call in political favors. From his enormous wood-paneled chambers in Staten Island Borough Hall he took steps to actualize his vision for the future of his borough. During his decade as president, Molinari negotiated the closing of the landfill at Fresh Kills, the largest garbage dump in the world and a lightning rod for Staten Islanders since its opening in 1948. He attracted investment and development dollars to the borough thanks to his close ties to Mayor Giuliani and New York State Governor George Pataki, which stood him in good stead once both Republicans ascended to power in the mid-1990s. In addition to run-of-the-mill patronage jobs, he also maneuvered his personal protégés into seats on the City Council, the State Legislature, the US Congress, and as judges and other elected officials.[2]

One of Molinari's most ardent goals was the development of the historic civic center neighborhood of St. George, located along the waterfront at the northeastern tip of the island and home to his Borough Hall offices. Originally known as New Brighton, the area was later renamed for nineteenth-century real estate developer George Law after he bought up most of its available waterfront property. Served by the Staten Island Ferry connection to Manhattan and three railway routes, St. George became densely developed and populated over the next several decades. But by the 1990s the neighborhood was plagued by soaring vacancy rates, a lack of new development, a falloff in railway usage, and depopulation as most of the borough's residents now lived along the South Shore and in central Staten Island. Once he was elected borough president, Molinari told anyone who would listen about his grandiose plans for what he called St. George Station on the North Shore. In plans that his office commissioned from a Staten Island–based architectural firm, Molinari laid out the building blocks of his vision to revitalize the area. The run-down Staten Island Ferry Terminal would be expanded and redesigned. New cultural institutions would be housed in St. George, including an institute for arts and sciences and a Lighthouse Museum. A pedestrian esplanade would attract strollers and tourists and businesses, offering unsurpassed views of lower Manhattan across New York Bay. And a state-of-the-art minor league baseball park would enhance the neighborhood and local revenues.[3]

In early 1998 the stars finally aligned for Guy Molinari's plans for Staten Island baseball and perhaps for St. George Station as well. At the very end of a busy New Year's Day, Mayor Giuliani traveled to the campus of the College of Staten Island to officially swear in Molinari to his fourth term as borough president. Late into the night the two men talked baseball, and two weeks later the mayor's Second Inaugural Address included a promise to construct "a Staten Island minor league baseball field." The mayor wasted no time before assembling an official task force to begin the process of achieving this goal, and he made sure to appoint Molinari to serve as its chair. Over the next three months the task force moved rapidly to assemble a list of possible sites for a Staten Island stadium, and by the end of April they had whittled down their choices to three finalists.[4]

The first was Homeport, a former US Navy Base approved by the Reagan administration that had been shuttered a mere four years after it opened due to military downsizing and budget cuts. Homeport was aggressively marketed to numerous developers and investors in subsequent years, but its abandoned barracks and remoteness from major highways and transportation access did little to recommend it. The strongest Homeport proposal prior to the idea of a baseball facility had come from the Circle Line Sightseeing Cruise company, which envisioned a retail and gaming plan that they claimed would yield direct returns to the city of over $93 million. Although the Circle Line argued that "gaming and baseball can co-exist" at Homeport, the stadium construction would preclude a portion of the retail project as well as a proposed motion picture production studio for the site. The grandiose nature of this multifaceted and possibly unrealistic plan ensured years of wrangling over all the details and necessary approvals, and ultimately none of it would ever come to fruition. As the Mayor's Office considered the Staten Island baseball stadium to be a high and immediate priority, the Homeport plan would not suffice.[5]

More attractive was an empty 120-acre parcel along the South Shore in Staten Island's Charleston section. In addition to its proximity to a thriving residential neighborhood, the site was also close to the Outerbridge Crossing and Goethals Bridge connections to New Jersey. It was hoped that a local professional baseball team might appeal to the many young families living nearby. The Charleston site was also already owned by the city and was entirely vacant, which would make it the cheapest of the three sites to develop. Furthermore, a developer had already secured the rights to constructing a retail and entertainment complex on another part of the parcel, and so a baseball stadium could complement these existing plans. Yet there was some concern that expanding the scope of the Charleston site plan to include a baseball stadium would cause unexpected delays in the required City Environmental Quality Review process, once again pushing off completion of the stadium that was so important to the mayor. There was also a more serious possible roadblock as the city was concerned that "significant community opposition is anticipated for any development project on this site." Although the Charleston site made the most economic sense, the task force evidently concluded that its negatives outweighed the potential positives.

In the end Guy Molinari's task force chose the third and final proposed option for the new stadium, the North Shore neighborhood of St. George. The group further suggested that the stadium should be part of a larger St. George Station rebuild as described in plans already commissioned by the borough president. From the outset, Molinari telegraphed this to the press the day he first announced the list of the three finalists. His remarks, specifically alluded to St. George's proximity to Manhattan baseball fans via the Staten Island Ferry and also lauded its "unique attractions, [especially] the waterfront facing the Manhattan skyline." Given Molinari's unwavering commitment to his St. George Station vision and the funding, time, and effort his office had invested into crafting his preexisting architectural plans, this did not come as a surprise to Staten Island's political cognoscenti.[6]

The chosen stadium site was directly along the waterfront, immediately adjacent to the Staten Island Ferry Terminal to the north. As Molinari noted, this location offered unimpeded views of Manhattan to the north and Brooklyn to the south. Its proximity to the terminal also guaranteed easy access to the largest intermodal transportation hub on Staten Island, which offered service via ferry, bus, rapid transit, van lines, and taxis as well as ample parking facilities for fans attending the games. However, the local streets and particularly the main arteries of Bay Street and Richmond Terrace were not very wide, which would likely lead to traffic congestion on game days. The typical weeknight game scheduling of a 7:00 p.m., starting time would also likely exacerbate the crush of ferry and public transit commuters returning home from work. But these concerns were deemed to be worthwhile tradeoffs for the benefits offered by the stadium and the future development of St. George Station that was sure to follow.[7]

Unfortunately the planned stadium site was not actually owned by New York City, which significantly complicated matters. Known as the "Chessie site" in city documents, the land was part of a larger parcel that was privately held by the former Chessie System, the onetime Chesapeake & Ohio Railway that was now part of the conglomerated CSX Transportation Corporation. The Chessie site in question was a fifty-two-acre site by the water's edge of New York Bay, with half of that acreage underwater. As for the remaining exposed half of the site, the New York City Department of City Planning described it as follows: "It contains a large commuter parking facility, the unused North Shore Rail Line (soon to be acquired by the city), deteriorating piers and nine, vacant, dilapidated and fire damaged structures formerly used as railroad storage facilities." In order to construct a ballpark, New York City would first have to purchase the site from CSX at market rates, then perform significant cleanup efforts to a site strewn with nearly a century of railroad detritus and possible industrial waste, and also resolve any shoreline issues where the stadium site met the waters of New York Bay. The total expenditures would far surpass the $20 million budget allocation for the ballpark itself, whose costs had not even been estimated yet. If Guy Molinari had been willing to situate the Staten Island Yankees' stadium on the municipally owned vacant site in Charleston, he'd have saved the city an awful lot of money and headaches.[8]

In mid-August 1998, as the Getzlers' Watertown Indians played out the string of their last season upstate, Mayor Giuliani announced that the New York City Economic Development Corporation (EDC) had signed a deal to buy the Chessie site from CSX for $13 million.[9] The mayor's press release mentioned the planned cultural center and Lighthouse Museum, and looked forward to "the opportunity to build on these cultural, civic and other projects to further promote economic growth in Staten Island." He also included a special commendation for Borough President Molinari, who stood behind him as he made the announcement. Although published reports did not take note, the purchase of the St. George railyard was one of several transactions that New York City completed with the CSX Corporation in the 1990s, all of them in Staten Island. In 1993 EDC bought the defunct Staten Island Railway, "a 15-mile stretch of overgrown, rusty tracks and ramshackle stations," from CSX for $10.3 million in the name of revitalizing the local economy. Five years later in May 1998, only a few months before the Chessie site purchase, New York State awarded a contract to create a new Staten Island Railroad to CSX in a deal that could potentially result in many millions of dollars in future profits. The arrangement allowed CSX to reap the financial rewards of selling their railroad to New York City and then circling back to get the rights to the future profits from rebuilding and operating the very same railroad they had just sold. This breathtaking deal was brokered by the chairperson of the House Railroad Subcommittee who just happened to be Guy's daughter, Republican representative Susan Molinari of Staten Island, characterized in the press as "an able broker and articulate voice for Republican solutions to problems facing railroads." The cozy relationship between the Molinari clan and CSX likely played some role in the decision to situate the ballpark on the St. George Chessie site, pouring another $13 million into the CSX coffers.[10]

The decision to purchase the site through EDC was another canny move by the experienced politicians. As opposed to land bought directly by the city, property acquired by EDC was exempt from the extensive and expansive approval process known as the Uniform Land Use Review Procedure (ULURP). This staged process, which could take up to two years to complete, included multiple levels of municipal review by the Department of City Planning, community boards, the City Council, and the Mayor's Office among others, as well as several rounds of public hearings. All of this, and any negative press or public pressure which might result from the ULURP, was neatly avoided by allowing EDC to take point on acquiring the St. George stadium site. Frank Chaney, the director of land use at Staten Island Borough Hall, dismissed any suggestion of impropriety. "It's not being done to circumvent or do an end run," he told a reporter from the *Staten Island Advance*. "It's being done to make sure we can close this deal and it doesn't slip through our fingers." And although stadium-building design firm HOK had been commissioned four months earlier by CSX to draft a stadium design for the site—which was promptly reviewed and approved informally by Borough President Molinari—local officials refused to confirm anything beyond a vague statement that they were "not sure if a stadium will end up at St. George."[11]

The haste and caginess of all the involved parties, as well as their pronounced reluctance to subject the deal to public scrutiny, may have stemmed from the serious environmental concerns hovering over the Chessie Railyard site like a greasy cloud. As the Department of City Planning had noted back in 1994, the surface of the parcel was strewn with abandoned structures and railroad miscellany that had accumulated over a century of railyard activities and several recent decades of disuse. Further toxins lay buried in the soil and sediments, which were suffused with chemicals and long-forgotten hazards. A breezy environmental study compiled in 1986 by hired Manhattan consultants Ethan C. Eldon Associates posited "that the detected concentrations were of no environmental health significance." Three years later in 1989, rival firm Fred C. Hart Associates was commissioned by the New York City Department of Environmental Protection to retest the same site, and they came to drastically different conclusions. Their results found "petroleum-impacted soils under a location where an aboveground fuel oil tank had been placed; elevated concentrations of semivolatile organic compounds and heavy metals; and hydrocarbon contamination in the ground water." These findings were corroborated in a third report by yet another consultant, Eder Associates, in 1995. Commissioned by CSX themselves in a failed effort to sell the site to New York City for $18 million—that deal was scuttled after CSX reportedly delivered a faulty legal title to the city—Eder's personnel found similar toxins as the Hart report, along with evidence of a leaking underground 550-gallon fuel storage tank, which they proceeded to seal off. While they neglected to include the tank's precise location in their own final report, they assured CSX that they had cleaned the tank and filled it with fresh soil to mitigate any further problems. But that sale had not gone through, and now EDC needed to do its own updated environmental impact study (EIS) to see what would need to be done to make the site suitable for a baseball stadium and public use.[12]

Over the next several months from August through November 1998, hired environmental consultants from the TRC Companies combed the site, took sediment and soil samples, completed borings, and monitored the ground water, all before the CSX deal was finalized. This raised hackles at CSX, whose lawyers served notice that "EDC has violated the contract by performing work on site without written request or approval from CSX." Throughout October and early November lawyers for both sides jockeyed with one another as CSX attempted to limit the scope of the environmental studies and EDC did its best to conduct full and thorough investigations. When TRC submitted its findings to EDC in mid-November, it became apparent why the sellers had been trying so hard to interfere with a complete EIS. Their findings included the following:

> low-level pesticides in the surface soils across the site; low level PCBs in the surface soils across the site; SVOCs consisting primarily PAHs in the soil and fill across the site; metals in the soil and fill across the site; petroleum contaminated soils and ground water in the north central portion of the site; elevated levels of several minerals in the site ground water; elevated

> PAHs [and] pesticides in the shoreline sediments near the central portions of the site; and elevated metals in the shoreline sediments primarily in the central portions of the site . . . Based on the identification of several other areas of concern at the site which have not been fully investigated and the historic nature of the site railyard operations, EDC should be aware that there may be other areas of contamination that may be discovered and have to be managed properly during future site development activities . . . At a minimum, TRC recommends that the petroleum contaminated soils and ground water in the north central portion of the site and contaminated shoreline sediments be remediated to levels acceptable to the NYSDEC and NYCDEP . . . We also recommend that provisions be made for the remediation of any other significantly contaminated materials (e.g. tanks, oily soils, drums) encountered during future site construction activities.

TRC had worked diligently to earn the $100,000 consulting fee they charged for their services, and their report revealed a host of problems at the site. Nevertheless, CSX's extended delaying tactics ultimately cost them nothing. All of the costs for environmental cleanup and remediation were passed on to EDC and New York City upon the transferal of the property, along with several years of unpaid property taxes. On Thanksgiving Eve 1998 EDC closed on the Chessie site purchase from CSX. Thirteen days later, EDC flipped the parcel and sold it to the City of New York for a purchase price of $19.37 million, well above the figure of $12.75 million that they'd paid CSX (who had knocked an extra $250,000 off their final asking price when the scope of the needed remediations became apparent). Throughout this process a great deal of money had changed hands between city agencies, railroad corporations, contractor and consultant firms, and lawyers. A pollutant-ridden eyesore along the waterfront was purchased at top dollar even after a range of careful and expensive studies revealed the presence of dangerous contamination, not that any of those findings were made public. The Staten Island stadium site was chosen based on political expediency, and by the end of 1998 the deal was done, the design approved, and the tenant identified and ready to move in. But many steps remained before construction could begin.[13]

On January 14, 1999, for the second straight year, Mayor Giuliani devoted part of his annual State of the City speech to the subject of minor league baseball.

Last year I promised that we would do something that I'm looking forward to when I retire: minor league baseball in New York City. My idea of retiring is to go to minor league baseball games in the morning and then to go see the Yankees and the Mets at night . . . Here are three agreements. I want to show you these three agreements. One agreement is an agreement with the Mets to use the site in Coney Island where we'll build a baseball field to put a minor league team. Another agreement is with the Yankees. This agreement is to put a minor league team in Staten Island. And that team will begin in May. They'll be playing at the College of Staten Island first for about two or three years while we build a field for them at the Ferry Terminal, while we build a tremendous development there. There's going to be a new terminal, there will be a museum, and there will be a baseball field where these young ballplayers will be trying to hit home runs in between the World Trade Center towers because the outfield faces the World Trade Center. And just think of the amount of business that this is going to bring from Wall Street. You can go by boat to the Yankee facility, to the Mets facility. Those teams hopefully could play each other. It would be great for Coney Island. It would be great for Staten Island.[14]

The mayor, Borough President Molinari, the City Council members, and the Yankees were all well aware of the bureaucratic procedures that would delay the Staten Island's stadium construction over the next year or more. When EDC sold the stadium site to New York City the previous December it had triggered the land use processes that were avoided previously during the parcel purchase from the CSX Corporation. Routing the initial buy through EDC had served its purpose, which was to speed the immediate acquisition of the land without delay. Once that was accomplished there was no further need for their involvement until after the stadium construction was completed, when EDC would return to take over the leasing and other economic arrangements associated with managing operational municipal facilities. The arduous processes associated with ULURP, the final environmental impact statement (FEIS), holding public meetings, and arranging governance votes were best delegated to the city agencies which existed to handle them. This would also preserve the illusion of governmental transparency and responsiveness, as the press and the public would be given the opportunity to express a modicum of input while the stadium project marched inexorably forward to its completion. Behind closed doors the city was already deep into negotiations over stadium lease agreements and arranging state permits to stabilize a deteriorating shoreline bulkhead adjacent to the stadium site. With the first stadium approval votes still months away, the project budget had already increased from $20 million to $29 million with much more to come.[15]

In the meantime, the newly rebranded Staten Island Yankees—"we were told that we were naming the team 'the Yankees' by Mr. Steinbrenner," Josh Getzler later explained—had games to play.[16] The Getzler family did not intend to sit out one or more seasons while they waited impatiently for their new stadium, and Mayor Giuliani was not willing to wait eighteen to thirty months to see them in action. With the team already packing up its supplies and selling its game-used uniforms back in Watertown, the Mayor's Office had already prepared to expedite the relocation by arranging temporary facilities until the St. George ballpark was completed. From the outset Mayor Giuliani (and likely Guy Molinari) determined that the team should play every one of its home games in Staten Island. Unlike the Mets' planned Brooklyn franchise, which would begin its tenure in a borrowed ballfield in a different borough, the minor league Yankees lacked the cachet of the legendary Brooklyn baseball heritage to create a groundswell of early publicity. They needed to build a local identity and presence right away, building their Staten Island fan base and heightening excitement and interest. Local support was also crucial in any upcoming battles over approvals and funding for their permanent stadium, since Molinari's Democratic rivals were already expressing some skepticism over its projected price tag. So it was important that a temporary facility be secured immediately and that it be in Staten Island.

The site chosen for interim play was the campus of the College of Staten Island (CSI), a senior college in the City University of New York (CUNY). Although the mayor regularly excoriated CUNY's educational shortcomings to the press (claiming that the university was "constantly serving all this failure and letting it play itself out year after year"), he was not averse to using its facilities for his own purposes now and then. CSI's Willowbrook campus was located conveniently adjacent to the Staten Island Expressway that bisected the island, allowing easy access for fans who could also take advantage of the plentiful campus parking facilities. The college's president, Marlene Springer, was happy to welcome in the baseball team along with crowds of Staten Islanders during the underutilized summer months, promoting the college among the residential families who provided the bulk of CSI's student body. She was also not averse to the Yankees' facility rental payments and ancillary revenues generated by their presence on campus, nor to Mayor Giuliani's promise that the city would provide extensive and expensive athletic field upgrades to accommodate the needs of their new minor league tenants. With the Getzlers also promising a major donation to the college's educational programs, Springer doubtless agreed with Stan Getzler's pronouncement "I think everybody's going to come out of this a big winner." The CSI stopgap plan was leaked to the press by the Getzlers as early as September 1998, the day after they announced that they would be moving to Staten Island. In a carefully orchestrated rollout, CUNY issued its own official press release in December, followed by an explicit reference in the mayor's State of the City Speech in January 1999. Two weeks later the Mayor's Office revealed that it had awarded "$3.5 million in contracts for bleachers, dugouts, field lights and other improvements at CSI's field," a mere formality in a process that had been meticulously planned and carried out over the previous several months.[17]

With cash in hand and armed in advance with a stadium design commissioned from HOK, the city and its hired contractors immediately began work on the new temporary stadium at CSI. The facility would feature 2,500 permanent seats along with another 2,000 seats in portable bleachers, lights for night games, sunken dugouts, and new dressing rooms, and the college would get to keep everything afterward. Only five months remained to get everything done before the season was set to begin on June 20, 1999, which was a major reason that the stadium was limited to so few permanent seats in its grandstand. By virtue of its small size the CSI facility would also circumvent New York City's zoning laws, which required special permits and a public review process to approve any stadium with more than 2,500 seats. The savvy experts at EDC who were overseeing construction knew they would save up to seven months or longer by limiting the size of CSI's permanent stadium and augmenting it with the additional temporary bleachers.[18] In the meantime the Staten Island Yankees' undersized front office was frantically hurrying to print and sell tickets and merchandise, market the team, and equip and open their new business office in the borough. As they discovered when the team's ticket windows opened in March, all that effort and haste would soon pay off.

The Getzlers' arrival in Staten Island could not possibly have gone any better if they had scripted it themselves. On March 1, 1999, tickets for the Staten Island Yankees' inaugural season went on sale at their temporary office in a nondescript strip mall called 2025 Plaza, prosaically named for its address along busy Richmond Avenue. Team General Manager Jeff Dumas, who had accompanied the Getzlers from Watertown, was flabbergasted to find a line of nearly one hundred ticket buyers waiting on the sidewalk before they even opened for the day at 10:00 a.m. Within the first hour the team had sold out all of its five hundred box seats for all thirty-eight home games at $10 per seat, a stark contrast to the thousands of unsold seats they had offered for only $1 in Watertown the year before. By 4:00 p.m. the team had sold more than half of its 1,500 season tickets. "We're thrilled," remarked Josh Getzler, as he and his father walked up and down the ticket line signing baseballs and chatting with new fans. After only three days of ticket sales they had sold 1,000 season tickets and many additional reserved seats. Before playing even a single inning in the 1999 season, the Getzlers had already outsold the entirety of their final year as the Watertown Indians at many times the price.[19]

By Opening Day the temporary stadium was completed, if barely. A sellout crowd of 4,547 packed the CSI ballpark to watch the team that the *Staten Island Advance* insisted on calling "Our Yanks." Mayor Giuliani and Borough President Molinari, who had been assigned the first two tickets issued by the team, both threw out ceremonial first pitches. The two men stayed for the entire game despite a rainy spell in the middle of the seventh inning. The fans cheered raucously for the team throughout, even after enduring pregame speeches by the politicians, the owners, and NY-PL President Bob Julian. While older fans rhapsodized about the family atmosphere and proximity to the game action, young attendees enthused about getting to meet the players and enjoyed the antics of mascot, Scooter the Holy Cow. Yankees colors and garb were on display everywhere in the stands. When the home team finished the game with a resounding 5–1 victory over Marv Goldklang's Hudson Valley Renegades, nearly everyone present agreed with the sentiments of Staten Islander Stan Ostapiak: "I think it's the greatest thing that's happened to Staten Island."[20]

Although interest flagged somewhat over the course of the summer, the inaugural season of the Staten Island Yankees was deemed an unqualified success. The unfinished and less-than-luxurious amenities at the CSI stadium were seen as quaint evocations of an earlier, simpler time when ballparks did not teem with distractions and loud noise. Attendance remained high throughout the season, with a final tally of 117,765 fans coming to see the seventh-place team. With an average just under 3,100 fans per home game, the Staten Island Yankees were attracting nearly four times the number they had the prior year in Watertown and all at a much more profitable price point. In the 2000 season the following year they continued to register strong attendance, although the total number fell off to a total of 102,697, or around 2,700 per game. This falloff came despite the team's on-field success with a .622 win-loss record, a playoff run that ended with a second-place finish as Championship runners-up, and a roster that boasted six future baseball major-leaguers including Taiwanese pitcher Chien-Ming Wang.[21]

Even though the ballpark was more than half-empty for the team's final game at CSI, neither the team's fans nor its owners seemed worried. Everyone had known from the beginning that the club's tenure at its first stadium was just temporary. After all, the team had only taken out a two-year lease at CSI in the first place. Fans were eagerly awaiting the chance to attend Staten Island Yankees games at their brand-new jewel of a stadium in St. George, even though it was not actually built yet. The 2001 season would be a spectacular success, they predicted. Ticket buyers would flock to the ballpark, drawn by the legendary Yankees name and the minor league club's recent on-field success. They would arrive by car or take the Staten Island Railway to the new Ballpark Station being built expressly for stadium-goers. Businessmen from lower Manhattan would pack the Staten Island Ferry to come see an entertaining ball game at the end of a long workday in the City. In Rudy Giuliani's oft-repeated words, in 2001 fans would be treated to the spectacle of ballplayers hitting home runs between the Twin Towers which rose up beyond the outfield fences that had yet to appear. Even as workers took down all signs of the Yankees' short tenure at CSI, the team's future seemed brighter than ever.[22]

Unlike the temporary facility at CSI, the ballpark at St. George would have to pass through a gauntlet of city agencies, committees, and public hearings before its official approval. With time ticking down on their tenure in office due to New York City's imposition of term limits, Mayor Giuliani and Borough President Molinari did not waste any time getting underway.

In March 1999, before the stadium's architectural plans had even been officially submitted by the HOK design team, the City Council passed a

Staten Island - CSX S...
Minor League Baseba...

Figure 7.1. Mayor Giuliani at the St. George Stadium site, February 1999. Photo credit: New York City Municipal Archives.

budget modification that shifted millions of dollars over to EDC "to pay for remediation and cleanup work at the [stadium's] 52-acre waterfront site." Several million would be allocated to stabilize the shoreline bulkhead where the stadium site would jut out into the waters of New York Harbor, as it was badly deteriorated. Several million more were designated "to eliminate contamination from the site," which was suffused with oil, chemicals, and refuse after a century of railroad use and neglect. Additional moneys would cover the bulldozing and contouring that would be necessary before the stadium could be built, and also the costs of the land review and environment impact review processes. All of this came in addition to the $29 million already allocated for constructing the stadium itself, whose design reportedly featured picturesque views of Manhattan and at least "10 to 20 luxury boxes" for the well-heeled fans and corporate sponsors the team expected to attract.[23]

A month later EDC held the first of several planned public hearings about the stadium, and it was well-attended by sixty Staten Islanders who were mostly St. George residents. After hearing from team co-owner Josh Getzler, senior EDC Vice President Robert Balder, and some local politicians, most of the crowd seemed supportive of the nascent ballpark plan. With the notable exception of senior citizen Helga Connor of Vine Street, who fretted about the loss of her neighborhood's residential character and an accompanying drop in her property values, the locals seemed chiefly concerned about traffic and parking issues. Although the presentation included a modified traffic plan as well as a new parking lot with spaces for 1,100 cars, several members of the neighborhood's St. George Civic Association expressed alarm at the prospect of game day crowding on the streets. "I can't revolve my life around a baseball game," complained one resident on behalf of many of those present. These concerns were taken seriously by EDC and the city administration, who would focus several studies on these issues over the next several months. When EDC's Final Environmental Impact Statement was released in October 1999, nearly 100 pages out of the 260-page report were devoted solely to traffic and transportation.[24]

Over the next few months the Giuliani administration put on a clinic in St. George demonstrating how to fast-track a high-priority major construction project. By July EDC and a host of city agencies had completed and scheduled the stadium's complex ULURP application for public review, a process that often took several years to complete. The sheaf of paperwork, which was forwarded to Staten Island's Community Board 1, bundled multiple documents, permits, arrangements, and requests into a single vote for public approval. This would allow the Community Board, followed by the borough president, the City Planning Commission, and finally the City Council to each vote for the entire package all at once in a single convenient session, hopefully without slowing down to examine each detailed application individually. These contents included the official selection of the St. George stadium site and permission for the city to purchase it from EDC; zoning amendments for the tall light towers and centerfield billboards that would obstruct views of the waterfront; the special permit to build a large sports stadium, which had been neatly avoided for the temporary Willowbrook stadium; a variety of construction permits that included the proposed public parking facility; and the team-friendly lease of the finished stadium to the Yankees. The ULURP application was immediately certified for public presentation, and a pair of public forums were hastily arranged to take place within a two-week span of the pro forma certification. Immediately after the end of the second meeting the Community Board would vote on the entire package, tying it up in a neat bow before sending it on to the next level and ultimately the City Council.[25]

As the accelerated approvals process hurtled forward in late July 1999, only one attempt was made to slow its progress. The voluminous ULURP documentation included some mention of soil contamination at the stadium site, referencing the findings from three environmental studies of the Chessie parcel conducted between 1989 and 1998. These were confirmed by new soil testing currently underway as part of the preparatory stages for planning the new stadium's foundation. Word of the presence of "toxic chemicals" and "poisonous substances" at the site was then leaked to the press by environmental lawyer Larry Shapiro, director of environmental programs at the crusading New York Public Interest Research Group. In a suggestive interview with the *New York Daily News*, Shapiro levied vague accusations that the city and state were hustling through a rushed second-rate cleanup process before proceeding to actual construction. "I think there's a lot of reason to be worried," he warned. "They run the risk of poisoning the next Rickey Henderson before he makes the major leagues." But the head of EDC brushed aside the criticisms as overblown, and a spokesman for the state Department of Environmental Conservation issued a terse statement that "none of this suggests cause for concern for the future use of the site." Lacking evidence that the official environmental reports were covering up any larger problem, no one questioned the official denials any further. At the public Community Board meeting the following week there were no questions and few statements about soil toxicity, with the exception of an EDC representative's terse assertion that "there is no serious environmental hazard on the site." In the October 1999 FEIS that came out subsequently, only 13 of more than 260 pages made any reference to environmental concerns and even then only in the mildest terms. As opposed to the more contentious issues of traffic and parking, there seemed to be virtually no public concern over toxic PCBs and chromium embedded in the soil of the former railyard.[26]

By the end of the summer the Staten Island Yankees were wrapping up a successful inaugural season at their temporary digs at the CSI campus in Willowbrook. In the meantime the ULURP public review process continued in St. George, where Staten Island City Councilman and Molinari rival Jerome X. O'Donovan made hay by raising the specter of parking congestion at every opportunity. O'Donovan refused to accept the placations of EDC and the City Planning Commission that ferry commuters would not be inconvenienced by stadium-goers. Instead he advocated for the purchase of an additional industrial site for parking use that happened to be nearby in his district of New Brighton: an abandoned gypsum plant that had once processed 500,000 tons of raw gypsum rock each year into wallboard, cement, and drywall. Undeterred by the added cost of purchasing and cleaning up this new parcel—which, unlike the Chessie railyard, had actually been designated as a toxically contaminated Superfund cleanup site—the councilman spent a few weeks on his own fruitless attempt to cash in on the St. George stadium project. Although O'Donovan's failed proposal made no headway at all, he continued to reiterate his parking concerns to the press and the irascible members of the St. George Civic Association. He also seemed downright gleeful when the news broke in late September that design and construction contracts issued for the stadium now totaled more than $40 million. O'Donovan, a Democrat, had been expressing skepticism regarding Mayor Giuliani's initial stadium price tag of $20 million ever since it had been announced the previous January. Each new announcement of cost overruns gave him a fresh chance to heckle the project, the mayor, and the Borough President's Office from the sideline.[27]

O'Donovan's next grandstanding opportunity came a few days later in early October, two months before he was to participate in the official City Council vote on approving the land-use terms needed for the new stadium. A letter of intent detailing the proposed stadium lease to the Yankees was leaked to the press by an anonymous source. The document, which contained business details that were only supposed to be accessible to "the Mayor's Office, the EDC and Staten Island Yankees," revealed that the Yankees' twenty-year minor league stadium lease was a sweetheart deal of epic proportions for the team. According to the terms being discussed, the city assumed all costs of stadium construction and would have use of the completed facility for twenty days each year, as well as one luxury box "reserved for their use at no charge." The city would also receive "an undetermined percentage of all ticket sales, luxury suites and tickets bought but not used," and an annual team contribution of $25,000 "to a sinking fund for capital repairs." For their part, the Staten Island Yankees would receive nearly all gameday parking revenues and 50 percent of the stadium's naming and signage rights, which might total hundreds of thousands of dollars each year. The letter did not detail any sharing arrangement for revenues from food concessions, suggesting that the team would keep most or all of the benefit for themselves from those highly lucrative sources.

In actuality, the lease being discussed behind the scenes was even more generous than the press knew or suspected. Back in October 1998, months before the mayor's public announcement of the Staten Island stadium plan, EDC and the Yankees organization were already formulating estimated and highly confidential projections for the lease terms. The two sides collaborated on several alternative models ranging from a 50/50 split of gross revenues after operation and maintenance costs to a 70/30 model where the Yankees kept the lion's share of the revenues. They also formulated scenarios where the Yankees would also keep 100 percent of all advertising revenues, which were estimated at $1.2 million per year including $950,000 in stadium naming rights. The most optimistic projection netted the city a total of approximately $6 million by the end of the first five years, while the most favorable deal for the Yankees side would reduce the city's intake to below $4 million in the same span. Either way, the options under consideration promised only a paltry direct return on the city's $40 million investment. The projections were also based on the Yankees' prediction that they would attract 5,000 fans to each game played in the 6,500-seat stadium, offering attractive seat packages that were bundled with tickets to see the major league team at Yankee Stadium in the Bronx. Yet despite their optimism regarding attendance, the Staten Island club hedged their bets as they negotiated their rent payments to the city just in case.[28]

The stadium's rent schedule did raise some eyebrows when it first appeared in the press, although the public's reaction to the news was negligible. According to the lease figures, if the Staten Island Yankees drew attendance figures of fewer than 125,000 per season—as they did in both the 1999 and 2000 seasons when they played their games at CSI—then they would pay no rent at all. Rental payments would only be triggered once the team managed to draw 3,290 fans, a little more than half of the stadium's 6,500 seating capacity, to each game. Once they reached that minimum attendance threshold of 125,000 their rent would increase on a sliding scale from $100,000 per year all the way up to a maximum of $510,000, reaching that top level only when they sold out nearly every one of their thirty-eight home games. A final clause indicated that if attendance sank to below 75,000 for three consecutive years, then the Staten Island Yankees could opt out of the remainder of their lease entirely with no penalty.

To the rest of the New York-Penn League and likely all of minor league baseball, this represented municipal magnanimity on an unprecedented scale. The estimated stadium budget of $29.5 million was nearly quadruple that of Erie's Jerry Uht Park (completed in 1995), almost six times that of Dutchess Stadium (built the year before that in 1994), and at least three times costlier than New Jersey's Skylands Park, which had been plagued by cost overruns and put its management company into bankruptcy. Despite the historically high price tag for this underused short-season facility the tenant team would be showered with a fantastical level of revenue rewards, no level of financial risk whatsoever, and an opt-out clause that would let them off scot-free if everything went wrong. Rather than sparking widespread disbelief or outrage, these revelations barely drew a collective shrug from New Yorkers or their political representatives, most of whom already planned to approve the stadium regardless of its ultimate cost. Even skeptical Councilman O'Donovan's office merely stated that he would "try to address certain concerns about the proposed lease agreement during a hearing before the Council" scheduled for the following month.[29]

Despite all the attention being paid to the potential drawbacks of the stadium and the lease terms, no one really wanted to derail the St. George stadium project. This was particularly true of O'Donovan, who spent the next two months wringing every possible financial concession from the city and EDC for his district. In November 1999, shortly after the stadium proposal flew through the Community Board and New York City Planning Commission approval votes, the legislation bogged down in the City Council Land Use Committee, which happened to include Councilman O'Donovan among its members. Over the course of several weeks of hearings, committee meetings, and negotiations, O'Donovan convinced and cajoled the city administration into multiple concessions. More money would be allocated for the additional costs of gameday police security and traffic, and also beautifying the area on Richmond Terrace outside the stadium with trees and shrubs, new lighting, and public benches. The planned waterfront esplanade behind the stadium would now boast additional exercise stations, two "tot lots" for kids, emergency phones, and "decorative waste receptacles." EDC even promised to conduct a study of O'Donovan's newest pet proposal, a two-tiered parking garage at the north parking lot adjacent to the ballpark. HOK tossed in a new picnic area inside the ballpark for fans, and EDC agreed to ask the Yankees for additional days over and above the twenty that were already reserved for community use of the facility. Although Guy Molinari griped to the press about the "unnecessary . . . hoopla and interrogation" and the "cosmetic" amenities tacked on by O'Donovan's efforts, the compromises won the day. In early December the Land Use Subcommittee approved the stadium project by a vote of 13–1, with only one member from Queens voting no on the grounds that "the price just keeps going up . . . I can't have my name associated with this." The following day the City Council reaffirmed that decision by nearly the same proportion, voting 39–5 in favor of building the ballpark in St. George. The fix had been in from the start, and Mayor Giuliani's promise to bring baseball to Staten Island was delivered in less than eleven months and apparently for only twice the price.[30]

Now that the approvals process had been completed in record time, the actual construction of the stadium could begin. As the new millennium loomed in December 1999, the city and EDC officials engaged in planning the project were well aware that its scope far outpaced public estimates of its $40 million cost. In actuality the city's Capital Program Project Budget had ballooned to more than twice that amount. Figures compiled several weeks prior to the December 1999 City Council vote cited costs of more than $80 million affiliated with all of the St. George construction. The federal government and New York State had promised more than $5.3 million in funding for a new Staten Island Rapid Transit station to serve the ballpark and the thousands of stadium-goers who were expected to arrive by public transportation. In excess of $71 million would be paid by the City of New York, including the $15 million already spent on acquiring and clearing the land. Another $13 million of the city's share would go towards repairing, strengthening, and remediating the shoreline and retaining wall, as well as the landscaping of the waterfront esplanade. St. George's residents and elected officials were doubtless pleased with the $4 million allocated for commuter roads and parking lots, and the firm of HOK expressed no dissatisfaction with the $10 million earmarked for site design and management. The remaining $29.5 million of the city's spending was dedicated to building the stadium itself, far and away the most expensive facility in the New York-Penn League.[31]

While the city handled all of the physical aspects of the stadium structure from beams to masonry to infrastructure, the Staten Island Yankees would contribute more than $3.5 million of their own. Nearly all of the team's expenditure went toward amenities that would benefit them in the short and long term. The Getzlers paid to fit out the luxury suites, restaurants and concessions, the retail space for the team store, the sound system and cable TV, and a $500,000 scoreboard that dwarfed the subsidized model that they had installed in Watertown years before. All of these contributions would enhance the stadium experience and team revenues. But they also became points of contention between the team and the city, which drew the line at fulfilling several Yankees requests. Team General Manager Jeff Dumas later recalled asking the city to fund the construction of year-round facilities in the vacant commercial space adjacent to the stadium, which would help attract prospective tenants such as pizza places, restaurants, or pubs. The city decided instead to carve out boxy no-frills cavities which lacked interior walls, plumbing or electrical connections. This eventually led to years of vacancies when EDC repeatedly failed to find willing tenants for these unfinished spaces. Some facets of the stadium's design also caused friction, such as the city's decision to build large gates rather than solid walls alongside parts of the stadium. While this provided view corridors to appease local residents, it reduced available concession space inside the stadium that would normally be built directly into the walls. While most observers characterized the Yankees as freeloaders benefitting from municipal largesse, they were unknowingly dismissing the team's admittedly limited contribution of several million dollars of their own, a sum that was substantial by minor league standards.[32]

In early 2000 the disparate aspects of stadium building came together nearly as quickly as the preliminary approval stages had the previous year. Actual construction began in February and March with the pouring of the stadium's concrete foundation and the erection of steel beams for its concourse level. By April, seventy workers employed by contractors and subcontractors worked steadily and swiftly to keep the project on schedule for its projected opening in time for the 2001 NY-PL season. In June a staged groundbreaking ceremony was held in front of the skeletal structure, featuring speeches and appearances by Mayor Giuliani, Guy Molinari, EDC President Michael Carey, Councilman Jerome O'Donovan, and a sprinkling of additional Staten Island politicians. Josh Getzler represented the team owners, accompanied by New York Yankees General Manager Brian Cashman, who represented the 49 percent of team ownership that remained in the hands of the Yankees. The event officially announced the finalization of the team's stadium lease and the Metropolitan Transit Authority's agreement to build a new transit station beneath the ballpark site, although the negotiations on both of these issues had been completed sometime earlier. The ceremony also included an announcement of the stadium's new name, Richmond County Bank Ballpark. This would honor Staten Island's own Richmond County Savings Bank, which would be paying annual naming rights of $400,000 for the next nine years in exchange for this privilege. As construction proceeded ahead of schedule and the stadium's remaining checklist items dwindled, only the owners and employees of the nearby Rapid Park car lot expressed any gripes. Business had fallen off during the months since the project began as the lot had to give up 250 parking spaces because of the construction, and it was uncertain if the city would choose a new lot operator once the project was completed. "The situation is not in favor of us," sighed one Rapid Park attendant. But for the Staten Island Yankees the situation seemed most favorable indeed.[33]

Although there was no reason for overt pessimism, there were some hints even at the outset that the Staten Island Yankees might not be able to meet the lofty expectations they were setting. The lucrative stadium naming agreement built positive relationships within the borough's business community and appeared to be a fair deal in terms of market value. Yet internal EDC and team projections had estimated an annual worth of $950,000 for the stadium's naming rights, a number that proved to be inflated and unrealistic. The rent schedule set out in the final lease agreement was identical to the one that had appeared in the original letter of intent, with its minimum threshold of 125,000 fans per season. But after falling short of that target in its first season in Staten Island, the team's attendance would actually drop further in the 2000 season that had just begun. Despite winning the NY-PL Championship that year, the Staten Island Yankees barely drew over 100,000 fans to their temporary stadium at CSI, playing their final home game in a "ballpark [that] was more empty than full." Although team officials and city politicians seemed confident that the new Richmond County Bank Ballpark's location and amenities would draw in thousands of additional fans, that remained to be seen.[34]

The stadium would be ready in time for the season opener in June 2001, that was certain. By New Year's Day construction was more than half completed, and the Getzlers went on a spree of press interviews and photo ops to drum up presales of season and game tickets. They touted the ballpark fan amenities such as seats with built-in cupholders and a picnic area with barbecue grills. They gave glowing testimonials to the major league resources that would be available to their minor league players, including high-grade video and weight rooms and an indoor underground batting tunnel impervious to inclement weather. In a nod to their own heritage there would even be a kosher food kiosk, the first of its kind in the minor leagues. The proud team owners consistently stressed the fact that ticket prices would remain at or below $10 apiece, the same low price they had been charging back at the CSI field. Local St. George businessmen soon caught the Getzlers' booster spirit, sprucing up their local eateries and bars in the hopes of attracting additional pre- and postgame customers from among the hoped-for crowds of fans. Although some skeptics continued to express dread of the traffic and parking nightmares they anticipated, most local interviewees preferred to be optimistic. As the head of Staten Island's Center for the Arts remarked about the stadium, "It's a tremendously exciting thing for Staten Island."[35]

But was Staten Island excited enough to maintain a successful ballclub, even at the minor league level? Perhaps the most unfortunate ill omen of the team's future was the fate of its temporary ballpark at the CSI campus in Willowbrook. Of the nearly $82 million spent on construction related to the Staten Island Yankees, $3.5 million had gone toward renovating and preparing that stadium where the club played out the 1999 and 2000 summer seasons. The team had ended its tenure at CSI on a tremendously high note, winning the League Championship and leaving behind a superbly manicured and well-tended facility for the college to inherit. The Getzlers had added a cash donation of $120,000 to the CSI Foundation on top of the field transformation that the college had received at no cost. This granted CSI a top-flight facility that it could use for its own college athletic programs, and also to generate additional revenue opportunities by renting it out to local organizations and school and youth groups.

Instead the College of Staten Island completely wasted the multi-million-dollar windfall it received. The college's charitable foundation did nothing with the Getzlers' monetary contribution and instead absorbed it into its general fund, applying none of the money to field maintenance or upkeep. CSI's custodial staff likewise gave little or no attention to the grounds during the months after the Yankees departed in September 2000. Although the team had bequeathed to the college an expensive Infield Pro machine to care for the infield dirt and keep it smooth, there was no evidence that the new groomer was ever powered up at all, let alone used for its proper purpose. The outfield grass was essentially abandoned, as CSI neglected to turn on the expensive built-in sprinkler system for eight long months until May 2001. By then one-quarter of the grass was dead, further worn away by its careless use as a parking area by denizens of the college. This devastation stood in marked contrast to the lavish care exercised by St. John's University toward the temporary Queens field bestowed upon them by the Brooklyn Cyclones when they departed the same year. For anyone paying attention, the subsequent treatment of the field at CSI helped form a cautionary tale of neglect, mismanagement, and how little the borough of Staten Island valued local baseball.[36]

In the meantime, Staten Island's muted excitement over its new minor league team and stadium drew little attention elsewhere. Despite the natural draw of the championship Yankees brand, few people off the island even seemed aware of the team's existence. Instead, everyone's attention was focused on the adjacent borough that lay at the other end of the Verrazano Narrows Bridge. To most New Yorkers, media members, and baseball fans, there might as well be only one minor league franchise on the horizon, promising to fulfill long-buried dreams, rekindle old memories, and reach into a shared nostalgic past.

Baseball was finally coming back to Brooklyn.

CHAPTER EIGHT

WE COULD NOT STAY IN ST. CATHARINES

B rooklyn's baseball history began in the 1850s, when teams like the Atlantics and the Excelsiors played in the pre–Civil War days of "bowlers" and "strikers" and "muffins" who tried to "show a little ginger" for their "cranks." After the formation of the National League in 1876, the then-City of Brooklyn remained without a professional team for fourteen years. Then in 1890 the Brooklyn Bridegrooms joined the league, subsequently renaming themselves the Superbas and finally the Brooklyn Dodgers. After moving into and out of various venues, the team finally found a home in 1898 in Washington Park, where it would play for the next decade and a half. The second stadium by that name, Washington Park was located at the corner of 3rd Avenue and 3rd Street in northwestern Brooklyn and seated nearly 19,000 fans. It was also frequently assailed by overpowering odors from the nearby Gowanus Canal which flowed around the park on two sides, as well as the omnipresent industrial factories that dominated the area.

Fifteen years later, the team's new owner, Charlie Ebbets, had bigger dreams for his Dodgers. Ebbets bought up a number of small adjacent lots to the west of Gowanus in an undeveloped East Flatbush neighborhood known as Pigtown. He then scraped together enough funding for a new facility and completed construction on his new Ebbets Field just in time for the 1913 season. The enclosed bandbox of a stadium had a seating capacity of 25,000 (expanded to 32,000 in the 1930s) and would be home to the club for the remainder of its time in Brooklyn until its final season there in 1957. At Ebbets Field the Dodgers would eventually win six National League pennants between 1947 and 1956 and one legendary World Series over the hated Yankees in 1955. Their famed "Boys of Summer" teams of that era featured legendary players including shortstop Pee Wee Reese, catcher Roy Campanella, right-handed pitcher Carl Erskine, and trailblazer Jackie Robinson. Together those Dodger teams had a permanent impact on an entire generation of young Brooklyn baseball fans of the post–World War II era. Lifelong New York City newspaperman Pete Hamill spoke for thousands of his contemporaries when he summed up his borough's bone-deep connection to and love for the Dodgers: "We always thought baseball was pure in Brooklyn—until they took it away from us."[1]

That happened in the 1950s. After more than four decades Ebbets Field had become too small for the demands of postwar baseball, with no facilities to accommodate automobile parking for the team's growing contingent of suburban fans. In 1952 owner Walter O'Malley announced plans for a domed stadium for his Dodgers at the intersection of Flatbush Avenue and Atlantic Avenue in Brooklyn, where a large market was being torn down. The stadium, which was to be privately funded and owned, would raise seating capacity to 52,000, would be more accessible to major roads nearby, and would ensure the team's future in the borough. But he had not reckoned on the unwavering opposition of New York City Planning Commissioner Robert Moses. The hugely influential power broker insisted that the city build a stadium on an alternative site in Flushing Meadows, Queens (where one day Shea Stadium would be erected). O'Malley refused to consider Moses's position, and Moses likewise refused O'Malley's. Shortly afterward O'Malley began public negotiations with Los Angeles, California, threatening to take his team there unless Moses and the city assisted him in acquiring the needed land to build his new stadium in Brooklyn. Ultimately O'Malley and Moses both refused to give an inch in their battle of wills and never came to an agreement. At the conclusion of the 1957 baseball season O'Malley's franchise packed up and moved west to be reborn as the Los Angeles Dodgers, leaving an entire borough bereft. The old Brooklyn ballpark was sold off to a local real estate developer, and in 1960 it was demolished in the name of urban renewal. In its stead the low-income Ebbets Field/Jackie Robinson Apartments went up on the site, at the time the largest state-subsidized housing complex in New York City. Baseball had left Brooklyn, and it looked like it was never coming back.[2]

Although it had grown run-down and outdated by its final years, Ebbets Field became a lost baseball icon of the golden era of the sport and a powerful symbol of baseball's good old days. This was especially true for the many Brooklynites who grew up in the borough before going out to accomplish bigger and better things in the world. Among those faithful were two Brooklyn boys who went on to achieve success, wealth, and power while maintaining their abiding love for Brooklyn baseball. Bill Gladstone and Fred Wilpon had never given up their fantasy of somehow restoring professional baseball to their home borough, maintaining what Bob Julian called their "misty-eyed" nostalgia many decades later in the 1990s. Just as importantly, both men were well aware of the enormous profit potential that their dream could generate in real dollars and cents. The opportunity to realize their dream came in late 1997, when Mayor Giuliani was feverishly sowing the seeds to fund a pair of major league stadiums for the Mets and Yankees. As the mayor's administration moved through the planning stages in concert with the Mets and Yankees organizations, they expanded the stadium package to include an additional minor league facility for each team's entry in the New York-Penn League (NY-PL).

For the Yankees, then ensconced in a thirty-two-year relationship with Sam Nader in Oneonta, this minor league component represented a welcome opportunity of only secondary importance. They were more than willing to embrace it for the sake of parity and power-sharing with the Mets, but it would cause them intra-organizational complications and was really just an intermediate step toward their true goal of a new, luxurious Yankee Stadium in the Bronx or Manhattan. As such, they were content to yield to the importuning of Giuliani's people and Borough President Guy Molinari that they situate their hypothetical franchise in Staten Island at a location to be chosen for them. On the other hand, the Mets were fixated on their minor league plans from the outset. Certainly they were willing to put in tremendous effort toward the planning and construction of their new major league stadium a decade or so down the road. But their plan to bring baseball back to Brooklyn was an independent priority with its own significance. At every preliminary stage over the next three years the Wilpon family and the Mets organization would play a major role in decision-making, asserting as much control as possible over the process. Unlike the Yankees, who were generally willing to let the local politicians do the heavy lifting on the Staten Island project, the Mets insisted on articulating and achieving their vision of their Brooklyn "Baby Mets."

By late 1998, as the Getzlers packed for their move from Watertown to Staten Island, the Mets were several months behind in their effort to recruit a minor league baseball team. After more than a year of negotiations and political groundwork, many of the largest hurdles had already been overcome. Both the Mets and Yankees had come to terms on waiving their exclusive territorial rights and allowing each other to operate their new affiliates within the city limits. Mayor Giuliani, riding high off his decisive reelection victory, was arranging millions of dollars in municipal funding through his administrative offices and EDC. He was also effectively bulldozing any political opposition that might stand in the way of his twin stadium projects. Press coverage and public opinion were overwhelmingly positive as they praised the long-awaited return of professional baseball to Brooklyn. Any one of these factors could have either derailed the plans completely or caused endless and frustrating delays, but everything had gone even more smoothly than anyone had expected. But a huge obstacle remained for Fred Wilpon and the New York Mets: they still had no NY-PL team to play in Brooklyn.

It had long been assumed that Brooklyn's team would be the Pittsfield Mets franchise owned by Bill Gladstone. A year of fruitless negotiations over team control had shown that to be impossible, and so the Mets were back to the drawing board. But with the help and intercession of NY-PL President Bob Julian, it would not be long before they too would be paired up with a different franchise that would soon be available for outright purchase. Like the Yankees, the Mets would look northward for a team trapped in an underperforming market and ready for relocation. That team, situated across the border and owned by a group of Canadian investors, was called the St. Catharines Stompers.

Before the NY-PL was renamed, it had begun its existence as the Pennsylvania-Ontario-New York (PONY) League. From its inception in 1939 until 1956 the league fielded a few teams in Canada, chiefly the Hamilton Redbirds of the St. Louis Cardinals organization. When minor league baseball suffered through the doldrums of the late 1950s into the 1960s, the Redbirds folded. The PONY League renamed itself the NY-PL, and any thought of a Canadian presence was abandoned for the next several decades.

The closest this iteration of the league came to Canada was the border city of Niagara Falls, New York, which was home to the NY-PL's Pittsburgh Pirates affiliate in the 1970s. The Niagara Falls Pirates continued to play there through 1979, two full years after the team lost its affiliation with its parent club. The challenges of running an independent franchise proved to be too much for the local owners, and so the club closed up shop. A few years later in 1982, Niagara Falls businessman George Wenz decided to try his hand at minor league baseball ownership. A onetime college basketball player and amateur pitcher, Wenz brought a White Sox franchise to his city's empty stadium and promptly won the league championship in his first year as owner and general manager. But the difficulties of maintaining the team and its aging facility proved too daunting for Wenz as well. Shortly after the end of the 1985 season, he reached a deal to sell the team to the Toronto Blue Jays organization. For the first time since the demise of the Cardinals' Hamilton Red Wings three decades earlier, a league team would now be completely owned by its major league parent. The new Blue Jays team would shortly be the first league team to play in Canada since those same 1956 Red Wings played out the last season of the original PONY League.[3]

Within six weeks of buying the franchise the Blue Jays announced its relocation to the city of St. Catharines, along the shores of Lake Ontario. Once the major industrial center of Canada's Niagara region, St. Catharines promised a much larger market share with a population of 130,000. Its relative nearness to Toronto (about seventy miles away, ten miles closer than Niagara Falls) was expected to benefit the club in terms of attendance and local support. The major league Blue Jays were on the rise, having just played in the American League Championship Series after nearly a decade of last-place finishes and expansion-team futility. By moving into the area known locally as St. Kitts, they hoped to capitalize on their growing popularity and make a success out of their new "Baby Jays" club. At the very least, they hoped to draw the 40,000 fans they would need in their first season to break even on their costs and expenses.[4]

One major and expensive hurdle was the renovation of the city's existing wooden baseball facility in Merriton Community Park at an anticipated cost of between $500,000 and $750,000. Despite the high price tag for the renovations, the contributions by the Blue Jays organization totaled only $80,000, with another $80,000 coming from Labatt Breweries, the corporate owner of the team. The city of St. Catharines forked over nearly $170,000, more than both of these private sources combined. The remainder was expected to come from further municipal and federal funding. Unfortunately neither the team or the city ever secured a definitive timetable or concrete commitment from the local or national legislatures, and most of the needed funds would never be allocated. In the meantime, constricted by the limited cash that was available, the physical improvements to Community Park were extremely slow to materialize. Even the erection of lighting standards took months, and they were delayed further by an unexpected electrical workers' strike in early 1986.[5]

Although the organization's direct costs were defrayed by the shared financing arrangement, Community Park's refurbishments were fairly pricey considering their limitations. Everything about the finished stadium seemed small, from its 2,000-seat capacity to the size of the dugouts to the narrow strips of foul territory that separated the playing field from the grandstands. The outfield fences were noticeably lacking in height, and the stands consisted mostly of plain aluminum benches with no seatbacks and a windowless wooden shed for the press. The overall effect was that of a cheap, cookie-cutter minor league park with no frills, which, of course, it was. Local fans called it "The Box." Nevertheless, by the time Opening Day took place as planned in June 1986, more than 500 season tickets had been sold for the inaugural season of the Baby Jays. The team responded by winning that year's NY-PL Championship, a precursor to the two world championships its parent club would win in the coming decade.[6]

The early success of the St. Catharines franchise sparked a minor Canadian renaissance within the NY-PL. In 1988 the St. Louis Cardinals moved their affiliate from Erie, New York, to Hamilton, Ontario, returning to the city where Cardinals executive Oliver French had helped establish an original PONY League club back in 1939. The following year the Pirates team owned by Eric Margenau abandoned Watertown, New York, for the city of Welland, Ontario, which built them a brand new 2,500-seat ballpark at a cost of $2.6 million. At the dawn of the 1990s the three proximate teams seemed to be poised for success, establishing a fan base and rivalries with the other teams in their Stedler Division, which included western New York teams from Niagara Falls, Erie, and Jamestown.[7]

Despite all of the money and effort that went into the formation of the three Ontario teams, Canadian expansion was short-lived. Under the terms of the Professional Baseball Agreement (PBA) negotiated in 1990, minor league teams were now absorbing a larger share of the costs of doing business. This represented a heavy burden for new clubs still struggling to pay off their startup outlays. Even more burdensome was a clause that applied specifically to Canadian teams, which were required to pay their personnel in American currency despite the fact that the majority of their revenues were earned in Canadian money. Since at the time the exchange rate for the Canadian dollar often dipped below 70 cents American, international team owners faced even more daunting economic challenges than their cash-strapped US counterparts. When they had to factor in the additional expenses of lodging and travel to the rest of the American-based league, the Canadian operators were in a no-win situation. They also struggled to raise local fan interest in baseball, which lagged far behind more popular sports like hockey.[8]

Both the Hamilton and Welland franchises succumbed to the financial pressures within only five seasons, the former folding in 1992 and the latter in 1994. At the same time the Blue Jays organization was also reevaluating its investment in St. Catharines. In late 1993 Bob Nicholson, the team's vice president for business, released a statement announcing that the Baby Jays were for sale. In part, he noted that "recent changes to the Professional Baseball Agreement have guaranteed the quality of the facilities and operations in the minor leagues and eliminated the need for the Blue Jays to continue to maintain ownership in these franchises." In a neat bit of public relations spin, Nicholson's comments not only solicited bids for the club but also reaffirmed MLB's official position that the PBA's restrictions and demands were for the benefit of all of professional baseball. They also glossed over the messy issues of dwindling attendance and revenues that plagued the St. Catharines operation.[9]

Although the Jays' asking price of $1 million Canadian was fairly steep, within a few months they found a group of buyers. The consortium was from London, Ontario, and it took only a matter of weeks before a deal was finalized that would move the team there. However, the Blue Jays had not reckoned with the directors of the NY-PL. Led by Sam Nader, the board vetoed the sale on the grounds that London was too far for any of the other teams to travel, since it was more than 100 miles west of its current St. Catharines location. By the time the 1994 season began the team was back on the block, and in the press Bob Nicholson raised the pressure on the league's last remaining Canadian team in an effort to attract local buyers. "We'd love to see the team stay there," he said. "But we can't guarantee it because we are of the mindset we don't want to own a club."[10]

Fortunately another investment group was waiting in the wings, led by a deep-pocketed real estate magnate who was also a Liberal Party politician: Ontario Cabinet Minister Greg Sorbara. Sorbara was a huge Blue Jays fan, and after attending a Jays fantasy camp in Florida in the early 1990s he conceived a plan to construct a baseball complex in the greater Toronto area. When the St. Catharines franchise became available, he gathered a number of investors and proposed to move the Baby Jays to a new facility to be built in Richmond Hill, just north of Toronto. But Richmond Hill was also eighty-five miles of additional travel from St. Catharines, and the rejection of the London sale made it clear that the league was unlikely to approve this expansion deal either. It seemed that the only way to keep an NY-PL team in Canada was if someone from St. Catharines were to pay an exorbitant price to do so. As a frustrated Bob Nicholson reiterated, "We would love to have local ownership run the team, [but] we can't hold out any promises."[11]

In the summer of 1994, as professional baseball tore itself apart during a protracted and acrimonious major league players' strike, the Blue Jays organization found a buyer among its own ranks. The general manager of the St. Catharines franchise had convened an advisory committee of local businessmen to assist with promotion and municipal relations. As early as 1992, several of the group's members had floated the idea of purchasing the team themselves. Nick Cannon, a British expatriate with a successful real estate firm, was the first to pitch the plan to his friend Mike Katz, owner of several nearby McDonald's restaurants. "I thought it was a riot," Katz recalled later. But as the sale arrangements continued to linger without any resolution, the two started to put serious effort into organizing their bid. They enlisted two more locals, advertising executive Terry O'Malley and hotelier Chris Nitsopoulos, whose St. Kitt's Howard Johnson hotel would be used to house visiting teams. To add professional credibility, the St. Catharines crew recruited recently retired Blue Jays catcher Ernie Whitt, an original team member since 1977 and one of the most popular and beloved baseballers in Canada.[12]

Armed with financial and organizational plans and a commitment to keep the team in St. Catharines, the only missing element was the million dollars needed to complete the purchase. A mutual acquaintance introduced O'Malley to Greg Sorbara, and the final pieces fell into place. As Nick Cannon recalled, "We got together, met Greg and said, 'We've got the facility, and we've got the viability, but we don't have the money. You've got the money, but no facility and no viability. If we put the two together, we've got a match.' And that's how it came about."[13] Sorbara, on the other hand, saw St. Catharines as merely a piece of his much larger plan to move the team in the near future, notwithstanding the opposition of the other NY-PL owners.

> Toronto had become a baseball city, just very high energy for baseball in Toronto. Kids were playing baseball everywhere, people were talking baseball. The SkyDome four years running, every game [drew] 50,000 plus in attendance. And I was thinking about building a true state-of-the-art baseball complex

in the Greater Toronto area. We would train baseball players, young kids from all over Ontario, tournament play and all of that stuff. Someone suggested that the critical component would be to have a pretty little minor league stadium with a minor league team, which would really anchor the whole complex. It just so happened at that time that the Toronto Blue Jays were looking to sell their franchise in St. Catharines . . .

The Blue Jays' interest was to sell the franchise to someone who would agree to keep it in Saint Catharines for at least two years. They didn't want the negative publicity of selling the franchise to someone who would get out of that camp. So the two groups got together and we actually expanded the groups, particularly in Toronto, so that we came together as a unit to buy the franchise. . . . My objective mostly was to build this baseball complex.

Negotiations proceeded smoothly, and in November 1994 the St. Catharines Blue Jays were bought for $920,000 Canadian (about $660,000 in American currency). As part of the new ownership arrangement Greg Sorbara was appointed team president, with the locally based owners taking charge of many of the day-to-day operations. The grateful city government of St. Catharines allocated another $100,000 to improve Community Park, adding club seats for season ticket holders, a patio deck, and expanding the overall seating capacity and the size of the locker rooms in an attempt to better meet PBA facility standards. After holding a naming contest in the media the new owners announced that the Baby Jays would now be known as the St. Catharines Stompers, a nod to the region's heritage in winemaking and grape-stomping. Terry O'Malley, the team's resident PR whiz and idea man, designed an adorable cartoon logo for the club's purple uniform caps and the Stompers were off and running.[14]

The inaugural 1995 season was a stellar one by St. Catharines standards. Attendance rose from 850 to more than 1,300 per game, and the season attendance total of 50,000 set a new Community Park record. The new owners increased the annual operating budget to $550,000, quadrupling the amount spent by the disinterested Blue Jays the previous year. Merchandising sales of team caps and custom purple baseballs were brisk, with inquiries from as far away as Japan for collectibles. Reportedly there was even an outside offer of $1.3 million to buy the resurgent club before its first season was done. At each game team co-owners Nick and Pam

Cannon greeted fans at the front gate, Mike Katz put his food service skills to work at the stadium concession stands, and Chris Nitsopoulos took care of all the visiting teams' needs at his nearby Howard Johnson's motel. The team was being run as a local family-owned business, trying to weave itself into the fabric of their community.[15]

Yet there were already disturbing signs for the future of the team. The team president remained Greg Sorbara, who lived at a remove in Toronto while he handled the business end of the team's operations. Nearly two-thirds of Community Park's 3,200 seats remained empty at every game, and the season ticket sales of only 285 fell far short of the levels set during the heyday of the Baby Jays in the late 1980s. Mike Katz tried to put a brave face on for the press, saying "the city of St. Catharines has a habit of not supporting its pro teams, but they're finding out we're for real." Unfortunately, being for real was not nearly sufficient. Although club spending was much higher than before, it comprised only a fraction of the $2.6 million (US) budgeted by multimillionaire Alan Levin's Erie SeaWolves, formerly the Hamilton Redbirds. Most ominous of all, the more money the Stompers spent the greater were their losses. In the first year alone the club lost between $100,000 and $150,000. Money "was flowing out in gushes," Nick Cannon recalled. Attendance continued to rise over the next few years; alas, revenues did not.[16]

As if their immediate troubles were not enough to deal with, in 1997 the Stompers' ownership and finances were further destabilized by developments on the major league level. At that time the Toronto Blue Jays organization was owned by the Labatt Brewing Company, a Canadian beer-making giant that had held the majority share in the team since 1976. In 1995 Labatt was acquired by a huge Belgian-based multinational conglomerate called Interbrew, which promptly put the Blue Jays on the block but could not attract serious bidders. The Blue Jays' offer was also meant to include the Toronto SkyDome, the team's brand-new retractable-roof facility that faced bankruptcy proceedings due to cost overruns and financial mismanagement. Sensing an opportunity, a consortium of Canadian and American investors made an attempt to buy out Interbrew's 90 percent stake in the Blue Jays and 49 percent stake in the SkyDome just after the 1997 baseball season ended in October. One of the most high-profile and vocal members of that investment group was Greg Sorbara, one of the politicians who had supported the construction of the SkyDome and also the president and part-owner of the St. Catharine Stompers.[17]

Ten days after news leaked of the consortium's formation, Labatt abruptly yanked the Blue Jays off the market, citing the tight deadline before the onset of major league free agency for the coming season. But a year later in 1998 rumors began to fly again after the SkyDome went into formal bankruptcy protection and the Blue Jays renewed their lease for another decade. Although Labatt and Interbrew made no public comments, insiders observed "the team will never formally be for sale again, but it will always be available." Now calling itself Sportsco, Sorbara's group again tried and failed to buy the Blue Jays. Several months later Sorbara and the rest of the Sportsco gang made a revised offer of $100 million to buy the SkyDome alone, figuring that would give them the inside track to purchase the team if the brewing companies ever decided to sell. After months of protracted wrangling, the bankruptcy court-appointed financial monitors awarded the SkyDome to Sportsco in early 1999. Less than ninety days later, internal fractures within Sportsco led to the ouster of several Canadian partners including Sorbara. Even as the reconstituted consortium renewed its efforts to acquire the Blue Jays, its ousted Canadian members were fighting bitterly to demand the best possible price for the shares they were being forced to relinquish. Leading the charge yet again was Greg Sorbara, who launched a lawsuit against his former Sportsco partners for damages of $18.5 million in June 1999.[18]

For Sorbara's partners in the St. Catharines Stompers, the organizational dysfunction of the Blue Jays and the high-stakes preoccupation of their wealthiest co-owner could not have come at a worse time. Canadian interest in baseball had sagged after the calamitous Major League Baseball strike of 1994. The Toronto Blue Jays, who had been on the verge of a coveted "three-peat" as World Series Champions after victories in 1992 and 1993, sank back into obscurity and regularly came in last in their divisional standings. Interest in the game was lagging, and attendance and revenues were way down. As Sorbara later recalled, "Baseball was getting hit very badly right across Canada—the air started to go out of the baseball balloon." This was especially true in St. Catharines, always a weak baseball market. And so even while he was vying to buy the Blue Jays and the SkyDome, Sorbara was simultaneously reaching out to other municipalities to build his planned baseball complex and move the Stompers. In 1997–1998, with no input from the St. Catharines faction, Sorbara and his Toronto partners had serious discussions with the cities of Mississauga and Brampton who were both "very excited to have a team in their jurisdiction." No matter what the Cannons, Terry O'Malley, Mike Katz, or anyone else from St. Catharines might think, Team President Sorbara had a very clear vision of the short-term future. "I was pretty convinced that either we were going to relocate the franchise in a stronger market with a stadium that had an attractiveness to it, or we were going to sell the franchise."[19]

The Stompers' options shrank further when the potential for a Brampton deal fell apart. Greg Sorbara blamed its failure primarily on competing visions for the proposed sports complex.

> The biggest impediment was that in the Sports Complex in Brampton the city had, in the power of public/private partnerships, vested the rights to continue developing the sports components of the land to a private-sector real estate entity in return for its participation in the in the stadium. And these guys just wanted too much. They were not doing very well with the hockey facility and so they thought they could extract it from us by granting us the rights to create a baseball complex on part of the land. We said, "Look, we're here to help you. You bring us here and give us space to put our baseball fields up and our stadium up, and this will give you the critical mass to make this place really happen. But they weren't having any fun and they didn't want us to have any fun, so the failure to be able to negotiate that was the final indication that the St. Catharine Stompers were not going to move to a new home.

At the same time the team also had zero chance of remaining in St. Catharines. With the market softening every year since the inception of the Stompers, the possibility of a new stadium was a nonstarter. Even with the initial bump in fan interest, the team consistently played in front of a half-empty ballpark and ranked tenth or lower in NY-PL attendance. With a tiny footprint and a maximum seating capacity of only 2,500 Community Park was cramped, outdated, and noncompliant with PBA requirements. The estimated cost of needed renovations was around $5 million, far beyond any sum they could reasonably expect to raise. So while the team had nowhere realistic to move, it was equally clear that they would not stay much longer in a city that did not provide adequate support and was also geographically remote from the rest of the league.

After a brief consideration of their options Sorbara and his out-of-town partners began making a serious effort to sell out. "We really could not stay indefinitely in St. Catharines," he later recalled. So in early 1999 he told his partners, "You know we've got no future here, this is just not going to happen in St. Catharines. We've had five years of fun, [but now] we can make a little bit of money." And they would in fact reap a significant windfall on their original $920,000 investment. But they could only realize those profits by viewing the franchise as "a piece to be moved rather than a piece to be kept," as Sorbara summed it up. So once he felt he had a consensus even among the St. Catharines people, Sorbara reached out to NY-PL President Bob Julian.[20]

The timing was serendipitous, because the Canadians' readiness to sell out came shortly after the Pittsfield Mets' plans to move to Brooklyn fell apart. Many millions of dollars had already been allocated for New York City's two proposed minor league stadiums in Mayor Giuliani's April 1998 budget, and the territorial negotiations between the Yankees and Mets organizations were long since satisfactorily completed. Up in Watertown the Getzlers had sold their old secondhand uniforms and packed their team's remaining possessions into moving vans bound for Staten Island, where their new facility's planning and construction were already underway. Only the future of the Brooklyn franchise, the linchpin of the entire New York City minor league deal, remained in doubt. The Mets organization had made it clear that they would accept nothing less than controlling interest in whichever NY-PL team they set up in their own territorial backyard. With Bill Gladstone's Pittsfield club out of the picture, they were actively searching for a team to purchase and relocate as soon as possible before the clock ran out on the plans they already had in place. Well aware of all of these moving parts, Bob Julian wasted no time in making a match between the eager-to-buy Mets and the ready-to-sell owners of the St. Catharines Stompers.

At the outset, some members of Greg Sorbara's faction hoped there might be a way to have their cake and eat it too. One partner hoped to convince the Mets organization to allow him to buy in and join them in their acquisition of the team, effectively allowing him to be a seller and a buyer at the same time. But from the beginning Fred Wilpon and his underlings made it clear to the Stompers owners, just as they had to Bill Gladstone in Pittsfield, that they were committed to sole ownership and control of their new team and the enormous profits they expected to make off it. Although the two sides reached an agreement in principle in mid-1999, nearly a year of protracted negotiation followed due to what Greg Sorbara called "the craziness of lawyering."

> The purchase agreement required us to transfer ownership rights to a gazillion things. We knew that, in the end, they knew that they *had* to buy the team. They already had a deal to build their stadium [in Brooklyn]. And they just should have said, "Thank you very much for selling us this franchise at a reasonable price, because we're going to make a shitload of money off of it." But we spent money on lawyers. It could have been simple and straightforward, but they wanted guarantees about liability. If anyone sued them because five years later they found out someone got sick from a hot dog [in St. Catharines], that they [were protected against] every conceivable possibility . . .
>
> The only thing that we were selling was the right to participate in the New York-Penn League and to enter into a player development contract with a Major League franchise, which for the first season was actually the Toronto Blue Jays rather than the Mets. We weren't even selling them any hard assets they had the right to come and take, except maybe some equipment out of the equipment room—which they never did. They weren't buying pop machines, they weren't buying popcorn makers, they weren't buying anything. They were just buying rights. It took far too long, and it was far too silly because they knew they had to buy it and we knew we had to sell it.[21]

The team's sale negotiations went on throughout the entirety of the 1999 NY-PL season. The Stompers' owners kept the news of the impending transaction tightly under wraps, fearing that any publicity at all might derail the entire plan. Whether any rumors leaked out or local support simply continued to ebb, that season turned out to be the worst in the Stompers' short history. On the field the team posted a losing record of 34–42, ending the year in second-to-last place in their division and eight games out of the playoffs. Attendance sank below 47,000 fans, a drop of nearly 9,000 from the previous year and only good enough to earn them thirteenth place out of their fourteen-team league. The team's continued deterioration only strengthened the owners' resolve to sell out to the Mets regardless of how many reams of paperwork their lawyers continued to generate. Finally in late September the sale of the St. Catharines Stompers to the New York Mets organization was announced to the media without much fanfare, attracting only a tiny ripple of attention. In the meantime, the deal would not actually reach completion until early 2000 at the end of a long winter of legal wrangling and billable hours.[22]

The final agreement sold the team to the New York Mets for around $2.5 million (US), nearly triple the amount that had been paid for the St. Catharines club only four years earlier. Although professional baseball would never return to Community Park, the facility did become home to the local Brock University Badgers baseball team. The amateur Central Ontario Baseball League also expressed interest, and its Niagara Metros began playing its home games there as well. So even though the dream of using the Stompers to anchor a developmental baseball complex had failed, their ballpark did play a small role in developing Ontario baseball for the next few decades.[23]

None of the Stompers' owners ever played a role in baseball again. The investors from the St. Catharines group went back to their day jobs a bit wealthier but far more disillusioned. Chris Nitsopoulos continued to run his hotel and branched out into real estate management. Nick and Pam Cannon found a second postretirement career escorting senior citizen tour groups on excursions to ninety countries around the world. Mike Katz expanded his Canadian McDonald's franchise empire to seven locations before he began to sell them off in 2006. Terry O'Malley, the most tenacious of the partners and the last to agree to sell out in 1999, continued his advertising work and made forays into local hockey and lacrosse sports ownership. Elected to the admittedly small St. Catharines Sports Hall of Fame in 2005, O'Malley went on to sponsor an ongoing lecture series and an archive of his professional papers at a nearby university.[24]

Of the Toronto partnership, Greg Sorbara would maintain the highest profile after the team was sold. Even as the sale was being negotiated in November 1999, Sorbara reignited his political career by winning election as president of the Ontario's opposition Liberal Party. When the Liberals took control of the Ontario provincial government in 2003 Sorbara rose to the position of cabinet minister of finance. A decade later he stepped down from active government service and returned to the family-owned Sorbara Group, then valued at more than $1.4 billion. But Sorbara's past legal wranglings as a would-be sports impresario foreshadowed a larger conflict in the late 2010s, when disputes over their father's legacy and the company's direction boiled over into a series of expensive high-profile lawsuits and countersuits between Sorbara and his older siblings. With so much on his plate, Sorbara never looked back at his brief forays into the sports business. Although he continued to maintain years afterward that "Canadian local ownership in baseball teams is very, very important," the onetime owner and finance minister had few concrete ideas on how that was to be achieved. Like his former small-town partners, who were mostly realistic and resigned to the fate of their onetime hometown team, Greg Sorbara was well acquainted with the increasingly cutthroat economics of professional baseball.[25]

The New York Mets, who were poised to make "a shitload of money" by bringing baseball back to Brooklyn, had no such concerns. Securing the team they needed had been a major hurdle, particularly after the Pittsfield deal fell apart in early 1999. The advent of the St. Catharines purchase, despite all of its subsequent delays, brought the Mets close to realizing Fred Wilpon's long-cherished dreams. What remained was the task of picking the site for the team's ballpark, a choice with enormous importance for its future. To capitalize on the inherent nostalgia and meaning already denoted by Brooklyn baseball, the stadium's location would be crucial in maximizing fan attention and interest in what was essentially near-amateur and low-level minor league play.

Fortunately the Wilpons and the Mayor's Office had already decided on the absolutely perfect spot to resurrect long-gone memories of the New York of the past. As early as January 1998 word had leaked through the press that the Mets' minor league stadium would be erected "at Old Steeplechase Park on the boardwalk" in historic Coney Island.[26] That site, beloved to generations of baseball fans and non-fans alike, carried its own deep significance for generations of New Yorkers and Brooklynites who had spent countless childhood summers along the wooden boardwalk at the beach, seeking thrills and adventures at bygone amusement parks. But raising the spirits of the dead came at a heavy price, and stadium proponents faced a gargantuan task to achieve what they sought. In addition to the high economic cost that would be associated with the project, they would face stiff opposition from borough and city politicians and would also be forced to overcome decades of history that mitigated against quick and easy solutions. It was anything but a foregone conclusion that the mayor and the Mets would succeed in getting everything they wanted.

CHAPTER NINE

CONEY ISLAND IS HOT RIGHT NOW

The connection between Coney Island and baseball was a relatively recent development that only came about in the mid-1980s. However, the deep significance of the neighborhood to millions of New Yorkers stretched back more than a century before that. More specifically, the history and imagery of Coney's Steeplechase Park conjured up especially powerful wellsprings of memory and emotion among those who were old enough to remember the park's heyday and later its ignominious end. For those reaching late middle age like Fred Wilpon and Bill Gladstone, the possibility of Brooklyn baseball at Coney Island irresistibly combined nostalgia for the Brooklyn Dodgers with memories of Steeplechase, a potent and powerful mixture indeed. In no small measure, this was due to the lengthy and contested history of a neighborhood and a site that was world-renowned before commencing a sharp and prolonged decline.

Coney Island is a narrow strip of land at the very southern tip of Brooklyn, about four miles long. Originally the westernmost of the Outer Barrier Islands along the southern shore of Brooklyn, Queens, and Long Island, a variety of nineteenth-century landfill efforts modified it into a peninsula attached to the mainland. By the 1850s its proximity to Atlantic Ocean sea breezes and easy accessibility made Coney Island a summer destination for poor and wealthy alike, and over the ensuing decades resort development exploded as the area's population surged. Steamboat, railroad, and eventually subway lines were established to serve the hundreds of thousands of summer patrons who flocked there to patronize its hotels, bathhouses, eateries, and innumerable entertainments. Many were drawn to Coney's gambling and drinking establishments, as well as the girlie shows and prostitution that earned it condemnation by the *New*

York Times as "Sodom-by-the-Sea" in the 1890s. But increasingly by the turn of the century, masses of people from around the globe and from all social classes packed into Coney Island to experience firsthand the three great amusement parks that spread its fame throughout the world: Steeplechase Park, Luna Park, and Dreamland.[1]

Steeplechase Park was the oldest and longest-lasting attraction at "The Playground of the World," as Coney Island became known. The park was first erected in 1897 along Surf Avenue by George C. Tilyou, a native New Yorker whose family had moved to Coney Island during his childhood. Inspired by the remarkable sights, attractions, and massive profitability of the 1893 Chicago World's Fair, Tilyou had returned home determined to replicate the amusements of the famed Midway Plaisance on an ongoing and permanent basis. After beginning modestly with a single show house called Tilyou's Surf Theatre, he acquired fifteen acres of land where he would construct an enclosed amusement park. Under the faintly naughty leer of the park's trademark "Funny Face" logo (known colloquially as "Tillie" by inveterate parkgoers), visitors thronged the rides, games, and amusements that allowed them temporary escape from propriety and respectability. In rough-and-tumble attractions like the Barrel of Love, the Human Pool Table, and the Human Roulette Wheel, men and women were bodily thrown together and twirled about before disentangling themselves afterward. Visitors seized the opportunity to view all of Coney Island from the dazzling height of 125 feet in the air aboard "The World's Largest Ferris Wheel," which was actually only half the size of its famous predecessor at the Chicago World's Fair. And perhaps the most famous attraction of all was the park's namesake Steeplechase Ride, a gravity-powered mechanical horse race special-ordered from Great Britain. Eagerly anticipating the promise of "a half a mile in a half a minute and fun all the time," couples straddled a metal horse and clutched at each other as they hurtled down a circular steel track at breakneck speed. After disembarking the riders traversed a stage called the Blowhole Theatre where a jet of air blew up the women's skirts and the men faced a paddling from a mischievous team of a clown and a midget. Audiences were delighted and clamored for more.[2]

They got exactly that in 1903, when architect Frederic Thompson and his business partner Skip Dundy opened their even grander Luna Park across Surf Avenue from Steeplechase. Eventually expanded to an enormous thirty-eight acres, Luna Park offered fantastic recreations of exotic locales and fairy tales, a "Trip to the Moon" and "20,000 Leagues under the Sea," acrobats and contortionists and dancing girls, and rec-reated disasters including a tenement fire multiple times each day. At its peak Luna Park drew more than four million visitors in the course of a four-month summer season, a staggering number. Its success prompted a group of local politicians to open Dreamland, a third huge amusement park further east along Surf Avenue. Following its opening day in 1904 the park became renowned for its 275-foot Dreamland Tower Observatory, festooned with more than 100,000 light bulbs and flashing an enormous searchlight that confused navigators aboard passing ships (one historian claims the tower was visible to new immigrants at sea before they even reached the Statue of Liberty). Dreamland featured a variety of strange and fascinating attractions including infant incubators housing premature babies, a Hell Gate display occupied by impish demons and devils, and the Bavarian village of Midget City where 500 little people lived. Fire eventually claimed two out of the three great parks, as Dreamland burned down in 1911 and Luna Park several decades later in the mid-1940s. By that time Coney Island's heyday had long since passed, although millions of visitors and especially servicemen continued to pack the area every summer through the end of World War II.[3]

Fire had threatened to destroy Steeplechase Park earlier than any of its competitors back in 1907, when a carelessly-thrown cigarette incin-erated almost the entire facility along with dozens of small hotels in the surrounding area. But George Tilyou salvaged everything by raising funds through a public stock offering to rebuild the entire park, this time under a giant glass and steel shed that he named the Pavilion of Fun. Immune to the vagaries of weather, his New Steeplechase Park far outlasted its rivals and even the passing of its own creator in 1914. Over the years Tilyou's heirs continued to add new attractions, the most notable being the 262-foot-tall Parachute Jump which was relocated there from the 1939 New York World's Fair. Steeplechase's ubiquitous Funny Face icon, Tillie, continued to grin all the way through 1964, when George's last surviving child, Marie, finally made the unilateral decision to close Steeplechase and sell the site. In a brief and uncommunicative interview with the press, Marie Tilyou admitted to receiving several offers for the property; one of those later turned out to be from the New York City Parks Department, which was supposed to receive a $2 million federal grant to turn it into a public park. Neither the city nor most of its rivals managed to get their acts together in any kind of organized way, and so the site was sold to a private developer instead.[4]

The sale and shutdown of Steeplechase came after a tumultuous year for the amusement park and the Tilyou clan. The provisions of the federal Fair Housing Act of 1949 had empowered the city to acquire blighted slum properties and hand them over to private developers to clear, redevelop, and construct residential housing. Under the direction of Robert Moses, Coney Island became one of the prime targets for more than a decade of relentless urban renewal. By the mid-1960s Moses had cleared most of Coney Island's amusement district away and replaced it with superblock high-rise housing projects. In the meantime many of the area's middle-class residents grew affluent and moved away to the suburbs, and with their departure much of the neighborhood was allowed to deteriorate and its infrastructure to collapse. Coney Island developed a reputation for poverty, crime, drugs, and a variety of social ills. In 1964 a *New York Times* article bemoaned many of the neighborhood's problems, including inadequate parking, unsafe subways, and "an influx of Negroes . . . [and] teen-age hoodlums." Not only did these perceived threats scare away potential residents but also summer visitors, and so even the remaining concessionaires reported a 30 to 90 percent fall-off in business and revenues.[5]

As the only large amusement park remaining in Coney Island, Steeplechase was deeply impacted by the social and economic changes engulfing the surrounding area. The park's difficulties were compounded by the death of its parent company's president Frank Tilyou in May 1964 at the age of only fifty-six years old. The last surviving son of George C. Tilyou, Frank had inherited the presidency after his older brother George had died six years earlier. Frank had been born on the very day that the Pavilion of Fun was completed in 1908, and he had spent his entire life in and around Steeplechase Park as its hands-on manager for decades. But his strength had been sapped by a string of illnesses culminating in his final battle with cancer, and his own deterioration had accompanied that of his amusement park and its neighborhood. Upon his death the park reverted entirely into the hands of his elder sister Marie, who had never married. Although some of her nephews reportedly wanted to keep the park going, she announced three months after Frank's death that she had decided to sell out.

Fearful of racial unrest and pressure over integration—Steeplechase had closed its pool entirely rather than to end its unofficial segregated-swimming policy—and pessimistic about the future of the neighborhood, Marie quickly moved to wrap up her family's commercial interests in Coney Island. She described her feelings at the time in a personal letter: "Naturally I feel very sad to even think of George C. Tilyou's Steeplechase Park closing but one night walking along Surf Avenue after dining at the Clam Bar and milling with the horrible types one sees in the summer now, I decided that Steeplechase, with all its splendor, drama and real beauty, stood out like a gorgeous rosebush in a garbage can." On September 20, 1964, the remaining family members gathered at Steeplechase for the park's final closing ceremonies, together with park employees past and present. The public address system played "Auf Wiedersehen," "There's No Business Like Show Business," and "Auld Lang Syne," and then bells tolled sixty-seven times to mark the years of the park's existence. As the tiers of lights were shut off, the family and friends of Steeplechase made their way out of the darkened amusement park for the last time.[6]

The man who bought Steeplechase was Fred C. Trump, a prominent real estate developer who was already heavily invested in Coney Island housing projects like the Trump Village complex along Neptune Avenue, Beach Haven Houses on West 2nd Street, and the Shore Haven Apartments in nearby Bath Beach. Twenty years prior to his purchase of Steeplechase, Trump had opportunistically jumped in and snapped up Luna Park after it burned down in the mid-1940s. He immediately shut down the amusement park, razing the property to build even more residential redevelopment. Trump's ascendancy was marred by a number of scandals and setbacks, however. In the 1950s it was discovered that Trump had been padding his construction costs and pocketing millions of government funding dollars earmarked to house war veterans. While his profiteering off the Federal Housing Authority did not lead to criminal prosecution, he was stripped of several sites including Luna Park and also blacklisted from federal funding for a time. Trump's questionable practices extended into mistreatment of poor and minority residents of his planned projects, as he relocated those families from his new building sites to substandard, dilapidated, unheated shacks. In the meantime Trump pocketed additional government fees which covered the costs of the relocations he himself had implemented. Trump's manipulation of the neighborhood and its residency patterns, particularly during construction of Trump Village in 1963–1964, created a poverty zone and urban blight that soon impacted quality of life all over the area, as the *New York Times* had observed. Coney Islanders came to loathe Fred Trump and blamed him for the demise of a once-thriving community. One of these was folk music pioneer Woody Guthrie, who resided for a time at Trump's Beach Haven complex in the early 1950s. In an unrecorded song he titled "Old Man Trump," Guthrie decried Trump's segregationist housing practices and "how much racial hate/He stirred up in that bloodpot of human hearts."[7]

Now in April 1965, acting through a front man in order to conceal his identity and possibly score a better deal, Fred Trump bought the Steeplechase Park site from Marie Tilyou for $2.5 million. He made no effort to reopen the amusement facility, which he intended to replace immediately with what he called a "modern, Miami beach-type high-rise apartment development" on the site. After selling off virtually all of the amusement machinery that remained, in September 1966 Trump staged an orgiastic public spectacle of destruction to commemorate a permanent end to the Steeplechase era in Coney Island. Dressed in a topcoat and hat, a grinning Trump inexpertly wielded a large axe and took a few desultory swings at the ruins of Steeplechase before an assemblage of invited news photographers. Accompanied by "six bikinied beauties" wearing plastic hard hats, Trump then invited participants to hurl large stones through the remaining windows of the vacant Pavilion of Fun, many of them directly through the fading Funny Face icon painted on the glass. Workmen then got down to business, bulldozing the building and razing all remaining Steeplechase structures to the ground. Trump's visible glee at literally destroying historic Coney Island further stoked the high levels of enmity against him. It was also perceived as an attempt to get rid of the building before it could be landmarked, further demonizing him as a greedy developer who would stop at nothing.[8]

This backfired dramatically when the Coney Island Chamber of Commerce and the New York City Planning Commission halted Trump's Steeplechase redevelopment plans in their tracks. Citing a lack of "sound city planning," they refused to waive the site's official amusement zoning status in order to allow residences to be built. Stymied by this political maneuvering, Trump sicced his attorney Abraham "Bunny" Lindenbaum on several local officials to revoke their decision, but to no avail. For the next several years Trump would take his fight to the courts, where Bunny was kept hopping with a variety of suits and complaints. In the meantime Trump and Bunny prevailed on city officials to allow them to lease out the site to Norman Kaufman, a seedy small-scale operator who lacked the required licenses to operate his amusement machinery. The ongoing wrangling came to a head in 1969 when New York City officially declared the site condemned and banned for use. Trump responded by reducing Kaufman's rental payments but allowing him to remain open.

He then sued the city in New York State Supreme Court after it tried to seize both the title and the property itself. In the end the city did manage to pry Steeplechase away from Trump, but at a heavy price. In a stinging rebuke to the city's bungling of the entire affair, the judge awarded a payment to Trump of $3.8 million, ensuring that he walked away from Steeplechase with a profit of at least one-third over his purchase price only four years earlier.[9]

In return the city leaders had paid dearly for a rubble-strewn lot littered with trash and abandoned car wrecks, which they could have originally purchased from the Tilyou family for far less money. They also inherited Norman Kaufman and his below-market rental agreements, as well as the many nuisance suits he would file after the city served him with multiple eviction notices over the next several years. For the next decade bureaucratic red tape strangled multiple leasing opportunities that would have netted the city over $100,000 per year, even as the courts allowed Kaufman to stay for less than half that rate due to innumerable delays, errors, and irregularities perpetrated by multiple city agencies. To add insult to injury, the federal government soon yanked its grant funding for a park on the property due to the New York City Parks Department's inefficiency and lack of a coherent plan. As the 1970s drew to a close, the Steeplechase site had become one of New York City's biggest boondoggles in recent memory. Its tribulations reflected the struggles of a city that had very nearly gone broke over the course of the decade. And the physical wreckage of the proud amusement center was emblematic of the state of Coney Island, once world-famous but now considered one of the most blighted neighborhoods in all of New York.[10]

In the 1980s the Steeplechase site changed hands yet again when it was leased by Horace Bullard, a Harlem-born entrepreneur who owed his success to his chain of Kansas Fried Chicken restaurants. A decade earlier Bullard had begun investing his fast-food profits in Coney Island real estate, beginning with the once-luxurious Shore Theater that had now been reduced to screening pornographic films. Bullard owned the entire ten-story office building that rose above the theater, a building that remained completely vacant except for a Kansas Fried Chicken restaurant that he had installed on the ground floor. Soon he added to his Coney Island portfolio the former Washington Baths abutting the beach and the defunct Thunderbolt roller coaster parcel which lay to the east of Steeplechase Park. Over time he accumulated enough Coney Island real estate that he became the biggest landowner in the neighborhood, purchasing several of the properties through local partners and a purported international shell company he disingenuously named Wantanabe Realty. Envisioning a revitalized Coney Island, Bullard spearheaded an effort to convince the New York State Legislature to legalize gambling and permit the construction of casinos. Although his Casinos for Coney Committee did everything they could, their efforts were reputedly killed in committee by none other than Fred Trump and his son Donald, whose Atlantic City casino interests would be jeopardized by Bullard's plan to establish gambling within New York City limits. The proposed casino referendum never even came to a floor vote, and so Bullard was forced to go back to the drawing board for new ideas to save Coney Island.[11]

By 1985 Bullard owned several parcels adjacent to and across Surf Avenue from Steeplechase, which was still city-owned and in complete disarray. Rather than develop each smaller property individually, Bullard crafted a combined plan which he pitched to Parks Commissioner Henry J. Stern. As a complement to a new federal grant aiming to develop the Boardwalk, Bullard would lease the Steeplechase site from the city and use it as the linchpin for a proposed $55 million amusement park. His vision depicted a "Disney-sized" attraction that covered twenty-seven acres from Surf Avenue to the reconstructed Boardwalk, featuring roller coasters, thrill rides, arcades, and all the "razzmatazz" of the vanished Coney Island of the past. It took a year of negotiation and delays before the New York City Council finally approved his lease in late 1986, and by that time Bullard had expanded his vision to grandiose extremes. Now tentatively budgeted at $100 million, the reborn Steeplechase would feature three roller coasters, a monorail, a two-tiered amusement structure, stages for live entertainment and festivals, a 6,000-space parking garage, and even a renovated Parachute Jump. But Bullard encountered a variety of difficulties in lining up his financing and then navigating New York City's paperwork and permit requirements. He continued to garner public support from politicians and city agencies for his ever-expanding plan, culminating in a ninety-nine-year lease agreement for an updated $220 million iteration of his vision in early 1989. Yet after years of talk and promises, not a single iota of actual physical development had taken place at Steeplechase. In the meantime a second plan was circulating that had the support of several local politicos, small business owners, and Brooklyn Borough President Howard Golden.[12]

Bullard's new competition was a group calling itself the Brooklyn Sports Foundation (BSF), which was initially championed on the state level by Democratic State Senator Thomas Bartosiewicz of Bushwick, Brooklyn. Although his district was nowhere near Coney Island, the well-connected party machine politician had plans of his own for the area. In 1982, several years before any of Bullard's plans became public, the senator had convinced the New York State Legislature to spend $30,000 on an initial study aimed at constructing a domed baseball stadium in Brooklyn. Born in 1948, Bartosiewicz was a Brooklyn native who had long bemoaned the fact that "Brooklyn hasn't been the same since the Dodgers left." Now that he had achieved some degree of political power, he hoped to bring professional baseball back to his home borough, and one of the primary focuses of the study was the feasibility of locating a stadium along Surf Avenue in Coney Island, among other possible locations. The intended study languished for several years until 1985, when Horace Bullard's Steeplechase plan burst on the scene. This in turn motivated Bartosiewicz to revive his dormant stadium study, which suddenly was re-funded to the tune of $75,000 and commenced immediately under the auspices of the New York State Urban Development Corporation (UDC) in conjunction with the Pratt Institute.

As Bullard's plans bogged down in red tape and staggered under the weight of their own expanding scope, Senator Bartosiewicz went to the media and assailed Bullard's ideas as unrealistic and "pie in the sky." While Bullard went back and forth with the city regarding his lease, UDC completed its work in less than a year and produced a full and polished report ready for review by the mayor and the City Council. At a December 1986 news conference UDC announced its recommendation to build a 15,000-seat arena and outdoor field that would house an as-yet unidentified minor league baseball team and would also host games and events for Brooklyn high schools, colleges, and community organizations. Several Triple A leagues expressed interest in moving a franchise to the proposed stadium, and Bartosiewicz claimed that he was about to meet with representatives of the New York Mets to gauge their interest as well. The project's $58 million budget would be raised through a combination of deferred loans, revenue bonds, and attendance receipts. It would also create nearly 600 local jobs and provide a much-needed boost to the depressed economy of Coney Island.[13]

The stadium would not even conflict directly with Bullard's proposals for a new Steeplechase Park, since it was located next door and not on the site itself and was presented only as a preliminary plan with the potential for further expansion. For the next few years Senator Bartosiewicz and

Borough President Golden shored up support for the BSF's planned facility, now known as the "Sportsplex." They also stocked the BSF board of directors with several of New York City's movers and shakers, including well-known real estate developer Bruce Ratner. Simultaneously they cast shade at Horace Bullard whenever possible. "He's had more than a year to develop it and nothing has happened," Bartosiewicz said about Bullard and Steeplechase in June 1987. "I don't think anything will happen."[14]

Over the next seven years nothing did happen for either side. The UDC report went into limbo for the remainder of the Mayor Koch administration and then for the entirety of Mayor Dinkins's term. Although Howard Golden raised the subject of the Sportsplex occasionally to the press, he did so alone and to no apparent avail.[15] It did not help that Golden could no longer count on Thomas Bartosiewicz to keep the issue alive in Albany, since the state senator had quit politics in 1988 in hopes of buying his own minor league baseball team. As for Horace Bullard, the erstwhile real estate tycoon rode a figurative roller coaster of his own making as his financing arrangements collapsed, were revived, and ultimately collapsed again in the early 1990s. Over the prior decade Bullard had fruitlessly spent over $6 million of his own money to bring his fantasy park into existence, and his most recent projected price tag had ballooned to more than $350 million. Then Rudy Giuliani was elected mayor of New York City, and less than two months after he took office the city abruptly terminated Horace Bullard's ninety-nine-year lease on the Steeplechase Park site. Although Bullard fought back in court, within a few years he had lost not only Steeplechase but several other parcels besides.[16]

The backers of a Coney Island Sportsplex hoped this was a sign that their long-awaited project would soon be built. Spearheaded by Golden and his political and economic contacts, they moved to amass funding and make their case to New York's legislative bodies and to the public.[17] In August 1993, seven months after Rudy Giuliani took office as the 107th mayor of New York City, the New York State Legislature passed a last-minute bill that seemed to confirm that years of BSF efforts were finally about to pay off. The bill created an eleven-member Brooklyn Sports Facility Commission, which would spend the next year developing a building plan for the Sportsplex. Based on BSF designs assembled over the previous seven years, the facility would include a 12,000-seat arena for hockey and basketball, an indoor track, gyms, a boxing ring, and training spaces for a wide variety of the borough's high school, college, and amateur athletes. Less than a year later in early 1994, the commission issued a very encouraging full report. Its strong recommendation to construct a $70 million Sportsplex was met with rapturous approval from the BSF, Borough President Golden, powerful State Assembly representatives, and officials from local high schools and colleges. Initial public hearings resounded with local support for the Coney Island facility. Mayor Giuliani remained conspicuously silent, but the BSF was confident that they had mustered overwhelming support for their plan.[18]

It took another year, but in 1995 a bipartisan team of Brooklyn state legislators introduced bills in their respective houses to fully finance the Sportsplex project. Situated on the site of the former Steeplechase Park, along Surf Avenue between 16th and 19th Streets, the 262,000-square-foot facility plan was loudly praised by a bevy of local politicians. Its construction would immediately create 5,000 jobs, they said, and the Sportsplex would eventually generate 500 additional permanent jobs for local Coney Islanders. Although its passage in the New York State Legislature was by no means guaranteed, Howard Golden pledged $7 million from his borough's upcoming annual budget to help defray the costs and another $7 million the year after that. New York State Assembly Speaker Sheldon Silver went on record calling the Sportsplex a "high priority." And finally a reluctant Mayor Giuliani lent his formal support to what he now termed "a good idea for Brooklyn," although he declined to offer a more concrete statement or financial backing of any kind.[19]

For the next two years the Sportsplex plan languished in bureaucratic limbo, much to the displeasure of Borough President Golden and his cronies. Then when New York State's 1996 budget was finally passed several months late that July, no money was allocated for a Brooklyn Sportsplex. "All we have ever gotten on this proposal was lip service," groused Democratic Assemblywoman Eileen Dugan, one of the representatives who had sponsored the state's funding bill. Golden and the BSF vowed to fight on, but as the calendar moved forward nothing changed. Albany politicians continued to insist that the Sportsplex was "by no means a dead issue," but little progress was made and Brooklyn's delegates seemed to lack the clout to move things forward. Unexpectedly, Governor George Pataki reversed this trend by included funding for the project in his 1997 budget proposal, albeit at a reduced level of $60 million. When a final budget deal was reached at the end of July—more than three months late yet again—Sportsplex proponents were pleased to note that it authorized a bond issue to effectively borrow money to build the facility. By this time the funding level had shrunk to a meager $30 million, less than half the original allocation recommended by the Brooklyn Sports Facility Commission just two years earlier. Nevertheless, the Sportsplex was on its way to becoming a reality. But no one seemed to know or care about making up the needed funds to build it.[20]

The unexpected savior of the Brooklyn Sportsplex initially seemed to be Rudy Giuliani. After months of reticence, the mayor announced that New York City would cover the massive shortfall that remained after the state had cut its contribution in half. He said so publicly at a Brooklyn Chamber of Commerce luncheon in mid-August 1997, assuring that the city "would plug the hole that was there so we finally got the Sportsplex done" and promising to pony up $30 million to supplement the State Legislature's allocation. Howard Golden hailed this late development, although he stopped short of openly thanking the mayor or giving him any credit. "Ten years ago I began the campaign to create a major sports facility for Brooklyn, and this year our dream became a reality," Golden crowed to the press. Equally exciting was the news that real estate magnate Bruce Ratner, a member of the BSF board of directors, was committed not only to the Sportsplex project but to developing and constructing a $100 million "virtual reality park and commercial complex" on a seven-acre tract adjacent to the facility. Everything was in place—funding, political backing, moneyed business interests, and a can't-miss plan for Coney Island.[21]

Unfortunately Golden and his allies did not realize that a second competing Steeplechase plan was already in the works and that Mayor Giuliani was deep in negotiations to shape that alternative dream into a very different reality. Around the same time that he made his public promises to support the Sportsplex—possibly even beforehand, but certainly over the ensuing months—Giuliani was already working surreptitiously to bring minor league baseball to New York City. Even as he ran his successful campaign for his November reelection, the mayor was arranging territorial agreements between the Mets and Yankees, scoping out possible sites for his pair of minor league stadiums, and working with Bob Julian and several minor league team owners to designate which clubs would shortly be relocated. By this time the Mets' Brooklyn stadium was already planned for the Steeplechase site currently set aside for the Sportsplex, a secret kept tightly under wraps by Giuliani's people. And so the confidence expressed by Golden and the BSF members was severely misplaced, as the mayor's bait-and-switch was well underway. Every aspect from the location to the city-provided funding to the needed City Council votes would soon be diverted away from Golden's pet project to Giuliani's instead.

The first hint of Giuliani's betrayal surfaced in January 1998, shortly after the mayor boasted of a new Brooklyn Sportsplex in his annual State of the City speech. In a series of carefully calibrated press leaks, the mayor and New York Mets owner Fred Wilpon revealed that they had an agreement in principle for the city to build a new minor league baseball stadium for the team in Coney Island. Their comments described a dedicated facility that was in no way part of the long-awaited Sportsplex plan but was instead a freestanding and separate stadium reserved for use by the Mets organization rather than a variety of community institutions and groups. The mayor referred to this new plan as expanding the Sportsplex rather than replacing it. While the respective chairmen of the BSF and Coney Island's Community Board 13 were initially taken by surprise, they soon warmed to the idea. "Coney Island is a very hot area right now," said CB13's chair Martin Levine. Al O'Hagen, chair of the Coney Island Chamber of Commerce, asserted there was more than enough space for both projects as well as even more additional development in the neighborhood since "there are plenty of vacant lots in Coney Island." Governor George Pataki agreed, telling the Brooklyn Chamber of Commerce, "Let's see if we can work that same kind of magic on Coney Island as we worked on Times Square."[22]

By May 1998 speculation reached a fever pitch with the news that the mammoth Disney Corporation had expressed interest in taking part in Coney Island's development. Not since the days of Horace Bullard's grandiose plans in the 1980s had there been so much attention on the future of the moribund amusement area. The Sportsplex remained at the epicenter of the conversation, especially now that the Forest City Ratner firm owned by Bruce Ratner was offering to build it at cost. The facility would be paired with Ratner's planned $100 million "entertainment-retail complex" next door, and now both projects would be augmented by the mayor's new minor league baseball stadium. No one knew what the Disney people would contribute, but it was sure to be a blockbuster. Even Horace Bullard's name resurfaced, as one of his few remaining Coney Island properties was the Surf Avenue site containing the ruins of the Thunderbolt roller coaster. Since that tract was adjacent to the Steeplechase site, he too could play a part in the plans swirling around the seashore. Al O'Hagen was ebullient, especially when he talked about the Sportsplex as the keystone for all the plans. "The mayor's behind it, the governor's behind it, the Borough President's behind it," he gloated. "There's no way it's not going to happen." Countered savvy Daily News columnist Bob Liff,

"I hope he's right, but he should hold on to his wallet. We've been this far down the road before."[23]

Over the summer of 1998 wild rumors about the nature and scope of Coney Island's development continued to swirl and grow. One account now had Bruce Ratner running his planned entertainment complex as a front man for the Disney Corporation. As Forest City Ratner dithered on presenting an official proposal to the city for consideration, a new player burst briefly on the scene. Westchester County New York developer Louis R. Capelli and his New Roc Associates were revitalizing downtown New Rochelle with their New Roc City complex, a 1.2-million-square-foot $190 million behemoth that boasted a nineteen-screen movie theater, a shopping center, an amusement park, and an ice-skating rink. With all the attention being focused on Coney Island, Capelli now pitched a similar large-scale project to New York City's Economic Development Corporation (EDC) that would encompass both the Steeplechase site and Horace Bullard's Thunderbolt parcel. Although EDC declined to pursue the offer, it was undeniable that Coney Island was indeed a very hot area that summer, one of the hottest on record weather-wise since the late 1960s.[24]

But as the weather cooled at summer's end, so did many of the plans for Coney Island including the Sportsplex. The rejection of New Roc City's proposal evidently sent a signal to Forest City Ratner that the Giuliani administration had moved on, and so the firm never did submit its own long-awaited formal Coney Island proposal. Although Bruce Ratner still expressed polite interest in the area, the well-connected developer doubtless realized that the mayor's intentions for Steeplechase likely blocked his own involvement. The Disney people never made any public comments at all about Coney Island, disappearing like a mirage concocted by Al O'Hagen. And Mayor Giuliani began taking decisive steps toward constructing his Coney Island baseball stadium, which had been allocated $20 million earlier in the year in the City's 1998–1999 annual budget. In mid-September he announced that the city had reached an agreement in principle with the Mets to move Bill Gladstone's Pittsfield franchise to Coney Island (a move which never actually took place thanks to his infighting with the Mets organization). Although the rival Yankees had yet to be convinced to approve this incursion into their territory, the mayor spoke with ebullient certainty regarding the stadium's construction, its potential benefits to the community and the city, and, of course, the ever-present thrill of "bringing baseball back to Brooklyn." City Council member and mayoral hopeful Peter Vallone, usually no friend of Giuliani's, also expressed public support for the minor league facility.[25]

Only Howard Golden publicly opposed Rudy Giuliani's vision, and he did so with every means at his disposal. In contrast to the positive spin being promoted by the mayor and his people, Golden groused, "It is disappointing to hear that the plan involves a single-A Mets team, the lowest minor league affiliate, since Brooklyn, the home of the world-champion Dodgers, is clearly a major league town." He also began immediately to demand more details about the financial and land-use arrangements between the Mets and New York City, hinting that the former might benefit far more than the latter. Then in early November 1998 the sharp-eyed borough president noticed a minor item buried deep in the agenda for an upcoming meeting of New York City's Franchise and Concession Committee, of which he was a member. The document, which was distributed less than twenty-four hours prior to the committee's scheduled meeting, announced that members would vote on for negotiating a "sole-source concession" to the Mets organization to operate a ballpark on the Steeplechase site. This would be unlike virtually all New York City concession arrangements, which usually solicited competitive bids from multiple sources. It also gave control of the entire Steeplechase parcel to the Mets, precluding the situating of the Sportsplex on all or even part of the site.[26]

Golden was generally known for maintaining a relatively low-key political style, but in this case he raised a ruckus that ended up postponing the meeting by more than a week. In the interim he and Giuliani's Deputy Mayor Joe Lhota sniped at each other through the press, with Golden protesting that he had been ambushed and Lhota riposting that "formal notification had been sent a month before." As reporters gleefully hectored the "high-level panic" brought about by "City Hall's penchant for secrecy and inattention from Brooklyn officials," it was difficult to determine if the Brooklyn Sportsplex would still have a future once the Steeplechase concession vote took place. The mayor's side refused to give any concrete assurances aside from a single noncommittal assertion: "Don't worry, there's room for everything." Although the administration was presumably referring to both the Sportsplex and the entertainment complex next door, no clarifications were issued.

In the end the vote was a foregone conclusion, since the six-member Franchise and Concession Committee was comprised of four mayoral aides, one neutral member, and Howard Golden. By an anticlimactic count of 5–1 the group duly granted the Mets Development Corporation full control of the whole twelve-acre Steeplechase site. Although the city acknowledged that the financial deal with the Mets might still fall through, officials steadfastly refused to guarantee that the Sportsplex might live on as a possible contingency plan. Newsman Bob Liff, who had foreseen this outcome six months earlier, reported with no pleasure that the mayor had "rammed through a sweetheart deal" for the Mets. Even as Liff echoed Golden's criticism of the sole-source deal and urged that the city consider other candidates to play in Coney Island, both knew their protests would be pointless. The fix was in and the Mets would be in the driver's seat when it came to the future of professional baseball in Brooklyn. As 1998 drew to a close, the Wilpons' organization made it clear that they insisted on full and complete control of the Coney Island stadium and the team that would ultimately play there.[27]

The sole concession award to the Mets effectively doomed the possibility of a Coney Island Sportsplex project. In January 1999 Bob Liff penned one last column about the shelved facility, excoriating the Giuliani administration for holding it hostage to his misplaced prioritizing of privately held baseball stadiums over community needs and services. For his part, the mayor blamed the Sportsplex backers for creating a half-baked plan that was incomplete and having "put the cart before the horse." Blithely ignoring the half-million visitors who regularly packed the Coney Island beaches on a daily basis all summer, the mayor confidently asserted that the new stadium would serve the greatest number of New Yorkers by bringing several thousand fans to the neighborhood for baseball games. In the meantime, Howard Golden spent most of 1999 trying to derail the stadium plans and keep the Sportsplex issue in the public eye. He continued to hammer away at the notion of building an expensive stadium for a short-season Class A minor league affiliate. Speaking on behalf of millions of Brooklynites, Golden accused the mayor of neglecting "our kids" and their need for communal sports facilities in favor of a private entity, the Mets. Working with his allies on Coney Island's Community Board 13, he reiterated the message that "this is not responsible economic development." On his weekly weekend radio show Giuliani responded by taunting Golden, telling him "get your head examined" for opposing the new stadium and the rich economic benefits that it would provide to the borough of Brooklyn. "He dodges the facts and engages in rhetoric," sniffed Golden's chief of staff in response.[28]

As opposed to Staten Island, where Republican Borough President Guy Molinari worked in near-perfect harmony with Republican Mayor Rudy Giuliani to hasten the birth of the Staten Island Yankees, Brooklyn was wracked by political conflict over baseball. Multiple hurdles had yet to be overcome, votes needed to be locked down, and the mayor's opponents were sharpening their knives. In particular, a spurned Howard Golden was now determined to delay and derail the best-laid plans crafted by the mayor and the Mets. In the end, the borough's minor league affiliate would languish for another year as the battle was fought out in the press, the political arena, and in multiple neighborhoods throughout New York City's most historic baseball borough.

CHAPTER TEN

AN INSULT TO THE PEOPLE OF BROOKLYN

The slow demise of the Sportsplex coincided with an all-out baseball war between Rudy Giuliani and Howard Golden, two men who never liked each other that much to begin with. Golden was a quintessential New York Democratic Party politician, ruling over his borough of Brooklyn for twenty-five years as borough president after first serving on the City Council from 1970 to 1977. It was a given that the powerful and connected Golden would not get along with the outspoken outsider Giuliani, particularly since the former US prosecutor was also one of New York City's rare Republican mayors. Over the course of his mayoralty the two tussled over a variety of issues including the disposal of Brooklyn's garbage, mass transit service cuts, several large polluting power plants, and the confirmation of multiple political appointees. But none of their battles approached the ferocity or complexity of their fight over the Mets' minor league stadium, which took place over several years and spread out to locations across Brooklyn and eventually Queens as well.[1]

When the Franchise and Concession Committee awarded the Mets sole-source concession rights to the Steeplechase site in November 1998, Golden immediately went on the warpath. In press conferences, newspaper op-eds, and his 1999 State of the Borough speech, he criticized the sole-source decision as undemocratic, short-sighted, and as a waste of millions of taxpayer dollars. Besides the issue of the endangered Sportsplex, Golden raised other objections to the mayor's deal with the Mets. Why restrict the new stadium tenancy to a short-season bottom-feeding single-A minor league team, Golden asked, when his office had received inquiries from

Figure 10.1. Mayor Giuliani and Brooklyn Borough President Howard Golden in happier times, 1994. Photo credit: New York City Municipal Archives.

two higher-level leagues that boasted longer playing seasons? Surely the residents of New York City's most populous borough deserved "better baseball" played by "the highest-caliber players" after waiting four decades since the departure of their beloved Dodgers. Golden also asserted that the longer season played by an independent league team would bring in "three times the amount of tax dollars" that would be generated by a New York-Penn League (NY-PL) Mets franchise during its truncated ten-week summer session. "The mayor's backward approach is an insult to the people of Brooklyn," he concluded as he vowed to fight on.[2]

Over the next six months the stadium project began to wend its way through the lengthy path towards city approval, and throughout that time Golden erected every stumbling block he could think of to delay the process and wring concessions from the Mayor's Office. In press interviews and at public events he maintained public pressure on Giuliani to unseat the Mets' rights to the planned stadium, completely disregarding the mayor's single-minded orchestration of that precise arrangement. In an attempt to block Giuliani's plan using data, Golden's office commissioned a study of the issue from sports-economist-for-hire Mark Rosentraub.

Unsurprisingly, the study's conclusion urged the mayor to solicit additional bids from other major league and independent league teams to come to Coney Island, reiterating the arguments Golden was making in the press. In the meantime, he marshalled his allies in Coney Island and on the City Council to join him in linking the stadium approval to construction of the Sportsplex, which still remained a real possibility in his mind. Friendly newspaper columnists were recruited to advocate the same positions and urge Giuliani to give in so they could "forestall months of delay before the ballpark can proceed." In June 1999 Golden proceeded to his political lines of defense, threatening that he and the members of Coney Island's CB13 would block the stadium's approval through a series of required land-use votes. Although the mayor could supersede this maneuver by bypassing the Community Board in favor of a direct City Council vote, the stadium's passage by a council stoked with a number of Giuliani rivals was by no means certain either. Perhaps prompted by Golden behind the scenes, Coney Island's local politicians also piped up with demands for an additional $400 million in infrastructure improvements as the price for their yes votes to support the mayor.[3]

For his part, Mayor Giuliani responded in measured but noncommittal tones to Golden's demands and delays. City and Economic Development Corporation (EDC) officials cautiously allowed for the possibility of the Sportsplex even as they refused to make it part of any package deal. They were especially cagey when it came to funding any project outside the ballpark itself, promising almost nothing concrete. But they were quick to stifle any talk of soliciting any other team to occupy the new stadium. To them the stadium for the Mets was already part of their own separate package deal, namely tying it to the ballpark planned for the Staten Island Yankees affiliate. The mayor's spokespeople stressed the natural Verrazano Bridge rivalry that would exist between the two new NY-PL franchises, who would travel back and forth across the span to face each other. This competitive relationship was a key selling point for the entire minor league baseball scheme, and it would be stillborn if an alternative organization or league replaced the NY-PL Mets in Coney Island. They also suggested that it would be extremely risky to pin the future of a multimillion-dollar facility to an independent or unaffiliated team that lacked the resources, track record, and local fan base of the Mets and Yankees. "When you build a $20 million stadium, it's critical you know the team will still exist in three years," the mayor's press secretary Sunny Mindel told the *Daily News*. "If you build it, you need to know they will stay."[4]

In fact, the public posturing of both sides was totally disingenuous. The Mayor's Office and EDC were fairly certain by this time that the Sportsplex plan was already dead in the water, no matter what platitudes they offered to the press and the public. And for all of his bluster over competitive bids, Howard Golden was well aware that the sole-source decision passed the previous November had effectively blocked any scenario where the stadium was occupied by anyone but the Mets. It was also obvious that the mayor's arrangement for a Mets franchise in Brooklyn and a Yankees franchise in Staten Island was the only realistic option on the table. It had been hard enough to get agreement from both teams to allow even this unconventional deal, and there was no way either team would waive their shared territorial rights for the sake of a third organization or independent operator. Even if they did, Sunny Mindel's points about staying power were well taken. Minor league baseball had a very spotty track record of success in markets across the country as the NY-PL's own past history in Pittsfield, Elmira, and Utica demonstrated, and independent leagues often performed even worse.

As for Mark Rosentraub's allegedly expert study, its figures and conclusions were based on profit projections that relied on lively local interest and high attendance, neither of which were guaranteed if the powerful New York Mets and Yankees brands were removed from the equation. Rosentraub also posited that potentially high economic benefits would flow from large numbers of fans hanging around and spending their money in Coney Island before and after the games, a questionable assertion. Among many of Rosentraub's contemporaries in the field of sports economics he was generally regarded as a paid advocate for publicly funded stadiums, and many opposing pieces were soon published that argued that his assumptions and conclusions were unwarranted. At the same time, Rudy Giuliani's own justifications for the city's two minor league stadiums relied on many of those same questionable assertions, and so his side did not utter a single public criticism of the study or its findings throughout the ensuing debate. In the end, Rosentraub's contribution to the Coney Island stadium struggle did not move the needle at all, although it doubtless earned him a substantial payment from the Office of the Brooklyn Borough President who had commissioned it.

As the Coney Island stadium plan trudged inexorably through the city's byzantine land-use procedures in 1999, Golden and Giuliani went to war on a second front. With the Mets purchase of the St. Catharines Stompers now complete, the team would need a temporary facility to play its home games over the next year or two until the stadium's completion.

Just as he had for the Staten Island Yankees, who were currently playing out the 1999 season in their temporary stadium at the College of Staten Island (CSI), the mayor already had a contingency plan in place for the minor league Mets. After compiling a list of Brooklyn sites, the Mayor's Office settled on the borough's Parade Grounds as the leading candidate for a 3,000-seat stadium to house the team in 2000 and possibly 2001. Established in the late 1860s along Caton Avenue in central Brooklyn, the Parade Grounds occupied forty acres just across the street from the southern boundary of Prospect Park. It was originally home to more than a dozen baseball diamonds where Brooklyn-born sports legends Sandy Koufax, Willie Randolph, and Joe Torre once honed their skills. The facility now boasted sports fields that were heavily used by hundreds if not thousands of children and amateur athletes every year. After decades of disrepair, the city now planned a multimillion-dollar upgrade that would outlive the short tenancy of the Mets' new minor league affiliate. One of those who lauded the offer was former New York State Governor Mario Cuomo, who had played semi-pro ball there himself many decades earlier. "If they're only going to use it for a year, and what you get is a magnificent field, that is a wonderful deal," he said.[5]

One of the primary advantages to temporarily situating the Mets club there was that the site was already designated for baseball fields, which meant that no tedious municipal land-use proceedings would be needed, at least not according to the mayor's legal experts. Giuliani promised a win-win deal to the borough of Brooklyn and its politicians: he asked that for the next year or two they set aside one of the existing baseball fields for the minor league Mets, along with several nearby soccer and football fields for game-night parking. In return the team and the city would pay for all-new fields upon their departure, just as they had already promised to do at CSI in Staten Island. The new facilities would be resodded with a new cutting-edge surface called FieldTurf, a vast improvement over the Parade Grounds' abused and uneven grass surfaces that were decades overdue for replacement. Local baseball leagues, teams, and youth organizations were thrilled with the plan, which would bequeath them $6.5 million in spanking-new baseball fields. Far less enthralled were local Youth Soccer players, their parents, and neighborhood residents who dreaded game-night traffic nightmares in an area already crowded to capacity throughout the summer.[6]

Sensing blood in the water, Howard Golden undertook a number of steps to deride and undermine the mayor and his plans for the Parade Grounds. Golden's first step was to call a public hearing on the issue, something the mayor had declined to do. His decision had been in keeping with his position that the preexisting zoning eliminated the need for a formal land-use process, and since the facility would only be temporary anyway there was no need to go to so much bother. Golden then scheduled the hearing for early November 1999, just before yet another preordained Franchise and Concessions Review Committee meeting was planned to hand the Parade Grounds over to the Mets and EDC. At this hearing, with Golden's blessing and careful prearrangement, there was a very high turnout among soccer families. Also in attendance was a nascent group called the Save the Parade Grounds Coalition, all packing into Brooklyn Borough Hall to speak against the Mets plan. Two weeks later, many of those same individuals joined with hundreds of additional supporters in a march across the Brooklyn Bridge to City Hall to register their opposition, featuring dozens of children dressed in soccer uniforms and, of course, borough president Golden. Golden and the community groups went so far as to file a pair of lawsuits to prevent the imminent construction of the Mets' field at the Parade Grounds. The community organizers joined the local chapter of the Association of Community Organizations for Reform Now (ACORN) to demand that the plans be submitted for community review. Abetted by local Community Board 14 and various other local politicians, Golden demanded much the same in his own separate suit which also cited his oft-repeated criticism of the sole-source concession of Steeplechase to the Mets a year prior. Within two weeks of the filings, a pair of injunctions were handed down and then upheld in Brooklyn Supreme Court, halting any further work or progress on the project. Giuliani and EDC were now temporarily stymied at the Parade Grounds, even as Golden continued his quixotic campaign to build his Sportsplex in Coney Island.[7]

With pressure building to secure a temporary stadium in time for the Brooklyn team's upcoming season six months hence, the Mets and EDC immediately backpedaled and offered significant incentives to end the lawsuits and injunctions. Within days the city doubled its financial offer, promising to upgrade the entire Parade Grounds in addition to the single field used by the Mets. EDC would also reduce the size of the temporary stadium and retract its plan to use adjacent fields for parking, sharply curtailing the impact on community athletics. The Mets' Dave Howard added that his organization would try to limit the team's tenure at the Parade Grounds to a single season if at all possible and promised extra funding for local schools and athletic programs to boost goodwill.

All of these offers were music to the ears of ACORN and its community partners, who would achieve every goal they had and then some by dropping their suit, which they immediately did. But the mayor's side was adamant that both lawsuits must be dropped as part of the bargain, and Howard Golden stubbornly refused to withdraw.[8]

The Parade Grounds were only one facet of Golden's take-no-prisoners assault on the mayor and the Mets, and in January 2000 he deployed every weapon at his disposal. First he cast his official vote as Brooklyn borough president against the Coney Island stadium, joined by his allies on Coney Island's Community Board 13 in refusing to approve the proposal in its current form. This was essentially a delaying tactic, since the final authority over the project rested not with the borough but the City Council. But council members would not be able to cast their deciding vote until after several more months of the land-use process were complete, now that Golden and the community board had forced the issue by rejecting the current draft and the proposed shortcuts it contained. Simultaneously Golden refused to drop his lawsuit over the Parade Grounds, which was proceeding alone in the courts after ACORN dropped its parallel suit. He continued to hold firm even when community activists began protesting against him instead of City Hall, enraged that his stubbornness could cost them millions of dollars' worth of Parade Grounds improvements being dangled before them by the mayor. Their anger was justified, because within days the entire plan was scrapped. New York City lawyer Christopher King informed the court that "the plan to build the Mets facility at the Parade Grounds is dead." EDC President Michael Carey chimed in, "It is a very sad day that the Parade Grounds will not be restored anytime soon because of the Borough President's utter refusal to negotiate in good faith . . . This is a lost opportunity, and it is the people of Brooklyn who will lose out as a result of the Borough President's recalcitrance and arbitrary refusal to compromise." Crestfallen activists bemoaned the lost opportunity, even as Golden's aides offered a halfhearted promise that the borough would somehow scrape together funding on its own.[9]

In the meantime, throughout early 2000 the mayor chipped away at any support for Golden's obstructionism. Giuliani continuously downplayed any direct opposition to the Sportsplex plan even as he offered millions of dollars' worth of alternative inducements to Coney Islanders. Helplessly Golden watched his former allies among neighborhood groups and community boards drift over to the mayor's side, wooed by $30 million in new shade pavilions, rest rooms, handicapped-access beach entrances, and a promised restoration of the landmarked Parachute Jump adjacent to the stadium site. These improvements would be featured elements of a $91 million Coney Island redevelopment plan that would be anchored by the Mets' new minor league facility. Dazzled by dollar signs, Coney Islanders withdrew all opposition and embraced the mayor's vision. "The Mets stadium should not be held up because of the Sportsplex mentality that has failed to proceed to development for 15 years," intoned Brooklyn Councilman Herbert Berman, possibly at the mayor's behest. Golden responded that Berman was "leading the Brooklyn delegation to turn its back on amateur sports and on the people of Brooklyn," but his prepared statement lacked the energy and vitriol of just a few months earlier.

By the time the City Council came together to vote on approving the new Coney Island stadium in April 2000, Howard Golden was a beaten man. Once the Council's Land Use Committee unanimously approved the stadium by a vote of 16–0 it was a foregone conclusion that the measure would pass by an overwhelming margin, as it inevitably did. The City Council agreed to budget the project at a generous $31 million for the stadium alone, along with all the additional neighborhood add-ins. "We took a [Sportsplex] plan that was dying on the vine and we made it into a package that will result in the redevelopment of Coney Island and all of south Brooklyn," crowed Herbert Berman to reporters in the aftermath. Construction crews broke ground on the stadium in Coney Island that very same day. As the owner of Deno's Wonder Wheel told the *Daily News*, "They had bulldozers sitting there like racing cars waiting for the flag to go down."[10]

Now that his pet project was fully approved and invested, Mayor Giuliani was free to exact revenge on his erstwhile gadfly. First he brought the hammer down on Golden's cherished Sportsplex plan. In testimony before the City Planning Commission, EDC president and Giuliani front man Michael Carey openly attacked the Sportsplex as being too large, impractical, and costly. Adding it to the existing stadium plan "would retard and kill all that went into the environmental review process to date," he said, suggesting that if both projects were forced into simultaneous consideration then neither one would ever be built. In a pointed critique of Golden, Carey added, "In the Steeplechase project, he is being close-minded." As part of the subsequent City Council deal to fund the stadium the council created a new local development corporation to "plan sports, recreation and entertainment programs in Coney Island and surrounding neighborhoods." This new body was formulated in such a way that the

Brooklyn borough president's office would have no input or impact on its membership or decisions, and its starting budget of $30 million was stripped away from the Sportsplex for which it had been earmarked.[11]

With no mandate, no citywide support, and no funding, the Sportsplex was scarcely heard from again. The Brooklyn Sports Foundation went dormant, its advocacy of the Sportsplex subsumed by the tide of money Giuliani made available for other Coney Island projects. The sole subsequent mention of a proposed Sportsplex came in 2003, buried in a 600-page bid created by the NYC2012 Committee to bring the Summer Olympics to the city. Deep in its description of proposed facilities for the games was a passing reference to a Coney Island Sportsplex that might possibly host indoor volleyball matches. When the $3.3 billion Olympic bid ultimately fizzled, so too did any faint hope that the Sportsplex would ever be built.[12]

With less than a year remaining before he was forced out by newly enacted term limits, Borough President Golden saw his budgets sharply reduced as Mayor Giuliani punished him for his public opposition. To add insult to injury Golden was forced by local pressure to make good on his commitment to refurbish the Parade Grounds out of his own office's resources. To mend fences with angry community members he expended considerable effort to shift the borough's capital budget funds to cover $12 million in Parade Grounds improvements. Of course, it did not go unnoticed that it was his own obstinacy over his stadium lawsuit that had spurned the mayor's largesse and forced Golden to provide the money instead.[13] In August the mayor pointedly disinvited Golden from the ceremonial stadium groundbreaking in Coney Island, sniping, "Why wasn't he here? Because he is against this project. I can't imagine why." By year's end an increasingly irrelevant Howard Golden found himself marginalized and lacking in political influence. The following year his handpicked successor and former Deputy Borough President Jeannette Gadsden was trounced in the race to succeed him, soundly beaten by state senator and Golden rival Marty Markowitz. Golden's taciturnity and crankiness were displaced by Markowitz's boundless enthusiasm and the Office of Brooklyn's Borough President transitioned from opposing minor league facilities to boosting for massive sports redevelopment projects like the Barclays Center arena.[14]

In the meantime, the Mets' new minor league franchise still needed somewhere to play its first summer season in New York City. With the Parade Grounds plan hopelessly tied up in the media and the courts and

Brooklyn's Borough President Golden actively trying to spike any alternative venue on his turf, Mayor Giuliani abandoned Brooklyn entirely to seek greener ballfields elsewhere. In early 2000, at the height of the Parade Grounds showdown between Giuliani and Golden, the mayor's minions hastily assembled a new plan to relocate the still-unnamed team to a temporary home in Queens. They put together a package similar to that successfully piloted at CSI a year earlier and pitched it without delay to the Mets organization, who took the lead in relaying this information to the local news media. This allowed the mayor and EDC to maintain their public position supporting the Parade Grounds plan even after they had privately decided to abandon it, saving face in Brooklyn and laying all blame at the feet of Howard Golden and his stubbornness.

And so on January 10, 2000, the day Golden's lawsuit was scheduled to be heard in Brooklyn Supreme Court, Mets officials leaked word in the morning papers that they were looking at several sites in Queens for their team. Fred Wilpon indicated that he would even consider having the team play in the Mets' own Shea Stadium if necessary, although the logistics of juggling teams from two different leagues in a single stadium would have been a nightmare. Two days later, with Golden obstinately proceeding with his lawsuit, Dave Howard told reporters that the team was now actively pursuing other sites outside Brooklyn, although for the moment "we're sitting tight and relying on the city to offer us guidance." It took less than a week before the news broke that the Mets were engaged in serious talks to relocate their team to St. John's University in Jamaica, Queens. The office of Queens Borough President Claire Shulman refused to comment, saying only that they were "sworn to secrecy" until an expected announcement. A high-ranking vice president at St. John's would only state that no lease had yet been signed. Reporters long accustomed to such noncommittal responses understood the coded message that a deal was imminent. It seemed that the city's guidance to the Mets had been to get as far away from Howard Golden as quickly as possible.[15]

Less than a month later, a group claiming to represent hundreds of Queens residents announced a lawsuit against the city to prevent construction of a new stadium at the St. John's campus. Despite the fact that no formal agreement was yet in place, it seemed to be common knowledge that EDC was planning to spend $5 million on a 3,500-seat ballpark on campus grounds. The Mets' temporary stadium would be slightly smaller than the Staten Island Yankees' temporary digs at CSI but $1.5 million more expensive and would likewise be gifted to its host campus after the departure of its minor league tenant in a year or two. This plan was completely unacceptable to local Republican State Senator Frank Padavan, who cited many of the same arguments Golden had used against situating a stadium at the Parade Grounds. Marshalling four neighborhood groups and 250 homeowners from nearby Jamaica Estates, Padavan led a hastily organized "Stop the Stadium" meeting that culminated in a protest march to St. John's. The protesters decried the excessive noise and light pollution that would destroy their peace and quiet on game nights and carped about the impact of excessive traffic on local roads and parking. When St. John's administrators attempted to reassure their angry neighbors that on-campus parking facilities would be more than adequate to handle the influx of baseball fans, local neighborhood associations questioned the ethics of using public tax dollars to pay for a facility at a private institution like St. John's University. In the words of dentist Barry Weinberg, chairman of the Jamaica Estates Residents' Association, "People here feel we must win for the survival of our community."[16]

Frank Padavan's vociferous opposition to the stadium's location was curious in light of the fact that he actually represented the district of Bellerose, a community several miles east of Jamaica Estates. Thus Barry Weinberg and his association members were not technically his constituents, and their concerns were not uppermost in his priorities. In a candid interview with the *New York Daily News*, Padavan admitted that his true interest was a real-estate deal he had previously brokered for St. John's University to acquire a long-abandoned parcel in Bellerose for a new baseball facility. That arrangement, along with the $1.1 million that St. John's was scheduled to pay for the Bellerose purchase, would go up in smoke if the mayor's minor league plans came to fruition. Padavan presented his site as a palatable alternative for all parties, from the local residents of Jamaica Estates to the university to the mayor himself. "I don't want to sue him," Padavan remonstrated, "I support him." But the single-minded Giuliani would brook no plan and no site except for the one he had already chosen, and he reiterated that position at a contentious town meeting in Queens in mid-February. "I'm happy to have people vote against me if they don't agree with me," he hectored the local residents who had gathered to hear him at a nearby public school. "We would love to find other alternatives, but there isn't one." Scores of angry attendees responded by marching out of the meeting in a huff.[17]

Undaunted, Mayor Giuliani proceeded to commence construction at St. John's over the next several months, citing the time pressures to have a facility that would be game-ready before the NY-PL season began in June. The Mets issued a blizzard of local public relations outreach efforts to dispel residents' misgivings, with Mets' Vice President Dave Howard promising to "eliminate or minimize any adverse effects" on nearby neighborhoods. The team, to be called the Queens Kings for the duration of its stay at St. John's, promised free tickets to youth groups, pledged to allow nearby youth sports teams to play on the new field once it was completed, limited the number of home night games, and even banned the sale of beer. Now budgeted at $6 million, the new facility would even serve as a potential venue for national NCAA tournament events. But Frank Padavan and his band of litigants were not mollified, and however reluctantly, they continued to press their legal case before their assigned judge in Jamaica Supreme Court. Like Howard Golden before them, they argued that the city's failure to conduct a conventional Uniform Land Use Review Procedure (ULURP) process disqualified the stadium project on environmental and legal grounds. They added a zoning claim that a commercial-use baseball stadium should be disallowed in a residential area and insisted that the city's building permit had been illegally obtained. And they asked repeatedly for an injunction to halt the construction or at least the occupancy of the rapidly developing stadium before Opening Day. Howard Golden wished them well from the sidelines, interjecting, "I want to assure those in Queens who are suffering under the mayor's autocratic philosophy of government that we in Brooklyn know how you feel."[18]

Alas, the wheels of justice turned far too slowly to aid the members of the Committee to Stop the Stadium. Their case did not even come before the judge until June 2000, less than two weeks before Opening Day at the nearly completed temporary stadium. Even then the court declined to issue any temporary injunction to delay the season, which had been the only potential leverage held by Padavan and his backers. In fact, the court refused to take any action whatsoever on the stadium until after a hearing by the New York City Committee on Standards and Appeals, which would decide weeks later on the legality of the St. John's permit, after the short summer season had already started. And so Opening Day came on June 21, with painters frantically touching up the dugouts, electricians finishing last-minute work on lighting, and soda dispensers and concessions being filled just prior to game time. Although rain threatened, it held off long enough for the home team to achieve a thrilling 10–9 come-from-behind win. Ceremonial first pitches were thrown out by Mayor Giuliani and Queens Borough President Shulman, and 2,407 fans came to enjoy the game, marvel at the beauty of the brand-new field ("This is class," enthused one of the Queens Kings pitchers), and to take pleasure in a family night out at the bargain price of $6–$10 per ticket. The only discordant note was sounded by Barry Weinberg as he led sixty protestors in a picket line outside the stadium parking lot before the game. "Traffic will be horrendous, the PA system will be blaring, and the lights will invade the homes of the neighboring blocks," he predicted, incorrectly as it turned out.[19]

In the end the lawsuit against the St. John's Stadium never got anywhere, but aside from the inevitable legal fees and court costs, it hardly mattered. The Queens Kings had always been intended to be a one-season wonder, and before the 2000 season even ended construction was already well underway on the franchise's future Coney Island stadium. For all of the dire predictions of unruly crowds and neighborhood gridlock, the Queens Kings drew only a meager 930 fans to each of their home games, never coming close to selling out their 3,500 available seats despite rock-bottom ticket prices and giveaways. Although the club finished first in its Stedler

Figure 10.2. From left: Jeff Wilpon, Queens Borough President Claire Shulman, Mayor Giuliani, and Fred Wilpon on Queens Kings Opening Day, June 2000. Photo credit: New York City Municipal Archives.

Division and made the league playoffs it ranked dead last in attendance with a final tally of 38,662, placing them behind small markets like Utica, Pittsfield, and even remote Batavia, which drew one additional fan for a total of 38,663 for the season. Meanwhile their closest geographical rival, the Staten Island Yankees, drew a robust 102,697 attendees to their own temporary stadium at CSI, far outclassing their fellow New York City club.[20]

One major factor in the failure of the Queens Kings was the uncertainty over the future of the franchise, which seemed less and less likely to remain in the borough past season's end. But the main reason behind the stadium's paucity of residents, particularly among the many Mets fans who were ubiquitous in Queens, was the simple fact that the Kings team was not an official affiliate of the New York Mets. To fulfill the terms of the league's Professional Baseball Agreement the Mets had to maintain their existing contractual agreement with Bill Gladstone's Pittsfield franchise until after the conclusion of the 2000 season. In the meantime, the transplanted St. Catharines team now operating as the Queens Kings had to play out its own arrangement with its parent organization, the Toronto Blue Jays. In a unique and strange quirk of timing and financial dealings, the Blue Jays' affiliate in the NY-PL was actually owned by the Mets organization. This prompted even less loyalty on the part of any potential Queens Kings fans, since the so-called "stars of tomorrow" they cheered for were most likely future Blue Jays, if they made it to the majors at all.[21]

The Queens Kings were also an afterthought for the Mets, whose entire focus was their Brooklyn franchise and the stadium being built for them in Coney Island. The general manager they installed for the Kings, Steve Cohen, was put in place chiefly to give him a season of experience under his belt before helming the team in its new home in Brooklyn. Even before his first successful season ended, Cohen was rhapsodizing to reporters about how next year "the possibility of watching future Mets stars will appeal to the people of the city of New York." Fred Wilpon was brutally honest in his assessment of the lost year, admitting, "We had no pre-time to promote it properly," adding "we're sort of putting all our efforts into Brooklyn." Even the Jamaica Estates stadium protestors ran out of steam, although technically they had not yet dropped their lawsuit. "Life around the stadium on game nights has been a lot quieter than people expected," they grudgingly allowed. Always one to look on the bright side, Barry Weinberg got in his last lick just before the season finally expired. "Thankfully, for whatever reason, the team hasn't drawn well," he said. But the dour dentist remained defiant even after the team packed up to leave his neighborhood for good: "What could have happened could have been a complete disaster."[22]

In contrast to the neglect demonstrated by CSI toward their donated field, St. John's University administrators, coaches, and players treated their new facility with reverence. Drawing on the significant resources of a private university with a sizable endowment, the college kept up its maintenance of the "substantial improvements" made by the Mets. St. John's now boasted one of the best stadiums in all of college baseball, complete with professional-caliber lighting, seating, public address amenities, and field conditions. In 2018, after nearly twenty years of use, the university even invested an additional $1 million of its own to convert the playing surface to state-of-the-art FieldTurf to better withstand the effects of annual snows and rains in the chilly northeast.

For their part, although they had only used the St. John's stadium for a year, the Mets continued to maintain a cordial relationship with their erstwhile landlords and Queens neighbors over the ensuing decade. And so in March 2009 when it came time for the Mets to test out their own new billion-dollar stadium at Citi Field, they invited the St. John's Red Storm baseball team to play the stadium's inaugural game. Despite rainy weather, more than 20,000 people showed up to watch the game and gawp at the pricey features of New York's new shiny retro-style ballpark. Meanwhile, across town in the Bronx the new $1.5 billion Yankee Stadium remained dark until the arrival of the major league club from Florida spring training several days later. There was no mention at all of the College of Staten Island, since the Yankees had utterly severed that relationship the moment their minor league team left the campus nine years earlier. By 2009 neither CSI nor the entire borough of Staten Island were of any great interest to the Yankees organization, which had far bigger fish to fry on its march toward a record twenty-seventh World Series championship. Not so for the Mets, who considered New York City's outer boroughs to be a major source of team support.[23]

The months between February and June 2000 were extraordinarily busy for New York City's stadium builders, subcontractors, and crews. In Queens, the campus of St. John's University buzzed with preparations for the upcoming (and only) season that would be played there by the Queens Kings. At St. George in Staten Island, workers poured the concrete foundation for the Staten Island Yankees' new facility, whose ceremonial groundbreaking in June coincided with the announcement of its official christening as Richmond County Bank Ballpark. Meanwhile at Coney

Island in Brooklyn, bulldozers were hard at work clearing away the long-abandoned wreckage of half-demolished Steeplechase Park. It took several months to remove the accumulated detritus of more than four decades of neglect on the part of successive generations of owners and leaseholders. Working steadily, they rid the site of the remnants of the unrealized fantasies of what George C. Tilyou had once promised long ago in 1907: "On this site will be erected shortly a better, bigger, greater Steeplechase Park." Fred Trump, Horace Bullard, Norman Kaufman, the New York City Parks Department, and even Howard Golden and his Brooklyn Sports Foundation never managed to complete that task. But Mayor Giuliani was determined to make the site part of his baseball legacy, and he was willing to spend upward of $30 million plus an additional $60 million in neighborhood improvements to accomplish that.[24]

Coney Island nostalgia was all the rage in the New York media as the new stadium began to take shape. Before the erstwhile Queens Kings even completed their single season of play, the New York Daily News and sports radio station WFAN announced a contest to choose a name for the new Brooklyn team. After casting the first vote—he promised he had not chosen "Yankees" despite his own well-known preferences—Mayor Giuliani casually revealed that the new stadium's cost had already ballooned to $39 million, double the figure of his initial appropriation. He attributed the price inflation to the rush to complete the facility in a single year instead of two, a decision he had made arbitrarily. A few reporters and politicians timidly suggested other uses for the $180 million in funds now earmarked for the baseball projects, including buying the city new police cars and fire trucks or increasing the capital budget for public libraries, but Giuliani brushed off the implied criticism. "This is a great use of City money," he insisted. As the media churned out puff pieces touting a long-awaited comeback and renewed hopes for Coney Island, few seemed to disagree.[25]

In November 2000 the naming contest closed with some fanfare. At a press conference hosted by Fred Wilpon and Mets officials, team General Manager Steve Cohen, legendary Mets relief pitcher John Franco, and, of course, Mayor Giuliani, it was announced that the team would be named the Brooklyn Cyclones. More than 1,000 of the 7,000 entries had chosen the moniker, which beat out less-popular suggestions like the Sweathogs, Honeymooners, the clearly off-limits Dodgers, and "every variation of the name 'dog'" one could imagine (presumably referring to the reputed invention of the hot dog at Coney Island more than a century before). Recalling the legendary wooden roller coaster that had been operating continuously at Coney Island since 1927, the instant recognizability, nostalgia factor, and huge branding value of the name Brooklyn Cyclones was not lost on anyone present. The connection between the team and the landmark was further strengthened by their proximity, as the high peaks and steep drops of the coaster track would be visible beyond the left-field fences and signage of the new stadium. Although the Cyclone ride was stationed along Surf Avenue at West 10th Street and the stadium was some distance away at West 16th Street, no obstacle existed in the six intervening blocks to impair the view of stadium-goers. At least, not anymore.[26]

Originally the parcel to the east of Steeplechase Park housed the Thunderbolt roller coaster, which occupied the block between West 16th and West 15th Streets. Built in 1925, the Thunderbolt was always less popular than its rival the Cyclone, and by the 1970s it was considered so moribund and decrepit that even a featured role in Woody Allen's popular film *Annie Hall* did little to attract visitors. After the death of its owner Fred Moran in 1982 the Thunderbolt was closed for use and subsequently it rusted, decayed, and was irreparably damaged by a major fire. Eventually the Thunderbolt parcel found its way into the possession of Coney Island's would-be impresario Horace Bullard who did nothing with it for a dozen years. Even as the Cyclone roller coaster found rejuvenation in a public "Save the Cyclone" campaign and achieved city landmark status, the Thunderbolt loomed over Surf Avenue as a hulking wreck. The actor Kirk Douglas, born in New York as Issur Danielovitch, had been a summertime carny wrestler in Coney Island in the 1930s. When he returned in the 1990s as a successful actor and author he observed,

> when I was ten years old someone brought me to Coney Island, and I went on the Thunderbolt, the biggest roller coaster in the world. I was so excited I wet my pants. "My God," I thought, "this is wonderful!" Now, when I went back and researched for the book, this is just a skeleton against the Manhattan skyline, and I can't believe it. I think, "My God, the Thunderbolt is dead?" I couldn't believe it. You know, I have a lot of those emotional feelings about Brooklyn.[27]

One person who did not share those "emotional feelings" was Jeff Wilpon, chief officer of development and construction at Sterling Equities and heir to the Mets empire controlled by his father, Fred. As a dry run for the Mets' major league stadium to come, the younger Wilpon was overseeing construction of the Brooklyn stadium when he noticed the unsightly remains of the Thunderbolt towering over what was soon to be left field. According to several Coney Islanders and Horace Bullard in particular, at the stadium groundbreaking ceremony on August 22, 2000, Jeff Wilpon dropped a not-so-casual remark to the mayor that "the Thunderbolt was an eyesore that looked dangerous." Mayor Giuliani apparently took this observation very seriously and spoke sternly to his aides, who contacted ranking members of EDC who were overseeing stadium construction, who promptly reached out to various city agencies including the Department of Buildings. They, in turn, sent inspectors to examine the Thunderbolt's remains, which they could only do at a distance due to fencing around the property. The examiners did take some photos (which were later allegedly misplaced by the city), and as a consequence of this supposed evidence, the buildings commissioner immediately "issued an emergency declaration to demolish without the benefit of a personal visit or any engineer's report on the structure's integrity." This all took place within the span of ten days as the emergency order was quietly signed and in place by September 1. After several months of delay—Horace Bullard's lawyer later claimed that "no one really wanted to demolish the Thunderbolt"—a representative of EDC upped the pressure on the Buildings Department. No sooner said than done. On November 17 work crews arrived without warning at dawn and methodically dismantled the ancient roller coaster track in less than a day. By the time Jeff Wilpon and the Brooklyn Cyclones announced their team's name at their press conference two weeks later, the remnants of the Thunderbolt had entirely vanished from view.[28]

Horace Bullard was absolutely livid. The first he heard of the demolition of his property was a phone call from one of his employees that morning saying, "Hey Boss, the City is tearing down your roller coaster." Even after arriving on the scene within a few hours he was physically restrained from entering the site and could only watch helplessly from outside the fences. Afterward Bullard fulminated to the press that Giuliani was "a dictator," recalling how six years earlier the mayor had seized the Steeplechase site to construct the stadium that had now deprived him of the Thunderbolt roller coaster as well. "He doesn't like that black people want to create major developments," Bullard fumed as he announced that he would be launching a lawsuit against Giuliani and the city. For their part, city spokespeople painted Bullard as a multimillion-dollar tax dodger who represented a threat to public safety. As Sunny Mindel said,

"Instead of making inflammatory comments, if Horace Bullard maintained the property so it wasn't dilapidated and dangerous, this wouldn't have happened."[29]

The razing of the Thunderbolt was eventually determined by the courts to have been wholly illegal. After years of litigation and depositions, the Manhattan Federal Court found for the plaintiff Horace Bullard that the City of New York had no right to demolish his property. But subsequent appeals exonerated then-Mayor Giuliani from any culpability, then rescinded a $3 million jury award of damages, and finally let the city off the hook for neglecting to inform Bullard of the imminent demolition order. In the end, Bullard never received a penny or just the satisfaction of assigning any blame for what he had undergone. Even five years later, the message was clear that the city's highest priority for Coney Island had been and continued to be professional baseball.[30]

With the Thunderbolt out of the way and the Mets in uncontested control of the stadium site, team preparations went into high gear over the winter and into the spring of 2001. Construction workers were on the job six days a week, with team officials maintaining an onsite presence in a trailer parked along Surf Avenue. Reporters brought in on tours conducted by the Wilpons admired the stadium's twelve luxury boxes, an unprecedented amenity at most minor league parks. Their genial hosts showed off the space allocated for upscale shops and even the high-quality shower tiles being installed in the clubhouses, a far cry from the primordial conditions in NY-PL sites like Pittsfield and Jamestown. Already by the end of January the team had sold more than 20 percent of all its seats for the entire season, with fan interest multiplying as Opening Day grew closer. The infield and outfield were laid out, the walls partially constructed, and blue plastic seats installed, even if much of the field still resembled "primeval ooze," in the words of a *New York Times* columnist. In addition to all the physical preparations, the team also revealed that it had successfully sold the stadium's naming rights to Keyspan Energy (formerly Brooklyn Union Gas) for an undisclosed amount, likely at least $500,000 per year for the next decade.[31]

The unwillingness of the mayor and the Wilpons to reveal the terms of the Keyspan Park naming arrangements raised the volume of financial criticism at a rather crucial moment. Mid-February was scheduled for one final meeting of New York City's Franchise and Concessions Review Committee to formally approve the Cyclones as sole tenant and rightsholder over the new stadium. Since the mayor controlled four of the six seats on the committee, with the exception of Borough President Howard Golden and City Comptroller and mayoral hopeful Alan Hevesi, this was widely regarded as a shoo-in. Nevertheless, the doldrums of winter and the fuzziness of many of the lease details provoked some pointed political grandstanding. When reporters and politicians inquired about how much Keyspan was paying and to whom, they were told only that the city would net $250,000 per year from the agreement. No information was made available as to how much the Mets would keep over and above the city's cut. It seemed likely that they would accept no less than the city's share or more, which in turn meant that Keyspan's agreement with Brooklyn was far more lucrative than the Staten Island deal for $400,000 per year from Richmond County Bank. Yet the documents provided to the committee revealed that the Cyclones' stadium rent payment schedule was identical to that of the Staten Island Yankees, with payments determined on a sliding scale based on attendance up to a maximum of $510,000 should they sell out every single game. Given the disparities in the valuation of the naming rights and the size and visibility of the Brooklyn market, it seemed to some that the Cyclones were receiving an extra-special sweetheart deal. Since the team would also pocket all additional advertising and parking revenue, rent payments from stadium stores and concessionaires, and a wealth of additional income, it was unsurprising that misgivings were expressed.[32]

The politician raising objections this time was Alan Hevesi rather than the embattled Howard Golden, who was beaten down after losing to Mayor Giuliani in every single ballpark-related confrontation between the two. Instead it was Comptroller Hevesi who insisted on delaying the Review Committee meeting for a day, so he had sufficient time to peruse the fine points of the 180-page agreement between EDC and the Wilpons. The following day at the committee meeting, it was Hevesi who denounced the deal as "egregiously one-sided to the city's detriment." It was also Hevesi who cast one of two fruitless no votes alongside a scowling Golden, who "sat mum" even as he watched the mayor's appointees ram the contract through. Yet it had also been Alan Hevesi who had voted yes on every previous committee vote that had brought the stadium to this point, without ever uttering a single public word in opposition to the project. Moreover, Hevesi's mayoral campaign had already received more than $17,000 in political contributions from the Wilpon family and their Sterling Equities firm, and those checks had long since been cashed. In the end, neither Golden's furious efforts nor Hevesi's token criticisms did anything to derail a project that was on the speediest of fast tracks.[33]

As winter turned to spring the construction of Keyspan Park proceeded exactly according to plan. The infield dirt was installed first, followed by high-quality grass and sod as the weather warmed. Large light stanchions were erected to encircle the stadium, their tiers of spotlights encased in round steel hoops which would pulse with colored neon lights after Cyclones home runs. Their modernity was balanced by the old-fashioned quaintness of outfield walls plastered with advertising billboards, evocative of bygone ballparks. Down the first-base line towered the repainted and reinforced Parachute Jump, and patrons could look out past centerfield at the vast Atlantic Ocean that had attracted millions of Coney Island beachgoers for more than a century. Over the leftfield fence the stadium's logo and scoreboard appeared on an ingenious backdrop which reproduced the Cyclone ride, perfectly placed in front of the actual roller coaster track which dipped, rose, and rattled with screaming riders six blocks away. By early April, Steve Cohen reported that the team had already sold half of the entire season's 247,000 available tickets. By mid-June that figure was up to two-thirds, and Cohen speculated that by the time the games actually started the Cyclones might very well have sold out up to 90 percent of all seats for their entire inaugural season.[34]

On June 25, 2001, New York-Penn League baseball finally arrived in Staten Island, and a day later it came to Brooklyn as well. It had taken years of planning and the combined involvement of at least four minor league teams and two major league organizations, countless city agencies, scads of lawyers, and one indomitable mayor to reach this moment. For New York City and its taxpayers, the costs of all of those efforts included nearly $120 million in public funds and the earmarking of large land tracts for private sports teams that paid nothing to acquire them. In the meantime, smaller baseball communities such as Oneonta, Watertown, Pittsfield, and St. Catharines had their loyalties tested and ultimately cast aside by the big business interests of minor league baseball. On these highly anticipated Opening Days the universal message communicated by team owners, politicians, media observers, and fans alike was that it had all most certainly been worth it. The truth of that assessment remained to be seen.

CHAPTER ELEVEN

WAITING FOR EXACTLY THIS:
THE INAUGURAL SEASON

As the spring of 2001 finally gave way to early summer, the excitement over a very special upcoming NY-PL season was palpable. This was particularly true in Staten Island, where Richmond County Bank Ballpark at St. George was preparing to open its rather expensive gates to the public. Rudy Giuliani and Guy Molinari had achieved their vision of bringing professional baseball to Staten Island, even as their final terms in public office were winding down. Stan and Josh Getzler relished the opportunity to make their mark in the biggest sports market in the country after their unsatisfying years in the baseball hinterlands. Only two years into their existence, the Staten Island Yankees had already achieved tremendous on-field accomplishments, won their first league championship, and taken significant strides towards short-term profitability. The imminent approach of Opening Day in the last week of June only heightened the interest and expectations surrounding the team.

During the months leading up to the season the franchise successfully negotiated six-figure partnerships with three different companies, including a local Staten Island brewery. Mayor Giuliani continued to beat the drum for the new stadium, announcing that he would be guest-conducting a July performance of Handel's "Fireworks Music" accompanied by a fireworks display launched from barges floating in the harbor beyond the outfield. Ticket sales were brisk, if not quite as impressive as the already league-leading Brooklyn Cyclones across the Verrazano Narrows Bridge. As summer commenced and the stadium neared full completion, owner

Stan Getzler took to going to the empty ballpark each morning to drink his coffee and watch the boats in New York Harbor from his vantage point along the third-base line. "In the Bronx, we grew up playing on the sandlots," he marveled. "The only view was the building next door. For somebody from the Bronx to wind up in partnership with the Yankees . . . There was so much serendipity, so much good fortune. I wish I could say I was smart enough to have planned it this way."[1] It remained to be seen how long the honeymoon would last and whether the team's early success would have actual staying power.

In the meantime, their rivals across the Narrows in Brooklyn showed every sign of standing on the brink of an unmitigated triumph. Tickets and merchandise continued to sell at a feverish pace, and positive press mounted as the season drew nearer. While the Staten Islanders were portrayed as a local story, the return of Brooklyn baseball was drawing national interest as well as fervent fan attention throughout the populous borough. Without yet playing a single game the Wilpons' new minor league venture was already a huge success. And despite the opposition of Howard Golden and his cronies, the irrepressible mayor was actualizing his baseball dreams in two boroughs simultaneously. On two consecutive picture-perfect nights in late June 2001 His Honor would celebrate his $120-million achievement at a pair of memorable Opening Day festivities at his brand-new minor league stadiums. He would make speeches and issue pointed digs at his political rivals and detractors, throw out the first pitches, and sign countless baseballs for the fans in the stands. There was nothing feigned about the megawatt grin Rudy Giuliani flashed at the cameras, his joy and pride at his "Edifice Complex" on full display.

On Sunday June 24, 2001, the Staten Island Yankees played their first game at Richmond County Bank Ballpark. After starting their season with a week of road games, they came home to defeat the Hudson Valley Renegades, coincidentally the same team that they had beaten two years earlier on their original Opening Day at the College of Staten Island (CSI) campus in Willowbrook. Inaugurating their new digs in St. George, the Yanks sold out every single seat in both general admission and the luxury suites, packing a capacity crowd of 6,854 into their shiny new stadium. New York baseball legend Dwight Gooden was on hand to hoist the NY-PL Championship Banner won by the new Baby Bombers, as they hoped to be known. Mayor Giuliani, accompanied by his "very close friend" (and future third wife turned ex-wife) Judi Nathan, sat in prime seating alongside Guy and Susan Molinari and a who's who of local Staten Island elected officials and business figures. Much to the consternation of

Figure 11.1. Mayor Giuliani signing baseballs at Saint John's University on Queens Kings Opening Day, June 2000. Photo credit: New York City Municipal Archives.

Figure 11.2. Mayor Giuliani signing baseballs at College of Staten Island on Yankees Opening Day, June 1999. Photo credit: New York City Municipal Archives.

Figure 11.3. Mayor Giuliani signing baseballs at Keyspan Park in Coney Island on Brooklyn Cyclones Opening Day, June 2001. Photo credit: New York City Municipal Archives.

the mayor, Councilman Jerome O' Donovan was also in attendance and enjoyed the game even as he openly criticized the stadium's inflated costs to the press. There was some grumbling among attendees about the long lines for admission and at the concession stands, the lack of skyline views from some of the seats, and the requirement of exact change for those riding the Ballpark Express rail shuttle from the new St. George Station. Local residents also griped about the loud noise levels produced by the booming fireworks display in the harbor after the game. But traffic and parking outside the stadium were smooth and trouble-free, the fans were rhapsodic about the sparkling new taxpayer-funded stadium facility, and the game was generally regarded as a triumph all around.[2]

Still, as Harvey Araton pointed out the following morning in the *New York Times*, something was missing from Staten Island on Opening Day. "As New York-Penn League openings go," he observed, "this one was practically a civic secret compared to the nostalgia convention scheduled for the Brooklyn Cyclones in Coney Island tonight." Despite the gorgeous vistas on display at the bayfront stadium, featuring "the ferries in the harbor, the Twin Towers looming in the distance, the Brooklyn Bridge framed like a photo, the skyline at dusk and the Statue of Liberty welcoming [the team] to its new home," a sense of rebirth and renewed excitement were undeniably lacking. It may have been "a view worth $71 million" as Araton noted, but that alone was no guarantee of sustained success for the team inhabiting New York City's most isolated borough. Stan Getzler put the best face on his team's debut that he could. "I think the press has been slow to what's going to happen here," he said. "When dusk settles and the lights go on, this is like any small town in America." Having previously failed to produce baseball success in an actual small town in upstate New York, the Getzlers were already growing fretful about their future in one of the biggest metropolitan areas in the country.[3]

Meanwhile, it only took a single day for the Brooklyn Cyclones to cast the Baby Bombers in the shade. On the following morning of June 25 at the dawn of a second consecutive picture-perfect summer day, viewers of multiple early-morning television news shows were treated to a series of onsite interviews with Mayor Giuliani at Keyspan Park. Prior to making a relatively bland appearance on the NBC *Today Show*, the feisty mayor first conducted a testy exchange with Bryant Gumbel on the *CBS Early Show*. When the longtime newsman sought to challenge him regarding the high costs of his minor league stadiums and questioned their benefits to the city and its residents, Giuliani countered with a lengthy flow of talking points and unverified claims and statistics. He said,

This will be the core around which the economic revival of Coney Island takes place. It's already taking place. You bring 7,000 people in here 40 times a summer, and there are going to be concerts here, we're going to have a major boxing match here in July. This is the core around which the economic revival of Coney Island, which used to be the most famous amusement park in the world, is going to take place. We already have two new developments going up, a hotel that someone is investing in. We're doing a whole new modernization work at the aquarium, which is right down the road. This will do for Coney Island what Disney did for 42nd Street in Times Square. Take that from the mayor who's done more to economically revive New York City than any mayor in 50 years. Property values here have already gone up 10 percent or 15 percent . . .

I grew up in Brooklyn. I used to come to Coney Island with my grandmother four or five times a year every summer. It was like one of the great outings of the year. You're going to see kids coming to Coney Island, using it. This is a great thing. And you'll see a rivalry between Staten Island and Coney Island that really helps the City of New York . . .

The newspapers don't understand economic development and they attack things like this. [But] people love it. Come and watch baseball and stop all the cynicism.

Unable to get a word in edgewise, Gumbel finally surrendered and muttered "we're getting out of here" as he cut to a commercial break, the only way to silence his voluble interviewee.[4]

As the day continued with sunny skies and a temperature just below 90 degrees, Coney Island was the perfect setting for a day at the beach and later for a ballgame at dusk. Prior to the game, an official Cyclones welcoming parade marched down Surf Avenue featuring local Little Leaguers, dozens of police officers, and the ever-present mayor. Every local media outlet sent cameras and reporters to cover the much-hyped return of baseball to Brooklyn and interviewed fans, local residents, elderly Brooklyn Dodgers veterans, and the ubiquitous politicians and would-be candidates who turned out for Opening Day. Their numbers were augmented by members of the national and international press who had come to cover the feel-good story of the summer. Outside the stadium gates men held up cardboard signs reading "I need tickets" as they fruitlessly sought entrée to the sold-out contest. Although gametime vehicular traffic was heavy, it moved along steadily, with traffic cops waving in fans who exited the Belt Parkway to park their sedans and SUVs in the stadium's spacious parking lot at a bargain price of $10. Few of these fans would spend any of their time or money in Coney Island either before or after the game. Their patronage was restricted to the Keyspan Park concessions that filled the Wilpons' coffers but no one else's.

Once inside, the fans oohed and aahed over the old-timey décor of the brand-new facility. The perfectly manicured field was adorned only with a painted Cyclones logo behind home plate, and it was circumscribed by colorful old-fashioned billboards reminiscent of the golden age of baseball in Fred Wilpon's youth. The field's dimensions mirrored those of the major leagues, such as its centerfield distance of 412 feet. Yet the design and feel of the stadium was cozy and intimate. Each of Keyspan's 7,500 seats felt closer to the field and the game action than one would find at Shea Stadium or Yankee Stadium, and at a fraction of the ticket price. During the hours before the game, fans drank their inexpensive $5 beers as they soaked up the atmosphere and enjoyed the refreshing sea breeze wafting through the stadium. They packed the two-story stadium souvenir shop to buy t-shirts, tchotchkes, and hats. Although the stadium's last-minute construction and touch-ups were by no means finished, those in attendance noticed only the considerable charms of their new ballpark. The grousing and mild complaints of the Staten Island crowd the night before were completely absent in Brooklyn, even as stadium employees privately admitted that much was left unfinished. Instead the fans cheered the pregame introductions of Cyclones coaches and ex-Mets players Bobby Ojeda, Howard Johnson, and manager Edgar Alfonso, and basked in the nostalgic glow surrounding Joan Hodges, widow of the beloved Dodgers player and 1969 Miracle Mets skipper Gil Hodges. The icing on the cake was the game itself, which boasted an unlikely ninth-inning comeback by the Cyclones that ended in an extra-inning victory for the home team. The capacity crowd which had largely stayed all the way through the end of the game went home happy and satisfied. As Brooklyn-based writer Ben Osborne observed, "A historic moment had rarely been this fun. Leaving Keyspan Park on this gorgeous night, most of the fans feel as if they've been given a gift . . . with the first game over, people act as if their lives have been waiting for exactly this."[5]

The Cyclones' epic Opening Day was the culmination of a great deal of planning and orchestration by the Mets organization and its enablers in the Mayor's Office. For several years they had spun a meticulous public narrative that had begun with Fred Wilpon in his shower, dreaming of the day that he could bring professional baseball back to Brooklyn. The loss of the Dodgers, the borough's beloved "Dem Bums," remained a gaping wound for Brooklyn-born fans far and wide even four decades later. Now they would have the chance to bring back those days thought to be gone forever. "Who'da thunk we'd really come to the day we'd see baseball again in Brooklyn?" asked Robert Catell, the Keyspan Energy CEO whose company name adorned the new stadium in white-and-blue block lettering. Added official Brooklyn baseball historian Tom Knight, "The best thing is that we can now say something we've wanted to say for more than 40 years: 'How'd Brooklyn do?' "[6]

Critics like author Roger Kahn, famed for his legendary Brooklyn Dodgers tome *The Boys of Summer* and a onetime NY-PL team owner himself, scoffed at the idea that these low-level minor leaguers could somehow fill that void. "It's like bringing back Camelot," he told the *New York Times*, "but instead you get a whole lot of dwarfs sitting around a very small Round Table. It has nothing to do with Reese, Robinson, Furillo." Instead of denying Kahn's cantankerous grumpings, everyone affiliated with the team hurried to agree with him loudly and repeatedly. "We're not replacing the Brooklyn Dodgers," Fred Wilpon averred a month before the season. "A short-season-A team is not going to replace the Brooklyn Dodgers," echoed his son Jeff. Former Mets World Champion and current Cyclones pitching coach Bobby Ojeda also stuck to the party line, observing, "We're not the Brooklyn Dodgers. But, you know what? We're something. And we're going to earn our following and maybe win back some of those ones who turned off baseball in 1957." Even some fans seemed to share the same attitude. As Gerritsen Beach resident Buddy Heffernan told one reporter, "I'll be watching these guys all season long, and nobody has to worry about the Dodgers anymore."[7]

Yet the Cyclones and their owner and the mayor and the media missed no opportunity to draw a clear and direct line of descent between the two teams. While the Dodgers name and cursive uniform logo were off-limits due to potential conflicts with their Los Angeles incarnation, no other aspect of Brooklyn Dodgerdom was out of bounds for the Cyclones. Space was set aside in the new stadium for a future Brooklyn Dodgers Museum to be constructed. The city also announced plans to erect a $600,000 statue at the stadium's main entrance featuring Brooklyn Dodgers Jackie Robinson and Pee Wee Reese in full Dodger regalia, embracing in friendship. On Opening Night the savvy Wilpons invited the surviving members of the Dodger Sym-Phony to join the crowd, serenading fellow fans and opposing players with a brassy cacophony unheard since the old days at their beloved bandbox stadium. Keyspan Park's outfield even featured a clothier's advertising sign that read "Hit Sign, Win Suit," an unmistakable nod to the legendary Abe Stark sign that had been one of Ebbets Field's most recognizable features for over a quarter-century. And in a marketing masterstroke the team's official caps sported a stylized white "Brooklyn B" with curlicues and flourishes indistinguishable from those worn by Duke Snider and Ralph Branca back in the 1950s, although the modern version interlaced a small red C for Cyclones.[8]

R. C. Reuteman, longtime general manager of the Binghamton Mets, had been brought in as a Cyclones senior vice president to oversee the launch of the franchise. He later explained that nothing about the team's Brooklyn baseball connection was accidental. Every aspect was calculated and painstakingly researched.

The marketing philosophy was that we would be foolish to turn our backs on the Brooklyn Dodgers. But at the same time, we needed to establish our own identity. So we actually got permission [to use the "Brooklyn B"]. We had asked permission from the Dodgers. Bob Graziano, who was a Brooklyn native, at the time was president of the Dodgers. So Fred reached out to him and they gave us permission to use it, and we worked with Major League Baseball to develop the fonts [for the team].

I also worked with a woman in Major League Baseball who did a hundred-year historical study of Coney Island, and she did boards for us. The colors we used, the yellow, the red, the blue, were predominant in Coney Island forever.[9]

Marketing the Wilpons' new franchise as the-Dodgers-return-but-not-really was just the beginning. It was the combination of Brooklyn baseball lore with the irresistible lure of Coney Island that imbued the venture with unprecedented nostalgic potency. For a generation of Brooklynites now ensconced in more placid middle age, Ebbets Field and Steeplechase Park both represented a bygone era of lost youth and carefree summer amusements. Shuttered within seven years of each other, the two iconic Brooklyn structures hearkened back to a time before New York City's perceived deterioration in the turbulent 1960s and 1970s. Trapped in a time before the deleterious effects of widespread urban renewal, teacher strikes, campus protests, and municipal near-bankruptcy, they were immune to the ravages of time, reality, and economic and population change throughout the borough and the city. As large numbers of white middle-class residents relocated to the suburbs of Long Island, New Jersey, and beyond, they took with them their memories of a vanished Brooklyn of the mind that they remembered as simple and wholesome. Those who remained behind nurtured the same nostalgic fantasies of days gone by. While the Brooklyn natives who detested Fred Trump were likely far fewer in number than those who cursed the memory of Walter O'Malley, in some ways the two men were hated for the same reason. Both had done their worst to destroy two of Brooklyn's dearest symbolic treasures.

Now the Cyclones had arrived to resurrect Brooklyn's fabled past in one fell swoop, at least according to the branding and publicity machines that toiled away throughout the months leading up to Opening Day. Besides bringing baseball back to Brooklyn and assuaging the hurt caused by the

Dodgers' departure, the team and its stadium were poised to revitalize Coney Island after decades of deterioration. The mayor stayed on-message and constantly referred to the project as the core of economic revival efforts, just as he did on Opening Day in the Bryant Gumbel interview. This sentiment was repeated over and over by his flacks at the Economic Development Corporation (EDC) and the local politicians who were benefiting from his largesse. Columnists touted the "synergy between boardwalk and baseball," so crucial to a neighborhood "where the once-thriving amusement park and beach have experienced a steady decrease in traffic in recent years." The sky would be the limit in the new Coney Island, and media members made mighty efforts to attach deep significance to what was being sold as the beginning of a new era. "Coney Island, all lit up and sparkling, was the first piece of New York old-time immigrants would see as they sailed toward Ellis Island," wrote one *Daily News* reporter. "These days, there is an energy around the famous boardwalk, a sense that the place is about to undergo another sea change."[10]

The canny Wilpons sensed the value of the Coney Island angle from the outset, and they made sure not to squander the marketing opportunities it afforded them. From the name of the team to the sinuous roller coaster reproduction adorning the left field scoreboard, references to Coney's historic Cyclone ride were inescapable. The Cyclones' crowd-pleasing mascot was Sandy the Seagull, a friendly version of the ubiquitous birds so familiar to beachgoers. A month before the season began, the team announced that it had signed a three-year concession contract with Nathan's Famous Hot Dogs, a Coney Island landmark for nearly a century. As a crowning touch, the Wilpons also told the press that they would be employing nearly two hundred Coney Islanders to work at the stadium throughout its inaugural season. In their press releases and in much of the public imagination the Brooklyn Cyclones were now the link between Coney Island's historic past and its rosy future, just as they were also the heirs to the long and storied tradition of professional baseball in Brooklyn.[11]

"When they went to Brooklyn, the Mets were going to create an old-time recreation of baseball on the boardwalk," Josh Getzler later recalled, not without some envy. "It was going to be lower-tech, it was going to be more of a carnival atmosphere. It was going to be honky-tonk." By leaning into those aspects of their product, the Wilpons not only tapped into a formidable wellspring of nostalgia but also saved themselves a great deal of money in expenses. Keyspan Park featured stadium signage consisting of "three layers of fence signs, board on top of board on top of board all over the ballpark like you had in *Bull Durham*," a choice that was both aesthetic and practical. Old-timey painted signs fit perfectly into the Cyclones' retro imaging and brand. But they also required only a bare minimum of maintenance and offered sponsors full-game exposure in front of capacity crowds.[12]

Perhaps the Cyclones' biggest advantage was their prominence within the Mets organization. The Wilpons were well aware that their new Brooklyn franchise had the potential to be the crown jewel of their entire minor league system. This was the reason they had insisted on complete ownership and control of the team, driving away their longtime partner Bill Gladstone once he had helped plant the idea. It was their motivation for bringing in R. C. Reuteman from Binghamton after his successful eight-year stint there as general manager, overseeing the construction of a pricy new stadium and even owning a piece of the Mets' AAA Binghamton affiliate. And so they stacked the deck with every advantage they could muster, from finagling a deal to bring back the Brooklyn B logo to assembling a coaching staff stocked with former members of the 1986 World Champion Mets. Those arrangements also came with a significant financial commitment to building the team and its brand. Although the huge burden of stadium costs had been assumed by Mayor Giuliani and New York City, there were still a wide array of ancillary expenditures required to get the entire enterprise off the ground. With the resources of the big club at their disposal, the Cyclones front office never doubted that every issue would be taken care of speedily and efficiently. "We did it first class, major league," Reuteman reminisced some years later. "The Wilpons gave us the opportunity to do it that way and spend the money. And we could spend money because we were making a lot of money. So they didn't question how we did things."[13]

The Yankees didn't question how the Getzlers were doing things in Staten Island either, but for different reasons and with different outcomes. Unlike the Wilpons, the Steinbrenner family did not consider their NY-PL affiliate to be a crown jewel of their organization, nor did they treat it as one. The major league Yankees owned only 49 percent of the Staten Island team and had zero interest in taking over full ownership. From the outset they had preferred a more traditional minor league model where the franchise would be under the control of a trusted partner, as they had for more than three decades with Sam Nader in Oneonta. Once Lonn Trost and Bob Julian matched the Yankees to the Getzlers, it was up to the latter to make the most of their Yankees connections to market and grow their team. Given the high profile of the new franchise and its expensive new stadium, it was expected that they would maintain regular contact with the parent organization. But the Yankees would mostly follow a hands-off approach to the club throughout the Getzlers' tenure in Staten Island. This was a stark contrast to the Brooklyn Cyclones, where no detail, from the ballpark views to the cap logo to the mascot, escaped the notice of the Wilpons, who owned the entirety of the team.

Unlike their National League counterparts, the New York Yankees were cresting the wave of one of the great dynasties in the history of modern professional sports. The 2001 team was headed to its fourth World Series in a row after winning three straight and four out of the past five championships since 1996. Although the Yankees would not actually win another for nearly a decade until 2009, they remained a perennially competitive playoff team just about every single year. During that span and throughout the Steinbrenners' ownership the organization was almost entirely focused on its dominance at the major league level. Minor league Yankees affiliates were primarily a means to that end, providing and training homegrown talent until they were ready to take their place on the big-league roster and play their assigned roles in bringing the team more victories. For also-rans like the Mets, who had appeared in only four World Series and won just two in their entire forty-year history, the Brooklyn Cyclones represented a huge opportunity to make their mark. The Yankees brand was so much more lucrative and recognizable—one contemporary study by *Forbes* magazine listed the Yankees as by far the most valuable organization in Major League Baseball, worth almost twice as much as the Mets—that the viability of a single minor league franchise would forever be a minor priority.[14]

The Yankees' laissez-faire attitude toward the entire Staten Island enterprise made them somewhat blasé about its day-to-day operations. The choice of the borough had been pressed on them by Mayor Giuliani and Borough President Molinari, as had the location of the new stadium in inaccessible St. George. This in turn had forced a shift of affiliation away from Oneonta, which the Yankees had previously shown no interest in abandoning. To accommodate the Mets' interest in Brooklyn and further their own future plans for an entirely new major league stadium in the Bronx, the Yankees had acceded to a move that had not really been their idea. So they did not devote many of their own formidable resources to proactive research into the potential market for their product in Staten Island, customer outreach, or profitability. They merely instructed the

Getzlers to slap the name Yankees on their new team and then handle all the details themselves. As it turned out, this would be the first in a series of costly mistakes and miscalculations.

It was the great success of the organization that had attracted the Getzlers to buy in from the outset, and that had an outsized impact on their marketing strategy. Josh Getzler was a lifelong Yankees fan who at the time was a freshly minted MBA with just a few years of baseball management experience. Dazzled by the potential of owning a Yankees franchise right in the team's backyard, his business plan for the team rested on a number of untested premises. His father shared his optimism, and when they ran their plans past their major league partners the Yankees brass expressed no immediate reservations with their approach. "We had assumed, and it was not an unreasonable assumption, that we could [just] open up shop and we would get an awful lot of people buying," Getzler later recalled.

> Everything would be fine and taken care of, because the Yankees were in the greatest hot streak dynasty of the generation. Why wouldn't it work? And the Yankees were going to be synergistic with us and it would be amazing. That's what we had to say—that we were the Yankees. I think we believed it, and I think that the Yankees believed it, and I think that the politicians believed it. I think everybody did, and I don't think it was a crazy assumption. But it didn't happen. Everybody was on the same page, but it was the wrong page.[15]

The team's most fundamental problem had been foisted on them by the politicians and their minions at EDC, namely the decision to situate the club's expensive new stadium in the relatively remote location of St. George. The team's previous temporary stadium at CSI had been less than a five-minute drive from the Staten Island Expressway, the borough's major artery. On the other hand, Richmond County Bank Ballpark was located along Staten Island's meandering North Shore and was far less easy to reach by car. Getting there from the expressway or the more populated family neighborhoods along the South Shore involved a lengthy trek along winding side streets, which were often crowded with traffic just prior to evening game times at 7:00 p.m. In fact, fear of traffic jams had been one of the primary objections of neighborhood groups like the St. George Civic Association back in 1999 throughout the ULURP process. At the time, representatives from the Mayor's Office and EDC had countered that vehicular congestion would be ameliorated by the availability of public transportation to the stadium. A new multimillion-dollar dedicated Staten Island Ballpark station was even built to transport gameday fans via Staten Island Rapid Transit.

As it turned out, none of these predictions ever materialized. The number of cars driving to the stadium for weeknight games turned out to be far fewer than the optimistic team estimates or even the pessimistic expectations of local residents. Whether that was a function of the long, convoluted drive to the ballpark or the result of poor marketing was uncertain, but either way it proved to be a rarity for a Staten Island Yankees game to create even a brief traffic jam. As for the railroad, the train proved inconvenient for ticketholders due to its demands for additional fares to be paid only in exact change, which many fans were not carrying. Furthermore, the entire transit system was chronically underutilized by Staten Islanders anyway. Within a decade the barely used Ballpark station was shuttered by New York City's Metropolitan Transit Authority in a budget-cutting maneuver that surprised no one and went entirely unmourned.[16]

The Getzlers' lack of familiarity with their new home borough meant that they did not comprehend the depth of their stadium problem for quite some time. "We didn't really understand the mentality on Staten Island or what the reality of traffic is," Josh Getzler would confess some years later. "What we did was very external analysis, and we made our assumptions based on raw numbers and not on psychology." After several seasons of declining attendance and revenues the Getzlers came to realize that their focus on individual ticket sales and walk-up buyers had been misplaced. A fatal flaw of the stadium was that the surrounding neighborhood was not inhabited by the middle-class families they hoped to attract. Compounding the issue was the lack of any additional development nearby. The mayor and the Staten Island borough president had portrayed the new stadium as the linchpin for a wealth of new cultural construction in the area. But Rudy Giuliani and Guy Molinari were both forced out of office by term limits within the year, and under their successors the promised Lighthouse Museum and Science Museum were never constructed. Most Staten Islanders viewed the underdeveloped downtown area as seedy and undesirable after dark, further inhibiting foot traffic and pregame sales. It became clear very quickly that the placement of the stadium was directly correlated to the team's attendance struggles, as Josh Getzler concluded: "We would have been considerably better off with a 4,500-seat facility at the College of Staten Island forever than 7,100 seats on the North Shore. [We could have reached] 500,000 people plus the occasional people from Jersey, but with all of Staten Island being able to get there easily."[17]

One justification for the stadium's location had been its closeness to the Staten Island Ferry, which was expected to bring in stadium-goers from out of the borough without clogging the roadways. Persuaded by the confidence of the mayor and EDC officials, the Getzlers incorporated the ferry as a cornerstone of their marketing approach to selling tickets. One of the team's primary goals as articulated by Josh Getzler was to target businesspeople and residents of Manhattan who were already Yankees fans and convince them to take a short half-hour ferry ride to see the future stars of their favorite team. It took several years before the realization dawned that he had not factored in all of the time and effort that would entail for the city dwellers he was trying to attract. "We figured that we would achieve market penetration in lower Manhattan just by working hard. [But] people didn't necessarily want to come home from their job in Manhattan, go out to Tottenville and come back in," he reflected many years afterward. "So either they had to meet the family at the ballpark or had to do that schlep in both directions." That round-trip would be well over an hour and perhaps as long as two hours once all was said and done, since it also encompassed travel time to and from the ferry terminals and the wait between ferry trips. Given the sheer number of entertainment options available to New Yorkers that did not require such a significant commute or time commitment, it was small wonder that the Staten Island Yankees failed to attract the Manhattan audience they most coveted.

The Getzlers' determination to attract wealthy, sophisticated Manhattanites led them down yet another blind alley of their own choosing. After considering what might best enhance their image among their chosen audience, and at the same time highlight the contrast between their team and their rivals in Brooklyn, they decided to make a particularly splashy and expensive statement.

> We knew that the Mets, when they went to Brooklyn, were going to create an old-time recreation of baseball on the boardwalk and it was going to be lower tech, that it was going to be more of a carnival atmosphere. Our goal was to be the most high tech, thinking of ourselves as being directly across from and trying to market to Wall Street. [To attract] the downtown techie kind of world, we had to be flashier. We had to be more

digital, more high tech. So we decided to really lean into that.

We spent over a million dollars on video boards to put on our outfield walls. Our marketing strategy was to sell half-inning sponsorships with exclusivity. Other than what was up on the scoreboard, we were not going to have any other advertising in the ballpark besides what was on those screens for half an inning at a time. Rather than trying to get a hundred or fifty-five bent signs and a whole bunch of [ads] on the top, we were going to just try to concentrate on seventeen very strong [sponsorships]. We were never going to need the bottom of the ninth, because when you win every game going away, you have nothing to worry about.

It was going to be a comprehensive sponsorship deal where you get your half inning, and you get a luxury suite, and X number of tickets, and advertising in the scorecard, and a whole bunch of things for $50,000 for the full season.

Like so many of the Getzlers' big plans, the high-tech approach ended up looking a lot better on paper than it ever did in reality. For one thing, the highest number of comprehensive sponsorships they ever sold in a single season was only ten or eleven, a far cry from the hoped-for seventeen. For another, several of those sponsors included existing business partners like Pepsi, Budweiser, and the company that had purchased naming rights to the stadium, Richmond County Bank. Instead of paying for their half-innings in desperately needed cash transactions, these companies accepted them as a form of barter instead. The beverage companies allowed the Yankees to pay off part of their bills as a sponsorship, while the bank applied the fee toward their annual naming right payments. Neither of these arrangements provided the team with the income it had planned to raise from their hypothetical sponsors. Worse yet, it took several years before they realized they had badly misjudged what their advertising clients had wanted all along. "It took us about four years to give up and to say 'what people really want are fence signs, and they don't care that the value is not as good. They want to be up all the time, even if it looks like the Yellow Pages. And they want to spend $3,700 for that, not $50,000 for a million things. That's not worthwhile.' We made a fundamental error in strategy with that." So the million-dollar video screens failed to satisfy existing sponsors or attract enough new ones to justify their cost.

The expensive screens soon became not only the most tangible symbols of their failed marketing plan, but also a financial boondoggle of towering proportions. The high-tech exterior video boards had been bought on credit, which became a burden as they failed to attract enough sponsors to pay for themselves. Because they were mounted above the outfield fences facing inward, anything mounted on the rear of the screens was exposed to the air to prevent overheating and allow ease of access for repairs. This meant that the screens' wires, power ports, and connections dangled on the outside of the stadium facing Upper New York Bay with little shielding or protection. When there was wind—and there was almost always wind swirling around the northern tip of Staten Island—saltwater kicked up and blew into the guts of the video boards, causing wire damage, corrosion, and electrical shorts on a constant basis. Underfunded, underutilized, and blinking constantly, the screens cost thousands of dollars in maintenance that only added to the team's budgetary woes. Sometimes they even had to be fixed during games in full view of the stadium, adding an extra layer of embarrassment to the injurious costs of going high-tech.[18]

The Yankees organization had signed off on the video screens just as they had agreed to nearly all of the Getzlers' plans, but with the underlying condition that they would pay for nothing above or beyond the players' salaries. Their vision was for the minor league affiliate to be self-sustaining by generating enough revenues to cover its expenses and pay down any debts incurred along the way. And those debts were piling up quickly even before the team's inaugural season began. Although New York City and EDC had assumed the construction cost of the ballpark, they provided the Getzlers little more than an empty concrete box with seats and stadium lights. Furthermore the city's architectural plans and cost-cutting measures precluded finished spaces for valuable commercial concessions, biting into potential revenue streams that the team desperately needed. The minor league owners were left responsible for constructing the offices, luxury boxes, clubhouses, and concession stands, as well as installing the plumbing, wiring and other electrical and computer connections, and a host of other needs. With the Yankees placing hard limits on their own contributions, the startup costs for the Getzlers were enormous even without factoring in the financial extravagances of their own devising.[19]

In their inexperience and naivete, Stan and Josh Getzler did not yet realize how deep of a hole they were already in. They were stuck with a stadium that was geographically inaccessible, unlikely to maximize much-needed revenue, and environmentally unsuited to the high-tech amenities that they sought to install there. Their home borough's customer base was limited and had a track record of apathy and lack of team support besides the additional hurdles imposed by the remoteness of their facility. Their own marketing myopia and misjudgments further reduced any burgeoning interest in their product. The imprimatur of the mighty Yankees brand raised high expectations within the front office, the parent organization, and New Yorkers in general, setting an unfairly high bar they could not hope to reach. The Yankees higher-ups had also made it clear that the team was a low priority for them in terms of resource allocation or hand-holding, and that the Getzlers were essentially on their own to make a go of it in Staten Island. All of this stood in stark contrast to the astronomic success, rapturous reception, and elaborate support system that sustained their closest rivals, the Brooklyn Cyclones.

Both teams continued to build on their early success throughout the 2001 season, although at times they almost seemed to be in different leagues. For the Staten Island Yankees the remainder of the inaugural season in St. George mostly followed the successful blueprint established on Opening Day. The team finished the year with a record of 48–28, good enough for second place in the NY-PL's Stedler Division behind only the Brooklyn Cyclones. That earned them a spot in the playoffs, although the Yankees lost in the first round to the Brooklyn Cyclones. By season's end the Staten Island Yankees had rung up 188,127 in ticket sales, averaging a healthy 4,951 per game and far surpassing their previous numbers at the CSI facility or in Watertown. They finished fourth in league attendance behind the Lowell Spinners, the Indians' new Ohio affiliate the Mahoning Valley Scrappers and, of course, the league-leading Brooklyn Cyclones. "I'm very positive with the reaction we've received," said Josh Getzler, repeating "I'm very happy" as if to convince himself. Mayor Giuliani seemed pleased as well, as he told the press that the Staten Island club had performed "beyond the expectations that anybody had for them at the beginning of the season." But he qualified even that muted praise, adding "the Staten Island Yankees are over 4,000 [per game]—although in comparison, that doesn't seem as good." In response to the constant contrasts between his club and the more successful Cyclones, Josh Getzler averred, "I don't think having another minor league team in Brooklyn has affected us . . . I don't think we're competing with Brooklyn at all. If anything, we're helping each other out." The Cyclones, who were bringing in 7,821 fans every time they played in Coney Island, didn't seem to need much help from the Yankees though.[20]

By the end of 2001 Staten Island's foray into minor league baseball could be deemed a mixed success at best. The Yankees had clearly established a position in the upper echelon of the New York-Penn League, averaging fourth in per-game attendance and second in total season attendance. The Getzlers also hoped to build on their New York City and Yankees connections and grow the business further in the upcoming years. But the constant comparisons to the unsurpassed achievements of the Brooklyn Cyclones were exhausting, as were the repeated press refrains recalling the high public costs attached to the Ballpark at St. George. The team's situation and future prospects were further shaken by the September 11 terror attacks on the World Trade Center, which the Getzler family watched collapse and fall from their unimpeded vantage point within their Staten Island stadium. Later that day and lasting for the next several weeks their "sparkling field of dreams" was converted into a staging area for rescue and emergency workers and eventually into a morgue for the remains of many who perished in the Twin Towers. When the team resumed playing nine months later in June 2002, more than the stadium view of the lower Manhattan skyline had changed. In the aftermath of 9/11 priorities had shifted for New York City's residents and political and financial leaders, and this would have a perceptible impact on the fortunes of entertainment-related businesses like minor league baseball and the Staten Island Yankees. Furthermore, their home borough had been hard-hit by the tragedy, which made it even more difficult for potential customers to block everything out and focus on what one fan called "the beauty of minor league baseball, [which is] all about youngsters looking forward to moving ahead."[21]

Although Staten Island's struggles were worrisome, the NY-PL scarcely noticed them in the rush to capitalize on the blockbuster success of the Brooklyn Cyclones. Over the next decade new teams would expand the league's geographical borders farther than ever before in the league's sixty-plus years of operation. New owners would infuse the league with cash and stadium deals, shifting the dynamic further away from the community-based approach of the old local teams of the past. The future of his legacy assured, Bob Julian would step down from the league presidency and hand it off to a successor with no ties to the NY-PL or its history.

With each passing year the league's independence and quirky uniqueness were shrinking. Over time it was settling into a reduced existence as a small cog in a professional baseball machine that was under the tightening control of major league ownership. While this brought the league to new prominence and a wider audience, it also increased its vulnerability to threats to its continued existence.

CHAPTER TWELVE
NOT EVEN A SMIDGEN OF SENTIMENT

Part One: What Goes Up

As the new millennium dawned, New York-Penn League (NY-PL) baseball seemed to be settling into a period of sustained growth and prosperity. Bob Julian's strategy of finding moneyed owners who would match NY-PL clubs to proximate parent organizations was paying off handsomely. The Cyclones were a phenomenon, reaching unprecedented levels of success and profitability unsurpassed by any other team in all of minor league baseball. While the Staten Island Yankees fell far short of that lofty benchmark, their opening season went well enough to engender cautious (albeit misplaced) optimism on the part of the Getzler family. Julian had done quite well for the league throughout his tenure as league president from 1992 to 2000. Under his stewardship seven of the league's fourteen teams had reached agreements for new stadiums while others had secured funding for substantial improvements, and several more stadium and ownership deals were in the pipeline. His departure came about not because of any dissatisfaction within the ranks but thanks to a golden opportunity. Over several decades as an attorney and legislator Bob Julian had cultivated important connections within state politics, and he now had a chance to run unopposed for a seat on the New York Supreme Court. In November 2000 Julian got his name listed simultaneously on four individual party lines, an electoral sure thing that resulted in his elevation to the bench. He would spend the next eight years building a reputation for pragmatism and decorousness, qualities that had served him well as he built up his baseball league over the previous eight years.[1]

213

Julian's successor as NY-PL president was Ben J. Hayes, who represented a new breed of chief executive for a league that had always been
intensely local. All of the Hayes's predecessors had deep roots in New
York State, including Buffalonians Robert Stedler and Vince McNamara,
Auburn native Leo Pinckney, and Utica's Bob Julian. Although Hayes too
was born in New York (in Niagara Falls), his family had long since relocated to St. Petersburg, Florida, and Hayes was basically an out-of-stater
through and through. Also unlike any of the league's previous presidents,
Hayes had played professional baseball. He even enjoyed a brief major
league career as a pitcher for the Cincinnati Reds before blowing out his
arm in 1983. After returning to South Florida to try his hand at college
coaching, he went on to earn a law degree at the University of Florida in
1992 and within a year had secured a job through his professional baseball connections. From 1993 to 2000 Ben Hayes served as secretary and
general counsel of Minor League Baseball (officially known as the National
Association of Professional Baseball Leagues), where his responsibilities
included vetting prospective team owners and negotiating stadium deals
with local municipalities. He struck out on his own to establish a private
law practice facilitating baseball team purchases and sales, only to be
drawn back into organized baseball when he was offered the opportunity
to run the NY-PL. Hudson Renegades owner Marvin Goldklang, who
chaired the search committee, was clearly satisfied with his choice. "Ben's
abilities and experience, particularly in areas relating to administrative,
legal and on-field baseball matters made him the leading candidate for
the job," Goldklang intoned. "The League is indeed fortunate to have Ben
Hayes as its next president." Fellow committee member Sam Nader was
less ebullient, adding only, "Bob Julian is leaving some big shoes to fill
and, while we look forward to welcoming Ben Hayes as our new President,
the League will miss Bob's leadership."[2]

As demonstrated by the differing reactions of Goldklang and Nader,
the selection of Hayes as president was clearly intended to move the league
into a big-time future and away from its rustic small-market past. Thanks
to Bob Julian's unstinting efforts the NY-PL was experiencing a period
of sustained and unprecedented prosperity and growth when Ben Hayes
took office in April 2001. In 1994 the New Jersey Cardinals (formerly the
Hamilton Redbirds) had moved into their new home at Skylands Park,
a $10 million facility plagued by cost overruns and construction delays.
A year later Marvin Goldklang's Hudson Valley Renegades celebrated
the opening of their own new ballpark, $5 million Dutchess Stadium

in Fishkill, New York. But under Julian's watch, the gold rush was just beginning. In 1996 the longtime Elmira Pioneers packed up their wagons to head hundreds of miles eastward to Lowell, Massachusetts, as the new affiliate of the nearby Boston Red Sox. Known henceforth as the Lowell Spinners (after the region's famed nineteenth-century textile mills), the team soon had a new local owner with deep pockets and a brand-new stadium, completed in 1998 at a cost of more than $8 million. They also had a second New England team as a neighbor, as the Vermont Expos relocated to Burlington from underperforming Jamestown, New York, in the mid-1990s (but not to a new stadium, unfortunately). In the year 2000, when the relationship between Pittsfield owner Bill Gladstone and the New York Mets soured over their plans for Brooklyn, Gladstone quickly arranged a relocation plan to Troy, New York, and its new $12 million Joe Bruno Stadium for his rebranded Tri City ValleyCats. A league that had once limited itself to New York and Pennsylvania now included teams reaching almost to the edge of the Atlantic Ocean.

Even as the league crept further east than ever before, it was also expanding into unprecedented territory to the west. The eviction of the league's Erie SeaWolves from its nearly brand-new facility Jerry Uht Park in 1999 could have been disastrous. Instead, a match was made between the homeless Erie club and the Cleveland Indians, whose Watertown affiliate was about to move to Staten Island to join the Yankees. With some deft politicking the team wrangled a move to the town of Niles, Ohio, where an $8 million ballpark was soon approved for a vacant corner of the Eastwood Shopping Mall. Located less than seventy miles from their new parent club, the Mahoning Valley Scrappers would enjoy two decades of uninterrupted affiliation with the Indians organization, just as the Lowell Spinners did with the locally venerated Red Sox. With five brand-new stadiums in addition to the imminent Opening Days in Brooklyn and Staten Island, the NY-PL was perfectly positioned for continued success when Julian stepped down to don his judge's mantle.

It took less than a year before Ben Hayes vindicated the search committee's faith in him. As the epic opening season of the Brooklyn Cyclones and Staten Island Yankees wound down and the immediate shock of the 9/11 attacks slowly began to ebb, the baseball world took notice of the approaching end of an era. Lifelong Baltimore Oriole Cal Ripken Jr., the legendary infielder known as the "Iron Man" for his streak of 2,632 consecutive games played, was retiring from play at the age of forty-one years old. Looking ahead to his life after the major leagues, Ripken had already dedicated extensive planning and money toward the construction of a youth baseball complex in his hometown of Aberdeen, Maryland. It would feature multiple facilities for instruction, dormitories, an array of little league fields modeled after iconic Camden Yards and Fenway Park, and its centerpiece would be 6,000-seat Ripken Stadium, a ballpark to house a minor league team owned by Ripken Baseball. Because Aberdeen was only twenty-six miles north of Baltimore the projected ball club would be situated in Orioles territory. Therefore it would have to be affiliated with the organization that just happened to boast Cal Ripken Jr. as its most legendary and bankable superstar. A deal was struck immediately between Ripken and Orioles majority owner Peter Angelos leaving only the identity of the minor league franchise in doubt. Given the complications of juggling multiple levels of little leagues, youth league instructional activities and now a minor league team, the short season Class A NY-PL seemed like an ideal fit for Ripken Stadium and its novice owners.[3]

In an act that firmly shut the door on the Bob Julian era once and for all, Ben Hayes helped seal a deal that offered Ripken ownership of Julian's hometown Utica Blue Sox. One of the last remaining small-town New York franchises in the league, the Blue Sox had fallen on hard times even as the majority of the NY-PL's teams moved on to wealthier ownership arrangements and new publicly funded stadiums. By this time the Blue Sox were an overlooked affiliate of the Florida Marlins and were beset by all of the bugaboos of small-market teams: sagging attendance, low revenues and underpriced game tickets, local apathy, and the ever-rising costs of operating a minor league franchise under the unfriendly conditions set by organized baseball. Blue Sox owner Bob Fowler, who said he had been dipping into his wife's retirement 401(k) to pay team bills, was only too happy to accept Ripken's $3 million offer for the franchise he had purchased for just $75,000 back in 1984. Once the sale was finalized in February 2002, Ripken immediately announced that the team would play its upcoming season in the brand-new, nearly completed $18 million Ripken Stadium in Aberdeen. Advance sales were brisk, and by May the team reported that it had already sold over 132,000 game tickets. Since the town of Aberdeen had only around 14,000 residents in total, it was clear that the synergy between the nearby Orioles brand and the popularity of the superstar Ripken name would propel the new franchise into the stratosphere. The new Aberdeen Ironbirds were named for a combination of "Iron Man" Cal Ripken, the local Orioles nickname "the Birds," and an Aberdeen military facility where jets were test piloted. They might not reach the level of the Brooklyn Cyclones, but they would soar nonetheless.[4]

It was unclear how large a role the new league president played in wooing future Hall of Famer Ripken to buy into his low-level short-season outfit. Based on his credentials and past experience, Hayes was certainly the perfect man to broker the arrangement. In his former role as general counsel for the minor leagues Hayes had a hand in multiple team sales and stadium deals in markets as far-flung as New Britain (Connecticut), Fresno (California), Modesto (California), and Provo (Utah). He had vetted multiple ownership candidates and served on baseball's Class AAA Expansion Committee alongside the top three executives in minor league baseball including Jimmie Lee Solomon, Major League Baseball's director of minor league operations. But the extent of Hayes' almost certain involvement was kept completely behind the scenes. His name was scarcely mentioned in any of the extensive media coverage of the Blue Sox sale and relocation to Aberdeen. Instead the focus remained entirely on new owner Cal Ripken Jr., which was exactly how the NY-PL owners and presumably Hayes himself preferred it. "It's huge," said Mike Veeck, co-owner of Goldklang's Hudson Renegades and a legendary minor league figure in his own right. Referring to Ripken, Veeck elaborated, "He is emblematic about what's right with the game. It provides a tremendous amount of pride to everybody in the league to get somebody of his stature." He might have said the same about Ben Hayes as well, but the latter's name never came up in the interview.[5]

When it came to media coverage in general, Hayes avoided the spotlight as much as possible and came off as a bit of a cipher. At ceremonial events and at public appearances throughout the league, Hayes smiled genially and offered positive platitudes about the health of the league and its history. Yet he almost never included anything substantive or revealing in his brief remarks, which were usually limited to just a few sentences. At times he would fall back on his own brief tenure in professional baseball, casually mentioning to reporters "baseball's been in my blood for a long time" or referring to himself as "someone who's been in baseball for thirty-some-odd years." Even in profile pieces solely about him, Hayes kept his answers bland and opaque. In a "Q&A with NYPL President Ben Hayes" for the official minor league baseball website he barely gave his own publicity people anything to work with. When asked what he looked forward to most in the upcoming season, Hayes replied,

"Just being able to go to the ballpark and enjoy baseball. It's that time of the year again." The next question was about which new minor league up-and-comers he'd like to see play, and his predictable answer was "all of them. They all hustle, they're all trying and they're all great kids." Perhaps his most masterful nonresponse came when he was asked to identify a "little-known fact about being a league president." Ben Hayes answered, "I don't really know about that one. I can't think of any specific thing."[6]

Hayes' lawyerly circumspection served him well among his league's owners, several of whom were already familiar with him from earlier encounters across the minors. Echoing his own favored themes, they praised him in positive if not glowing terms. "He understands the inner workings of baseball teams, the business side of things," said one businessman-turned-team-owner. "He's seen things from all different perspectives," added the general manager of the New Jersey Cardinals, who felt that Hayes's playing career gave him insight into dealing with players and umpires (neither of whom were under his direct authority as NY-PL president). Most of the plaudits for Hayes came from the newer breed of owner-entrepreneurs, the ten with shiny new or refurbished stadiums who now made up the majority of the fourteen-team league. Their elders from the historic markets of Oneonta, Jamestown, and Batavia—the ones dismissed by Brooklyn's R. C. Reuteman as "mom-and-pop operators in small towns" outmoded by a new era of "a more sophisticated ownership group"—spoke little about their new leader.[7]

In fact, it was unclear exactly who was responsible for ensuring that Hayes applied for and was then selected as president of the NY-PL. The league's representatives on the search committee gave him their imprimatur, and the league-wide vote appointing Hayes as president was unanimous, so he clearly had widespread approval. At the same time, Hayes's closest baseball connections were within the administrative apparatus of minor league baseball and not to any of the members or communities of the NY-PL. Perhaps most telling was his long-standing relationship with Jimmie Lee Solomon, Major League Baseball's enforcer of minor league compliance since 1995. While Ben Hayes was the league's consensus choice to be president, there was little doubt that baseball's organizational power structure approved of his selection as well. It remained to be seen where his loyalties would ultimately lie if and when any conflicts arose.

In 2002, Hayes' second year as president, the NY-PL had a combined attendance of 1,890,053 over its short seventy-six-game season, the highest the league had ever or would ever achieve. The Brooklyn Cyclones drew 317,124 fans to their thirty-eight home games, a record topping any short-season team in professional baseball history. Their tremendous turnout at Keyspan Park placed them in the top forty minor league teams in the country, outpacing more than eighty long-season franchises who played twice as many games at home over the course of their AA and AAA campaigns. Behind the Cyclones came the Aberdeen Ironbirds, who drew 231,935 in their inaugural season, followed by the Lowell Spinners with approximately 185,000 fans. The Staten Island Yankees placed fourth with an attendance figure of 181,936, presaging several years where they would drop to the middle of the pack in the NY-PL. Close behind were the Hudson Renegades and Mahoning Valley Scrappers, and then after a severe drop of another 20,000–30,000 fans came the lower half of the league.

For more than a decade, league attendance would continue to follow much the same pattern. Brooklyn remained far and away the number one team, and Aberdeen came in second with about 25 percent fewer fans in attendance. The Staten Island Yankees fluctuated between fourth and fifth place, competing on a similar level with Hudson Valley and Mahoning Valley. Inevitably bringing up the rear were the four teams that most exemplified the small-market upstate New York origins of the league: the Auburn Doubledays, Jamestown Jammers, Oneonta Tigers, and Batavia Muckdogs. Still in the hands of their longtime local owners, none of these clubs had gotten on board with the strategy of seeking out moneyed buyers and close ties to big-market major league parents. Of course if they had, they would have already abandoned their constrictive markets and aging facilities.

On one hand, the league was prospering. From 2001 to 2015 attendance was well over 1.5 million fans every single year, a benchmark the league had never attained even once before. Despite a noticeable downturn across the minors that began in 2016, the NY-PL's annual attendance still remained above 1.3 million as it had throughout the entire Ben Hayes era. But at the same time the gap between the league's haves and have-nots had grown so wide that there was scarcely any comparison between the two. In 2004 attendance at Brooklyn Cyclones games totaled 294,261, good enough for best in the league as always. Meanwhile in Batavia attendance was a combined 37,086, barely 13 percent of the league-leading Cyclones. As Brooklyn recorded sellout after sellout with more than 7,500 fans at every game, Batavia barely attracted 1,100 including ticket giveaways and no-shows. With the league territory now stretching into seven states and the harsh economics of baseball devolving travel and other additional expenses onto the franchises themselves, it seemed less and less plausible for the bottom-feeders to foresee any future at all. Their inability to compete financially also impacted their success on the field in terms of win-loss records and playoff appearances. From 2001 and on Auburn made only five playoff appearances in nineteen years, while Oneonta, Jamestown, and Batavia had but two apiece. Although this was generally attributed to the relative quality of talent bequeathed by each team's organizational system, Brooklyn and Staten Island each made around ten playoff appearances each over the same two-decade period.[8]

As president of a bifurcated league Ben Hayes would soon be forced to make some hard choices. It was his intention to keep the NY-PL on an upward trajectory, and that likely meant more deals like the highly successful transplantation of the outmoded Utica Blue Sox to Aberdeen. Yet doing so would trample the few remnants of the league's historic beginnings and would require the rankling or ouster of its most revered old-timers. The NY-PL had played continuously in Jamestown and Batavia since 1939, one of the longest streaks in professional baseball. Leo Pinckney remained a co-owner of the Auburn franchise he had founded back in 1958 and was a former NY-PL president with a league division named after him. The inimitable Sam Nader remained devoted to his Oneonta team and the league alongside his co-owner Sid Levine, despite the fact that both were well into their eighties and nineties by this time. For Hayes to realize his vision of the league's future he would have to approach each of these situations individually, waiting them out until changes could no longer be avoided. Eventually Pinckney, Nader, and Levine would age out or pass on. Eventually Jamestown and Batavia would be crushed by the financial exigencies of baseball economics. Eventually the team owners of the majors would enact some new facilities requirement that would force the few small-market teams to close up shop. Eventually change would become inevitable, and Ben Hayes would shepherd the last holdouts into the future.

What Ben Hayes did not and could not know was that he and his league had already peaked in 2002 in only the second year of his presidency. League attendance and profitability would never again reach the heights they had just recently attained. Several of the newest ownership groups and stadiums would lose their luster much more quickly than anyone had anticipated. Upcoming relocation deals would never match the spectacular splashes of Brooklyn or Aberdeen. And the lords of baseball had a long-term reorganization scheme that would ultimately render the NY-PL obsolete. They were just waiting for the optimal moment to implement their plans.

Part Two: Must Come Down

By any ordinary metric, the Staten Island Yankees ought to have been deemed a success. Despite the challenges of their location and their problems attracting and retaining fans, the Baby Bombers regularly placed in the top third of the league in attendance. The team secured a postseason berth in the playoffs in four of its first six years at Richmond County Bank Ballpark, winning the league championship three times in 2002, 2005, and 2006. It also fulfilled its marketing promise to fans that they would watch the Yankees stars of tomorrow play in Staten Island. Ticket holders were treated to nearly a full season of nineteen-year-old second baseman Robinson Cano in 2002, only three years before he was called up to the major league squad and became one of the team's mainstays. Other future Yankees who got their start in Staten Island in the early 2000s included pitcher Chien-Ming Wang, centerfielder Melky Cabrera, and catcher Francisco Cervelli. In 2005 a young outfielder named Brett Gardner got off the bus from South Carolina, where he had been a standout player for the College of Charleston. "He was beautiful to watch," Josh Getzler later remembered. The fresh-faced rookie promptly informed his new team owner, "Mr. Getzler, just sit back and enjoy yourself. You have nothing to worry about. We're going to win and it's not going to be close." His words were not just bravado, they were prophetic. That season Gardner helped lead a superb Staten Island club to a 52–24 record and then a playoff sweep enroute to a championship. Brett Gardner's confidence and ability eventually led to a fourteen-year major league career with the Yankees that included a World Series ring in 2009, an All-Star appearance in 2015, and a Gold Glove in 2016. Small wonder that Getzler summarized the 2005 team by declaring, "Wow, they were brilliant."[9]

Unfortunately the Staten Island Yankees were not judged by their on-field merits or their comparative success relative to Mahoning Valley. Expectations ran far higher than those for a team that had been gifted an $80 million stadium and boasted one of the most valuable brand names in sports. Everyone from Mayor Giuliani to the Steinbrenners to the press to the Getzler family themselves expressed dissatisfaction with the team's financial performance over its first half-decade. And looming over Staten Island was the ever-lengthening shadow cast by the Brooklyn Cyclones, who were turning into one of the top franchises in all of the minors. "The Cyclones were the extreme example of what works when you have all the confluence of great things," Josh Getzler observed. "And we were kind of an example of a really good idea. When things didn't work out, and when the Mets thrived, and when we were having issues, then their disappointment was significant." Although Getzler was referring specifically to the Yankees organization at the time, the same sentiments were true across the board.[10]

Between 2002 and 2006 things definitely didn't work out for the Staten Island Yankees. As Josh Getzler would later admit, the front office made more than its share of mistakes in terms of its marketing approach, audience targeting, misjudgments on stadium technology, and overreliance on the Yankees' name to sell tickets. They were also hamstrung by their remote St. George location and the stadium deficiencies that the city had bequeathed them. But the disasters really started to pile up when the summer rains came in 2003 and 2004. In the 2003 season Staten Island had eight games rained out, a catastrophic number for an underperforming team that only played thirty-eight home games in the first place. The following year, by Getzler's estimate, twenty-two games were impacted by rain and were delayed or canceled entirely. In all of these cases walk-up ticket sales were devastated, as were concession sales. On top of those losses, the team had to pay an estimated 230 game employees for the hours they spent at the ballpark, whether the games were ultimately completed or not. For a team already on the brink of financial ruin, these sunk payroll costs were another crippling blow to a reeling franchise.[11]

The team's fiscal weakness was exacerbated by a pair of publicly reported audits conducted by New York City's Comptroller in 2003 and again in 2006. The first report was fairly damning, concluding that the Staten Island Yankees owed the city in excess of $373,000 for not paying their utility bills on time, fudging their attendance numbers, and accruing more than $35,000 in late fees for missed payments. The Getzlers, who had cooperated fully with their auditors and admitted to some of the charges, objected that the Economic Development Corporation (EDC) was responsible for delaying many of the arrangements that had caused the payments to be late in the first place. Three years later, the subsequent audit was even worse. While the city acknowledged that the team owners had paid down over $340,000 of the previous charges, Comptroller William Thompson claimed that the Getzlers now owed a whopping $570,000 including even more late fees. The new document also included a series of terse comments from EDC, who took little responsibility for any confusion and asserted that they intended to collect every penny that was owed.[12]

One of the chief issues at play was game attendance and how it was recorded and reported. Unlike Watertown, where the team had paid the city a flat fee for each game they played at the Duffy Fairgrounds, the Yankees' lease payments on Richmond County Bank Ballpark were calculated on a sliding scale based on total fan attendance for the season. It was understood that if attendance fell below a threshold of 125,000 per season, not including complimentary giveaway tickets which were excluded from the total, then the team would pay no rent. The audits revealed that the number of comp tickets was so high and actual sales so low that the Yanks only paid rent for a single year in their new stadium. Because the facility had been so expensive to construct and could easily turn into a massive public boondoggle, this arrangement quickly became politicized. From Josh Getzler's vantage point, the city was out to get his family because they needed somebody to blame.

> Every other year the city came to us to audit tickets because the lease was based on whether you hit thresholds of ticketed attendance. So we kept our stubs and put them in bags, put them in boxes. When they came at the end of the season, we gave them the boxes and said, knock yourselves out. In Watertown we paid $2500 a game, it was just rent. [But in Staten Island] the question was always whether we were going to hit the thresholds for additional payments, which only [happened in] the first year.
>
> We knew they were going to hammer us because we just didn't have the attendance to support paying more, and they had to say that we were not doing it right. The attendance was the attendance. We didn't mess around with it at all in 2003 when they came in. It took them months to figure it out. We had days of meetings with them.
>
> [Eventually] we just said the report is going to kill us because it makes sense for the city as a political matter. If people are saying to them, "You suck, you spent all this money on the stadium and you're not making enough on rent," they could say, "Well, it's their fault, OK?" So we ducked and covered and did the best that we could, and we knew what we needed to

do to try to pay all the bills. We worked our way through it as much as we possibly could.

We knew we were going to start to try to sell at that point.[13]

In the middle of the magical Brett Gardner championship season of 2005, the Getzlers threw in the towel on the Staten Island Yankees. Attendance remained stubbornly low and their debts were mounting, the second straight negative Comptroller's Audit Report was already in the works, and the beleaguered owners had tried everything they could think of and "thrown everything we had at 2005" but to no avail. While they were fielding offers from outsiders, the Getzlers were hamstrung by a clause in their ownership agreement that they were first required to offer the Yankees organization an option on 2 percent of their own stake. If and when the Yankees pulled the trigger on that option, they would become majority owners of the team with 51 percent ownership and the Getzlers would only be offering prospective buyers a far inferior minority stake in a foundering franchise. In the end, Stan and Josh Getzler's only choice was to sell their entire interest in the team to the Steinbrenners at a far lower price than they might have attracted on the open market. Not only that, but virtually all the money from the sale went toward paying down the debts already incurred by the team to the city and their vendors.

Poorer but wiser, the Getzlers walked away from the Staten Island Yankees with no cash money but with their bills paid and their slate clean. Stan returned to a well-earned retirement, and Josh applied his business degree and experience to a career as a well-regarded literary agent for novelists and authors of young adult fiction, a far less stressful pursuit. Soured by several years of perceived failures, the Staten Islanders who had once been their boosters now bid good riddance to the Getzlers. The writers of the *Staten Island Advance* editorial page summed up the prevailing attitude in the borough: "After such great expectations, the Staten Island Yankees have evolved into a major disappointment, at least in the front office, not on the field . . . The lion's share of the blame, especially in view of what we've seen in Coney Island, must be laid at the feet of the complacent ownership. We think it's in the best interest of all parties that the Getzlers sell their interest and move on. Thanks for everything, but it's time."[14]

As soon as they took full control of the ballclub, the Yankees flipped the Getzlers' share and resold it. Their new partner was the Mandalay Baseball Group, a California-based consortium that already owned all or part of a half-dozen teams across several minor leagues including a half-share in the Yankees' AAA affiliate in Scranton-Wilkes Barre, Pennsylvania. The "marketing wizards at Mandalay," as the *Advance* admiringly described them, "have had plenty of experience turning chicken parts into chicken salad" and were expected to turn the sagging operation around within just a few years. Right off the bat the Yankees offered the new bosses the kind of cross-brand support they had denied to the Getzlers, offering Staten Island season ticketholders free souvenirs and Yankee Stadium visits as well as priority access to premium New York Yankees regular-season and playoff tickets. The new incentives had an immediate impact. Between 2005 and 2006 Staten Island's attendance had fallen from an all-time low of 155,531 to an even lower low of 115,395 as fans waited for the Getzlers to be put out of their misery. The following year attendance rebounded to 164,207, rising to 189,876 in 2008 and surpassing 200,000 for the first time ever in 2009 and 2010. The number of sellouts per season skyrocketed from a meager five games to a high of twenty-six out of the thirty-eight home games played by the team. Not only that, but the City Comptroller's Audit released in 2007 pronounced the ballclub completely solvent and cleared of all past debt, and Richmond County Bank forked over additional millions of dollars to keep their name on the stadium in a new multiyear pact. Over the course of three to four years, precisely the timeline that Mandalay had given for turning around a minor league franchise, the Staten Island Yankees had finally come to realize the potential that Guy Molinari and Rudy Giuliani had envisioned from the beginning. And so, of course, Mandalay and Hal Steinbrenner chose that precise moment to sell the team once again.[15]

This decision likely had more to do with the Yankees' AAA affiliate in Scranton Wilkes-Barre (SWB) than it did with any concerns over the Staten Island club, which was operating under greatly improved circumstances. Beginning in 2010 a rumor began to spread that the Yankees and their partners at Mandalay sought to buy the SWB franchise outright from its current owner, the Lackawanna County Multipurpose Stadium Authority. Two years of horse trading followed. The county demanded an asking price of $14.6 million, which the Yankees partnership granted on the condition that the team's frequently waterlogged facility receive a $43 million makeover and renovation at public expense. With intense lobbying and a sizable contribution from Pennsylvania Governor Ed Rendell, matters came to a lucrative and satisfactory conclusion. The Yankees agreed to a thirty-year lease for their SWB Yankees franchise (soon to be rebranded the SWB Railriders at the recommendation of Mandalay), and the whole deal was tied up in a neat bow by 2012.[16]

In the meantime, the suddenly successful Staten Island Yankees had doubled their valuation just when their co-owners needed an infusion of cash to finance some of their SWB investment. The Yankees' relationship with Staten Island had always been a matter of business in service to organizational priorities; the franchise's creation was purely an offset for the Mets' plans for Brooklyn, the new stadium was a dry run for a planned billion-dollar Yankee Stadium in the Bronx, and the St. George location was accepted to placate city politicians. There was no emotional connection akin to the Wilpons' sentimental ties to the Brooklyn Cyclones, and the Yankees had never even considered sole ownership of their single-A franchise the way the Mets had. So when the opportunity arose to sell 95 percent of their NY-PL affiliate for an unprecedented $8.4 million in 2011, the organization did not hesitate. The team would maintain its affiliation to the Yankees and keep its staid buttoned-down name in place, only now it would be owned by a group of young and inexperienced hedge-fund millionaires with no baseball experience whatsoever. The salad days of the Staten Island Yankees were over.[17]

In the limited press coverage of the ownership changes in Staten Island, the name of NY-PL President Ben Hayes remained conspicuously absent. Given the Yankees' prodigious ability to handle their own business and also their tendency to play their cards very close the vest, this was unsurprising. At the same time, his leadership style differed markedly from his predecessor's loyalty to his owners and history of mediating league business. Hayes may very well have sympathized with the worsening plight of the Getzlers, but there was not even a whisper that he made any sort of intercession on their behalf as they exited the league. Of course, there was little he could do for them due to the ownership clause that required them to cede majority control of the franchise to the Yankees rather than to seek buyers on the open market. Hayes' strong suit was finding and wooing candidates to pay top dollar for available teams, and in this case the Yankees were handling every aspect of the sale in-house together with their partners at Mandalay.

At any rate, Hayes was already preoccupied with a surfeit of league business. In 2005 he helped organize and launch the first annual NY-PL All-Star Game, which was played at Keyspan Park in Brooklyn. As the league's crown jewel and most recognizable venue, this was a no-brainer. As Cyclones General Manager Steve Cohen put it, "To put the game on the map, it was important that we host the first one," and more than 9,000 fans showed their agreement by packing a stadium that was only meant to hold 7,500. The following year the game moved to Aberdeen to showcase Ripken Stadium and the Ironbirds, the league's second-biggest draw. By the time the All-Star Game found its way to Richmond County Bank Ballpark in 2010 it was far too late to help the Getzlers, but doubtless the folks at Mandalay Baseball appreciated the attention less than a year before they sold the team off for a record haul. At the games Hayes posed dutifully for the cameras, uttered a few canned remarks to the press that said very little, and generally departed early once the games were underway.[18]

Hayes' negotiating experience was also useful for a number of team relocations and sales—aside from the Staten Island Yankees, that is—in his first decade as head honcho. After barely ten years at brand-new and unexpectedly overpriced Skylands Park, New Jersey Cardinals principal owner Barry Gordon was already dissatisfied with facility maintenance and attendance in his current location. After attracting only 115,129 fans in 2005, Gordon and his partners summarily sold the team to Curve Baseball Partners who already owned the Class AA Altoona Curve. Curve President Chuck Greenberg promptly announced that his new team would be moving to the Penn State University campus in State College, Pennsylvania, effective immediately. In a deal that had already been in the works for two years, the rebranded State College Spikes would play in a brand-new $28 million baseball stadium co-financed by the state, the university, and prominent donors. The arrangements had been complex and involved many months of negotiations, the ceding of territorial rights by the NY-PL's Williamsport Crosscutters, and the involvement of the Pittsburgh Pirates and St. Louis Cardinals as well as their affiliates. They also had Ben Hayes's fingerprints all over them, although he did not say a word publicly beyond welcoming another new market to the league. Meanwhile the NY-PL expanded past yet another geographical frontier that required additional travel time and expense from its poorest teams.[19]

All of the recent expansions and changes to the league under Hayes finally proved to be the last straw for the historic Oneonta franchise. In July 2008, after nearly a decade as an affiliate of the Detroit Tigers and over forty years with their team, Sam Nader and Sid Levine called it quits. Shortly after a multimillion-dollar renovation of Damaschke Field was completed, it was announced that the team had been sold to a New York City investment group headed by lawyer E. Miles Prentice III, owners of the Class AA Huntsville (Alabama) Stars and Midland (Texas) Rock-

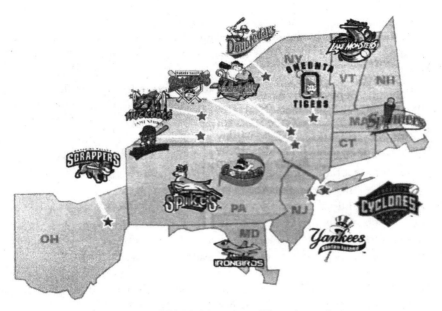

Figure 12.1. NY-PL Map, 2009. Photo by author.

hounds. The exact terms of the sale were not disclosed, but the purchase price was estimated to be in the range of $1.8 million, a far cry from the $7,500 originally invested by the members of the Oneonta Athletic Corporation four decades prior. Although the team's future in Oneonta was extremely shaky, the new owners made a commitment to stay for at least the duration of its current lease through 2010 and said they hoped to "keep the team in Oneonta into the indefinite future." Even after the sale was announced, the two-man front office of Nader and longtime Assistant General Manager Bob Zeh finished out the 2008 season alongside young Andrew Weber, the team's brand-new general manager and son of one of its minority partners.[20]

The transfer of ownership soon revealed the full extent of Sam and Sid's beneficence to their hometown crowds. Under their regime, a full fourteen out of the team's thirty-eight regular-season home games had featured free fan admission under local sponsorship deals.[21] Season ticket prices were kept artificially low thanks to subsidies from the owners, which may or may not have been augmented by nearby businesses. The Oneonta Athletic Corporation was also willing to absorb the financial losses that accrued due to its no-alcohol policy. But for the new Prentice group these conditions were untenable. "I have investors," said Miles Prentice in his first interview in Oneonta, "so what I have to try to do is make it successful." Before the 2009 season the new owners announced plans to apply for a beer license and nearly tripled the price of season tickets for the locals. They also watched with grim disquiet as attendance and revenues remained abysmally low. Even Sam Nader Bobblehead Night did nothing to boost attendance, leaving the club with more than three hundred undistributed figurines out of the thousand they had made.[22]

The axe finally fell in January 2010, a full season before the team's agreement to remain in Oneonta expired. After losing the previous Class AA tenant of its $9.3 million Dodd Stadium, the city of Norwich, Connecticut, reached out to the NY-PL about relocating one of its struggling clubs. After some negotiation and a letter of intent that set lease payments at $100,000 a year—quite an increase from the $6,000 in annual lease fees they paid to Oneonta—the Oneonta Tigers signed on to move there, effective immediately. The team would now play in a stadium that had eighteen skyboxes and averaged more than 3,000 fans per game the prior season, compared to the 692 that the Tigers drew to the aging Damaschke Field in 2009. The club estimated its new market size at 260,000, more than quadrupling that of the area surrounding Oneonta. With some regret but little hesitation, the soon-to-be Connecticut Tigers paid a nominal $7,500 penalty and bolted for the greener outfield pastures of the Nutmeg State. Ironically, the Tigers' reception by the residents of Connecticut was lukewarm, and in 2010 they again ranked in the bottom three in league attendance.[23]

Only three franchises now remained in the New York state environs where the league had been created back in 1939: Auburn, Batavia, and Jamestown. Only a short time after the NY-PL abandoned Oneonta, it came time for the Jamestown Jammers to face the music. For decades the franchise had placed third from last in annual attendance, shuffling its major league affiliations on a constant basis in a desperate attempt to stay alive and maintain its position in the NY-PL. Then in 2012 Ben Hayes attended an economic conference in Morgantown, West Virginia, at the campus of West Virginia University (WVU), some seventy miles south of Pittsburgh. Shortly afterward it was announced that the Pittsburgh Pirates, who had been connected to the NY-PL's State College Spikes for the previous six years, were shifting their affiliation to the Jamestown club instead. That same day Ben Hayes told Morgantown's *Dominion Post* newspaper that the league would be very interested in bringing a franchise there, if only a new stadium were built on the WVU campus. Although he cautioned that "it could be a considerable amount of time before a club is identified" and that any theory regarding the relocation of the Jammers was "total speculation," he then spent several minutes extolling the proximity of Morgantown to the Pirates' home in Pittsburgh and how "there are lots of benefits of having a ballclub close by." In October 2013 the university broke ground on $21 million Monongalia County Ballpark. Ten months later in August 2014, it was announced that the Jamestown Jammers would be moving there at the end of the season. In his usual noneffusive manner, Ben Hayes made an appearance in Morgantown and called it "an outstanding location" and expressed how "thrilled" the league was to be expanding there. The following season, the first for the new West Virginia Black Bears, attendance rose by nearly 60,000 over the Jammers' final tally of 24,246 the year before.[24]

Although no one knew it at the time, the league's relocation from Jamestown to Morgantown would be the last substantive change the NY-PL would ever make. Ben Hayes had doggedly done his duty for longer than a decade as league president, and he had done it well by the standards of professional baseball. Nearly every one of his fourteen clubs played in a stadium built or renovated within the past fifteen to twenty years. The majority of the teams in the NY-PL were now owned and operated by multimillionaires who had significantly raised their individual valuations and the profile of the league as a whole. The league's newest entries—the Aberdeen Ironbirds, State College Spikes, and West Virginia Black Bears, along with the slightly more senior Hudson Valley Renegades—were the property of cartels who controlled multiple minor league affiliates throughout organized baseball. The Brooklyn Cyclones and Mahoning Valley Scrappers had the additional advantage of being wholly owned by their respective major league parents, the New York Mets and Cleveland Indians. These arrangements enhanced the stability of both the teams themselves and the entire league. They carried the implicit promise that affiliation agreements would now remain intact for the long term and that the welfare of these franchises would remain a high priority for their influential and powerful owners. Meanwhile, the old local-ownership model persisted in Auburn, Batavia, Lowell, and Vermont, connecting the league with its historic roots and obscuring its upmarket sheen with a coating of nostalgia. It was difficult to discern many hints of the original PONY League in its modern incarnation, which was now stretched to eight states and lacked any cohesive regional or community identity. Yet the NY-PL remained the oldest continuous minor league in all of baseball, a fact Ben Hayes usually mentioned by rote when he addressed the media.

In 2019 the New York-Penn League was preparing to celebrate its eightieth anniversary. However, behind the scenes worrisome signs abounded. Overall minor league attendance had remained fairly stable across the board, totaling between 41 and 42 million every year since 2010. In the meantime the NY-PL was experiencing a steady decline of 50,000–100,000 fans each year, dipping from 1,829,755 in 2010 to 1,316,873 in 2019. Not only did that indicate a 28 percent drop over the course of the decade, but it also represented the league's lowest attendance since the 1998 season. Not even the charmed Brooklyn Cyclones were immune as they dropped from 264,441 to 174,522 during this period, their per-game average plummeting from 7,147 in 2010 to a far less impressive 4,848 in 2019. The league had weathered more challenging times before, but its higher profile owners and expensive facilities made it more vulnerable to public criticism.[25]

The timing could not have been worse, because the league was facing the biggest threat in its long history: minor league contraction. The diminishment of the minor leagues had first been raised during the Professional Baseball Agreement (PBA) negotiations of 1990–1991, when White Sox owners Jerry Reinsdorf and Eddie Einhorn began to beat the drum to reduce the existing number of 170 minor league clubs. They argued that baseball organizations were wasting valuable money and effort developing a large number of players who would never have the opportunity to reach the major league level. After acrimonious talks the majority of major league owners were satisfied by a variety of cost-cutting measures, increasing the financial burdens on their minor league part-ners, and imposing stricter facilities requirements that prompted a boom in stadium construction at all levels of baseball. This ushered in a new era of moneyed ownership and team relocations, accompanied by tighter control by major league organizations over their affiliates. Having achieved virtually all of their objectives, the major leagues backed off over the next several rounds of PBA renewals. The talks were relatively uneventful, and new deals extended for longer periods than the original four-year terms typical of previous decades. The 2005 PBA reached all the way to 2014 and was eventually renewed three years early in 2011. The current deal would last all the way until September 2020, and the majors agreed to field at least 160 minor league teams through either direct ownership or Player Development Contracts with their affiliates. Pat O'Conner, president of the

National Association of Professional Baseball Leagues that governed the minors, hailed the agreement as a classic case of "if it ain't broke, don't fix it." He said, "The fact that everyone is so comfortable with this speaks volumes about our relationship with Major League Baseball and speaks volumes about our stability as an industry. For us, that stability comes from the guarantee of 160 PDCs."[26]

O'Conner spoke too soon. As the end of the extended PBA loomed, rumors began to leak that Major League Baseball (MLB) was planning a drastic contraction of the minor leagues for its next iteration. One of the first to be informed of the coming disaster was O'Conner himself, who first found out about the plan in mid-2019. According to a *New York Times* account published a few months later, O'Conner first registered a blistering protest and then sent a letter to all of his minor league members "warning of significant impending changes and advising teams not to make any financial commitments, new lease agreements or schedules beyond 2020." The news went public in October 2019, shortly after all of the minor leagues had completed their seasons: MLB intended to reduce its number of minor league affiliates by more than forty teams and would distribute the remaining clubs into fewer leagues with fewer contracted players. This newest version of consolidation was said to be the brainchild of the Houston Astros organization, champions of analytics and ruthless operational efficiency. The arguments remained the same as they had three decades before, as proponents cited the need for facilities upgrades and cost-cutting on travel expenses and especially excessive development expenses. As one reporter noted, "It was the contention of the Astros and most of the smaller market clubs, that there is too much money being wasted on players who will never come close to reaching the majors." In the end it hardly mattered who had authored the so-called "Houston Plan," since the owners voted unanimously 30–0 to adopt it in advance of the PBA negotiations moving forward.[27]

At first some observers suggested that the contraction plan was just an opening salvo in the PBA negotiations, and that MLB would eventually back off their harsh demands. They were disabused of any such notion as the first few weeks passed and more details were released to the press and the public. Major league owners were dead set on the number of teams that would be contracted and cut loose to be independent and unaffiliated in the future. They even proposed a so-called Dream League of independent clubs who would be wholly responsible for all of their own expenses and procuring and paying their own amateur players. For nearly all minor league teams this dream would be a nightmare, requiring scouting and financial resources far beyond their means. Life without a major league affiliation also denied clubs the name recognition and income they desperately depended upon to attract fans to come to their ballparks to see future major leaguers in their formative years. Their PDAs with parent organizations also played a huge role in their franchise valuation, which meant that the cost to their net worth was enormous. For owners who had recently bought into baseball at inflated prices, the cumulative potential damage they faced was estimated at around $300 million. According to sources present at the negotiations, MLB representatives dismissed these concerns as overstated. Minor league owners quickly realized they could not expect any sympathy from the lords of baseball. They were on their own.[28]

One of the most contentious issues between the two sides was the amount of money at stake. Throughout the process MLB executives pleaded poverty, arguing that the current system with 160 minor league affiliates was costing them nearly a half-billion dollars per year to "subsidize." Minor league owners immediately took issue with the characterization of MLB's own player costs as a "subsidy," especially in light of the growing number of affiliate franchises owned completely or in part by major league parent organizations. Furthermore, one baseball writer found that 80 percent of that $500 million figure was eaten up by massive signing bonuses offered to top prospects and would not be reduced one iota by eliminating one-quarter of minor league affiliates as per the Houston Plan. MLB also declined to discuss how much actual money would be saved by the proposed contraction of all of these affiliated teams, and the accompanying reduction of each MLB club's affiliates to four from a current level of six or seven apiece. Muckraking blogger Neil deMause asserted in multiple sports media outlets that "Stanford University economist Roger Noll estimates the true savings of cutting 42 teams at about $22.5 million, or slightly more than the combined cost of one minimum-salaried player on every major league team." Whether or not that figure was precisely accurate, many minor league lifers wholeheartedly agreed with the sentiment. As Dave Baggott, president and owner of the Ogden (Utah) Raptors put it, "They are saving a little money, but for the New York Yankees it is the equivalent of the cost of our napkins for one season."[29]

As 2019 gave way to early 2020 both sides dug in and began to wage a war for public opinion. Pat O'Conner and some of his owners spoke out in the press, and they also enlisted a group of 105 Congressional members to decry the Houston Plan and start a groundswell to overturn baseball's long-standing antitrust exemption which protected MLB from many labor laws and restrictions. Senator Bernie Sanders promised to support the minor leagues in this affair, tweeting "closing down Minor League teams like the Vermont Lake Monsters would be a disaster for baseball fans, workers, and communities across the country. We must protect these teams from corporate greed." Taken aback by the massive wave of public backlash, MLB officials cut off all negotiations and refused to budge on a single one of their demands. In the meantime, some minor league owners whose teams were safe from any threat of contraction were wavering in their support for O'Conner and had strong doubts about his strategy of refusing to consider any compromise position to conciliate with MLB. Then in March 2020 came the onset of the COVID-19 pandemic, public lockdowns all across America, and the complete shutdown of baseball.[30]

The cessation of all baseball activity only increased the pressure on the minor leagues since many teams were shoestring operations imperiled by the lost income alone. Rather than reinstate negotiations or temporarily extend the PBA until after the end of the pandemic, MLB tightened the screws even further by announcing that the annual amateur draft would be cut back from forty rounds to five. Slashing the number of developmental players effectively choked off the supply to the affiliates, rendering many of them unnecessary in the absence of enough young players to fill all of their rosters. Over the remainder of the spring and summer of 2020 the minor leagues' position weakened markedly, especially once the season was officially canceled at the end of June due to ongoing pandemic restrictions on communal activities and events. Facing economic catastrophe and MLB intransigence, more and more owners were joining a growing faction favoring complete integration into what MLB executives were terming "One Baseball": a corporatized structure where they would have a hand "in all things baseball from cradle to grave" with Commissioner Rob Manfred as CEO. After offering some halfhearted counterproposals MiLB caved in completely in the fall. Pat O'Conner was ousted under the guise of retirement, his minor league negotiating team replaced by a new "transition team" instead. On September 30 the existing PBA expired, and one week later MLB announced that it was dissolving the minor leagues' former governing body, the National Association of Professional Baseball Leagues, and was taking over full and complete control of Minor League Baseball operations. It was clear that there was no longer any question of "if" when it came to minor league contraction, only a question of "when."[31]

From the outset it was clear that the teams most endangered by contraction would be those at the lowest level of organized ball, namely Rookie and short-season Class A leagues. This placed the NY-PL directly in the crosshairs, which was confirmed in November 2020 when MLB's official list of contracted teams was finally released. To no one's surprise the New York-Penn League was to be dissolved after playing eighty years as an affiliate league. It is unlikely that Ben Hayes and his constituent owners were capable of surprise by this time, after spending an entire season in operational shutdown and more than a year being roasted over the coals by MLB executives.

Equally unsurprising was Hayes's near-total public silence throughout the crisis and even now as his presidency of a defunct league came to a sudden end. Several months earlier in June, a week before minor league baseball operations shut down in the midst of the raging pandemic, Hayes had given a single interview. In it he revealed that all of the NY-PL's teams had developed a reopening plan under his guidance, and that he had been "traveling around the league" and holding conference calls with owners about how to safely resume play. In light of the unlikelihood of that happening, along with the mounting certainty that contraction was imminent and would decimate his league, he articulated a kind of vague powerlessness. Hayes said that he had asked Minor League Baseball's negotiators not to fight to spare his league or his teams but only to request a one-year delay of contraction. "That's my hope," Hayes sighed to a reporter in Batavia, where Dwyer Stadium's field was overgrown with weeds, the phones disconnected, and the Muckdogs team placed in receivership because it could not find a buyer. "There are 42 clubs out there that if that plan were to go through, they would have never gotten a chance to have a last season, and that would be very, very sad."[32]

Sad though it may have been, the NY-PL's last season had already taken place, and the majority of its teams would never again play a game as major league affiliates. The news was not all bad, however. The Brooklyn Cyclones, one of the most lucrative minor league franchises in history and most recently the final champion of the NY-PL in 2019, received an invitation from the New York Mets to move up as the team's new high A affiliate.

Given that the Cyclones were completely owned by the Mets already, an invitation was hardly necessary. But in keeping with the protocols of the new One Baseball structure, the Cyclones agreed to take their

Figure 12.2. Maimonides Park, Coney Island today. Photo credit: Dan Sokolow.

place as the Mets' "Class A+" representative in the reconstituted South Atlantic League (or Sally League), replacing the Port St. Lucie franchise which would move down to the low A level. Marv Goldklang's Hudson Valley Renegades were the beneficiaries of the same offer from the New York Yankees, along with the Aberdeen Ironbirds who would continue their long-standing relationship with the Baltimore Orioles as their high A affiliate. These three franchises, all among the most successful in the NY-PL, would be the sole survivors out of the league's fourteen members to continue to compete in baseball's official minor league system. Each of them had a stellar attendance record, with the Cyclones and Ironbirds consistently registering top results in the league and the Renegades selling out every single one of their home games for more than twelve years in a row. All of their owners had strong ties to their parent organizations, as the Cyclones were owned outright by the Mets, Goldklang was a minority owner of the Yankees, and Cal Ripken Jr. was an Orioles living legend. Few of their former league mates were as fortunate.[33]

Having eliminated the NY-PL as a partner, MLB and its transition team now made a concerted effort to find new homes for its bereft members. Throughout the pandemic shutdown most minor league front offices had expended significant time and effort to ensure their continued existence, whether inside organized baseball or outside it in some new capacity. As part of the restructuring effort, MLB had created one such opportunity in the form of a new MLB Draft League, which would begin play in the summer of 2021. The league would be open to post–high school and college players, focusing on top prospects eligible for the player draft that would now take place in July in mid-season. It would be run by a new outside operator named Prep Baseball Report that had no previous baseball league experience, would be noticeably more costly for teams than NY-PL membership had been, and offered no estimates of how much revenue teams could expect to make. The new league's FAQ also promised that "the league would be free for players," which was a disingenuous way of saying that they would not get paid for what was essentially a pre-draft internship. For MLB this was essentially a gesture of magnanimous self-interest, cutting their developmental expenses to almost zero while allowing their former minor league partners to shoulder the burden of showcasing their draft picks. Few NY-PL owners were enticed by this self-serving offer, but four teams with no other option took the bait. The West Virginia Black Bears, Williamsport Crosscutters, State College Spikes, and Mahoning Valley Scrappers all signed on the dotted line, comprising the bulk of the new five-team Draft League along with the Trenton Thunder, a former AA affiliate of the Yankees.[34]

Of the remaining teams from the NY-PL, two of the league's New England members followed the example of Pittsfield, Massachusetts after Bill Gladstone abandoned the city twenty years before. The Vermont Lake Monsters and Norwich Sea Unicorns (formerly the Connecticut Tigers) joined the Pittsfield Suns in the Futures Collegiate Baseball League, a wood bat summer league for college players willing to play without pay. Redirecting the bulk of college-aged players to these leagues forced them to play as unpaid amateurs, which suited MLB just fine. But not all former minor league clubs were willing to step down from professional to amateur status. Disgusted by these limited options and what they saw as a lowering of their standards, the Tri-City ValleyCats opted to cut all ties with MLB but to remain part of professional baseball outside their control. The team chose instead to join the independent Frontier League, which fielded sixteen teams across the East Coast, Midwest, and Canada.[35]

Meanwhile in Massachusetts, the Lowell Spinners took an opposite tack. Rejected as a Red Sox affiliate mainly due to the suboptimal conditions at their stadium LeLacheur Park, Spinners ownership decided to bide their time and see if they could beg or borrow their way back into the diminished minor leagues. Relying on their good relationship with both the Red Sox organization and Lowell's political establishment, the Spinners suspended their baseball plans while negotiating with both sides for an eventual return into the Red Sox fold. Unfortunately, after two years of talks that began with a guarantee of $10 million in federally funded stadium upgrades, the Red Sox increased their demands to nearly $40 million in improvements with no contribution at all on their part. While MLB had pledged that it would kick in funding to keep baseball in abandoned markets, there was conspicuous silence when that possibility was raised on behalf of Lowell. As of April 2022 the team remained dormant, although on again-off again negotiations continued on a sporadic basis. The last word from Red Sox CEO Sam Kennedy was noncommittal and not especially promising: "We don't have any specific plans to come back there with an affiliated team right now, but we never rule anything out in the future."[36]

While most of the NY-PL entered contraction with a great deal of uncertainty, the owners of the Staten Island Yankees were supremely confident that they would survive and prosper under the new regime. Hedge-fund managers Glenn Reicin, Nick Tiller, and their partners had purchased the team for an NY-PL record $8.3 million in 2011, save for 5percent of the ownership stake which remained in the hands of the New York Yankees organization. Since then they had endured an extended streak of poor performance, bad luck, and conflict with the parent club. Attendance had cratered since they bought the team, collapsing from 192,568 in 2012 to an alarming 85,513 in 2016, and finally to an anemic 66,520 in their final 2019 season. Despite low ticket prices and an abundance of gimmick nights, Richmond County Bank Ballpark was barely one-third full for games that drew a measly 1,848 fans on average. One reason for the downturn was the commencement of two massive construction projects that sandwiched the stadium between them. On one side grew an outlet mall plagued by delays and on the other was the doomed New York Wheel project, a planned ferris wheel that ran out of funding and never got built but left behind 100-ton chunks of wheel components to blight the St. George landscape. In the meantime nearly 1,000 parking spaces were sacrificed for the sake of all of this lingering construction, spots which might otherwise have served Staten Island Yankees fans on game nights.[37]

Meanwhile, inside the stadium conditions were deteriorating rapidly as the cash-strapped front office began to neglect basic upkeep of the grounds and the facility. According to damaging information later leaked by the Yankees organization, the turf was improperly cared for, stadium drainage clogged up for days after storms, and as the outfield wall padding grew worn and torn it was simply duct taped and painted over rather than replaced. Players were said to complain that they were being treated worse in Staten Island than they had in lower-level amateur leagues. It was even alleged that the new owners never replaced the team uniforms once they bought the team, and by 2019 the garments were falling apart after seven years of hard use. But the biggest source of acrimony between Staten Island and the hierarchy in New York was their three-year battle over promoting and possibly rebranding the team as the Staten Island Pizza Rats. Seizing on a viral video of a rat dragging a slice of pizza through a New York subway station, the minor league front office sought to generate much-needed publicity and merchandise sales by endowing the team with its new moniker beginning in 2016. Yankees officials were horrified by what they saw as a demeaning image, even as a short-term promotional gimmick let alone as a new, permanent team name. Yankees COO Lonn Trost sent a livid email saying that the organization had "absolute distain [*sic*]" for the notion of dressing Staten Island Yankees players in Pizza Rat uniforms, which would be "an embarrassment to the New York Yankees franchise." Trost even threatened the future of the Yankees' PDA with Staten Island over the controversy, and the team backed down but not without some resentment over what they saw as a missed opportunity.[38]

Despite the friction between themselves and the Yankees brass, Staten Island's owners as well as Team President Will Smith had no doubt that they would be spared the axe once contraction took place. They had heard no hint of negativity from the organization—in fact, they had heard nothing at all from the Yankees for months—and perhaps the good news of the Cyclones' promotion to the high A minor leagues bolstered their assumption that they would be invited to join their natural rivals from Brooklyn.[39] So they were flabbergasted when they discovered in November 2020 that Staten Island would not be chosen to remain as an affiliate club, since the Yankees had transferred their allegiance to the Hudson Valley Renegades instead. Even more galling was the way they found out the news on social media after no one from the organization reached out to tell them personally. The Yankees organization never made direct contact with anyone from Staten Island afterward, either. Instead they issued a pro forma statement thanking the franchise for its years as a Yankees affiliate and went on to assure Staten Islanders that a new independent Atlantic

League team would likely take up residence in the near future once the ballpark received a much-needed renovation. Without fully explaining their reasoning, the organization took another swipe at their former partners on their way out the door. "The Yankees carefully considered hosting their High Single-A affiliate in Staten Island," they wrote. "However, as the number of our minor league affiliates have been limited, we did not have the confidence that the organization could continue to allow us to develop our players in the best possible way . . . We found it essential that the people of Staten Island continue to have baseball, and we appreciate and thank them for their support. The borough of Staten Island will always be a part of the Yankees family."[40]

Although they would have first crack at securing the Atlantic League slot, Reicin and his co-owners at Nostalgic Partners LLC decided not to affiliate with any professional or amateur league in the absence of their Yankees connection. Unlike all of their NY-PL peers, they decided to go out of business rather than to maintain a baseball team under severely altered circumstances. But they made no secret of the fact that they were extremely upset at what they saw as shoddy treatment at the hands of the Yankees and Major League Baseball, and they swore vengeance over the losses they had suffered. As the spurned Staten Islanders made their plans

Figure 12.3. Community Park, Staten Island today. Photo credit: Dan Sokolow.

and consulted with attorneys, MLB moved quickly to acquire rights to an Atlantic League club and then secured a buyer in supermarket magnate John Catsimatidis. New York City's Economic Development Corporation agreed to spend yet another $8 million on refurbishing Richmond County Bank Ballpark for its new tenants, the Staten Island Ferryhawks, who promised to provide "community-focused, year-round affordable entertainment" for their "loyal and strong-willed fans."[41]

Baseball would continue, but for so many leagues and teams like the New York-Penn League and the Staten Island Yankees, it was the end of the line. One of the icons of both the league and its Yankees franchise had been Sam Nader, who lived just long enough to see their dissolution before he passed away at the age of 101 in his Oneonta home on February 9, 2021.[42] Whether or not Sam was aware of the end of the NY-PL when it finally happened, he had seen it coming long before. Back in the summer of 2006 Sam remarked to me, "I'm sure that down the road, when they'll have a realignment, Brooklyn will probably be in the AA league." That prediction had come true, or near enough. He also had this to say about reciprocity: "Mostly in the old days we were concerned with our own communities, we were from the community, and had some loyalties to the community. Now there is very little loyalty to the communities . . . That loyalty isn't in existence with players, with everything else. It's all money."[43] In the end, organized baseball demonstrated its lack of loyalty to communities, owners, players, and even entire leagues. It was all money.

AFTERWORD

Three teams from the former New York-Penn League refused to go quietly in the wake of minor league contraction. In December 2020 the owners of the Staten Island Yankees, Nostalgic Partners, sued the Yankees organization for breach of contract. In addition, they argued that the Yankees had made false promises, among a host of other complaints including bullying and costing them their business and its entire value. In their court filing they claimed that the Yankees had guaranteed them an ongoing affiliation when they made their offer to sell them a 95 percent interest in the franchise nearly ten years earlier. They included the full text of the offering memo as proof, demonstrating how the Yankees had promised that "the SI Yankees were a wonderful investment opportunity, had a guaranteed affiliation with MLB, were part of the best MiLB league in the country, and were affiliated with an MLB team so committed to the SI Yankees that it insisted on keeping a financial interest." Although attorneys for the New York Yankees succeeded in getting a dismissal of some aspects of the full complaint, New York State Supreme Court Justice Barry Ostrager ultimately decided that the breach of contract suit would proceed.[1]

One month later in January 2021, Tri-City ValleyCats owner Doug Gladstone sued the Astros organization on much the same basis. Gladstone, who had inherited the team when his late father Bill Gladstone died of complications from COVID-19 in April 2020, was taking on the architects of the infamous plan that had yanked away his team's MLB affiliation. Like the Staten Islanders, Tri-City had received no warning or any sort of contact from its parent organization before or after the full list of surviving affiliates was released to the media in late 2020. While the lawsuit did not claim the same breach of contract as Nostalgic

Partners, it did share the same charges of "breach of fiduciary duty and tortious interference" on the part of the Astros organization. The team also had an additional claim in that the Astros had made several public statements in 2019 promising that the ValleyCats were on the safe list and that their affiliation would remain intact after contraction, promises that were "reneged on at the eleventh hour." Not only did the ValleyCats share many of the same arguments and the same attorneys as the Staten Island Yankees (namely the firms of Weil, Gotshal & Manges and Berg & Androphy), but because their case was brought in New York State where the ValleyCats played, it too ended up before Judge Ostrager. He ruled the same way as he had in the Yankees case, dismissing some of the individual claims but permitting the bulk of the case to move forward.[2]

Nearly a year after filing their as-yet unresolved separate suits, the two teams joined forces with their former league mate the Norwich Sea Unicorns and Oregon's Salem-Keizer Volcanoes to file an even bigger suit against Major League Baseball. The plaintiffs charged MLB with violating the Sherman Antitrust Act by illicitly reducing competition through illegal collusion. In short, their lawsuit aimed to challenge one of MLB's most cherished privileges, the antitrust exemption it had enjoyed for a full century.

Baseball's unique exemption to the Sherman Act dates back to 1922, when an upstart competitor called the Federal League sued MLB for colluding to take away their players and put them out of business. The case reached the United States Supreme Court, and in an opinion penned by legendary jurist Oliver Wendell Holmes the court ruled that baseball did not qualify as interstate commerce and so was not regulated by federal antitrust legislation. Over the ensuing decades MLB took full advantage of their immunity to oversight and the usual rules that governed all other sports leagues. Baseball's notorious reserve clause allowed teams to bind their star players to a single club in perpetuity, with no free agency permitted at all until the Curt Flood case of the 1970s. Wages were suppressed to scandalously low levels in the minor leagues, where they languished far below minimum wage requirements (as they still do today). And, of course, in 2020 MLB made the unilateral decision to contract and reorganize the minor leagues without regard for MiLB interests or concerns.

There had been an array of challenges to baseball's antitrust exemption over the years, but all were brushed away by the Supreme Court or lower courts unwilling to challenge their long-enshrined ruling. Yet a change in the wind seemed to be brewing recently, especially after the Supreme

Court issued a landmark ruling against the NCAA in mid-2021. The formal decision in that case included the following statement by Justice Neil M. Gorsuch: "To be sure, this Court once dallied with something that looks a bit like an antitrust exemption for professional baseball [in Federal Baseball] . . . But this Court has refused to extend Federal Baseball's reasoning to other sports leagues—and has even acknowledged criticisms of the decision as 'unrealistic' and 'inconsistent' and "aberration[al]." Never before had a sitting justice spoken with such disapproval of the MLB exemption, let alone had his or her skepticism echoed by another justice, in this case Brett Kavanaugh. Attorneys for the four jilted minor league franchises took this as an invitation to challenge the exemption. As one of the legal partners told the media, "We've decided we're going to accept that invitation."[3]

In October 2022, a ruling was issued in the Staten Island Yankees' legal case by Judge Andrew L. Carter of the U.S. District Court of the Southern District of New York. Judge Carter found that the four minor league plaintiffs had presented a cogent argument in their case, and explicitly rejected MLB's argument that these former affiliates lacked the standing to bring their lawsuit. He even went so far as to assert that they had successfully demonstrated that MLB was guilty of restraint of trade and adversely inhibiting competition. However, based on decades of precedent in the federal courts that protected MLB's antitrust exemption, Carter ruled that he had no choice but to dismiss the lawsuit filed by the Staten Island Yankees, Tri-City ValleyCats and their fellow clubs. At the same time, he noted: "Plaintiffs believe that the Supreme Court is poised to knock out the exemption, like a boxer waiting to launch a left hook after her opponent tosses out a torpid jab. It's possible. But until the Supreme Court or Congress takes action, the exemption survives; it shields MLB from Plaintiffs' lawsuit."[4]

As of this writing, the case has yet to be petitioned to the Court of Appeals, let alone reach the Supreme Court for a hearing. MLB maintains a strong lobbying presence in Washington DC and has powerful friends in Congress to protect its interests. As recently as 2018 the legislature passed the disingenuously named Save America's Pastime Act as part of an omnibus federal spending bill. This law specifically exempted organized baseball from compensating its minor league players according to federal minimum wage and overtime pay standards, denying the players a living wage even as baseball's annual revenues topped $10 billion per year.[5] Past precedent also suggests that it would be a tall order for any lawsuit to overturn a century-old antitrust exemption that has already overcome multiple challenges.

Still, it would be one of the great ironies in the history of sports if Major League Baseball's decision to undo the New York-Penn League sowed the seeds for the remnants of the New York-Penn League to undo the sovereignty of Major League Baseball. In an even more dramatic twist, an embittered and rejected Astros affiliate would then share credit for avenging the contraction plan attributed to none other than the team's onetime parent, the 2022 World Series Champion Houston Astros. So although the history of the NY-PL is ended, it may not be complete. To put it another way, while the New York-Penn League's regulation nine innings have come to an end, it remains to be seen whether extra innings will yet be played.

NOTES

Chapter One

1. French was still president of the Rochester club as late as 1942. See Jim Mandelaro and Scott Pitoniak, *Silver Seasons: The Story of the Rochester Red Wings* (Syracuse University Press, 1996), 61, 74; *Batavia Clippers Score Book*, 1987.

2. Leo Pinckney, "History of P.O.N.Y. New York-Penn League," reprinted in *Utica Blue Sox 1994 Yearbook*, 14–20; *1985 Geneva Cubs Program*, 8; *1987 Batavia Clippers Score Book*; *1989 Utica Blue Sox Scorecard*, 19; Dan Winegar, "Return of Clippers," *Batavia Daily News*, March 26, 1987, 4; "Batavia Muckdogs/New York-Penn League History" at the Batavia Muckdogs website, batavia.muckdogs. milb.com (accessed June 2010, website no longer active). Please note that many of the sites belonging to Minor League Baseball have been reorganized (and in some cases scrubbed) following the MLB takeover of MiLB operations in October 2020. It is unknown if much of the content I accessed prior to that date will ever appear online again, or has been completely deleted.

3. Neil J. Sullivan, *The Minors* (St. Martin's Press, 1991), 18, 42–46; "General History: The History and Function of Minor League Baseball," https://www.milb. com/milb/history/general-history.

4. "1939 Register League Encyclopedia," https://www.baseball-reference. com/minors/league.cgi?year=1939.

5. Sullivan, *The Minors,* 65; Ben Fanton, "How It Was in the Old Days of Class 'D' Baseball," *Baseball Digest,* March 1981: 93.

6. Sullivan, *The Minors,* 93–114; Lee Lowenfish, *Branch Rickey: Baseball's Ferocious Gentleman* (University of Nebraska Press, 2007), 203–205, 325–326.

7. Sullivan, *The Minors,* 104–107; Pat Doyle, "Branch Rickey's Farm," https:// www.baseball-almanac.com/minor-league/minor2005a.shtml.

8. "1939 Pennsylvania-Ontario-New York League," https://www.baseball-reference.com/minors/league.cgi?id=13538 and "1939 Minor League Affiliates," https://www.baseball-reference.com/minors/affiliate.cgi?year=1939.

9. Winegar, "Return of Clippers"; see also articles in the *Batavia Daily News* dated June 8, 1937; August 23, 1937; January 9, 1939; February 14, 1939; March 6, 1939; April 4, 1939; April 11, 1939; April 12, 1939; April 25, 1939; May 10, 1939; June 1, 1939; June 14, 1939; "A Brief History of Baseball in Batavia," from Batavia Muckdogs website ca. 2005 (accessed June 2010, website no longer active).

10. "70 Years of Jamestown Pro Baseball to Be Celebrated," *Jamestown Post-Journal*, August 18, 2009; Frank Hyde, "The 1939 Pirates 'Threw Out' First Pro Baseball Here," *Jamestown Post-Journal*, August 20, 2009; Scott Kindberg, "Honoring Jamestown's Professional Baseball Origins," *Jamestown Post-Journal*, August 26, 2009.

11. "70 Years of Jamestown Pro Baseball"; "Pennsylvania-Ontario-New York League (D) Encyclopedia and History," https://www.baseball-reference.com/minors/league.cgi?code=PONY&class=D; articles from the *Batavia Daily News* dated May 5, 1941; October 23, 1941; October 25, 1941; October 30, 1941; November 8, 1941; November 11, 1941; November 27, 1941; February 16, 1942; February 25, 1942; April 13, 1942.

12. Fanton, "Old Days of Class 'D,'" 90–92.

13. Pinckney, "History of P.O.N.Y.," 14–15; "Pennsylvania-Ontario-New York League (D) Encyclopedia and History"; *Batavia Daily News*, articles dated November 11, 1941; November 27, 1941; February 15, 1943; March 10, 1943; October 19, 1943; December 10, 1943.

14. John P. Rossi, *The National Game: Baseball and American Culture* (Ivan R. Dee, 2000), 148–149; Jules Tygiel, *Past Time: Baseball as History* (Oxford University Press, 2000), 148–149; Sullivan, *The Minors*, 235; "General History: The History and Function of Minor League Baseball."

15. James A. Percoco, "Baseball and World War II: A Study of the Landis-Roosevelt Correspondence," *OAH Magazine of History* 7, no. 1: 55–60.

16. Cramer quoted in Robert Elias, "A Fit for a Fractured Society: Baseball and the American Promise," in *Baseball and the American Dream: Race, Class, Gender and the National Pastime*, ed. Robert Elias (M. E. Sharpe, 2001), 13. See also Tygiel, *Past Time*, 148.

17. Ron Briley, "Baseball and the Cold War: An Examination of Values," *Magazine of History* 2, no. 1 (Summer 1986): 15–18.

18. John P. Rossi, *A Whole New Game: Off the Field Changes in Baseball, 1946–1960* (McFarland, 1999), 1; Tygiel, *Past Time*, 148; George McGlynn, "Beyond the Dugout: Reassessing the Baseball Dream," in *Baseball and the American Dream: Race, Class, Gender and the National Pastime*, ed. Robert Elias (M. E. Sharpe, 2001), 189.

19. Rossi, *The National Game*, 158–160; Rossi, *A Whole New Game*, 1–3, 218–220; Tygiel, *Past Time*, 149–150.

20. Rossi, *The National Game*, 158–159; Rossi, *A Whole New Game*, 58, 93–94; Tygiel, *Past Time*, 151–156; Jim Owens, "Television Sports Milestones—A

Chronology of an Industry," (accessed June 2010, website no longer active); James L. Baughman, "Television Comes to America, 1947–57," *Illinois History*, March 1993, 41–44.

21. Rossi, *A Whole New Game*, 58, 114–115; Rossi, *The National Game*, 159; Sullivan, *The Minors*, 235–244.

22. Pinckney, "History of the P.O.N.Y. League," 15–16.

23. Quoted in Sullivan, *The Minors*, 238.

24. http://www.baseball-reference.com/minors/league.cgi?code=PONY& class=D; http://www.baseball-reference.com/minors/team.cgi?city=Buffalo&state= NY&country=US; http://www.baseball-reference.com/minors/team.cgi?city= Rochester&state=NY&country=US; *Seventeenth Census of the United States—1950— Population, Volume I: Number of Inhabitants* (U.S. Government Printing Office, 1952), 32-8-21 and 38-10.

25. "1956 Pennsylvania-Ontario-New York League," https://www.base-ball-reference.com/minors/league.cgi?id=13555; Pinckney, "History of the P.O.N.Y. League," 16.

26. Roger Kahn, *Good Enough to Dream* (Doubleday, 1985), 72–73.

27. https://origin.milb.com/milb/history/presidents.jsp?mc=_trautman.

28. Pinckney, "History of the P.O.N.Y. League," 16–18.

29. Lloyd Johnson and Miles Wolff, eds., *The Encyclopedia of Minor League Baseball*, 2nd ed. (Baseball America, 1967); Pinckney, "History of the P.O.N.Y. League," 16–17.

30. There is some difference of opinion as to who proposed the short season solution for the league. Minor league baseball's official website credits National Association President Phil Piton, a longtime assistant to both his immediate predecessor and commissioner Landis. The New York-Penn League version suggests that the decision originated within the league itself, which seems more credible to me. See https://origin.milb.com/milb/history/presidents.jsp?mc=_piton ; Pinckney, "History of the P.O.N.Y. League," 14–18.

31. Pinckney, "History of the P.O.N.Y. League," 17–19; https://www.milb.com/about/awards.

32. Author interview with Sam Nader, July 17, 2006; Brad Rogers, *Testimony before the New York State Senate Committee on Tourism, Recreation and Sports Development*, "Hearing re: The Well-Being of Minor League Baseball in New York State," February 9, 1993 (Roy Allen & Associates, 1993), 31, 44.

33. Gera, a Queens, New York, native and certified graduate of a Florida umpiring school, got the job over the objections of league president Vince McNamara only after she threatened to sue the league for gender discrimination. Even after her signing, it took three years and a court action before minor league baseball's National Association would approve the contract and her appointment. Gera's umpiring career lasted precisely one game in Auburn on June 24, 1972, at the end of which she tendered her resignation. Reportedly this was because the

other umpires refused to cooperate with her on the field. See Pinckney, "History of the P.O.N.Y. League," 17; "Baseball Admits Curves Are Now Legal, Signs Woman Ump to Minor League Pact," *Palm Beach Post-Times*, July 25, 1969, 19; "Woman Wins Umpiring Job after Suit," *Lodi (California) News-Sentinel*, July 26, 1969, 8; Milton Richman, "Lady Ump Gets Chance Friday," *The Bulletin* (Bend, Oregon), July 28, 1969, 8; "Obituary of Bernice Gera," *New York Times*, September 25, 1992.

34. Interview with Sam Nader; Sam Nader testimony, "Well-Being of Baseball in New York," 31; population figures from *Eighteenth Census of the United States—1960—Population; Volume I, Part A: Number of Inhabitants* (Washington, D.C.: U.S. Government Printing Office, 1961), 34–11.

Chapter Two

1. By way of comparison, four other films earned over $100 million each that season: *Big, Coming to America, Who Framed Roger Rabbit,* and *Crocodile Dundee II*.

2. *Sports Illustrated*, "Sports Illustrated's Greatest Sports Movies," August 4, 2003; "Ron Shelton: From the Red Wings to *Bull Durham*," interviewed in 2008 by Jon Zelazny, http://thehollywoodinterview.blogspot.com/2009/06/ron-shelton-hollywood-intervew.html; historical box office figures compiled at https://box officemojo.com/.

3. Steve Wulf, "Diamond Film with Clout: 'Bull Durham' Is a Movie with Something on the Ball," *Sports Illustrated*, July 4, 1988; Zelazny, "Ron Shelton"; *Bull Durham* (Orion Pictures, 1988); Chris Sprow, interview with Ron Shelton, *ESPN the Magazine*, https://sports.espn.go.com/espnmag/story?id=3433411.

4. Jules Tygiel, *Past Time: Baseball as History* (Oxford University Press, 2000), 198–222; Steve Kettmann, "Profile of Roger Angell," August 29, 2000, https://www.salon.com/people/bc/2000/08/29/angell/.

5. "Profitable Days Down on the Farm for Pro Baseball," *St. Louis Post-Dispatch*, September 24, 1989; "Minor League Baseball Is a Home Run for North Carolina," http://www.insidersportsmarketing.com (accessed June 1, 2010, website no longer active).

6. "Profitable Days"; "The Presidents in the History of Minor League Baseball," http://web.minorleaguebaseball.com/milb/history/presidents.jsp (accessed June 3, 2010).

7. Leo Pinckney, "History of P.O.N.Y. New York-Penn League," reprinted in *Utica Blue Sox 1994 Yearbook*, 14–20.

8. "New York-Pennsylvania League (Short-Season A) Encyclopedia and History," https://www.baseball-reference.com/minors/league.cgi?code=NYPL&class=A-; Roger Kahn, *Good Enough to Dream* (Doubleday, 1985), 46–47.

9. George Gmelch and J. J. Weiner, *In the Ballpark: The Working Lives of Baseball People* (University of Nebraska Press, 2006), 61.

10. Kahn, *Good Enough to Dream*, 74–77; John Merwin, "The Most Valuable Executive in Either League," *Forbes*, April 12, 1982, 129–138.

11. See the following articles by Murray Chass: "Baseball; Dollars and Sense, or Collusion?," *New York Times*, February 1, 1987; "Baseball Owners Lose Arbitration on Free Agents; Football Players' Union Strikes on a Parallel Issue; Ruling Backs Players on Collusion Charges against Teams in '85," *New York Times*, September 22, 1987; "Players Said to Hit Collusion Jackpot," *New York Times*, November 4, 1990; "With No Ceremony, Collusion Agreement Is Reached," *New York Times*, December 22, 1990; see also "Ueberroth Had Owners Share Free Agent Status Reports," *Washington Post*, July 5, 1988; "Baseball Owners Lose 1987 Collusion Ruling," *Chicago Sun-Times*, July 18, 1990; Steve Berkowitz, "Arbitrator Leaves Baseball Owners 0–3 against Union in Collusion Cases," *Washington Post*, July 19, 1990.

12. "Chicago White Sox Front Office," https://www.mlb.com/whitesox/team/front-office; David Greising, "The Toughest #&?!%* in Sports," *Business Week*, June 15, 1992.

13. Vic Ziegel, "The King of Junk Sports," *New York Magazine*, December 10, 1979, 9–12; Jack Buck, Rob Rains, and Bob Broeg, *"That's a Winner!"* (Sports Publishing, 2002), 99.

14. Curt Smith, *Storied Stadiums: Baseball's History through Its Ballparks* (Carroll & Graf, 2003), 349–350; Curt Smith, *Voices of Summer: Ranking Baseball's 101 All-Time Best Announcers* (Carroll & Graf, 2005), 159; Rich Wolfe and George Castle, *I Remember Harry Caray* (Sports Publishing), xxxii–xxxiii; Bob Logan, *Bob Logan's Tales from Chicago Sports: Cubs, Bulls, Bears and Other Animals* (Sports Publishing, 2002), 138.

15. Greising, "The Toughest #&?!%* in Sports"; Edward Kiersh, "Playing Hardball," *Cigar Aficionado* online profile, https://www.cigaraficionado.com/article/playing-hardball-6085; Laura L. Enright, *Chicago's Most Wanted: The Top 10 Book of Murderous Mobsters, Midway Monsters, and Windy City Oddities* (Potomac Books, 2005), 184; Dan Bickley, " 'A Lot of People Don't Like Me': Owner Reinsdorf Conquers Negative Public Opinion in His Pursuit of Winning," *Chicago Sun-Times*, September 27, 1993.

16. Ed Sherman, "Reinsdorf Had Unique Relationship with Steinbrenner," Chicago Business Online, www.chicagobusiness.com (accessed July 2010, website no longer active); Kiersh, "Playing Hardball."

17. Mark Liptak, "Expect the Unexpected: A White Sox History, Part Four: The Reinsdorf Years," http://www.whitesoxinteractive.com (accessed July 2010, website no longer active); Rick Bozich, "Fregosi Begging for Trouble with White Sox Job," *Chicago Sun-Times*, June 22, 1986.

18. Bozich, "Fregosi Begging for Trouble"; Dan Pompei, "Owners Probe Farm System," *Chicago Sun-Times*, June 21, 1986.

19. Dave Van Dyck and Joe Goddard, "Einhorn Figures It Out: Sox Co-Owner Renews Attack on Player Development Costs," *Chicago Sun-Times*, January 26, 1986.

20. Bozich, "Fregosi Begging for Trouble"; Simpson study cited in Sam Lazzaro, *More Than a Ballgame . . . An Inside Look at Minor League Baseball* (Pocahontas Press, 1997), 264.

21. Van Dyck and Goddard, "Einhorn Figures It Out"; Jack Sands and Peter Gammons, *Coming Apart at the Seams: How Baseball Owners, Players, and Television Executives Have Led Our National Pastime to the Brink of Disaster* (Macmillan, 1993), 98.

22. John Powers, "Majors Sow $75M Crop: Costs Rising, Farms Shrinking, but Minors Still Essential," *Boston Globe*, June 7, 1989.

23. John Helyar, *Lords of the Realm: The Real History of Baseball* (Ballantine Books, 1995), 413; McIlvaine quoted in Neil J. Sullivan, *The Minors* (St. Martin's Press, 1991), 264–265.

24. "Minor Leagues Approve Final Offer to Major Leagues," PR Newswire, November 19, 1990.

25. "Majors Using Antitrust Immunity to Break Up Minors, Charges Wolff," PR Newswire, November 21, 1990; Sands and Gammons, *Coming Apart*, 98.

26. Claire Smith, "Baseball Is Scouting Minor League Homes," *New York Times*, November 20, 1990; Larry Whiteside, "Major Problem with Minors Clubs May End Working Agreements and Start Own Farms," *Boston Globe*, October 9, 1990; "Dispute Cancels Winter Meetings," *Washington Post*, November 1, 1990; Associated Press, "Talks on Minors Turn Bitter," November 19, 1990; Sands and Gammons, *Coming Apart*, 4–5.

27. Steve Berkowitz, "Majors' Accord Is Near with Minors," *Washington Post*, December 3, 1990; Toni Ginnetti, "Settlement Reached for Minors, Majors; Tentative Pact Gives Big Leagues Greater Control," *Chicago Sun-Times*, December 3, 1990; "Minors Cautiously Approve New PBA with Majors," PBA Newswire, December 13, 1990.

28. Cassandra Hayes, "America's Favorite Pastime has a New Face: Jimmie Lee Solomon Heads Baseball's Minor League," *Black Enterprise*, February 1, 1995; Mensah Dean, "Baseball Executive in League of His Own," *Washington Times*, June 5, 1996.

29. Thomas Boswell, "Baseball's Greediest at It Anew," *Washington Post*, December 5, 1990.

30. See testimony by Robert Julian, Sam Nader, and Andrew Zimbalist in Brad Rogers, *Testimony before the New York State Senate Committee on Tourism, Recreation and Sports Development*, "Hearing re: The Well-Being of Minor League Baseball in New York State," February 9, 1993 (Roy Allen & Associates, 1993).

Chapter Three

1. Jim Kevlin, "As Mayor, He Sought Help for Oneonta Wherever He Could Find It: Born in 'League of Nations,' Oneonta Ex-Mayor Embraced Full Range of Friends, Allies," and "Sam Nader Recounts 'Wonderful Journey': Sam Nader Piles Praise on Oneonta," both online at www.hometownoneonta.biz (accessed April 2010, websites no longer active); I. Jeremiah Palmer, "Scintilla—A Famous Name in Sidney," July 2008, http://www.dcnyhistory.org/Scintilla.pdf.

2. Kevlin, "As Mayor"; Author interview with Sam Nader, July 17, 2006.

3. Author interview with Sam Nader; Robert Julian, Sam Nader, and Andrew Zimbalist in Brad Rogers, *Testimony before the New York State Senate Committee on Tourism, Recreation and Sports Development*, "Hearing re: The Well-Being of Minor League Baseball in New York State," February 9, 1993 (Roy Allen & Associates, 1993), 31.

4. Author interview with Sam Nader.

5. Author interview with Sam Nader.

6. Oneonta Tigers 2006 Program, 26, 30; http://www.enotes.com/topic/Oneonta_Yankees#Notable_alumni.

7. Author interview with Sam Nader.

8. Nader testimony, 33; Oneonta Tigers 2006 Program, 30; population figures from http://www.census.gov/geo/www/gazetteer/1990gazetteer.html and http://www.clrsearch.com/RSS/Demographics/NY/Oneonta/Summary.

9. Author interview with Sam Nader; author interview with Robert Julian, July 18, 2006.

10. "1977 New York-Pennsylvania League," https://www.baseball-reference.com/minors/league.cgi?id=13016. One of the local franchise owners was Bob Blumberg, a middle-class town alderman, community volunteer, and District Deputy Grand Exalted Ruler of the Elks (New York State Central District)—by no means a millionaire owner. His obituary appeared in the *Little Falls Evening Times*, December 23, 2006 (archived online at https://eneafuneralhomes.com/tribute/details/5204/Robert-Blumberg/obituary.html).

11. Stadium particulars at http://www.timandjillstravelogue.com/veteransmemorialpark.html and Charles O'Reilly, "The Little Vet," https://www.charliesballparks.com/st/NY-LittleFalls-Veterans.htm. An unflattering and not entirely accurate review appears at http://ballparkreviews.com/template2.php?in_name=Veterans%20Memorial%20Park&in_city=Little%20Falls&in_state=New%20York; and some spectacular photos of the facility are archived online at http://www.frontiernet.net/~rochballparks4/littlefalls/littlefalls.htm. For a prose description of the "Little Vet" written by a contemporary, see Roger Kahn, *Good Enough to Dream* (Doubleday, 1985), 202–203.

12. Population figures from U.S. Census Bureau, *1990 Census of Population, Social and Economic Characteristics: New York* (1990 CP-2-34), 8, 10.

13. Bill Everhart, "Casey, Murphy May Bring Baseball to Binghamton, NY," *Berkshire Eagle*, May 20, 1990, and "Casey Gets Franchise for Binghamton Park," *Berkshire Eagle*, June 1, 1990; Hugo Kugiya, "Marlins Sold: It's a Miracle," *South Florida Sun-Sentinel*, March 1, 1989; Maya Bell, "Miami Hopes for Miracle in Base-ball—Owners: Class A Team Could Be Springboard," *South Florida Sun-Sentinel*, March 1, 1989; Dave Joseph, "The Bad-News Boys," *South Florida Sun-Sentinel*, July 9, 1989; "Business of Baseball," *Orlando Sentinel*, September 20, 1985; "Base-ball," *Orlando Sentinel*, March 20, 1986. In the end Goldklang and Revo's group would lose out on major league ownership to Blockbuster Video tycoon Wayne Huizenga, who even had the gall to name his new team the Marlins—a name they had cast off when they came to Miami. See Ed Giuliotti, "Huizenga Goes Fishing for 'Marlins,'" *South Florida Sun-Sentinel*, May 31, 1991.

14. John Kekis, "Little Falls Cries Foul over Losing Their Mets," *Albany Times-Union*, June 18, 1989; Bob McDonough, "Mets Approve Pittsfield," *Berkshire Eagle*, January 12, 1989; Bill Everhart, "Batter Up! It's Casey and the Mets," *Berkshire Eagle*, January 15, 1989; author interview with Rick Murphy, August 10, 2006.

15. See the following articles by Bill Everhart in the *Berkshire Eagle*: "Pittsfield Mets Talking Baseball," February 8, 1990; "Casey, Murphy May Bring Baseball to Binghamton, NY," May 20, 1990; "Casey Gets Franchise for Binghamton Park," June 1, 1990; "How Pittsfield Could Host AA Baseball in '91," September 9, 1990.

16. Howard Herman, "Mike Casey out of Baseball for Now," *Berkshire Eagle*, December 16, 1990; Bob McDonough, "Michael Casey's World Unraveling," *Berkshire Eagle*, December 19, 1990 and follow-up on December 31, 1990.

17. See the following articles from the *Berkshire Eagle*: Howard Herman, "Pittsfield Mets Planning for 1991: Ownership Unsettled, but Murphy Moves Ahead," February 23, 1991; Lewis C. Cuyler and Bob McDonough, "Creditors Accept Casey's Repayment Plan," June 29, 1991; three more articles by Howard Herman: "Pittsfield's Link with Binghamton," June 30, 1991; "Mets Ownership Battle May Drag Beyond February 1," January 5, 1992; "Mets Down to the Wire," January 31, 1992; and Bill Everhart, "Dream Dies, but Team Remains," February 9, 1992. For Casey's subsequent history, see Nick Cafardo, "Worcester May Have a Ball with This," *Boston Globe*, December 3, 1995, and "Former Minor League Owner Arrested on Fraud Charges," *Albany Times-Union*, January 8, 1999.

18. See the following articles from the *Berkshire Eagle*: Herman, "Mike Casey out of Baseball for Now" and "Pittsfield Mets Planning for 1991: Owner-ship Unsettled, but Murphy Moves Ahead," February 23, 1991; Lewis C. Cuyler and Bob McDonough, "Creditors Accept Casey's Repayment Plan," June 29, 1991; Howard Herman, "Murphy Declares Mets' Season a Success," September 22, 1991; Bob McDonough, "Top County Story," January 1, 1992; Howard Herman, "Mets' Ownership Battle May Drag Beyond February 1," January 5, 1992.

19. Herman, "Mets Down to the Wire"; see also Gladstone's official profile at the minor league baseball website, https://www.milb.com/news/gcs-157976280;

"Anatomy of a Merger: Ray Groves and William Gladstone," *Connect: The Magazine for Ernst & Young Alumni* (Winter 2009/10), www.ey.com (accessed July 2011, website no longer active); for S&L involvement and Gladstone's testimony before Congress, see Michael C. Knapp, *Contemporary Auditing: Real Issues and Cases*, 7th ed. (South-Western Cengage Learning, 2009), 91–95.

20. Herman, "Mets Down to the Wire" and "Pittsfield Mets Sale Is Completed," *Berkshire Eagle*, April 5, 1992, A1; Ronald Rosenberg, "Diamonds in the Rough: Minor Leagues Attract Fans, Investors and Dollars in a Major Way," *Boston Globe*, July 10, 1994, 75; author interview with Rick Murphy.

21. Howard Herman, "Mets, League Set Four More Years," *Berkshire Eagle*, September 3, 1992 and "Mets, Mayor Open Talks to Renew Lease of Park," *Berkshire Eagle*, September 5, 1992; author interview with Rick Murphy.

22. https://sports.espn.go.com/mlb/news/story?id=1799618.

23. Brief histories of Wahconah Park can be found in Rebecca A. Morris et al., "Considerations on the Pittsfield Stadium Issue," Williams College Center for Environmental Studies student paper, December 12, 1997, archived at web. williams.edu/wp-etc/ces/pittsfield-stadium.pdf; and David Pietrusza, *Baseball's Canadian-American League: A History of Its Inception, Franchises, Participants, Locales, Statistics, Demise & Legacy, 1936–1951* (McFarlane, 2005).

24. Pietrusza, *Baseball's Canadian-American League*; "Canadian-American League (C) Encyclopedia and History," https://www.baseball-reference.com/minors/league.cgi?code=CAML&class=C.

25. Morris, "Considerations"; Pietrusza, *Baseball's Canadian-American League*; Paul A. Witteman, ""The Only Game in Town," *Time Magazine*, August 22, 1994, 76–77; Charles O'Reilly, "Wahconah Park," http://www.charliesballparks.com/st/MA-Pittsfield-Wahconah.htm.

26. Morris, "Considerations"; Pietrusza, *Baseball's Canadian-American League*; Palmiero quoted in Bob Ryan, "Fading into Sunset? Pittsfield's Quirky Wahconah Park, Open Since 1919, May Not Be Able to Delay the Inevitable Much Longer," *Boston Globe*, August 30, 2001.

27. Mark McGuire and Michael Sean Gormley, *Moments in the Sun: Baseball's Briefly Famous* (McFarland, 1999), 231; author interview with Rick Murphy; Ty Quillin quoted in Howard Herman, "New Mets Face Quirky Outfield," *Berkshire Eagle*, June 15, 1992.

28. "Lights Are Installed at Wahconah Park," *Berkshire Eagle*, August 10, 1978.

29. McGuire and Gormley, *Moments in the Sun*, 229–231; Morris, "Considerations"; attendance figures 1984–2004 provided to the author by Debbie Carlisle, League Administrator, New York-Penn League, February 24, 2006. Burks quoted in Mark Leinweaver with Ryan Bradley, *Minor Moments, Major Memories: Baseball's Best Players Recall Life in the Minor Leagues* (Lyons Press, 2003), 186; Ryan, "Fading into Sunset?"

30. Howard Herman, "Mets, League Set Four More Years," *Berkshire Eagle*, September 3, 1992, and "Mets, Mayor Open Talks to Renew Lease of Park," *Berkshire Eagle*, September 5, 1992; author interview with Rick Murphy.

31. Jack Cavanaugh, "Season Ends as a Profitable One for Many Baseball Farm Clubs," *New York Times*, September 20, 1989; Daniel Okrent, "Just A Little Bit of Heaven: Pittsfield's Wahconah Park is Baseball as It Oughta Be," *Sports Illustrated*, July 23, 1990.

32. Howard Herman, "Mets, League Set for Four More Years," and "Mets, Mayor Open Talks to Renew Lease of Park"; author interview with Rick Murphy.

33. Howard Herman, "PMets Renew Freiling; Lease Is Next," *Berkshire Eagle*, November 22, 1993.

34. See the following articles in the *Berkshire Eagle* by Howard Herman: "As Snow Melts, Pittsfield Mets Prepare," April 7, 1993; "Mets Negotiating to Stay in Pittsfield," October 13, 1993; PMets Renew Freiling; Lease is Next"; "Off the Field, Pittsfield Mets Enjoyed '94," September 5, 1994; "Will the Mets Stay? Lease Expiring at Time $2.5 Million to Rehab Park Falls Through," August 6, 1996. Mayor is quoted in Greg Sukiennik, "Reilly Begins Lease Talks with Mets," *Berkshire Eagle*, August 8, 1996.

Chapter Four

1. Attendance figures provided by Debbie Carlisle, league administrator of the NY-PL to the author via an email sent on February 24, 2006.

2. League information from *New York-Penn League Media Guide and Record Book*, produced for the league's Inaugural All-Star Game, August 23, 2005, at Keyspan Park, Brooklyn New York.

3. Goldklang from Dave Beal, "Career Timeline: Marv Goldklang," *Twin Cities Pioneer Press*, October 25, 2015, https://www.twincities.com/2015/09/05/career-timeline-marv-goldklang/, and Alan Schwarz, "Businessperson's Special," *Wharton Magazine*, June 1, 2006, https://magazine.wharton.upenn.edu/issues/summer-2006/businesspersons-special/; Alan Levin from NY-PL website (accessed November 2020, website no longer active), and Terry Armour, "Pilots Not Up for Bid, But Owners Selling Their Other Baseball Teams," *Daily Press* (Hampton Roads, Virginia), February 28, 1990; Clyde Smoll from www.neimansportsgroup.com (accessed November 2020, website no longer active), and David Pevear, "In Their Ballpark, Fun Came First," *Lowell Sun*, July 2, 2016; Barry Gordon from NY-PL website (accessed November 2020, website no longer active), and Jack Cavanaugh, "How a Yankees Farm Team, Newly Named, Landed in Norwich," *New York Times*, March 26, 1995. Since the dissolution of the NY-PL by MLB in 2020, nearly all of its official web content has been scrubbed from the internet.

4. "Erie's Ainsworth Field—Baseball Archaeology in a Minor League Time Capsule," at https://deadballbaseball.com/2015/03/eries-ainsworth-field-baseball-archaeology-in-a-minor-league-time-capsule/; Mary Kay Melvin, "Baseball Team, Ballpark Boost Excitement in Erie," *Amusement Business*, May 8, 1995, 13; Bernd Franke, "New IBL Team Paying Tribute to Welland Pirates," *St. Catharines Standard*, July 17, 2019; "Erie SeaWolves UPMC Park" at https://www.baseballpilgrimages.com/minors/erie.html.

5. Jacques Steinberg, "In Fishkill, a New Team Steps Up to the Plate; Minor League Club Excites Baseball Fans in the Economically Ailing Hudson Valley," *New York Times*, February 5, 1994; population from https://www.citypopulation.de/en/usa/metro/39100__poughkeepsie_newburgh_/.

6. Richard Sandomir, "Field of Dreams Turns into Nightmare in New Jersey," *New York Times*, August 23, 1994; "Looking Back at 20 Years of Skylands Park History," *New Jersey Herald*, January 15, 2011. Harvey Araton, "The Farm Calls Out to the Fan," *New York Times*, May 4, 1995.

7. "In Memoriam: Bill Gladstone," *Ballpark Digest*, May 1, 2020, https://ballparkdigest.com/2020/05/01/in-memoriam-bill-gladstone/; William Gladstone obituary, May 1, 2020, https://www.legacy.com/obituaries/nytimes/obituary.aspx?n=william-gladstone&pid=196147281.

8. Rebecca A. Morris et al., "Considerations on the Pittsfield Stadium Issue," Williams College Center for Environmental Studies student paper, December 12, 1997, archived at web.williams.edu/wp-etc/ces/pittsfield-stadium.pdf; and the following articles from the *Berkshire Eagle*: Howard Herman, "Mets Want New Stadium," November 23, 1996; "Mets, City Reach Accord," November 20, 1996; "Council OKs Mets Lease," November 27, 1996; "Board to OK Funds for Ballpark Site Study," January 23, 1997; Theo Stein, "City Strikes Out on Deadline, but Mets Still Game," February 20, 1997.

9. Letters to the editor quoted in Morris, "Considerations on the Pittsfield Stadium Issue." See also *Berkshire Eagle* articles by Greg Sukiennik, "Field of Dreams or Nightmare," October 28, 1997 and "Convention Project In, Stadium Out as Convention Center Bill Passes," November 7, 1997, and D. R. Bahlman, "Proposed New Stadium Is Voted Down," November 5, 1997.

10. Letter from Charles Millard, President of NYC EDC to Paula M. Dagan and Aaron M. Barman at Prudential Securities, May 7, 1996. From NYC EDC baseball files, accessed by the author in 2006.

11. This anecdote appeared in several news pieces on Giuliani during the late 1980s and early 1990s; for examples, see Bob Herbert, "Giuliani the Bully," *New York Times*, April 13, 1994, A21, and a reference in Sam Roberts, "Yanks Win! City Loses! Or, 1977 Repeats Itself," *New York Times*, August 16, 1993, B2.

12. Among the biographies of Giuliani are Wayne Barrett, *Rudy!: An Investigative Biography of Rudolph Giuliani* (Basic Books, 2000); Andrew Kirtzman, *Rudy*

Giuliani: Emperor of the City (HarperCollins, 2001); his own 2002 autobiography by Rudolph Giuliani with Ken Kurson, *Leadership* (Miramax Books, 2002); and Fred Siegel, *The Prince of the City: Giuliani, New York, and the Genius of American Life* (Encounter Books, 2005). Perhaps the most jaundiced take on Giuliani's mayoralty was penned by one of his predecessors; see Ed Koch, *Giuliani: Nasty Man* (Barricade Books, reissued 2007).

13. See the following articles by Richard Sandomir in the *New York Times*: "Yankee Stadium's Future: New Players, Same Old Game," November 6, 1993, 26; "Stadium Waiting Game Adds a Pair of Players," November 12, 1993, B13; "Yankees Show Little Interest in Old-Style Stadium Renovation," March 19, 1994, 26.

14. Sandomir, "Stadium Waiting Game."

15. Quoted in Richard Sandomir, "A 3rd Pitch on Ruth's House," *New York Times*, December 5, 1993, 51.

16. Sandomir, "Yankee Stadium's Future," "Yankees Show Little Interest," and "Mayoral Aides and Yankees Meet to Discuss Stadium Plan," *New York Times*, February 18, 1994, B7. Also from the *New York Times*, see "A Budget: Delayed and Deficient," June 9, 1994, A24; Matthew Purdy, "Design Team Chosen to Set Stadium Plan," August 5, 1994, B1, and " 'Theme Park' Atmosphere Is Part of Proposal for Yankee Stadium," January 25, 1995, B1; David Firestone, "Giuliani's Spending Plan: Services, the Most Dependent Are Hardest Hit," April 28, 1995, B4; Vivian S. Toy, "Streak Alive as Yankees Veto 13th Stadium Plan in a Year," September 6, 1995, B3; Matthew Purdy, "Yankees Look Away from Bronx," September 24, 1995, 45. See also "New York Offers a Stadium Face-lift," *Chicago Sun-Times*, November 18, 1993, 6; Mel Antonen, "Stadium Debate Engulfs the Bronx: Steinbrenner Complains of Crime, Traffic," *USA Today*, June 24, 1994, 5C; Malcolm Gladwell, "Yankees Hurl Big League Knockdown Pitch at Politicians," *Washington Post*, August 7, 1994, A3; Bill Madden and David L. Lewis, "Boss' Squeeze Play on City Stadium Deal," *New York Daily News*, September 6, 1995, 3.

17. Richard Sandomir, "Mets' Owners Divided on Future Playing Site," *New York Times*, June 22, 1995, B9.

18. " 'Ebbets Field with Dome' Would Cost $457 Million," *Daily Mail*, Charleston (West Virginia), September 14, 1995, 5; Pam Belluck, "Mets and City Discussing a Domed Stadium," *New York Times*, September 15, 1995, B3.

19. Bob Liff and Frank Lombardi with Dick Sheridan, "Report: Jersey Wooing Yanks," *New York Daily News*, September 15, 1995, 8; Murray Chass, "New Jersey Is Said to Have Plan to Build Stadium for the Yankees," *New York Times*, September 15, 1995, A1; Purdy, "Yankees Look Away"; Sandomir, "Mets' Owners Divided"; "Mets Look to East, All Around New York," *St. Petersburg Times*, June 22, 1995, 5C.

20. Matthew Purdy, "Resentment Zone; Officials' Courtship of Yankees Stirs Anger in the Bronx," *New York Times*, May 2, 1994, B1; Mike Lupica, "Destroying a Tradition: One George Built Yankee Stadium; Another Will Leave It," *The*

Sporting News, July 18, 1994, 8; Gladwell, "Yankees Hurl Big League Knockdown Pitch"; Richard Sandomir, "Yankee Stadium Plan Stirs Criticism," *New York Times*, February 15, 1995, B3; Eugene G. Brennan, "Don't Spend $1 to Move Yankees to Manhattan," *New York Times*, Letters to the Editor, March 18, 1995, 22; Donald Bertrand, "Pol Takes Cut at a Yankee Stadium Plan," *New York Daily News*, April 4, 1995, 1.

21. This was particularly true for the Yankees, whose on-field performance in recent years did little to justify vast expenditures on a new facility. At the time, the erstwhile Bronx Bombers were mired in a fourteen-year playoff drought that stretched back to a devastating loss in the 1981 World Series. Despite their successful run in the late 1980s, the Mets had not yet made the playoffs in the 1990s either.

22. Paul J. Gessing, "Public Funding of Sports Stadiums: Ballpark Boondoggle," Policy Paper, No. 133, National Taxpayers Union Foundation, February 28, 2001; Roger G. Noll and Andrew Zimbalist, "Sports, Jobs, and Taxes," *Brookings Review*, Summer 1997, 35; Adam M. Zaretsky, "Should Cities Pay for Sports Facilities," *Regional Economist*, April 2001 (Federal Reserve Bank of St. Louis). Jacksonville's $134 million Memorial Stadium was actually approved for municipal underwriting before the city had even been awarded a pro sports franchise, which eventually became the NFL's Jacksonville Jaguars.

23. David M. Selden, "New Sports Facilities in the 1990s—A Tale of Elephants and Blind Men," *Real Estate Issues* 21, no. 3 (December 1996).

24. Zaretsky, "Should Cities Pay for Sports Facilities"; Gary R. Roberts, Stephen F. Ross, and Robert A. Baade, "Should Congress Stop the Bidding War for Sports Franchises?" Hearing before the Subcommittee on Antitrust, Business Rights, and Competition, Senate Committee on the Judiciary (November 29, 1995); Raymond J. Keating, "Sports Pork: The Costly Relationship Between Major League Sports and Government," Cato Institute, Cato Policy Analysis No. 339 (April 5, 1999).

25. By the late 1990s the facility was abandoned by both its baseball and football teams, and it has struggled since then to find long-term tenants of any kind. See Paul Taylor, "Jury Still Out on Benefits of Stadiums as Cities across Continent Follow Fad," *The Globe and Mail* (Canada), June 3, 1986, A18; Richard Korman et al., "Reaching for a High-Flying Market: Stadiums, Arenas Find New Forms and Offer Luxury," *Engineering News-Record*, July 14, 1988, Special Report on Sports Construction, 221, no. 2: 36; Associate Press, "'New' Astrodome Still Evocative of Great Events," *The Globe and Mail* (Canada), April 9, 1990; Michael A. Lutz, "Historic Astrodome Prepares for Final Season of Baseball," Associated Press, April 5, 1999.

26. For a sampling on retro ballparks of the 1990s, see Herbert Muschamp, "Baseball for the Birds, and Everyone Else," *New York Times*, April 6, 1992, C3; Thomas Stinson, "Arlington's Part of the Move to New Parks with an Old Feel,"

Atlanta Journal-Constitution, July 11, 1995; Steve Halvonik, "Three New Ballparks' Architecture Pays Homage to Old Fields," *Pittsburgh Post-Gazette*, August 19, 1994; David Conrads, "Baseball's Big Hit—Intimate, Luxury Parks Designed for the Sybarite in You," *Christian Science Monitor*, May 9, 1997, 10.

27. Richard Sandomir, "Yankees Show Little Interest in Old-Style Stadium Renovation," *New York Times*, March 19, 1994, 26; Charles V. Bagli, "So Many Seats, So Many Tax Breaks," *New York Times*, July 11, 2018.

28. Charles V. Bagli, "'96 Stadium Study Found Fewer Benefits," *New York Times*, April 23, 1998, B3; Peter Passell, "Economic Scene; Local Payoff on a Stadium Is Uncertain," *New York Times*, April 30, 1998, D1. The bulk of the criticism and negative coverage came after Mayor Giuliani announced specific plans and budgetary figures for his stadium proposals in late April 1998.

29. Roger G. Noll and Andrew Zimbalist, "Are New Stadiums Worth the Cost?," November 25, 1998, breadnotcircuses.org/brooking.html (accessed February 2003); Dale Krieger, "Build It and They Will Come?," *Johns Hopkins Magazine*, February 1999.

30. Thomas V. Chema, "When Professional Sports Justify the Subsidy," *Journal of Urban Affairs* 18, no. 1 (1996): 20.

31. Noll and Zimbalist, "Are New Stadiums Worth the Cost?," 2.

32. Robert A. Baade, "Stadiums, Professional Sports, and Economic Development: Assessing the Reality," Heartland Institute Policy Study No. 62, April 4, 1994; Robert A. Baade, "Professional Sports as Catalysts for Metropolitan Economic Development," *Journal of Urban Affairs*, 18, no. 1 (1996): 1–17; Robert A. Baade and Richard F. Dye, "The Impact of Stadiums and Professional Sports on Metropolitan Area Development," *Growth and Change*, Spring 1990; John L. Crompton, "Economic Impact Analysis of Sports Facilities and Events: Eleven Sources of Misapplication," *Journal of Sports Management*, no. 9 (1995): 14–35; and Mark L. Mitchell, "To Build or Not to Build: An Analysis of the Benefits of New Sports Facilities," *Real Estate Issues* 21, no. 3 (December 1996).

33. "The Agenda For Permanent Change," Second Inaugural Address of Mayor Rudolph W. Giuliani, January 1, 1998, http://www.nyc.gov/html/records/rwg/html/98a/secondinaug.html (accessed October 2020); Dan Barry, "The Inauguration of Rudolph W. Giuliani: The Overview; At Inauguration, Giuliani Outlines Police Expansion," *New York Times*, January 2, 1998, 1. Press coverage of the inauguration speech generally overlooked the mayor's references to baseball and keeping the city's teams in New York.

34. Jesse Drucker, "Kill the Watchdog: Mayor Seeks an End to Budget Monitor," *New York Observer*, January 12, 1998, 1, 9; Norimitsu Onishi, "Giuliani Sued over Access to City Data," *New York Times* April 2, 1998, B5; Independent Budget Office, "Living Dangerously," 1998 annual report, https://ibo.nyc.ny.us/annualreport98/AR99dangerously.html.

35. Office of Bronx Borough President Fernando Ferrer, "The Perfect Pitch: The Bombers in the Bronx," October 22, 1996; Matthew Purdy, "New Old Yankee Stadium?," *New York Times*, December 14, 1994, B3; Charlie LeDuff, "Giuliani Plans to Bypass Referendum on Stadium Financing," *New York Times*, April 30, 1998, B3. All subsequent notes on the IBO report are from city of New York Independent Budget Office, "Double Play: The Economics and Financing of Stadiums for the Yankees and Mets," April 1998, https://ibo.nyc.ny.us/iboreports/doubleplay.html.

36. Dan Barry, "Giuliani's Plan for Stadiums Uses Tax He Planned to End," *New York Times*, April 21, 1998, A1; Michael Finnegan with Maureen Fan, "Mayor's Ballpark Figures," *New York Daily News*, April 21, 1998, 3; Daniel Kruger, "Giuliani Would Use Old Tax, Not Bonds to Build Stadiums," *Bond Buyer*, April 21, 1991, 1; Norimitsu Onishi, "Giuliani Proposes $34 Billion Budget with Cut in Taxes," *New York Times*, April 25, 1998, A1.

Chapter Five

1. David Firestone, "Labor Chief for Giuliani to Leave for Baseball Job," *New York Times*, September 19, 1995, B3; Reginald Patrick and Warren Hines, "A Promise Kept: Two Teams Coming," *Staten Island Advance*, January 15, 1999, A1.

2. Christopher Sciria, "Leo Pinckney, Auburn's 'King of Baseball,' Passes Away at 89," *Auburn Citizen*, November 20, 2006, https://auburnpub.com/news/local/leo-pinckney-auburns-king-of-baseball-passes-away-at-89/article_2056be85-c48d-5851-bb25-d3a978709e69.html.

3. Leslie Eaton, "Party Politics Hold Sway in Choice of Judges Upstate, Too," *New York Times*, November 17, 2003, B1.

4. Quote from author interview with Robert F. Julian, July 18, 2006.

5. Interview with Julian; Robert Harding, "25 Years Ago, Minor League Baseball in Auburn Faced Extinction—Until NY Stepped In," *Auburn Citizen*, December 15, 2019, https://auburnpub.com/news/local/25-years-ago-minor league-baseball-in-auburn-faced-extinction-until-ny-stepped-in/article_80eb0d36-024a-5995-840a-b2bd2ed6933b.html; Jacob Weisberg, "Remembering Mario Cuomo's First 4,000 Days in Office," *New York Magazine*, August 8, 1994, https://nymag.com/intelligencer/2014/12/mario-cuomos-first-4000-days-in-office.html.

6. Interview with Julian.

7. Minor League Baseball, "Lowell Spinners: Franchise History," www.milb.com (website accessed June 2010, no longer active as site has since been scrubbed by MiLB).

8. Profile of Barry Gordon, see Larry Moko, "Gordon: A Wheeler, Dealer; Redbird Owner Is All Business, Collects Lucrative Baseball Cards," *Hamilton Spectator* (Ontario, Canada), March 12, 1992, E2. For Albany-Colonie Yankees

move to Long Island, see UPI, "Long Island Makes Pitch for Minor Leagues," *Sports News*, September 15, 1992; "Suffolk Authorizes Outlay of $500,000 for a Ball Park," *New York Times*, September 24, 1992, B7; Charles Strum, "Back to the Minors; It's a Major New Market for Baseball," *New York Times*, October 8, 1992, B1. Committee rejection of Yankees proposal, see "Sports News" Press Releases, Associated Press, February 16, 1993 and February 17, 1993; Jim Donaghy, "Sports News," Associated Press, February 21, 1993. For Pittsfield stadium vote, see *Berkshire Eagle* articles by Greg Sukiennik, "Field of Dreams or Nightmare," October 28, 1997, and "Convention Project In, Stadium Out as Convention Center Bill Passes," November 7, 1997; and D. R. Bahlman, "Proposed New Stadium Is Voted Down," November 5, 1997.

9. Interview with Julian.

10. Wilpon comment quoted in Dan Barry, "Feverish Dreams of Baseball as Mets Look at Brooklyn," *New York Times*, January 17, 1998, B3.

11. Andrew Rice, "Sultan of Spending: Mayor Goes on Spree Constructing Stadiums," *New York Observer*, July 17, 2000, 2.

12. Bill Madden and Michael Finnegan with Thomas Hill, "Yanks' S. I. Team May Strike Out," *New York Daily News*, January 3, 1997, 7; "State of the City Address," Mayor Rudolph W. Giuliani, January 14, 1998, http://www.nyc.gov/html/om/html/98a/pr022-98.html; Dan Barry, "What Staten Island Needs, Mayor Says, Is Baseball," *New York Times*, January 14, 1998, B3; Molinari quoted in Bill Madden, "A Team Grows in Brooklyn: Mets Eye Farm Team in Borough," *New York Daily News*, January 16, 1998, 79.

13. Madden, "A Team Grows in Brooklyn"; Mike Lupica, "Sweet Summer Dreams Flicker in Coney Island," *New York Daily News*, January 16, 1998, 78; Barry, "Feverish Dreams of Baseball."

14. See these articles by Greg Sukiennik: "Big Apple Beckons Mets," *Berkshire Eagle*, January 17, 1998, A1, "Pittsfield Mets 'Likely' To Play Here Through '99," *Berkshire Eagle*, January 22, 1998, A1, and "Mets Appear Coney Bound," *Berkshire Eagle*, September 16, 1998, A1. For November 1998 developments, see articles by Bob Liff: "Borough Bigs Nearly Whiff on Rudy's Ballpark Curves," *New York Daily News*, November 12, 1998, 8, and "Rudy's Minor League Stunt Door Open to Mets on Coney Island Ballpark," *New York Daily News*, November 23, 1998, 6. For Jeff Wilpon, see David Waldstein, Kevin Draper, and James Wagner, "Fans Didn't Like the Way Jeff Wilpon Ran the Mets. Neither Did Some of His Relatives," *New York Times*, December 6, 2019, B7; David Waldstein, "With Wilpons Set to Cede Control, the Mets End an Era of What-Ifs," *New York Times*, September 27, 2020, D1.

15. Greg Sukiennik, "Mets to Stay in Pittsfield through '00," *Berkshire Eagle*, January 5, 1999, A1; Associated Press, "Mets to Stay in Pittsfield for at Least Next Two Years," *Sports News*, January 5, 1999; Bob Liff, "Here's Another Fine Mets,"

New York Daily News, January 7, 1999, 2; Bill Madden, "Minor Moves," *New York Daily News*, January 10, 1999, 71; Interview with Julian.

16. Erik Arvidson, "City Losing Minor League Team: Franchise Plans Move to Troy" and Howard Herman, "Gladstone Seizes Opportunity," both in *Berkshire Eagle*, May 9, 2000, A1; Jim Luttrell, "Charm Might Not Be Enough," *New York Times*, August 2, 2000; author interview with Rick Murphy, August 10, 2006.

17. Interview with Julian.

18. Author interview with Sam Nader, July 17, 2006.

19. Interview with Julian, Interview with Nader.

20. Although such arrangements were highly unusual, there were rare precedents for a major league club to maintain two franchises in a single minor league. For example, at the time the San Francisco Giants fielded two teams in the Class A California League.

21. See the following articles from the *Press and Sun-Bulletin* (Binghamton, New York): Dan Rafael, "Oneonta Yankees' Owner Says Team Isn't Moving," May 10, 1998, 68; Dan Rafael, "NY-P Says Yanks Could Have 2 Teams in League," May 12, 1998, 9; Charlie Jaworski, "O-Yanks Give Birth to Tradition," June 14, 1998, 6; Maurice Thomas and Linda Jump, "Yankees Leaving Oneonta; New Team Expected," September 18, 1998, 1, 40; Jim Howe, "End of Baseball Era: N.Y. Affiliation Yanked from Oneonta," September 18, 1998, 37; and John W. Fox, "Baseball's Downstate Trickle Sparks Nightmarish Thoughts," November 1, 1998, 79.

22. Thomas and Jump, "Yankees Leaving Oneonta," 40; interview with Nader.

Chapter Six

1. Quote from Bob Liff, "Borough Bigs Nearly Whiff on Rudy's Ballpark Curves," *New York Daily News*, November 12, 1998, 8. For 1998 budget and ensuing controversy, see: Dan Barry, "Giuliani's Plan for Stadiums Uses Tax He Planned to End," *New York Times*, April 21, 1998, A1; Michael Finnegan with Maureen Fan, "Mayor's Ballpark Figures," *New York Daily News*, April 21, 1998, 3; Norimitsu Onishi, "Giuliani Proposes $34 Billion Budget with Cut in Taxes," *New York Times*, April 25, 1998, A1; Henry Goldman, "Critics Cry Foul over New Move to Move Yanks' Park," *Philadelphia Inquirer*, April 26, 1998, E1; Tom Pedulla, "N.Y. Stadiums: Controversy Is All That's Building," *USA Today*, May 20, 1998; Juan Gonzales, "Going to Bat for Fans Rudy Strikes out with Stadium Judge," *New York Daily News*, October 8, 1998, 18; Beth Gardiner, "Stadium Vote May Tilt NY Sen. Race," Associated Press, October 11, 1998; Supreme Court, Appellate Division, First Department, New York, *The Council of the City of New York, et al., v. Rudolph Giuliani, etc., et al.,* decided October 16, 1998, https://caselaw.findlaw.com/ny-supreme-court-appellate-division/1229249.html.

2. Thomas J. Lueck, "Baseball Entrepreneurs Score in Bush Leagues," *New York Times*, August 24, 1987, 1, 53; Mark Zwolinski, ""Baby Jays Open Their Season Tonight," *Toronto* Star, June 16, 1989, B3. See also the following articles in the *Watertown Daily Times*: "Baseball Fans: Where Are You? Pirates Fans Dwindle," July 10, 1988, F3; "Dearth of Paying Fans Alarms Pirates' Owner: Attendance for First 10 Games Averages 762," July 10, 1988, A1; "City Fans Insist Owners at Fault, Lack of Promotions Cuts Crowds," August 2, 1988, 17; "Watertown Officials Say They've Had It with Pirates Brass," August 2, 1988, 17; "Ontario City Signs Pirates: Welland Wins Ball Team," August 19, 1988, 30; "Watertown Fans Tell League Boss Pirate Owners Should Just Go Away," August 21, 1988, F3; "Top Pirate Talks but Says Nothing," August 30, 1988, 22; "Pirates Gone NY-Penn OKs Welland Move," September 11, 1988, A1; "City Seeking to Lure NY-Penn Team In '89," September 12, 1988, 28; "Pirates Clean Out Clubhouse: Batting Cage, Generator, Washer Gone from Fairgrounds," September 20, 1988, 28; "Ball Field to Receive Facelift," April 20, 1989, G1; "Indians' NYP League Trial in City Going to Jury This Week," June 11, 1989, G6 (source for Margenau quote); and "Indians Must Buck History against Longevity," June 14, 1989, T6. See also the Eric Margenau profile that calls him "a fun-loving guy with glasses," Michael Lewis, "A Man for All Seasons," *Glens Falls Post-Star* (New York), January 25, 2004. For the sale of the teams to Alan Levin, see Curt Rallo, "South Bend Sox Still Mum on Sale," *South Bend Tribune*, February 6, 1990, C1 and Curt Rallo, "No Problems Anticipated on Sale Approval," *South Bend Tribune*, February 23, 1990, B1, B3.

3. See the following articles in the *Watertown Daily Times*: Paul Foy, "Team Owners Pitch in Money: Deal Slams Baseball over Fence," April 14, 1989, 28; "The Bottom Line for Indians Is to Improve the Bottom Line," June 14, 1992, G1; "Cities in NY-P Grapple with Issue: Can They Afford to Meet Ballpark Standards?," October 18, 1992, G8; "Indians Hope City Looks at Fairgrounds," January 7, 1993, 18; "Owners Intend to Sell Indians Team, City Can't Reach Accord," September 11, 1993, 32; "Indians Deal Clarified," September 13, 1993, 18; "Indians Now Feature a First-Rate Facility," June 13, 1994, 15; "Financially, Indians Optimistic," September 11, 1994, D8.

4. See the following articles from the *Watertown Daily Times* by Rob Oatman: "Want to Buy Indians? You Must Make Offer by Sept. 24," September 12, 1995, 15; "Indians Are Champions, but Franchise Is a Mess," September 17, 1995, D1; "Deadline Extended for Potential Buyers of Watertown Indians," October 7, 1995, 17; "Getzlers Optimistic about Offer to Buy Indians," November 2, 1995, 15; "Getzlers Wait to Buy Indians," November 5, 1995, D1. See also these articles from the *Watertown Daily Times*: Mark Houck, "Acting President Gardner: Indians Buyers Down to 3," October 17, 1995, 18, and Keith Button, "Indians Owners Agree to Sell Baseball Team: Father, Son Vow to Keep Club in City 5 Years," November 11, 1995, 34.

5. Steve Popper, "Dreaming of Baseball on Staten I.," *New York Times*, May 11, 1999, D2; Wedding Announcement of Phyllis Resnick and Stanley Getzler, *Asbury Park Press*, April 17, 1961, 27; Stanley Getzler, "Recollections of LSS' Early Days by Stanley Getzler, LSS President 1978–1981," https://www.lss.org/memories.html?post_id=17270.

6. Getzler, "Recollections"; Richard Wilner, "Getzler's Double Play: Father-and-Son Team behind the Staten Island Yankees," *New York Post*, May 13, 1999.

7. Interview with Josh Getzler, January 21, 2021.

8. Interview with Josh Getzler; see also Oatman, "Getzlers Optimistic" and "Getzlers Wait to Buy Indians." Background on Kuhn and Sports Franchises Inc. from Woody Anderson, "Kuhn: Sports Teams Vital to Bridgeport," *Hartford Courant*, February 12, 1993. Kuhn's business was based in Norwalk, Connecticut, although he lived in Ponte Vedra Beach, Florida, where he had moved to prevent his home from seizure during bankruptcy proceedings over a failed law firm from his post-commissioner days. See Richard Goldstein, "Bowie Kuhn, 80, Former Baseball Commissioner, Dies," *New York Times*, March 16, 2007.

9. Oatman, "Getzlers Optimistic" and "Getzlers Wait to Buy Indians"; Button, "Indians Owners Agree to Sell Baseball Team"; Mark Houck and Rob Oatman, "Problem with Tribe Sale: Stocks vs. Assets," *Watertown Daily Times*, December 7, 1995, 17; Rob Oatman, "Sale of Indians Still Waiting on Lawyers," *Watertown Daily Times*, February 18, 1996, D9; Rob Oatman, "Steady at the Top: General Manager Tracz Stays with Indians through Uncertain Times," *Watertown Daily Times*, February 20, 1996, 15.

10. Interview with Josh Getzler; Rob Oatman, "Getzlers Visit, Challenge City: New Indians Owners 'Continuously Evaluating Situation,'" *Watertown Daily Times*, November 16, 1995, 17.

11. Rob Oatman, "Duffy Fairgrounds' Scoreboard Should Light Up Watertown Fans," *Watertown Daily Times*, April 8, 1996, 15; John Day, "Indians Drop Home Opener: In Minor League Towns, Summer Begins at the Park," *Watertown Daily Times*, June 19, 1996, 15; Rob Oatman, "Where Have All the Fans Gone? Watertown Club Ranks Last in NY-P Attendance, First in the Pennant Race," *Watertown Daily Times*, August 25, 1996, D1.

12. Wayne Parry, "A Dream of Shore Baseball," *Asbury Park Press*, February 18, 1997, 1, 12; Wayne Parry, "Owners Touch Former Home Base: Minor league Team Envisioned at Shore," *Central New Jersey Home News* (New Brunswick, New Jersey), February 18, 1997, 3.

13. See the following articles by Rob Oatman in the *Watertown Daily Times*: "Selling Seats to Save the Indians: Group Tries to Bring in Tribe Fans," June 15, 1997, D1; "Indians Owner Hopes Second Time Around Brings More Success," June 16, 1997, 15; "Getzler: No Plans to Move Tribe to New Jersey," September 4, 1997, 17; "Indians Losing Money: Tribe Requires More Fans in '98," D1; "Tribe

Owners on the Move: Getzlers Hold Meetings with Cape May Officials," November 20, 1997, 17; "Cape May Keeps Pitching, Lawmaker: N.J. Competing against Albany for Indians," December 6, 1997, 15; Lois R. Shea, "Baseball Beckons In N.H.: Concord Group Makes Pitch to Attract Minor League Team," *Boston Globe*, August 12, 1997, B2. See also these additional articles in the *Watertown Daily Times*: Roy C. Goodwin, "Indians Baseball: Great Affordable Fun," June 16, 1997, 5; Clayton Gordon D. Cerow Jr., "Fan Support Crucial for Baseball's Survival," July 1, 1997, 5; Thomas Fillhart, "Support Baseball," August 2, 1997, 5; John O'Donnell, "Watertown's Athletics Recalled during Historical Society Program," August 9, 1997, 19; Jow Flynn, "Tribe Owners to Meet with N.J. Group," November 13, 1997, 17; and "Tribe Owner Meets N.J. Group Again," January 7, 1998, 15.

14. Quotes from Rob Oatman, "Owner Getzler Assures Decision Hasn't Been Made on Relocation," *Watertown Daily Times*, June 14, 1998, D1; see also Rob Oatman, "Talk of Tribe Move Concerns Diehard Followers," *Watertown Daily Times*, June 14, 1998, D1, and Kelly Tomlinson, "Tribe Increases Promotion Days in Bid to Entertain, Attract Fans," *Watertown Daily Times*, June 14, 1998, D1.

15. Quote from author interview with Josh Getzler, March 2, 2021.

16. Kelly Tomlinson, "Getzler Mum on Move," *Watertown Daily Times*, August 29, 1998, 15; Rob Oatman, "Fans Bid Tribe Uncertain Farewell," *Watertown Daily Times*, September 2, 1998, 15, and "Although Tribe Through, Getzler Has Work to Do," *Watertown Daily Times*, September 6, 1998, D1.

17. Interview with Josh Getzler.

18. Justin Ritzel, "Riding the Storm Out: A Look Back at the 1998 Auburn Doubledays," *Auburn Citizen* (Auburn, New York), August 9, 2018, https://auburn-pub.com/sports/local/riding-the-storm-out-a-look-back-at-the-1998-auburn-dou-bledays/article_bf713111-0876-5fd5-a366-d24ea7093e10.html; "Oneonta Will Stay in NY-P League Despite Losing Yankees Affiliation," *Watertown Daily Times*, September 18, 1998, 17; Kelly Tomlinson, "Yankees Land Getzler," *Watertown Daily Times*, September 19, 1998, 15; "Getzler Wraps Up Yanks Deal," *Watertown Daily Times*, October 2, 1998, 19; Rob Oatman, "Athletics Decide to Shed Old Nickname after Acquiring Ex-Indians' Uniforms," *Watertown Daily Times*, October 22, 1998, 17, and "Getzler Buys Time at Fairgrounds: Lease Expiring, But Still No Decision from Owner of Watertown Franchise," *Watertown Daily Times*, October 30, 1998, 15.

19. See these two articles by Rob Oatman in *Watertown Daily Times*: "Local Sports Fans Turn Away from Baseball at Every Level," August 9, 1998, D1; "The Final Exit: Pro Ball Dies Again in Watertown," January 10, 1999, D1. See also Greg Lavine, "Council Mourns Loss of Pro Ball in City," *Watertown Daily Times*, January 5, 1999, 28; and Kelly Tomlinson, "As New NY-P Season Arrives, Some Miss Pro Game, Others Don't Care," *Watertown Daily Times*, June 13, 1999, D1. Stan Getzler quoted in Warren Hynes, "Profile: Stanley and Josh Getzler," *Staten Island Advance*, January 24, 1999, A21.

20. Popper, "Dreaming of Baseball"; Oatman, "Getzlers Visit, Challenge City"; Warren Hynes, "On June 20, Play Ball! Yankee-Style," *Staten Island Advance*, January 21, 1999, A1.

Chapter Seven

1. Tom Wrobleski, "Obituary: Guy Molinari, 89, a Giant Who Transformed Staten Island's Civic and Political Landscape," *Staten Island Advance*, July 25, 2018; Daniel C. Kramer and Richard M. Flanagan, *Staten Island: Conservative Bastion in a Liberal City* (University Press of America, 2012), 88.

2. Robert D. McFadden, "Guy V. Molinari, Power Broker in New York and Beyond, Is Dead at 89," *New York Times*, July 25, 2018, A24. For the effects of the charter revision, see Alan Finder, "The Fight over Changing the Borough Presidents' Role," *New York Times*, October 19, 1989, B1.

3. http://www.vincemacdermot.com/planning.html, illustration and depiction of St. George Station as commissioned by the Office of the Borough President Guy V. Molinari. Tish Durkin, "Mayor's Big Plan: Baseball, Gambling, More Crime Fighting," *New York Observer*, January 19, 1998 attributes the minor league ballpark plan to Molinari: "Staten Island Borough President Guy Molinari has been talking about building a minor league ball park in his borough for years, and now it seems he will get his wish. 'I can't think of a favor that I sought that was turned down!' exulted Mr. Molinari on the subject of life with the Giuliani administration. It was New Year's night at the College of Staten Island, after the freshly reinaugurated Mayor had sworn in the Borough President for his third term-and though it would be un-American to equate a baseball team with a political favor, Mr. Molinari did seem awfully bubbly about the idea."

4. Durkin, "Mayor's Big Plan"; Jacques Steinberg, "The Inauguration of Rudolph W. Giuliani: Inaugural Notebook; a Borough-Hopping Tour," *New York Times*, January 2, 1998, B5; State of the City Address, Mayor Rudolph W. Giuliani, January 14, 1998, https://www1.nyc.gov/html/rwg/html/98a/stcitext.html; Dan Barry, "What Staten Island Needs, Mayor Says, Is Baseball," *New York Times*, January 14, 1998, B3; Judy L. Randall, "5 Baseball Sites Named; Mets In Brooklyn," *Staten Island Advance*, January 16, 1998, A1.

5. Matthew Goldstein, "Staten Island Gets Ready for Its Own Opening Day: Minor League Site Will Be Picked," *Crain's New York Business*, April 27, 1998, 29. The details on the advantages and disadvantages of the three Staten Island sites are provided in an internal EDC document titled "Site Analysis of Proposed Minor League Stadium on Staten Island." It is undated but almost certainly from early 1998 during the process of whittling down the list of proposed sites to three finalists. Six sites are listed in the document including the three eventual finalists as well as Willowbrook Park, Mariners Harbor I & II, and Father Capodanno

Boulevard Site. For Homeport's closure, see Kimberly J. McLarin, "Opening a Wound on Staten Island," *New York Times*, June 26, 1993, section 1, 7.

6. Quote from Goldstein, "Staten Island Gets Ready."

7. The history and overall development plan for St. George was laid out in detail several years earlier in a New York City study. See "Plan for the Staten Island Waterfront: New York City Comprehensive Waterfront Plan," New York City Department of City Planning (Spring 1994), document NYC DCP 94-04, particularly p. 23.

8. "Plan for the Staten Island Waterfront," 50.

9. Archives of the Mayor's Press Office, "Mayor Giuliani Announces City Will Acquire CSX Site in Staten Island," Press Release #394-98, August 15, 1998.

10. James C. McKinley, Jr., "Restoring the Rails on Staten Island: Plans for Economic Revival Stretch Along 15 Miles of Track," *New York Times*, November 11, 1994, B1; William Roberts, "Gender Mender," *Journal of Commerce*, July 22, 1996; "Republicans and Railroads," *Traffic World*, May 18, 1998, 25; Frank N. Wilner, "CSX, NS Win SIRR: Conrail Partners Exchange Extension of N.J. Shared-Assets Area For 7-Mile Line, Port Access," *Traffic World*, May 18, 1998, 25.

11. Karen O'Shea, "City Buys 26 Acres in St. George, Former Rail Yard Is Purchased from CSX for $13 Million," *Staten Island Advance*, August 16, 1998, A1.

12. All EIS reports cited in TRC Preliminary Draft Report, Supplemental Site Investigation Report, Ballpark at St. George Station, TRC Project #14638-0310, dated August 31, 1999; from EDC documents Box NE000519, "Ballpark at St. George." See also Memo from Jim Peronto, P. E., Senior Consulting Engineer, TRC Environmental, to EDC, "re: Conclusions and Recommendations . . . Former CSX St. George Railyard," dated November 18, 1998. For faulty CSX title, see Judy L. Randall, "Rail Yard Tract Back in Running as Stadium Site," *Staten Island Advance*, January 20, 1998, A1.

13. TRC Preliminary Draft Report; TRC Revised Cost Estimate, dated August 5, 1998, followed by Memo from Jim Peronto P. E., TRC Environmental Corp., to Kay Zias, EDC, dated August 12, 1998, containing italicized addition at end of memo that "TRC is hereby authorized to complete the scope of work presented in this letter dated August 12, 1998 for the CSX/St. George Railyard site for the estimated amount of $100,761 in accordance with our current retainer contract. [signed] Ms. Kay Zias, 8/13/98." From EDC documents Box NE000291. Sale figures from Closing Statement for EDC sale of block 2, lot 20 (52.73 acres of land) to the City of New York, signed by David Farber, dated December 8, 1998 (referring to a contract dated December 7, 1998) for a purchase price of $19,374,291. Purchase already approved in a letter from Deputy Mayor Joseph Lhota to Hon. William J. Diamond, Commissioner, Dept. of Citywide Administrative Services, dated December 4, 1998. EDC documents Boxes 11318 and 11328. For the CSX sale, see Reginald Patrick, "City Now Owns Railyard Track; CSX Knocked 250Gs Off," *Staten Island Advance*, December 2, 1998, A1.

14. Office of the Mayor of the City of New York, "An Agenda to Prepare for the Next Century: 1999 State of the City," January 14, 1999, http://www.nyc. gov/html/rwg/html/99a/stcitytext.html (web page no longer active).

15. Lease Terms Proforma/Revenue Projections (First 5 years), Alternatives 2A-2E "based on Conversations with the New York Yankees," draft versions dated October 14, 1998. From EDC documents; Reginald Patrick, "Officials Plan Repairs to Stadium Property," *Staten Island Advance*, December 26, 1998, A1.

16. Author interview with Josh Getzler, July 8, 2021.

17. 1999 State of the City address; Reginald Patrick and Warren Hynes, "A Promise Kept: 2 Teams Coming," *Staten Island Advance*, January 15, 1999, A1; Joe D'Amodio, "At CSI, A New Team Brings New Changes," *Staten Island Advance*, January 27, 1999, B1; Stan Getzler quoted in Warren Hynes, "Profile: Stanley and Josh Getzler," *Staten Island Advance*, January 24, 1999, A21.

18. Karen O'Shea, "Reinforced CSI Stands Deemed Safe—Zoning Law," *Staten Island Advance*, June 22, 1999, A1.

19. Tom Topousis, "S.I. Yanks Tix 'A' Hot Item," *New York Post*, March 2, 1999; "New Staten Island Team Big Draw with Fans," *Watertown Daily Times*, March 3, 1999, 16; Warren Hynes, "Hottest Ticket in Town," *Staten Island Advance*, March 2, 1999, A1; Warren Hynes, "S. I. Yanks Guaranteed to Outdraw Watertown Team," *Staten Island Advance*, March 4, 1999, A4.

20. Jim Waggoner, "Our Yanks Hit a Home Run with a Sellout Crowd," *Staten Island Advance*, June 21, 1999, B1; Warren Hynes, "Ballpark's the New Town Hall," *Staten Island Advance*, June 21, 1999, A1.

21. Staten Island Yankees attendance, players, record and statistics for 1999 and 2000 from https://www.thebaseballcube.com/content/stats/minor~1999~10400/ and https://www.thebaseballcube.com/content/stats/minor~2000~10400/.

22. Jay Price, "Our Yanks' Fans Bid Farewell to Willowbrook," *Staten Island Advance*, September 13, 2000, A1.

23. See the following articles in the *Staten Island Advance*: Cormac Gordon, "Stadium Birth Starts with Baby Step," February 17, 1999, A6; Reginald Patrick, "Council Expected to OK $11M for S. I. Yanks' Sites," March 4, 1999, A5; Reginald Patrick, "Site of St. George Ball Park to get $7.6M Facelift," March 6, 1999, A4; Reginald Patrick, "Funds Allotted for S. I. Yanks Ballpark Site," March 17, 1999, A16.

24. Rebecca Cavanaugh Warren-Hynes, "Some St. George Residents on Stadium," *Staten Island* Advance, April 14, 1999, A1; NYCEDC, "The Ballpark at St. George Station in Richmond County, New York: Final Environmental Impact Statement," October 7, 1999.

25. See the following articles from the *Staten Island Advance*: Karen O'Shea, "Public Review Process Begins for Stadium," July 19, 1999, A15 and "Soil Testing Conducted for Stadium Project," July 20, 1999, A7; "Forum Scheduled on Baseball Stadium," July 28, 1999, A22.

26. Michael Finnegan, "Tainted Soil Present at Ballpark on S. I.," *New York Daily News*, July 29, 1999, 8. See also Karen O'Shea and Judy L. Randall, "Ballpark Soil Tests May Be a Little Noisy," *Staten Island Advance*, July 16, 1999, A1; O'Shea, "Soil Testing"; Reginald Patrick and Don Gross, "Stadium Site Toxins Raise Little Concern," *Staten Island Advance*, July 30, 1999, A1; Eileen AJ Connelly and Jodi Lee, "Views, Parking Questioned at St. George Stadium," *Staten Island Advance*, July 30, 1999, A12.

27. See the following articles from the *Staten Island Advance*: Robin Eisner, "Concerns Aired about St. George Stadium Parking," September 9, 1999, A15; Eileen AJ Connelly, "City Hearing on St. George Stadium Stirs New Protests," September 21, 1999, A13; Reginald Patrick, "Councilman Tosses Out Curve Ball," September 23, 1999, A12; Reginald Patrick, "Stadium Concerns Aired at Hearing," September 23, 1999, A12; and "St. George Stadium Price Could Top $40M," September 29, 1999, A2. For U.S. Gypsum Plant, see James G. Ferreri, "From Wallboard to Street Salt in Staten Island's New Brighton," *Staten Island Advance*, January 15, 2013, silive.com.

28. "Proposed Minor League Baseball Stadium Lease at CSX Site, Staten Island," dated August 27, 1998 and "Lease Terms Proforma/Revenue Projections (First Five Years)," Alternatives 2A-2E. EDC Executive VP Robert Balder copy, dated October 14, 1998, from EDC documents accessed May 2006.

29. Karen O'Shea, "Lease Deal a Steal for Our Yanks?," *Staten Island Advance*, October 7, 1999, A1; Cormac Gordon, "Silence on Stadium Deal Speaks Volumes," *Staten Island Advance*, October 7, 1999, A6.

30. See the following articles from the *Staten Island Advance*: Reginald Patrick, "Plan Board OKs Stadium; Council Next," October 21, 1999, A1; Reginald Patrick, "Council to Modify Stadium Plan?," October 24, 1999, B3; Karen O'Shea, "A New St. George—City Study of Stadium Project," November 7, 1999, A1; Reginald Patrick, "Ballpark Plan No Hit with City Council Panel," November 17, 1999, A1; Jodi Lee Riefer, "BP Would Toss Critics Out of Stadium Game," November 18, 1999, A1; Reginald Patrick, "Stadium Plan Looking More Like a Team Effort," November 21, 1999, A1; "Stadium Stumbling," November 28, 1999, B2; Reginald Patrick, "Stadium Plan Looks Like a Winner Today," December 7, 1999, A1; Reginald Patrick, "Stadium Breezes to Council Approval," December 8, 1999, A1; Reginald Patrick, "Was Stadium Approval Ever in Doubt," December 8, 1999, A1.

31. "Ballpark at St. George: Capital Program Project Budget," drafts dated September 28, 1999, November 18, 1999, and December 1, 1999, from EDC documents accessed May 2006.

32. "Capital Program Project Budget"; Arden Sokolow interview with Jeff Dumas, October 16, 2002.

33. See the following articles from the *Staten Island Advance*: Karen O'Shea, "Our Yanks' Goal: Filling New Stadium," February 22, 2000, A13; "Our Opinion:

EDC and Full Disclosure," March 10, 2000, A26; Eileen AJ Connelly and Reginald Patrick, "Bank to Hang Its Name on Island Stadium," April 13, 2000, A1; Karen O'Shea, "Beam Topples over on Worker at Stadium Site," June 1, 2000, A1; Eileen AJ Connelly, "Ballpark Banks on New Name: Staged 'Groundbreaking' of Richmond County Ballpark at St. George Is a Home Run," June 9, 2000, A1; Eileen AJ Connelly, "Stadium Construction Is Ahead of Schedule," June 30, 2000, A8.

34. Jay Price, "Our Yanks' Fans Bid Farewell to Willowbrook," *Staten Island Advance*, September 13, 2000, A1.

35. Frank Donnelly, "Getzlers' 'Vision' Is on Target for June Opening," *Staten Island Advance*, January 7, 2001, A8; Frank Donnelly, "Businesses See New Ballpark as a Potential Home," *Staten Island Advance*, January 21, 2001, A1.

36. See the following articles from the *Staten Island Advance*: Jack Minogue, "CSI Strikes Out with Baseball Field," May 12, 2001, C9; Ryan Lillis, "CSI's Ballfield on Losing Streak," June 1, 2001, A17; "Our Opinion: What Happened Here?," June 2, 2001, A11.

Chapter Eight

1. Burton A. and Benita Boxerman, *Ebbets to Veeck to Busch: Eight Owners Who Shaped Baseball* (McFarland, 2003); John G. Zinn, *Charles Ebbets: The Man Behind the Dodgers and Brooklyn's Beloved Ballpark* (McFarland, 2019). Wilpon and Hamill quoted in Mike Lupica, "A Team Grows in Brooklyn: Sweet Summer Dreams Flicker in Coney Island," *New York Daily News*, January 16, 1998, 78.

2. "Ebbets Field," https://www.ballparksofbaseball.com/ballparks/ebbets-field/; Steven Zinger, "The History of Ebbets Field Apartment Complex," https://patch.com/new-york/new-york-city/history-ebbets-field-apartments-complex.

3. David Staba, "Falls in League of Its Own; Chances of Comeback Slim," *Niagara Falls Reporter* (online), Jan/May 2001, http://www.niagarafallsreporter.com/fallsleague.html; Tom Schmitt, "Making the Minors: Falls Not Quite Ready for Pro Baseball," *Tonawanda News*, June 30, 2006, https://www.niagara-gazette.com/sports/making-the-minors-falls-not-quite-ready-for-pro-baseball/article_f1d3a7e6-35fc-5c79-a847-96122b664e0d.html; Associated Press, "Toronto Wants to Buy Niagara Falls Team, Move the Franchise to a Canadian City," *Los Angeles Times*, September 22, 1985, http://articles.latimes.com/1985-09-22/sports/sp-18260_1_niagara-falls.

4. Canadian Press, "Jays Choose St. Kitts for Team Site," *Toronto Star*, November 6, 1985, F1.

5. Garth Woolsey, "Lights, Jays Are Ready in St. Kitts," *Toronto Star*, June 5, 1986, D3; Allan Ryan, "Blue Jay Time in St. Catharines," *Toronto Star*, June 18, 1986, F8; Mike Rutsey, "St. Kitts Adopts Baby Jays, Young Prospects Find 70 Miles Long Way to Majors," *Globe and Mail*, June 19, 1986, C12.

6. Woolsey, "Lights, Jays Are Ready in St. Kitts"; Author interview with Greg Sorbara, August 21, 2006; "A Look Back at 1986," Niagara Metros Archive Website (accessed July 2011, website no longer active); Eric and Wendy Pastore, "Community Park, St. Catharines," http://www.digitalballparks.com/NYPenn/StCatherines_640_1.html, http://www.angelfire.com/games2/canuckball/Community.html; Charles O'Reilly, "Where a Certain Lady Sang," http://mysite.verizon.net/charliesballparks/stadiums/stcath.htm.

7. Paul Patton, "Hamilton-Welland in Line for Baseball Expansion," *Globe and Mail*, October 29, 1987; Neil A. Campbell, "St. Catharines Jays' Success Spur for Hamilton's New Team," *Globe and Mail*, June 16, 1988; "1990 New York-Pennsylvania League," http://www.baseball-reference.com/minors/league.cgi?id=602a436e; Bernd Franke, "Fields of Dreams Home to Little More Than Memories: Hockey Hot Bed Remains Cool to Minor League Baseball," *Welland Tribune* online, 2009 (accessed July 2011, website no longer active).

8. Franke, "Field of Dreams"; Steve Cannon, "Pro Baseball Hopes Alive: Money Is Still the Key to Kitchener's Chances," *The Record* (Kitchener-Waterloo, Ontario), July 3, 1992, E1; Larry Millson, "Take Me Out to the (Minor League) Ballpark: Interest Piqued but Not Profound as Majors Strike Out," *Globe and Mail*, August 17, 1994.

9. Allan Ryan, "Jays to Sell Two Teams in Minors," *Toronto Star*, September 3, 1993, E3; Larry Millson and Neil A. Campbell, "Jays Sell Teams in St. Catharines, Knoxville Club Now Owns Only Dunedin Class A Squad, Citing Looming Revenue Shortfall," *Globe and Mail*, September 3, 1993.

10. "St. Catharines' Loss London's Gain," *Financial Post* (Toronto), December 23, 1993, section 4, 40; Steve Milton, "Baby Jays Must Fly or Face Losing Their Nest," *Hamilton Spectator*, June 4, 1994, C2.

11. Christina Blizzard, "A Man of Many Talents," *Toronto Sun*, May 9, 2004, 28; Milton, "Baby Jays Must Fly."

12. Author interview with Nick Cannon, July 18, 2006; Jim Byers, "Whitt May Buy St. Kitts Farm Team," *Toronto Star*, June 7, 1994, E1; John McHutchion, "Execs of Summer: New Owners Are Using Fun, Games and Love of Baseball to Revive St. Catharines' Minor League Team," *Toronto Star*, July 8, 1996, C1.

13. Interview with Nick Cannon.

14. Steve Milton, "Whitt Has Plans for Ex-Baby Jays," *Hamilton Spectator*, January 28, 1995, C6; Jim Byers, "Ex-Jays' Farm Team Looks for New Identity," *Toronto Star*, December 21, 1994, SE3; "New Name for Jays' Farm Team," *Globe and Mail*, December 21, 1994; McHutchion, "Execs of Summer"; Rob Malich, "Blue Jay Name Is Stomped Out in Image Change," *Toronto Star*, July 13, 1995, D1; Cannon interview.

15. Steve Milton, "Baby Jays Are Long Gone but St. Kitts Club Survives," *Hamilton Spectator*, June 17, 1995, C2; Malich, "Blue Jay Name Is Stomped Out"; McHutchion, "Execs of Summer."

16. Malich, "Blue Jay Name Is Stomped Out"; Milton, "Baby Jays Are Long Gone"; Cannon interview.

17. Tony Van Alphen, "2 Named in Bid to Buy Blue Jays; Former Liberal Minister Part of Consortium," *Toronto Star*, October 23, 1997, A1.

18. Bob Elliott, "Not Easy to Come Up with a Deal for the Jays," *Financial Post*, August 12, 1998; Larry Millson, "Owner Denies Sale Is Brewing; Rumours Rampant; Observers Feel Club Is Back on Market," *Globe and Mail*, August 12, 1998, S1; Michael Grange, "Jays More Attractive to Buyers New Lease, Debt Moves May Make Purchase Easier," *Globe and Mail*, November 27, 1998, S1; Tony Van Alphen, "New Bid to Buy the Jays," *Toronto Star*, November 29, 1998, 1; Paul Brent and Brenda Bouw, "Gillick Group Bids For SkyDome: $100-Million Offer Seen as a Sidelong Way of Buying the Blue Jays Too," *National Post* (Canada), December 5, 1998; Paul Brent and Brenda Bouw, "Sportsco Looks Set to Win Battle for SkyDome: Court Ruling Tomorrow: Partnership with Tenant Labatt Likely to Be Strained," *National Post* (Canada), February 10, 1999; Tony Van Alphen, "SkyDome Chief Fired in Power Play," *Toronto Star*, May 27, 1999; "Ex-Cabinet Minister Sorbara Sues SkyDome Owners," *Toronto Star*, June 12, 1999.

19. Interview with Greg Sorbara.

20. Interview with Greg Sorbara. Attendance figures from http://www.thebaseballcube.com/minors/teams/history.asp?T=10396. Team valuation and Community Park renovation estimate from Mark Zwolinski, "Stompers Leaving St. Kitts," *Toronto Star*, September 23, 1999 and "Sports in Brief: Stompers Off to Brooklyn," *Globe and Mail*, September 23, 1999, S4.

21. Interview with Greg Sorbara.

22. See Zwolinski, "Stompers Leaving," "Stompers Off to Brooklyn," and "Sports Brief: St. Kitts Loses Team," *The Record* (Kitchener-Waterloo, Ontario), September 23, 1999, C2.

23. https://www.niagarametros.com (accessed July 2011, website no longer active).

24. Interview with Nick Cannon; https://craigtravel.com/users/nick-cannon; Pam Cannon, "Hometown Traveller: Centuries of History and the Welcoming People of Iran," *Niagara Now*, January 19, 2020, https://niagaranow.com/entertainment.phtml/3300-hometown-traveller-centuries-of-history-and-the-welcoming-people-of-iran; Michael Katz and Laurie Cooke, "One Brand, Three Generations: The Shared History of McDonald's and the Katz Family," *Canadian Business Franchise Magazine*, March/April 2008, 69–81; Brandon James, "Terry O'Malley Fonds, n.d.," March 4, 2016, https://silo.tips/download/terry-o-malley-fonds-nd; St. Catharines Sports Hall of Fame, https://scshof.com/terry-omalley/ (accessed November 2020, website no longer active).

25. Sorbara interview; The Canadian Press, "Liberal MPP Greg Sorbara Resigns," CBC News, August 1, 2012; Sandro Contenta, "Greg Sorbara in the

Middle of Ugly Feud That Threatens Family's Billion-Dollar Company," *Toronto Star*, October 5, 2018.

    26. Lupica, "A Team Grows in Brooklyn."

Chapter Nine

    1. John S. Berman, *Coney Island* (Museum of the City of New York, 2003); John F. Kasson, *Amusing the Million* (Hill & Wang, 1978); Michael Immerso, *Coney Island: The People's Playground* (Rutgers University Press, 2002). Especially helpful was Juan Jorge Rivero Souss, "Coney Island: Planning Nostalgic Space," a Columbia University master's thesis (2004), which provides an excellent recounting of many local politicians and groups in the effort to develop Keyspan Park in particular and Coney Island in general in the 1990s–2000s.

    2. Judith A. Adams, *The American Amusement Park Industry: A History of Technology and Thrills* (Twayne, 1991); Immerso, *Coney Island*.

    3. David A. Sullivan, "The Comprehensive History of Coney Island," https://www.heartofconeyisland.com; Immerso, *Coney Island* (see p. 4 for his observation about immigrants and the Dreamland Tower); Kasson, *Amusing the Million*.

    4. Jeffrey Stanton, "Coney Island—Second Steeplechase Park" (revised May 1998), https://www.westland.net/coneyisland/articles/steeplechase2.htm; Sullivan, "Comprehensive History." New York City Parks Service, "Steeplechase Park," https://www.nycgovparks.org/parks/steeplechase-park/highlights/12477.

    5. Souss, "Coney Island," 32–35; "Coney Island Slump Grows Worse; Decline in Business Since the War Years Remains Steady," *New York Times*, July 2, 1964, 33.

    6. "Frank S. Tilyou of Coney Island; Head of Steeplechase Park Dies in Arizona at Age 56," *New York Times*, May 9, 1964, 27; Stanton, "Coney Island—Second Steeplechase Park," based on the recollections and diaries of Steeplechase General Manager James Onorato. Tilyou letter quoted in Charles Denson, *Coney Island: Lost and Found* (Ten Speed Press, 2004), 135.

    7. Denson, *Coney Island: Lost and Found*, 138–140, and Charles Denson, "Fred Trump's Coney Island: 50th Anniversary Exhibit" (July 5, 2016), https://www.coneyislandhistory.org/blog/news/fred-trumps-coney-island-50th-anniversary-exhibit; Alden Whitman, "A Builder Looks Back—and Moves Forward," *New York Times*, January 28, 1973; Gwenda Blair, "Fred Trump Slays the King of Cooperative Housing," Gotham Center for New York City History, February 8, 2018, https://www.gothamcenter.org/blog/fred-trump-slays-the-king-of-cooperative-housing. Woody Guthrie, "Old Man Trump," https://woodyguthrie.org/Lyrics/Old_Man_Trump.htm.

    8. "Six Bikinied Beauties Attend Demolishing of Coney Landmark," *New York Times*, September 22, 1966, 49; Dennis Lynch, "Remembering the Day

Trump's Dad Destroyed a Coney Icon," *Brooklyn Paper*, May 23, 2016, https://www.brooklynpaper.com/remembering-the-day-trumps-dad-destroyed-a-coney-icon/.

9. Martin Tolchin, "Coney Landmark Is Sold to Trump," *New York Times*, July 2, 1965.

10. Marcia Chambers, "New York, after 10 Years, Finds Plan to Create a Coney Island Park Is Unsuccessful," *New York Times*, April 3, 1977, 42.

11. Denson, *Coney Island: Lost and Found*, 162–166; Owen Fitzgerald, "Casinos For Coney at Top of Chamber's List," *New York Daily News*, March 19, 1981, K3; Stephen Kurutz, "Chicken Little," *New York Times*, August 15, 2004.

12. The fullest treatment of Horace Bullard and his plans appears in Denson, *Coney Island: Lost and Found*, 211–219. See also "Activity and Hope Rising at Coney Island," *New York Times*, April 7, 1985, 20; Dierdre Carmody, "Reborn Steeplechase Park Planned At Coney I.," *New York Times*, August 5, 1985, B1; Jesus Rangel, "Broad Redevelopment Is Urged for Coney Island," *New York Times*, June 5, 1987, B3.

13. Fred Lebow, "Politicians Should Run with Amateurs," *New York Times*, February 28, 1982, sec 5, p. 2; Mervyn Rothstein, "Follow-Up on the News: Brooklyn Stadium," *New York Times*, September 5, 1982, 41; Beth Sherman, "State Approves Stadium Study," *New York Times*, October 25, 1985, B1; Jesus Rangel, "State Proposes Baseball Stadium for Coney Island," *New York Times*, December 5, 1986, A1. An early version of the Sportsplex concept is explored at length in Judie Glave, "Coney Island Stages a Comeback," *Journal-News* (Rockland County, New York), September 2, 1990, H1–H3.

14. Tom Raftery, "Sportsplex Eyes Coney Again," *New York Daily News*, June 19, 1991, 62; Betty Liu Ebron, "Apple Sauce," *New York Daily News*, September 27, 1990, 6.

15. In 1993 the BSF and Golden organized a petition, rally, and a children's march across the Brooklyn Bridge to drum up support, but to little avail: see Michael O. Allen, "Petition Rolled Out for Sports Center," *New York Daily News*, June 18, 1993, KSI 2, and "Borough President Gets Ball Rolling for Sportsplex," *Canarsie Courier*, July 1, 1993, 10.

16. Rangel, "Broad Redevelopment"; Elizabeth Kolbert, "Albany Notes; Mario Cuomo Rediscovers 'Real People,'" *New York Times*, June 26, 1988, 28.

17. The Brooklyn Sports Foundation also attempted to raise public awareness and funds by selling merchandise like t-shirts and sweatshirts proclaiming "Brooklyn Attitude." In 1990 they regularly published mail-in ads in *New York Newsday*; for one example, see June 3, 1990, p. 473, under the heading "Support Sports in Brooklyn."

18. Roger Rubin, "Sportsplex Plans Under Way," *Newsday*, August 1, 1993, B15; Manuel Perez-Rivas, "Sportsplex Surviving Cuts," *Newsday*, April 12, 1994, B7; "Hearing Held on Brooklyn Sportsplex," *Canarsie Courier*, November 24, 1994, 12;

Paul Moses, "Dream Arena: Panel Pitches Plan for Brooklyn Sportsplex," *Newsday*, December 8, 1994, A3; Annette Fuentes, "Field of Dreams Plan," *New York Daily News*, December 9, 1994, KSI 2; Austin Evans Fenner, "Sportsplex—Landmark of the Future," *New York Daily News*, December 15, 1994, KSI 4; Darcy Frey, "When Hoops Are Handcuffs," *Newsday*, December 20, 1994, 34.

19. James Harney, "Pols Go to Bat for Sportsplex," *New York Daily News*, May 9, 1995, KSI 1; Dena Bunis, "Don't Bet Money on Sportsplex," *Newsday*, May 16, 1995, B7; Tara George, "Sportsplex Gets Rudy's Nod," *New York Daily News*, May 18, 1995, KSI 2; Paul Moses, "Rudy Gives Coney Island Arena a Ride," *Newsday*, May 18, 1995, A32; James Harney, "Pols Rally to Save Sportsplex," *New York Daily News*, June 13, 1995, KSI 1; "Plans Heating Up for Boro Sportsplex," *Canarsie Courier*, March 14, 1996, 9.

20. See the following articles in the *New York Daily News*: Bill Farrell, "1 for L.I. in Arena Struggle," July 23, 1996, 81; "Sportsplex Fans to Go for It Again," September 10, 1996; "Pols Give Sportsplex Top Priority," November 29, 1996; "Pols' Plan: 120M & Jobs," April 8, 1997, KSI 1. Also Austin Fenner, "Sportsplex Hopes Up," March 20, 1997, KSI 2; Kimberly Schaye and Jon R. Sorenson, "State Pols Finally KN a Budget," July 30, 1997, 2; Jon R. Sorenson and Kimberly Schaye, "Albany End Game," August 5, 1997.

21. Michael Finnegan and Stephen McFarland, "Coney Sportsplex—Yes!," *New York Daily News*, August 15, 1997, KSI 2; "City & State Ready to Complete Funding for Brooklyn Sportsplex," *Canarsie Courier*, August 21, 1997, 8; Bill Farrell, "Rally for Coney Venue," *New York Daily News*, January 21, 1998, KSI 1.

22. Bill Madden, "A Team Grows in Brooklyn: Mets Eye Farm Team in Borough," *New York Daily News*, January 16, 1998, 79; Dan Barry, "Feverish Dreams of Baseball as Mets Look at Brooklyn," *New York Times*, January 17, 1998, B3; Mike Lupica, "Sweet Summer Dreams Flicker in Coney Island," *New York Daily News*, January 16, 1998, 78; Farrell, "Rally for Coney Venue"; Bill Farrell, "Big-Bucks Presents from Gov to Coney," *New York Daily News*, January 30, 1998, KSI 6.

23. Bob Liff, "The Mouse That Roared Eyes Coney Island," *New York Daily News*, May 7, 1998, KSI 13.

24. Bob Liff, "Borough Bigs Nearly Whiff on Rudy's Curves," *New York Daily News*, November 12, 1998, KSI 8; Mary McAleer Vizard, "In the Region / Westchester; When Developers, and City Officials, Think Big," *New York Times*, June 20, 1999, sec. 11, p. 9; Souss, "Coney Island," 57–58. New York City recorded thirty-five consecutive days warmer than 80 degrees Fahrenheit in the summer of 1998, a string unmatched since 1966; see https://thestarryeye.typepad.com/weather/2012/02/new-york-weather-highlights-1998.html.

25. The Associated Press, "Mets Farm Team May Play in Brooklyn," September 15, 1998; United Press International, "Mets' Coney Island Team Held Up," September 16, 1998; Daniel Kruger, "Brooklyn Stadium Brings Baseball Back," *The*

Bond Buyer, September 16, 1998, 35; Andy Newman, "Mets Accord Could Return Pro Baseball to Brooklyn," *New York Times*, September 16, 1998, B3.

26. Liff, "Borough Bigs."

27. Liff, "Borough Bigs" as well as his additional *New York Daily News* articles "Ballpark Bidders Limited to 1: Mets," November 20, 1998, KSI 11, and "Rudy's Minor League Stunt Door Open to Mets on Coney Island Ballpark," November 23, 1998, KSI 6.

28. See the following *New York Daily News* articles: Bob Liff, "Mayor Truly Has a Complex about Plans for Sportsplex," January 11, 1999, KSI 4; Bill Farrell, "Giuliani Snubbed Boro, Golden Sez in Speech," February 11, 1999, KSI 2; Howard Golden, "Call Strike on Stadium in Brooklyn," March 28, 1999, 98; Bob Liff, "Coney to City: Sportsplex for Ballpark," June 16, 1999, KSI 4; Frank Lombardi and Bob Liff, "Rudy Pitch Beans Beep on Ballpark," June 19, 1999, KSI 4.

Chapter Ten

1. Press Office of the Mayor, "Mayor Giuliani Delivers Remarks at Swearing In of Brooklyn Borough President Howard Golden," January 27, 1998, Release #045-98; "A Brooklynite's Sway," *New York Times*, September 25, 1995, B3; Howard Golden, "Giuliani Disses Brooklyn," *Newsday*, October 27, 1999, and "Punishment by Budget," *New York Times*, May 3, 2000, A26; Jonas Sagalnik, "The Battle for Borough Hall," *The Brooklyn Rail*, July-August 2001, https://brooklynrail.org/2001/08/local/the-battle-for-borough-hall; Carl Campanile, " 'Golden' Rule: Spoil It for Next Brooklyn Beep," *New York Post*, December 18, 2001; Bob Liff, "Golden Days Spent in Shadow of Rudy," *New York Daily News*, October 15, 1998, 72.

2. Bob Liff, "Here's Another Fine Mets," *New York Daily News*, January 7, 1999, KSI 2; Bill Farrell, "Giuliani Snubbed Boro, Golden Sez in Speech," *New York Daily News*, February 11, 1999, KSI 2; Howard Golden, "Call Strike on Stadium in Brooklyn," March 28, 1999, 98. See also Bob Liff, "First Pitch on Coney Island Ballpark," *New York Daily News*, June 14, 1999, QLI 6; Julian E. Barnes, "Neighborhood Report: Coney Island; Just How Minor Should a Minor League Baseball Club Be?," *New York Times*, June 20, 1999, sec. 14, p. 10.

3. Liff, "First Pitch"; Barnes, "Neighborhood Report"; Mark S. Rosentraub, "Out at First! The Giuliani Administration's Missed Opportunity," study prepared for and released by the Office of the Brooklyn Borough President, June 14, 1999; see also Robert Hardt Jr., "Hizzoner Takes Swing at B'klyn Beep," *New York Post*, June 19, 1999, and Norman Oder, "Flashback, 2000: The Borough President Criticizes the Mayor over a Sports Facility," August 8, 2007, https://atlanticyardsreport.blogspot.com/2007/08/flashback-2000-borough-president.html.

4. Bob Liff, "Coney to City: Sportsplex for Ballpark," *New York Daily News*, June 16, 1999, KSI 4.

5. Sergey Kadinsky, "The Story of Brooklyn's Parade Ground," June 13, 2018, https://forgotten-ny.com/2018/06/parade-ground-flatbush/; Bob Liff, "Mets Farm Team May Use B'klyn Ballfield for Year," *New York Daily News*, May 23, 1999, 18; Andrew Paul Mele, "Remembering the Parade Ground: A Field of Dreams and Dreamers," *New York Daily News*, July 28, 2008.

6. Bob Liff, "Mets Farm Team May Use Ballfield for a Year," *New York Daily News*, May 23, 1999, 18; Neil DeMause, *The Brooklyn Wars: The Stories behind the Remaking of New York's Most Celebrated Borough* (Second System Press, 2016), 214–216.

7. Kit R. Roane, "In Brooklyn, Neighbors Balk at a Ballpark Plan," *New York Times*, November 1, 1999, B3; Associated Press, "Plans for a Ballpark Challenged in Court," *New York Times*, November 23, 1999, B4; Bob Liff, "Suits Target Stadium Plan: Double Play on Forcing Review," *New York Daily News*, November 23, 1999, KSI 1; DeMause, *Brooklyn Wars*, 218–220.

8. See the following *New York Daily News* articles by Bob Liff: "City Throws a Curve: Tie Parade Grounds Plan to Mini-Mets OK," December 9, 1999, KSI 2; "Ballpark Plans Still on Hold," December 14, 1999, KSI 1; "Bklyn Beep Knocks Pitch for Coney Island Ballpark," December 20, 1999, KSI 2; "Money Talk Sways Foes of Ballpark," December 29, 1999, KSI 1; "Mets Mull New Farm Team Sites," January 12, 2000, KSI 1.

9. See the following *New York Daily News* articles by Bob Liff: "Boro Prez Votes No on Ballpark," New York Daily News, January 6, 2000, KSI 2; "Mets Eye Shift from Brooklyn Site," January 10, 2000, KSI 1; "St. John's Eyed for Mets Farm Team," January 19, 2000, KSI 10. See also Julian E. Barnes, "Brooklyn Groups Back Use of Park by Mets Farm Team," *New York Times*, January 1, 2000, B1 and "City Drops Plan to Build Stadium in Parade Grounds," *New York Times*, January 19, 2000, B3.

10. See the following *New York Daily News* articles by Bob Liff: "Mayor-Beep Rub May Kill Coney Plan," January 31, 2000, KSI 1; "Sportsplex Push Fizzling," April 7, 2000, KSI 1; and "At Coney, Diamond in the Rough," May 5, 2000, KSI 1. See also Tania Lopez, "In Brooklyn, It's Play Ball," *New York Newsday*, June 25, 2001, A8.

11. Bob Liff, "City Big Rips Plan for Sportsplex," *New York Daily News*, January 21, 2000, KSI 5; Julian E. Barnes, "Deal Gives Coney Island a Ballpark, and a Team That Some Didn't Want," *New York Times*, April 12, 2000, B5.

12. Frank Lombardi, "Hevesi: Giuliani in Payback Mode," *New York Daily News*, May 18, 2000, 36; Associated Press, "City Submits $3.3B Bid to Host 2012 Olympics," December 16, 2000, reprinted in *The Journal-News* (White Plains, New York), 3.

13. Tara Bahrampour, "Rebirth at Historic Brooklyn Field," *New York Times*, March 31, 2000, B3; and these Bob Liff articles in the *New York Daily News*:

"Reviving Field of Dreams: 12M Plan to Rehab Ballfields," March 30, 2000, KSI 2, and "11 Sports Fields in Park Plan," March 31, 2000, KSI 2.

14. Thomas J. Lueck, "Opposition Precedes Arrival of Teams at New Coney Island Stadium," *New York Times*, August 23, 2000, B1; The following *New York Times* articles by Jonathan P. Hicks: "A Radically Altered Race for Brooklyn Borough Presidency," January 10, 2000, B1; "Brooklyn Politicians Ponder Borough President's Exit," April 17, 2000, B6; and "In Brooklyn, 3 Candidates Battle in Close Race for Borough President," July 31, 2001, B4. See also David Seifman, "Is B'klyn Beep Trying to Stick It to Old Foe?," *New York Post*, April 15, 2000; "Searchlight on Campaign 2001: Brooklyn Borough President," *Gotham Gazette*, www.gothamgazette.com (accessed December 2020, website no longer active); Gail Robinson, "How Sweet Was It? Marty Markowitz's Boro Hall Legacy," *The Brooklyn Bureau*, March 25, 2013, https://citylimits.org/2013/03/25/how-sweet-was-it-marty-markowitzs-boro-hall-legacy/.

15. See the following articles by Bob Liff: "Mets Eye Shift from B'klyn Site," *New York Daily News*, January 10, 2000; "Mets Mull New Farm Team Sites"; "St. John's Eyed for Mets Farm Team"; "Ballfield Deal Likely Lost: Mets Team Set to Play in Queens," *New York Daily News*, January 18, 2000, QLI 1.

16. Charles V. Bagli, "Queens Groups Plan to Sue to Stop a Baseball Stadium," *New York Times*, February 19, 2000, B2.

17. Michael R. Blood and Bob Liff, "Pol Pitches Ballfield Plan for Mets Farm Team," *New York Daily News*, February 28, 2000, CN4.

18. Bagli, "Queens Groups"; Blood and Liff, "Pol Pitches Ballfield"; Donald Bertrand, "Ballfield Plan Suits Are Merged," *New York Daily News*, April 6, 2000; Jim O'Grady, "Groups Sue to Toss Team out of a Park," *New York Times*, June 25, 2000, sec. 14, p. 11; Dennis Waszack Jr., "St. John's Feeling Effects of Season-Long Road Trip," Associated Press, May 5, 2000.

19. See these articles by Donald Bertrand in the *New York Daily News*: "Bid to Stop St. John's Ballpark Is Thrown Out," June 14, 2000; "It's a Kingly Realm: Minor League Field Wins Pats and Pans," June 21, 2000; "Queens' Kings Make a Hit: Fans Love New Minor League Nine," June 23, 2000. See also Jim O'Grady, "Groups Sue to Toss Team Out."

20. Bob Liff, "City, Mets Raise Cry: Batter Up," *New York Daily News*, August 23, 2000; "2000 New York-Penn League Standings," http://www.thebaseballcube.com/minors/leagues/review.asp?Y=2000&L=NYPL.

21. In the meantime, the Mets' own estranged affiliate in Pittsfield was waiting anxiously for their own divorce to be finalized, so that Bill Gladstone and Rick Murphy could pack up, leave town, and rebrand the P-Mets as the Tri-City ValleyCats in Troy, New York. For the failure of the Queens Kings, see Donald Bertrand, "Now It's Time To Play Ball! Minor League Kings a Major Draw," *New York Daily News*, July 25, 2000, and Sarah Kershaw, "Minor League Ball in

Queens: So Far, Everything but Crowds," *New York Times*, August 27, 2000, sec. 1, p. 31.

22. Liff, "City, Mets, Raise Cry"; Kershaw, "Minor League Ball in Queens."

23. Adam Rubin, "With New Stadium, Storm Safe at Home," *New York Daily News*, March 21, 2001; "Jack Kaiser Stadium," https://redstormsports.com/sports/2018/6/12/facilities-stjo-ballpark-html.aspx; "Iconic St. John's Baseball Stadium Converting to AstroTurf," January 26, 2018, https://www.prweb.com/releases/2018/01/prweb15135862.htm. For Red Storm game at Citi Field, see Dennis Waszak Jr., "Georgetown Beats St. John's as Mets' New Ball Park Opens," Associated Press, March 29, 2009, and "St. John's, Georgetown Play First Ever Game in Citi Field," St. John's University press release reported by Targeted News service, March 29, 2009.

24. David Barstow, "Facing the Ghost of Summers Past; Hope Dies Hard at Coney Island, and So Does Nostalgia," *New York Times*, June 9, 2000, B1. Text of Tilyou's sign at Steeplechase from the Coney Island History Project, https://www.facebook.com/ConeyIslandHistoryProject/posts/2736895579673639?comment_id=2737468146283049.

25. Liff, "Diamond in the Rough"; Barstow, "Facing the Ghost of Summers Past"; Andrew Rice, "Sultan of Spending: Mayor Goes on Spree Constructing Stadiums," *New York Observer*, July 17, 2000, 2; Bob Liff, "City, Mets Raise Cry: Batter Up!"

26. Bob Liff, "Meet the Cyclones: That's Name of Mets' New B'klyn Farm Team," *New York Daily News*, November 30, 2000.

27. Alfred E. Clark, "Obituary of Fred Moran, Owner of Thunderbolt Ride at Coney Island Park," *New York Times*, January 10, 1982, sec. 1, p. 32; Susan Chira, "The Talk of Coney Island; At Coney I., Symbols of Heyday Fading Away," *New York Times*, August 20, 1983, sec. 1, p. 23; Glenn Fowler, "Fire Guts House on Coney I.; Was in '77 Woody Allen Film," *New York Times*, May 16, 1991, B6; Douglas quote from "Make-Believe versus Reality," National Press Club Luncheon With Kirk Douglas at National Press Club, Washington, DC, June 30, 1994, transcript by Federal News Service.

28. Bob Liff, "Coney Is. Coaster Tumbles to Ground," *New York Daily News*, November 18, 2000; Associated Press, "Famous Coney Island Rollercoaster Is Demolished," November 18, 2000; Peter Duffy, "Relic of a Faded Playground Meets the Wrecking Ball," *New York Times*, November 18, 2000, B1. The full account of the behind-the-scenes maneuvering to destroy the Thunderbolt appears in Dan Barry, "About New York; Giuliani Razed Roller Coaster, and the Law," *New York Times*, October 4, 2003, B1. That article was written with significant input from Horace Bullard, who also shared his detailed recollections and reactions in Raanan Geberer, "The Legacy of Horace Bullard, Coney Island's Would-Be Developer," *Brooklyn Daily Eagle*, July 25, 2014, https://brooklyneagle.com/articles/2014/07/25/opinion-the-legacy-of-horace-bullard-coney-islands-would-be-developer/. Finally,

the alleged comments by Jeff Wilpon at the groundbreaking are mentioned in Robert Gearty, "Flash! Decision Due Today in Thunderbolt Suit," *New York Daily News*, September 22, 2003, as well as Barry, "About New York."

29. Liff, "Coney Is. Coaster"; Barry, "About New York"; Geberer, "Legacy of Horace Bullard."

30. See the following articles from the *New York Daily News*: Robert Gearty and Bill Hutchinson, "Judge: Rudy Must Answer Touchy Question," September 19, 2002; Hugh Son, "Judge Lets Giuliani Coast in Coney Suit," July 18, 2003; Robert Gearty, "Thunderbolt Hurled: City Not Liable in Coaster Raze," January 30, 2004. See also Gearty, "Flash!"; Barry, "About New York"; and Associated Press, "After Hilly Fight, City Found Not Liable for Demolished Coaster," December 7, 2005.

31. George Vescey, "Sports of the Times; Brooklyn, Blinis, Baseball," *New York Times*, January 31, 2001, D1; Michael O. Allen, "Keyspan's Pitch Is a Hit Coney Isle Ballpark Gets Name," *New York Daily News*, February 1, 2001.

32. See the following articles by Bob Liff in the *New York Daily News*: "Lil' Return In Lil' Mets Park: City's Guaranteed only 250G," February 13, 2001; "Coney Ballpark May Be Done Deal," February 14, 2001; "Coney Isle Ballpark Vote Is Tomorrow," February 15, 2001.

33. See the following articles by Bob Liff in the *New York Daily News*: "Coney Ballpark May Be Done Deal"; "Coney Isle Ballpark Vote Is Tomorrow"; "Lil' Mets Score Park as Hevesi Cries Foul," February 17, 2001; "Pol Calls Defector in Speaker Bid: Let's Go Mets," February 25, 2001.

34. See the following articles by Bob Liff in the *New York Daily News*: "Coney Builds Hopes Along with Stadium," March 20, 2001; "Thunderous Welcome for Cyclones Coney Hails Return of Pro Baseball," April 6, 2001; "Stadium Grows in Coney Will Be Ready for Mets Farm Opener," April 19, 2001. See also Michael O. Allen, "Cyclones: Overnight Sensation," *New York Daily News*, April 29, 2001; Mark Hochstein, "Hardball in Coney Island," *Business and Industry* 3 no. 4 (May 2001); Bill Farrell, "Sun Shines on Coney Opening: Beach May Not Face Lifeguard Shortage," *New York Daily News*, May 25, 2001; Larry McShane, "After 44 Years, Baseball Returns to Brooklyn," Associated Press, June 13, 2001.

Chapter Eleven

1. See the following articles from the *Staten Island Advance*: "Our Opinion: Games and Priorities," June 4, 2001, A14; Jay Price, "St. George Ballpark Turns on the Charm," June 18, 2001, A1; Maura Grunlund, "When You're Rooting for the Home Team," June 20, 2001, D6.

2. See the following articles from the *Staten Island Advance*: Frank Donnelly, "Grand Slam: A Sellout Crowd Turns Out to Root," June 25, 2001, A1;

Ryan Lillis and Stephanie Slepian," For Openers It's See and Be Seen," June 25, 2001, A6; David Andreatta, "They Built It, and 6,854 Came," June 25, 2001, A7.

3. Harvey Araton, "A Ballpark a Skeptic Can Love," *New York Times*, June 25, 2001, D5.

4. "Mayor Rudolph Giuliani Discusses the Return of Minor League Baseball to Brooklyn and Coney Island," transcript of the *CBS Early Show*, June 25, 2001 at 7:00 a.m., accessed via Lexus-Nexis.

5. Osborne's account of Opening Day is detailed and absolutely thrilling. See Ben Osborne, *The Brooklyn Cyclones: Hardball Dreams and the New Coney Island* (NYU Press, 2004), 5–28.

6. Bill Farrell, "Baseball's a Big Hit: Pols and Fans Enjoy Cyclones' Opening Win," *New York Daily News*, June 27, 2001; for more on Tom Knight, see Bruce Weber, "Tom Knight, Brooklyn's Baseball Sage, Dies at 89," *New York Times*, March 5, 2016, A22.

7. Kahn quoted in Larry McShane, "After 44 Years, Baseball Returns to Brooklyn," Associated Press, June 13, 2001; Wilpons quoted in Bill Farrell, "Cyclones Breathing New Life Into Baseball," *New York Daily News*, May 22, 2001; Ojeda quoted in Adam Rubin, "Minor League Parks Creating Major Buzz: New Diamonds Sparkle in Brooklyn, Staten Island," *New York Daily News*, June 20, 2001; Heffernan quoted in Josh Getlin, "Ploys of Summer," *Los Angeles Times*, June 26, 2001.

8. T. J. Quinn, "Camping Out," *New York Daily News*, March 28, 2001; Frank Lombardi, "Robinson, Reese Statue to Stand at Coney Island," *New York Daily News*, March 24, 2001; Wayne Drehs, "Brooklyn Baseball Memories Rekindled," September 3, 2001, https://www.espn.com/mlb/s/2001/0831/1246362.html.

9. Author interview with R. C. Reuteman, February 21, 2006.

10. Rubin, "Minor League Parks"; Lorraine B. Diehl, "A Coney Comeback: Brooklyn's South End Adds Baseball to Its Recreational Lineup," *New York Daily News*, June 24, 2001.

11. "Hot Dog Deal," *Crain's New York Business*, May 14, 2001; Joyce Shelby, "Sparkling Diamond Is Ready for Cyclone Fans," *New York Daily News*, June 15, 2001.

12. Author interviews with Josh Getzler, March 17, 2021 and July 8, 2021.

13. Interviews with Josh Getzler and R. C. Reuteman.

14. "MLB Valuations: Double Play," *Forbes*, April 26, 2004, at https://www.forbes.com/forbes/2004/0426/066tab.html?sh=3421888d4a70; see also Marquette Law School, "A Comparison of Team Values in Professional Team Sports" at https://law.marquette.edu/assets/sports-law/pdf/sports-facility-reports/Forbes.pdf.

15. Interview with Josh Getzler, March 17, 2021.

16. "MTA Board Approves Service Changes," press release by the Metropolitan Transit Authority, May 15, 2010, https://web.archive.org/web/20100515110640/

http://www.mta.info/news/stories/?story=24; "SIR *BALLPARK* station photos & R44 pix (729588)," https://talk.nycsubway.org//perl/read?subtalk=729588.

17. Interview with Josh Getzler, July 8, 2021.

18. Interview with Josh Getzler, July 8, 2021.

19. "Ballpark at St. George: Capital Program Project Budget," drafts dated September 28, 1999, November 18, 1999, and December 1, 1999, from EDC documents accessed May 2006; Arden Sokolow interview with Jeff Dumas, October 16, 2002; Getzler interviews March 2021 and July 2021.

20. Stephen Hart, "Staten Island Yankees: Attendance Is Just Fine," *Staten Island Advance*, July 17, 2001, A1; attendance information for NY-PL clubs from https://www.statscrew.com/minorbaseball/stats/; league records and playoff results from http://www.thebaseballcube.com/minors/leagues/review.asp?Y=2001&L=NYPL.

21. Harvey Araton, "Keeping Eye on the Ball, Not the Skyline; At a Staten Island Ballpark, the View Has Changed, but Dreams Endure," *New York Times*, June 19, 2002, B1; interview with Josh Getzler, March 2, 2021.

Chapter Twelve

1. Author interviews with Robert F. Julian, July 18, 2006, and R. C. Reuteman, February 1, 2006. See also Teri Weaver, "Cash Sets Off Run for 120th Assembly," *Syracuse Post-Standard*, November 6, 2000, A1; Leslie Eaton, "Party Politics Hold Sway in Choice of Judges Upstate, Too," *New York Times*, November 17, 2003, B1; Mark Thompson, *New York Judges Reviews and Court Directory 2007/2008* (James Publishing), 477–480; New York-Penn League press release, "New York-Pennsylvania League Has New President," April 25, 2001, https://www.oursportscentral.com/services/releases/nypl-names-new-president/n-2708122.

2. See "Vince McNamara, Professional Baseball Administrator," https://www.buffalosportshalloffame.com/member/vince-mcnamara/; "Ben Hayes," *Baseball Almanac*, https://www.baseball-almanac.com/players/player.php?p=hayesbe01; "Ben J. Hayes, '87," https://www.usfalumni.org/show_module_fw2.aspx?sid=861&gid=1&ecid=6443&control_id=644&nologo=1&cvprint=1&page_id=252&crid=0&scontid=-1&viewas=user; Gary Haber, "Major Minors," *Tampa Tribune*, February 12, 2002; "Ben Hayes," *Arkansas Democrat-Gazette*, March 27, 1986; Rick Stroud, "Coaches' Dilemma: How Much Rest Do Young Pitchers Need?," *St. Petersburg Times*, July 2, 1988, 4.; Roberto Gonzalez, "Minor League Details; A Weekly Report," *Hartford Courant*, August 27, 1999, E13; Brian Richesson, "New York-Penn League: New President, Growth Good Signs," https://vindyarchives.com/news/2001/jun/18/new-york-penn-league-new-president-growth-good/; press release, "New York-Pennsylvania League Has New President."

3. Peter Schmuck, "Angelos: He, Ripken Are Getting Along Fine; Owner Close to Putting Half-Year Single-A Club in Aberdeen Complex," *Baltimore Sun*, June 22, 2001; Mechelle Voepel, "Ripken Now Is Giving Kids Their Turn at Bat; Father Inspired Him to Share Love of Baseball," *Kansas City Star*, August 8, 2001; Mel Antonen, "Taking Their Final Bows," *USA Today*, October 5, 2001; Mark Kram, "Cal Tech; At Baseball Academy, Ripken Will Teach Kids What His Dad Taught Him," *Philadelphia Daily News*, October 10, 2001.

4. Associated Press, "Orioles Add Minor League Franchise in Aberdeen," February 6, 2002; Mark Zuckerman, "Cal's Group Buys Club for Aberdeen," *Washington Times*, February 7, 2002, C2; Jonathan Allen, "Bye-Bye Baseball: Ex-Owner Boehlert Becomes Just a Fan," *Congressional Quarterly Daily Monitor*, February 7, 2002; Associated Press, "Utica Hopes Baseball Will Return," February 7, 2002; David Ginsburg, "Ripken Enters New Career as Owner of Orioles' Minor League Affiliate," *Canadian Press*, February 13, 2002; David Ginsburg, "Ripken Names Minor League Team: Aberdeen IronBirds," Associated Press, April 11, 2002; John Lindsay, "A Minor Miracle; Ripken's Aberdeen Project Is a Perfect Pitch for His Small Hometown," *San Diego Union-Tribune*, June 16, 2002, C2; Sean T. McMann, "Ripken Joins N.Y.-Penn League," *Poughkeepsie Journal*, June 18, 2002, 7C.

5. The following articles directly cite Hayes's involvement in team sales and stadium negotiations: Gonzalez, "Minor League Details"; Jeff Davis, "Fresno Takes Aggressive Approach in Baseball Chase; City's Presentation to Expansion Committee Called 'Impressive,'" *Fresno Bee*, February 16, 1996 (including expansion committee membership); Jeff Jardine, "Deal May Keep Li'l A's in Modesto," *Modesto Bee*, June 10, 1994, A1; Chris Schulte, "No Truce in Provo Baseball Tug of War," *Salt Lake City Tribune*, March 13, 1996, D1. Veeck quote in Gary Haber, "Major Minors," *Tampa Tribune*, February 12, 2002.

6. Haber, "Major Minors"; "Sights and Sounds: Batavia Muckdogs 2019 Home Opener," *The Batavian*, filmed June 15, 2019, https://www.youtube.com/watch?v=wRn0WlGAFKY; Nick Cammarota, "Q&A with NYPL President Ben Hayes: Head of the Short-Season Circuit Answers 10 Questions from MiLB.com," June 17, 2008, https://www.milb.com/news/gcs-414076.

7. Haber, "Major Minors."

8. Attendance figures furnished by the New York-Penn League and also available at: thebaseballcube.com, ballparkdigest.com, ballparkwatch.com, and also *New York-Penn League 2019 Media Guide & Record Book*, http://www.milb.com/documents/8/8/6/308024886/Media_Guide_final_copy.pdf. See also https://newyorkpennleaguenews.wordpress.com/page/2/, entry dated September 10, 2019. While I believe it is certain that the "bottom-feeder" league teams were impacted by the paucity of resources, one cannot completely exclude organizational ineptitude at the top either. The Aberdeen Ironbirds were an affiliate of the Baltimore Orioles and were absolutely affected by the putrid state of the Orioles farm system. That is doubtless the main reason the Ironbirds made the playoffs only once in their

entire NY-PL existence from 2002 to 2020. On the other hand, that makes their attendance success all the more remarkable.

9. Author interview with Josh Getzler, July 8, 2021; Ken Rosenthal, "Farewell to Gardner?," *The Athletic*, May 13, 2022, https://theathletic.com/330 9703/2022/05/13/angels-trade-deadline-no-hitter-mlb-baseball/.

10. Interview with Josh Getzler.

11. Interview with Josh Getzler. Getzler noted that the same rains impacted the Brooklyn Cyclones as well, as they were located in the same city. However, the ultrasuccessful Cyclones had an easier time absorbing those costs as their tremendous resources enabled them to better weather these storms, figuratively and literally.

12. Office of the Comptroller of the City of New York, *Audit Report on the Compliance of Staten Island Minor League Holdings, L.L.C., (Staten Island Yankees) with Their Lease Agreement May 1, 2001–December 31, 2002, Report FN03-116A,* June 27, 2003 and *Audit Report on the Compliance of Staten Island Minor League Holdings, L.L.C., (Staten Island Yankees) with Their Lease Agreement May 1, 2003–December 31, 2004, Report FN05-106A,* April 21, 2006.

13. Interview with Josh Getzler.

14. "Time to Move On—Our Opinion," *Staten Island Advance*, April 26, 2006, A18.

15. See the following stories from the *Staten Island Advance*: quotes taken from Jay Price, "Heavy Hitters Launch a New Era for S. I. Yanks," November 10, 2006, A1; see also Karen O'Shea, "New Season Dawns, with Ownership Change on the Horizon," June 20, 2006, A3; Kevin Flood, "Just Ignore the Name on the Door," June 22, 2006, B6; Rob Hart, "S. I. Yanks Still Owe City Big $$," August 10, 2006, A1; "Time to Move On"; "H'Wood Producer May Take Over S. I. Yanks," September 5, 2006, A10; Jim Waggoner, "New Hope for S. I. Yanks' Empty Seats," October 30, 2006, A1; Sally Goldenberg, "City: Baby Bombers Cleared of Debt," June 20, 2007, A3; Dean Balsamini, "Staten Island Yankees Played before Record Home Crowds in '09," September 15, 2009; Bernie Augustine, "Record Crowds Filled Ballpark to See Staten Island Yankees This Summer," September 16, 2009; Frank Donnelly, "S. I. Yanks, Richmond County Savings Bank Reach New Naming-Rights Pact," January 14, 2010; "Staten Island Yankees Appear Likely to Be Sold as Bronx Bombers Look to Unload," September 15, 2011.

16. Chris Hine, "A Sodden Field Is Fixed as a Quagmire Remains," *New York Times*, July 18, 2009; Benjamin Kabak, "Details Emerge in Scranton Yanks Sale Dispute," November 15, 2010, riveraveblues.com (accessed May 2022, website no longer active); Neil deMause, "Yankees' Purchase of Scranton Affiliate a "Losing Proposition" for Taxpayers?," November 16, 2010, https://www.fieldofschemes.com/ category/minor leagues/minor league-baseball/scranton-wilkes-barre-yankees/; Stacy Lange, "Scranton/Wilkes-Barre Yankees Sold," April 26, 2012, https://www. wnep.com/article/news/local/lackawanna-county/scrantonwilkes-barre-yankees-

sold/523-5dfd0aad-ad6e-4c97-b90b-dd8ba8a388ba; Kevin Reichard, "SWB Yankees Sold," April 26, 2012, https://ballparkdigest.com/201204264789/minor league-baseball/news/swb-yankees-sold; Mike, "Triple-A SWB Yankees Sale Finally Final," April 28, 2012, riveraveblues.com (accessed May 2022, website no longer active).

17. Kevin Reichard, "NY Yankees Making Moves with Minor League Teams," *Ballpark Digest*, September 14, 2011, https://ballparkdigest.com/201109144195/minor-league-baseball/news/yankees-making-moves-with-minor-league-teams; Scott Beaulieu, "Connecticut Group Buys Yankees' Affiliate," October 4, 2011, https://www.nbcconnecticut.com/news/local/connecticut-group-buys-yankees-affil-iate/1892984/; Jim Waggoner, "New Ownership Group for Staten Island Yankees Talks about Future Plans," *Staten Island Advance*, May 17, 2012.

18. US States News, "First Ever New York-Penn League All-Star Game Hits Home Run in Brooklyn," February 14, 2005; Charles Cassy, "Baseball Lures People Back to Brooklyn," *Palm Beach Post*, August 23, 2005; *New York-Penn League 2019 Media Guide & Record Book*.

19. See the following items from the Associated Press: "New Jersey Cardinals Sold; Team to Be Moved to Pa.," *New Jersey Herald*, October 5, 2005; AP, "Altoona Curve, PSU Propose New Single-A Team in State College," December 6, 2003; "Curve, Crosscutters Deal Clears Way for Proposed State College Franchise," July 2, 2004; Genaro C. Armas, "New Ballpark to House Minor League and Penn State Teams," May 18, 2005; "Owners Unveil Name, Logo of Minor League Team in State College," November 23, 2005; see also Office of the Governor of Pennsylvania, "Governor Rendell Continues to Deliver on His Commitment to Create Jobs in PA; Announces $12 Million for Centre County; 300 Jobs to be Created as the Result of a New Baseball Stadium," Press release, May 18, 2005.

20. See the following stories in the *Daily Star*: P. J. Harmer, "Rojas: Damaschke Changes Are Top-Notch," June 28, 2008, and "O-Tigers Are Set to Be Sold," July 1, 2008; "Nader, Levine Kept It Simple," July 2, 2008 (no byline); "Future Uncertain for Team," July 5, 2008 (no byline); Rob Centorani, "Prentice: O-Tigers to Stay Put," July 9, 2008; P. J. Harmer, "NY-Penn Approves Sale of O-Tigers," August 20, 2008. Also, author interview with Connecticut Tigers General Manager Andrew Weber, August 2010.

21. Interview with Andrew Weber.

22. See the following stories in the *Daily Star*: "New Owner of Tigers to Face Tall Task in Oneonta," (no byline), July 9, 2008; Denise Richardson, "O-Tigers Still Applying for Beer License," June 1, 2009; Dick Powell, "O-Tigers Games Are Great Value," Letters to the Editor, August 21, 2009; "There Should Be More Fans Than Bobbleheads" (no byline), July 10, 2009.

23. Rob Centorani, "We're Giving the Tigers No Reason to Stay in Oneonta," *Daily Star*, August 15, 2009; Pat Eaton-Robb, "Team's Move Has Dodd Stadium Looking for a Tenant," *New Haven Register*, September 28, 2009; Claire Bessette, "Norwich Moves Closer to Regaining Minor League Baseball Team," *The Day*

(Connecticut), January 5, 2010; P. J. Harmer, "Is O-Tigers' Future Pro or Conn.?," *Daily Star*, January 11, 2010; Denise Richardson, "They're Out!," *Daily Star*, January 28, 2010; Rob Cipriani, "League Facing a Few Minor Issues," *Centre Daily Times* (Pennsylvania), August 15, 2010.

24. Todd Murray, "N.Y.-Penn Official: Rumor of Morgantown Move 'Speculation,'" *Morgantown Dominion Post*, September 21, 2012; "Potential of Professional Baseball in Morgantown, W.Va. (featuring Ben Hayes)," filmed March 26, 2013, https://www.youtube.com/watch?v=9wBuCwpAQNU; "A Grand Slam for Mon County," *Daily Athenaeum* (West Virginia University), August 25, 2014, 1; "Morgantown Lands Pirates Affiliate," *Charleston Daily Mail*, August 25, 2014; Anthony Pecoraro, "Luck Announces Professional Baseball Coming to Morgantown," *Daily Athenaeum*, August 26, 2014, 1; David Schlake, "Baseball Stadium a 'Game Changer' for WVU," *Daily Athenaeum*, September 22, 2014, 1.

25. *New York-Penn League 2019 Media Guide & Record Book*, 39; https://www.statscrew.com/minorbaseball/stats/t-bc10608/y-2010; J. J. Cooper and Josh Norris, "MiLB Sees Attendance Increase in 2019, Reversing Last Year's Drop," September 11, 2019, https://www.baseballamerica.com/stories/milb-sees-attendance-increase-in-2019-reversing-last-year-s-drop/. For a comprehensive analysis of MiLB attendance figures, see David P. Kronheim, *Minor League Baseball Attendance Analysis* for 2010 through 2019 at his incredible website, https://www.numbertamer.com/minor league-baseball.

26. Kevin Reichard, "NA, MLB Extend Agreement for Six More Years," *Ballpark Digest*, March 8, 2011, https://ballparkdigest.com/201103083626/minor-league-baseball/news/na-mlb-extend-agreement-for-six-more-years; Benjamin Hill, "Minors Extend Agreement through 2020," March 8, 2011, www.milb.com (accessed May 2020, website no longer active and may have been scrubbed).

27. J. J. Cooper, "MLB Proposal Would Eliminate 42 Minor League Teams," *Baseball America*, October 18, 2019, https://www.baseballamerica.com/stories/mlb-floats-proposal-that-would-eliminate-42-minor-league-teams/; David Waldstein, "M.L.B. Said to Be Pushing for Overhaul of Minor Leagues," *New York Times*, October 18, 2019, B11; Evan Drellich, "'If We Are Forced to Defend Ourselves and Fight for Our Mere Survival, We Will': MiLB President Responds to MLB Plan," *The Athletic*, October 19, 2019, https://theathletic.com/1306272/2019/10/19/if-we-are-forced-to-defend-ourselves-and-fight-for-our-mere-survival-we-will-milb-president-responds-to-mlb-plan/; Dan Barry, "Across the Country, Minor League Towns Face Major League Threat," *New York Times*, November 16, 2019, SP2; Bill Madden, "Rob Manfred's Plan to Destroy Minor League Baseball," *New York Daily News*, November 17, 2019.

28. Madden, "Rob Manfred's Plan"; Waldstein, "MLB Said to Be Pushing."

29. J. J. Cooper, "Dueling Letters Highlight Dramatic Differences Between MLB, MiLB on Elimination," *Baseball America*, November 20, 2019, https://www.baseballamerica.com/stories/dueling-letters-highlight-dramatic-differences-between-

mlb-milb-on-elimination/; Neil deMause, "Why MLB Declared War on the Minor Leagues," December 19, 2019, https://slate.com/culture/2019/12/mlb-minor-league-baseball-contraction-kill-milb-teams-collusion.html, and "Why MLB Declared War on the Minor Leagues" (separate and different article), December 22, 2020, https://defector.com/why-mlb-declared-war-on-the-minor-leagues/; Doug Robinson, "Changes on the Minor League Landscape Jeopardize Important Slice of Americana," *Deseret News*, October 17, 2020.

30. Cooper, "Dueling Letters"; Bernie Sanders tweet, November 19, 2019, https://twitter.com/BernieSanders/status/1196858220507226113; Kevin Reichard, "Legislators, Elected Officials, Owners React to MiLB Contraction Plan," *Ballpark Digest*, November 21, 2019, https://ballparkdigest.com/2019/11/21/legislators-elected-officials-owners-react-to-milb-contraction-plan/ and "Manfred: We Don't Need No Stinkin' Minor Leagues," *Ballpark Digest*, December 16, 2019, https://ballparkdigest.com/2019/12/16/manfred-we-dont-need-no-stinkin-minor-leagues/.

31. For a full month-by-month timeline of the 2019–2020 progress of MiLB contraction (complete with links to many additional sources), see J. J. Cooper, "A Complete Guide to MLB and MiLB's Negotiations," *Baseball America*, November 27, 2020, https://www.baseballamerica.com/stories/a-complete-guide-to-mlb-and-milbs-negotiations/; for One Baseball, see Maury Brown, "Under Manfred, MLB Is Swallowing the Minors—and Extending Its Reach into Every Level of Baseball," *Forbes*, September 10, 2020.

32. Howard B. Owens, "NY-Penn League President Hopeful the Muckdogs Will Take the Field at Dwyer Again," *The Batavian*, June 24, 2020.

33. Jim Dolan, "Cyclones Will Stay in Brooklyn as High-A Team," *Brooklyn Eagle*, November 20, 2020; Timothy Healey, "Brooklyn Cyclones Move Up a Notch in Mets' Minor League Restructuring," *New York Newsday*, December 9, 2020; Randy McRoberts, "Aberdeen IronBirds to Play High-A Baseball as Part of MLB's new Minor League Agreement, Unsure on Timetable," *The Aegis* (Bel Air, Maryland), February 12, 2021.

34. Kevin Reichard, "MLB Draft League to Launch with Five Teams," *Ballpark Digest*, November 30, 2020, https://ballparkdigest.com/2020/11/30/mlb-draft-league-to-launch-with-five-teams/ and "MLB Draft League Return In 2022 With Six Teams, 80-Game Schedule," *Ballpark Digest*, November 9, 2021, https://ballparkdigest.com/2021/11/09/mlb-draft-league-return-in-2022-with-six-teams-80-game-schedule/; https://www.mlbdraftleague.com/about/faq; deMause, "Why MLB Declared War."

35. See the following articles by Mark Singelais in the *Albany Times-Union*: "ValleyCats Not Part of Amateur MLB Draft League," November 30, 2020; "ValleyCats Still Mulling Their Options," December 10, 2020; "ValleyCats: No Contact from Astros since Losing Affiliation," December 15, 2020; "Tri-City ValleyCats Join Frontier League for 2021 Season," January 7, 2021.

36. Mac Cerullo, "Play Ball? Return of Lowell Spinners a Possibility," *Eagle-Tribune* (North Andover, Massachusetts), April 13, 2022.

37. Attendance figures from "Staten Island Yankees Franchise History (1999–2019)," https://www.statscrew.com/minorbaseball/t-sy14772; see also Aaron Elstein, "The Staten Island Yankees Are Having a Minor Identity Crisis," *Crain's New York Business*, June 11, 2017. For numerous photos and details of the New York Wheel project, see https://skyscraperpage.com/forum/showthread.php?t=200152.

38. Adam Weinrib, "Yankees: Reasons behind NYY Ditching Staten Island Affiliate Are Wild," https://yanksgoyard.com/2020/11/07/yankees-reasons-behind-ditching-staten-island/ and "Staten Island Yankees Go Scorched Earth in Lawsuit against NYY," https://yanksgoyard.com/2020/12/03/staten-island-yankees-lawsuit/; Rich Calder, "Yankees Were 'Embarrassed' by Staten Island Team's Pizza Rat Promotion," *New York Post*, January 1, 2022; Nick Regina, "Pizza Rat-Gate: Drama Ensues between New York Yankees Brass and Former Staten Island Franchise," *Staten Island Advance*, January 3, 2022. See also these articles in the *Staten Island Advance*: Joe D'Amodio, "Staten Island Yankees to Change Name to Pizza Rats for Five Games," June 11, 2018; Matthew Angell, "Future for Pizza Rats Unclear, but Rebranding Paid Off for S. I. Yankees," September 7, 2018; Joe D'Amodio, "Staten Island Yankees to Bring Back Pizza Rats for Second Straight Season," May 14, 2019.

39. Ken Davidoff, "Staten Island Yankees Fold, File $20M Suit against MLB, Big-League Club," *New York Post*, December 3, 2020.

40. "Press Release: New York Yankees Announce New Minor League Affiliation Structure," November 7, 2020, https://www.mlb.com/press-release/press-release-yankees-announce-new-minor-league-affiliation-structure; Eric Bascome, "Yankees Officially Axe Staten Island Affiliate; New Team Expected at Richmond County Ballpark," *Staten Island Advance*, November 7, 2020. For the lack of contact between the organization and Nostalgic Partners, see *Nostalgic Partners, LLc, vs. New York Yankees Partnership*, 72 Misc. 3d 1224, 151 N.Y.S.3d 862 (N.Y. Sup. Ct. 2021), 17.

41. Davidoff, "Staten Island Yankees Fold"; Joe D'Amodio, "Staten Island Yankees Cease Operations, Sue New York Yankees, MLB," *Staten Island Advance*, December 4, 2020; Neil deMause, "Friday Roundup: Everywhere from Reading to NYC Is Coughing Up Minor League Stadium Cash, Just Like MLB Planned It," July 2, 2021, https://www.fieldofschemes.com/2021/07/02/17580/friday-roundup-everywhere-from-reading-to-nyc-is-coughing-up-minor-league-stadium-cash-just-like-mlb-planned-it/; Oli Coleman, "John Catsimatidis, Others Founding Baseball Team to Replace the SI Yankees," *New York Post*, July 14, 2021; "Introducing Your Ferryhawks!," November 17, 2021, https://ferryhawks.com/news/2021/11/17/Your_FerryHawks_2.aspx.

42. Mark Simonson, "Oneonta Icon Sam Nader Dies at Age 101," *Oneonta Daily Star*, February 9, 2021, https://www.thedailystar.com/news/local_news/oneonta-icon-sam-nader-dies-at-age-101/article_6617302b-aab3-5bf5-a3f9-16515b52f39c.html.

43. Author interview with Sam Nader, July 17, 2006.

Afterword

1. *Nostalgic Partners, LLc, vs. New York Yankees Partnership*, 72 Misc. 3d 1224, 151 N.Y.S.3d 862 (N.Y. Sup. Ct. 2021); Staten Island Yankees Press Release: "Staten Island Yankees Cease Operations, Seek Legal Remedy," December 3, 2020, https://www.oursportscentral.com/services/releases/staten-island-yankees-cease-op-erations-seek-legal-remedy/n-5654944; Ken Davidoff, "Staten Island Yankees Fold, File $20M Suit against MLB, Big-League Club," *New York Post*, December 3, 2020, https://nypost.com/2020/12/03/staten-island-yankees-fold-sue-mlb-ny-yankees/; Mike Rosenstein, "Staten Island Yankees Whiff on Lawsuit vs. New York Yankees, MLB," September 10, 2021, https://www.nj.com/yankees/2021/09/staten-island-yankees-whiff-on-lawsuit-vs-new-york-yankees-mlb.html.

2. Obituary for William Gladstone, https://www.legacy.com/us/obitu-aries/nytimes/name/william-gladstone-obituary?id=13903190; Mark Singleais, "ValleyCats Sue Major League Baseball, Houston Astros for $15M," *Albany Times-Union*, January 15, 2021, https://www.timesunion.com/sports/article/Valley Cats-sue-Major-League-Baseball-Houston-15874082.php; Mike MacAdam, "Val-leyCats Suing MLB, Houston Astros," *Daily Gazette* (Schenectady, NY), January 16, 2021, https://dailygazette.com/2021/01/15/valleycats-suing-mlb-houston-astros/; Kevin Reichard, "ValleyCats Lawsuit against MLB, Astros to Proceed," August 25, 2021, https://ballparkdigest.com/2021/08/25/valleycats-lawsuit-against-mlb-astros-to-proceed/; Michael McCann, "Minor League Club Scores Win in Contraction Lawsuit," September 7, 2021, https://www.yahoo.com/video/minor league-club-scores-win-160042340.html.

3. Charles Anzalone, "UB Sports Law Expert Sees Possible SCOTUS Chal-lenge to Baseball Antitrust Status," December 22, 2021, https://www.buffalo.edu/grad/news.host.html/content/shared/university/news/expert-tipsheets/2021/029.detail.html; Chelsea Janes, "A Newly Filed Lawsuit Is Trying to Upend Baseball's Century-Old Status Quo," *Washington Post*, January 8, 2022, https://www.washing-tonpost.com/sports/2022/01/08/mlb-antitrust-lawsuit/; Olafimihan Oshin, "Sanders Calls for End to MLB Antitrust Exemption," *The Hill*, March 10, 2022, https://thehill.com/regulation/business/597767-sanders-calls-for-end-to-mlb-antitrust-exemption/; James Yasko, "Everyone Hates Baseball's Antitrust Exemption, But What Is It?," Chron, March 16, 2022, https://www.chron.com/sports/astros/article/Major-League-Baseball-antitrust-exemption-explain-17004658.php.

4. Nostalgic Partners, LLC et al v. The Office of the Commissioner of Baseball, Docket No. 1:21-cv-10876 (S.D.N.Y. Dec 20, 2021), Opinion Granting Motion to Dismiss, at https://aboutblaw.com/5tp. See also Mike Leonard, "Staten Island Yankees Lose Challenge to MLB Farm System Overhaul," October 26, 2022 at https://news.bloomberglaw.com/antitrust/staten-island-yankees-lose-challenge-to-mlb-farm-system-overhaul and Michael McCann, "Sea Unicorns Score Despite

Dismissal in MLB Antitrust Suit," October 31, 2022 at https://sports.yahoo.com/sea-unicorns-score-despite-dismissal-140000860.html.

5. "What Is the 'Save America's Pastime Act'?" Marketplace, https://www.marketplace.org/2021/03/17/what-is-the-save-americas-pastime-act/; Mitchell Williams Law, "Saving America's Pastime Means Not Paying Minor League Players," January 24, 2019, https://www.jdsupra.com/legalnews/saving-america-s-pastime-means-not-45220/.